THE OPERA

THE
OPERA

Joseph Wechsberg

The Macmillan Company
New York, New York

To the former Schostal Claque
at the Vienna Opera – where it all started

The Macmillan Company
866 Third Avenue, New York, N.Y. 10022
Collier-Macmillan Canada Ltd.
Toronto, Ontario

*Library of Congress Catalog
Card Number: 72-88013*

First Printing

Printed in the United States of America

Contents

Foreword

After almost four hundred years, the art of opera, often said to be dead and buried, is gloriously alive. More people than ever before discover the excitement of this allegedly "irrational" dramatic art form, in which people sing when they ought to speak, and vain tenors come up stage to display a high C.

Sometimes called a "hybrid" art, opera adds a new dimension to drama. The scenes of love and jealousy in Verdi's *Otello* create an impact which Shakespeare's *Othello*, despite its greatness, cannot convey. Shakespeare's poetry dramatizes Othello's and Desdemona's passions. Verdi's music unveils the abyss of their souls. At its very best, opera is powerful and timeless and incredibly beautiful. But as an art form it is very demanding. It isn't just "entertainment". At the opera house novices are often bothered by the absurd plot and their inability to understand the words while those who don't like music (is it true that there are such people?) may become bored. Opera is enjoyed only by those who know something about it.

This is the idea behind this book, which doesn't pretend to be a text-book or an encyclopaedia of opera. It was written for people who love opera and want to know a little more about its history and evolution, its lore and lure, and the people who create and re-create it.

Opera is sung; thus singing and the singers are discussed. Opera lovers are interested in the world's leading opera houses, the managers, the conductors, the producers. The orchestra will be discussed, the chorus, and the anonymous cogs in the machinery of an opera house. And on the other side of the orchestra pit are the audience, the claque, the critics. Without them, there would be no opera. Finally, opera is analysed as big business – probably the only business that always loses money and yet continues to thrive. But there certainly exists a crisis in modern opera and this will be discussed.

Of the forty-two thousand operas that are said to have been written, less than a few hundred have survived. Perhaps a hundred give opera lovers lasting pleasure. This is a unique phenomenon in the performing arts. I don't know anybody who, having seen seventy performances of Beaumarchais' *Le Mariage de Figaro*, would still enjoy this comedy. But I know a few (including myself) who have heard Mozart's *Le Nozze di Figaro* for the seventy-first time, and still enjoy it immensely because there is always something new and beautiful to find in it.

This book is for fellow opera fans (in Vienna they call them *Opernnarren*, opera fools) who love opera. There is nothing like A Night at the Opera – even without the Marx Brothers.

A note on the nomenclature: In most cases, the titles of operas are given in the language in which they were created. Thus it is Mozart's *Le Nozze di Figaro* and also Mozart's *Die Zauberflöte*. It is Boito's and Verdi's *Otello*, not Shakespeare's *Othello*. Italian, French, German and English (or American) operas are listed under the original titles. Other works are sometimes called by their English title. Instead of the original (Czech) *Prodaná nevěsta* it is *The Bartered Bride*. When in doubt, I always use the original title: *Die Walküre*, not *Walkure* or *Walkuere*.

I would like to thank the following for allowing me to reproduce passages from their books: Paul Henry Lang, *Music in Western Civilization* (W.W. Norton & Company, New York and J.M. Dent, London); Henry Pleasants, *The Great Singers* (Simon and Schuster, New York); George R. Marek, *The World Treasury of Grand Opera* (Harper & Row, New York); Wallace Brockway and Herbert Weinstock, *The World of Opera* (Pantheon Books, New York); W.J. Baumol & W.G. Bowen, *Performing Arts – The Economic Dilemma* (The Twentieth Century Fund, New York); Irving Kolodin, *The Musical Life* (Alfred A. Knopf, New York). I am also indebted to Harold Rosenthal and to *Opera* magazine, London, and to William Shawn, Editor of *The New Yorker*, who first published several of my articles dealing with opera.

Prologue: Tonight Figaro

Tonight's performance of Mozart's *Le Nozze di Figaro* is about to begin. The overhead lights dim, and go out. For one long, miraculous moment, one light remains on in every box, transforming the vast auditorium of the beautiful opera house into a magic grotto. The sounds of a thousand chattering voices have died down. Suppressed excitement is distilled into tense silence – a silence alive with anticipation.

Every opera lover cherishes this moment. He senses, instinctively, that this is going to be a great evening. How does he know? This is one of opera's many irrational phenomena. There are vibrations in the air that were not there the other night when one settled back in one's seat waiting for the overture. What creates the difference? The same musicians sit in the orchestra. On the stage, the same singers will perform under the same conductor. And backstage, hundreds of people will do the job they always do.

Perhaps this is one secret that makes opera the most fascinating and most complex of all musical art forms. Tonight's performance is the result of the precisely synchronized efforts of hundreds of people – dramatists, poets, librettists, composers, coaches, conductors, chorus masters, singers, instrumentalists, dancers, scenic designers, stage directors, painters, carpenters, stagehands, lighting technicians, property men, seamstresses, wigmakers, make-up men, producers, choreographers, supers, callboys, prompters, and the members of the management's administrative staff. At least four hundred people are involved in the performance you're going to see and hear. Somehow they've worked together for months to bring it off, despite enormous musical, dramatic, and technical difficulties. And there are emotional tensions that you won't notice if all goes well. The orchestra and the chorus habitually accuse each other of doing too little for too much money. The stage director and the conductor have aroused resentment by the amount of work they are demanding. And the singing stars, who get most of the money and most of the fame, are unpopular with most people who work in the house. For tonight's performance to come off at all is something of a miracle.

"There are two sighs of relief every night in the life of an opera manager", confessed Rudolf Bing, general manager for over twenty years of the Metropolitan Opera in New York. "The first comes when the curtain goes up and one knows that there is going to be a performance – that hundreds of people, artists, musicians, and technicians from all over the city are in the exact spot where they are supposed to be, each waiting for his cue to do his special job. The second sigh of relief comes when the final curtain goes down without any disaster, and one realizes, gratefully, that the miracle has happened once again."

Tonight the miracle will be a super-miracle: there is going to be a *great* performance. An especially "good" audience – demanding but knowledgeable, critical but enthusiastic – will give the performers that mysterious lift that makes all the difference between an ordinary performance and a great one (a bad audience is almost as bad as a bad cast). Between the audience and the performers the invisible spark will originate. A chain reaction is building up that will make the evening a success. It is an unanalysable phenomenon that makes opera an unpredictable entertainment – and the entrance fee a gamble. The conductor is inspired, the singers are in top form, there is a happy mood about the house.

It is very quiet now in the large auditorium. Several thousand people are in complete stillness, there is not even a cough. The lights in the boxes go out. The conductor steps into the orchestra pit. Applause. He raises the baton, gives the up-beat, and the strings and bassoons start the overture's exhilarating D major theme. Presto and pianissimo – pure musical vintage champagne.

Le Nozze di Figaro is for me the perfect opera. Its joyful spirit exists from the first note of the overture until the last note of the D major finale. (All of Mozart's operas begin and end in the same key.) Everything in *Figaro* is perfect – the libretto, the music, the musical characterization, the mixture of sadness and humour, the great arias and especially the ensembles. In the finale of the second act Mozart creates the exhilarating madness that explains the opera's subtitle *La Folle Journée*. "This piece exhibits a mastery of the counterpoint of characterization such as has been attained by few and surpassed by none", writes Alfred Einstein, the great Mozart scholar. Of some forty-two thousand operas written in the past four hundred years, less than half a dozen humorous masterpieces survive: *Figaro*, Rossini's *Il Barbiere di Siviglia,* Wagner's *Die Meistersinger von Nürnberg,* Verdi's *Falstaff.* Possibly Pergolesi's *La Serva Padrona,* Smetana's *The Bartered Bride,* Richard Strauss' *Der Rosenkavalier. Figaro* remains one of the most popular works of the repertoire. Of 565 operas played in Germany, Austria and Switzerland during the 1958–59 season, *Figaro* led all the rest. It is always at the top of the list.

Figaro is so perfect that it would be impossible to cut a single bar in the first three acts, and very difficult to shorten the fourth. Good as Beaumarchais' play was from which da Ponte's libretto is taken, the opera is better than the play. Mozart's magnificent music gives Beaumarchais' characters a new dimension, revealing more than even the best dialogue could convey of the subtle psychological complications of the plot. Mozart's inventive genius creates wonderful bits of melody which he uses once and never again. Richard Wagner would use his leitmotifs time and again, and even Verdi repeats certain themes. Mozart is more generous. Cherubino's "Voi che sapete", one of the greatest melodies ever written, delights us and is never heard again.

The story behind the story of *The Marriage of Figaro* begins, long before Mozart, in Paris, where Pierre Augustin Caron was born in 1732. His father was a watchmaker in the St Denis district, and Pierre started out as an apprentice in his father's shop, but soon left for much greener pastures. He played the harp and so delighted Mesdames de France, the four daughters of Louis xv, that at the age of twenty-three he became *Contrôleur clerc de l'office de la maison du Roi,* and on state occasions was permitted to carve and serve the meat course to the Royal Family. Later he married the widow of a high court official and took her name, Beaumarchais, though another version claims that he "purchased ancestry". Pierre had become acquainted with a financier who collected decorations. The young man supplied the decorations and the financier gave him valuable tips. Pierre made so much money that in 1761 he could afford to buy the title of a *Secrétaire du Roi.* In 1763, he purchased a better title, *Lieutenant-Général des Chasses et la Capitainerie de la Varenne du Louvre.* (That year, Wolfgang Mozart, then eight years old, came to Paris with his family, where he surprised everyone as a harpsichord performer. He was already composing. Mozart composed music before he learned to write.)

Beaumarchais became a banker, owned a paper factory, a timber firm and a shipbuilding enterprise, and built himself a *palais* on the Boulevard Beaumarchais. During the American War of Independence, he sold forty merchant vessels and a warship to the Colonies, and smuggled arms from Holland to America (at his death in 1799, his estate had claims against the United States Government for over a million dollars). Beaumarchais also became a secret double agent for Louis XVI and an intriguer for Madame de Pompadour and Marie-Antoinette, published a complete edition of his beloved Voltaire, and organized a union of playwrights. In between he was three times arrested in Paris and once in Vienna; his fortune was confiscated and then released; he was involved in a number of lawsuits, some of them defence actions in adultery and bribery cases, and was involved in a poison affair involving two married women. Later he published the details of these lawsuits in brilliant pamphlets. Came the Revolution, and the former self-made aristocrat became Citizen Beaumarchais, and managed to survive the first eight years of terror. He died peacefully in bed, not under the guillotine.

He had written plays *pour s'amuser,* and after a false start came up with the farcical *Le Barbier de Séville,* a sort of operetta interpolated with Spanish folk songs. It was successfully performed in 1775 at the Comédie Française. Five years later, Beaumarchais wrote a serious, satirical play, *Le Mariage de Figaro.* In between there had been the American Revolution which meant much to Beaumarchais – not only in terms of making money. It took courage to write this play which was accepted by the Théâtre Français in 1781. Each of the five censors turned it down. Beaumarchais read his new play to Louis XVI who thought it was "detestable". He also read it to several princes, duchesses and members of the Court's inner circle. They loved it because His Majesty detested it. The Court was divided into two factions. The intrigues around *Le Mariage de Figaro* lasted three years, during which it was several times scheduled and cancelled, once only an hour before the première.

On 27 April 1784 *Le Mariage* was at last performed, a great day in the annals of the French theatre. There was such a crowd that the gendarmes were unable to keep the people back and they stormed the doors and occupied the corridors and galleries. Some members of the aristocracy had their dinner served in the performers' dressing rooms so that they would be certain to be in the house when the performance started. *Le Mariage de Figaro* was a *succès fou* in Paris, performed sixty-eight times. Ten months later, several German translations were circulating in Vienna. Emperor Joseph II forbade the performance of the play that "everybody" had read by the time Mozart decided to turn it into an opera. The Emperor, though proud of his "liberal" ideas, found this play just too much for him.

For a long time, the French considered Beaumarchais one of the great writers of the French Revolution. Danton said, "*Le Mariage* has finished off the aristocracy and *Charles ix* finished off royalty", referring to Marie-Joseph de Chenier's *Charles ix*, a genuinely revolutionary play of the period. Later, Napoleon agreed when Danton said, "*C'était la révolution déjà en action.*" Yet nothing in the life or the philosophy of Beaumarchais indicates that he wrote *Figaro* as a social or political tract. However, he had sound dramatic instinct; he sensed the new ideas that were in the air, and he wrote an autobiographical play, identifying himself with Figaro, the servant who outwits his aristocratic master. Yet Beaumarchais was not a snob: he remembered his childhood as did Mozart, who had hated his early years at the Court of the Archbishop of Salzburg.

Mozart had read, and discarded, almost a hundred plays before deciding on *Le Nozze di Figaro*.* He knew Beaumarchais' earlier play *Le Barbier*, which introduces the characters (Count Almaviva, Rosina, Figaro) that we meet again later in *Le Mariage*. In *Le Barbier*, a farcical play, Almaviva, the youthful Spanish nobleman, with the help of the wily barber Figaro, tries to win the heart of the lovely Rosina, the ward of old Dr Bartolo. Almaviva uses different disguises – a commoner, a drunken soldier, a music master – and goes to a lot of trouble to marry Rosina. Here *Le Barbier* ends. In *Le Mariage*, Count Almaviva, about to be appointed as Ambassador to England, begins to chase his wife's chambermaid, Susanna, who happens to be engaged to Figaro. *Cherchez les hommes.* But in the meantime, the little barber has come up in the great world. Figaro is now Count Almaviva's "confidential secretary", an older, wittier, wiser man (whether he still shaves his master remains an open question). The Count, on the other hand, is more foolish than in the earlier play when he was just a nice young man in love. Now he is an arrogant philandering nobleman. Rosina, once a pretty, happy girl, has become the ladylike, charming, melancholy Countess, very unhappy and very human.

Six weeks after Mozart had decided on *Le Mariage de Figaro*, his eminently gifted librettist, the Abbé Lorenzo da Ponte, completed his difficult task. Being the Latin secretary and official court poet of Joseph ii, da Ponte presented the libretto to His Majesty. The Emperor reminded

* *The Marriage of Figaro* is a false literal translation from the Italian. The correct English translation is *Figaro's Wedding* as G.B. Shaw called it.

him that Mozart had written only one opera, "and nothing remarkable". Da Ponte replied that without His Majesty's clemency he (da Ponte) might not have written "but one drama" in Vienna. According to da Ponte's memoirs, the conversation continued:

> That may be, the Emperor answered. But *Le Mariage de Figaro!* I have just forbidden the German troupe to use it.
>
> Yes, Sire, I said, but I was writing an opera, and not a comedy. I had to omit many scenes and to cut others quite considerably. I have omitted or cut anything that might offend good taste or public decency at a performance at which Your Majesty might be present. The music, I may add, so far as I may be judge of it, seems to me marvellously beautiful.
>
> Good! said Joseph II. If that be the case, I will rely on your good taste as to the music and on your wisdom as to the morality. Send the score to the copyist.

Beaumarchais' *Figaro* was social-political dynamite, a challenge for Lorenzo da Ponte, a post-Renaissance adventurer, converted Jew and unfrocked priest, the friend of princes and princesses, poets and revolutionaries, and of Giovanni Jacopo Casanova. Da Ponte was often involved in scandals; his own life would have made a fascinating libretto. After the death of his protector, Joseph II, he had had to get out of Vienna; he went to London, wrote more libretti and went broke as a book dealer, finally escaping to New York where he sold tobacco, groceries and "strong waters". In 1825, he worked with Manuel del Pópolo Vicente García, one of the legendary singers of all times, when the first Italian opera company in New York performed *Don Giovanni*. He became a teacher of Italian at what is now Columbia University, where a da Ponte professorship remains in his memory. Among his close friends was Clement C. Moore, the author of *The Night before Christmas*. Da Ponte died in 1838, at the age of eighty-nine.

Mozart, who had an instinctive sense of the dramatic stage, *knew* that the Beaumarchais play would make a fine musical comedy. In *Figaro*, the dramatic complications reflect life; the characters are real human beings (much more so than in Beaumarchais' earlier *Barbier*), while the situations are never contrived. There is wonderful fun – and also deep sorrow. Mozart was not interested in the social philosophy of Beaumarchais' play, in which the low-born servant outwits his aristocratic master. "There is not a word in his letters ... about the French Revolution, which began when he was still alive – it did not touch him", writes Alfred Einstein. "Mozart ... saw through people, despite the fact that he was continually taken in by them". Mozart was also attracted by the opportunity to write a fine part (Figaro) for the bass Francesco Benucci whom he much admired. Two years earlier, he'd written to his father, "The Italian *opera buffa* has made its reappearance here and is extremely popular. The *buffo* is particularly good, his name is Benucci".

Da Ponte, on his part, understood what Mozart wanted: a *commedia per musica* – life, real human beings, sorrow and fun, with almost no political and social undertones. He gave Mozart exactly that. As da Ponte saw it, the real story in *Figaro* tells of how Count Almaviva is taught the facts of life by his wife and his servants. This da Ponte and Mozart did skilfully. The audience at the Vienna première didn't realize that Almaviva, a rather unpleasant character, represented themselves and all that they stood for – their arrogance, their privileges, their prejudices.

Da Ponte was no fool. He expected problems with the Emperor over his version of the Beaumarchais play. He also knew that Mozart could write subtle meanings into his music that were not in the text. Figaro's first-act aria, "Se vuol ballare", sounds harmless enough but the revolutionary spirit is there – in the orchestra. In the Beaumarchais play, Figaro asks the audience in his fourth-act monologue, "How did you become the mighty Count Almaviva?" and answers, "You took the trouble to be born". Da Ponte deleted this leaving only the unpolitical complaint about "those women", but there are serious undertones in the music of "Aprite un po'quegl'occhi".

Some biographers have called da Ponte a vain man, though there is no evidence of this in his preface to the libretto of *Figaro*. He writes:

The duration prescribed for a stage performance by general usage, and the given number of roles to which one is confined by the same, as well as several other considerations of prudence, place, public, constituted the reasons for which I have not made a translation of that excellent comedy (Beaumarchais' *Le Mariage de Figaro*) but rather an imitation, or let us say an extract.

For these reasons I was compelled to reduce the sixteen original characters to eleven ... and to omit in addition to one whole act, many highly effective scenes and many witty sayings, with which the original teems ... In spite, however of all the zeal and care on the part of both the composer and myself to be brief, the opera will not be one of the shortest that has been performed on our stages. We hope ... to paint faithfully and in full colour the divers passions that are aroused, and to realize our special purpose, which was to offer a new type of spectacle, as it were, to a public of such refined taste and such assured understanding.

Da Ponte's libretto in its own way is almost as good as Mozart's music. It has been called a "transfiguration" of the Beaumarchais original, which is still performed and remains a masterpiece of wit and revolutionary spirit.

Mozart was always completely involved with his librettists as were all the great and successful opera composers. Earlier, when he was working on his *Idomeneo* in Munich, and his librettist, Giovanni Battista Varesco, was in Salzburg, Mozart wrote his comments and requests to his father, who passed them on to Varesco. In a letter of 8 November, 1780, Mozart objects to a spoken aside which seems "unnatural" to him:

> In a dialogue all these things are quite natural, for a few words can be spoken aside hurriedly; but in an aria where the words have to be repeated, it has a bad effect, and even if this were not the case, I should prefer an uninterrupted aria. The beginning may stand, if it suits him, for the poem is charming . . .

Mozart often wanted cuts and shorter dialogue, understanding that the music would slow up the words. And Mozart knew (long before they preached it on New York's Broadway) that if the audience is bored for five minutes, the evening may be a total failure. On November 29, he writes about the oracle in the last act of *Idomeneo*:

> Don't you think that the speech of the subterranean voice is too long? Consider it carefully. Picture to yourself the theatre, and remember that the voice must be terrifying – must penetrate – that the audience must believe it really exists. How can this effect be produced if the speech is too long? The listeners will become more and more convinced that it means nothing. If the speech of the Ghost in *Hamlet* were not so long, it would be far more effective.

Varesco agreed to shorten the speech but it was "still far too long" and Mozart wrote to his father, "I have therefore shortened it but Varesco need not know of this, because it will all be printed as he wrote it."

All successful opera composers have treated their librettists as junior partners since Mozart's famous letter to his father of 13 October 1781, in which he stated that "in opera the poetry must be altogether the obedient daughter of the music". And he goes on,

Why do Italian operas please everywhere – in spite of their miserable libretti – even in Paris, where I myself witnessed their success? Just because the music reigns supreme and when one listens to it all else is forgotten.

Which is exactly what generations of opera lovers have felt when they listen to the impenetrable nonsense and the "supreme" music of Verdi's *Trovatore*.

Mozart concludes that "the best thing of all is when a good composer, who understands the stage and is talented enough to make sound suggestions, meets an able poet, that true phoenix". His dictum that poetry must be "the obedient daughter of the music" is not based on aesthetic theory but on instinct. He never took himself seriously as Richard Wagner did, overwhelming his contemporaries with his aesthetic theories. Mozart could express drama, action and character more deeply through his music than any librettist could through words, but he needed a libretto that contained a dramatic situation with various crises and an eventual denouement. There had to be touches of gaiety and of irony. In *Die Zauberflöte*, which contains some very serious music, the profundity is occasionally interrupted by the light-hearted nonsense of Papageno and Papagena; Don Giovanni's terrifying departure for Hell is balanced by the ironic finale wherein Leporello announces that he is going to the nearest inn to look for a new master. In short, life goes on.

Mozart wanted characters that deeply interested him and they had to act like human beings. Rossini, using the same characters in his *Barbiere*, made them physically alive and farcically amusing whereas Mozart made them psychologically and spiritually alive, giving each character his own musical speech, almost a dialect. He knew how they spoke and he expressed the subtle inflection of their voices in his music. A superb stage craftsman, he could create a complete unity of words and music, using music both to deepen character and to intensify the action. Often he does this by intercepting an aria with an unexpected, meaningful turn of the music. The ensembles are full of such sudden surprises. Even his recitatives contain highlights of this kind.

In his famous 'letter' duet in the third act of *Figaro*, the sole oboe and bassoon play together when Susanna is writing but not while the Countess is dictating, except at the end of the duet when the women re-read the letter together. In his astonishing ensembles, Mozart didn't just compose a number of beautifully woven parts but managed to develop and preserve the dramatic individuality of each person.

Does that sound as though we try to read too much into Mozart's music – his humour and irony and how he did it? I don't think so. On one occasion he writes to his father about his favourite aria in *Die Entführung aus dem Serail*, Belmonte's "Oh wie ängstlich,"

> I wrote it expressly to suit Adamberger's voice. You feel the trembling, the faltering, you see how his throbbing breast begins to swell; this I have expressed by a crescendo. You hear the whispering and the sighing – which I have indicated by the first violins with mutes and a flute playing in unison.

Once, Mozart's father told him "not to think in your work only of the musical public but also of the unmusical . . . You know that there are a hundred ignorant people for every ten true connoisseurs, so do not forget what is called popular and tickle the long ears" (nothing has changed in this respect in the two hundred years since Mozart Senior wrote this letter). Mozart replied, "As to the matter of popularity, be unconcerned. There is music in my opera for all sorts of people – but none for long ears".

A good composer of opera must be both dramatist and musician. He will not create a truly successful opera by simply setting the words of a libretto to music. Able composers have done it and failed because they couldn't visualize dramatic situations or were unable to identify themselves completely with their characters. The composer creates character and drama through music, somewhat as the dramatist creates drama and character with words. Good operatic libretti make good plays, even without music (both *Meistersinger* and *Rosenkavalier* have been performed as plays). But a great composer adds an entirely new dimension. To prove it, read the first-act monologue of the Marschallin, and then listen to the sung monologue which reveals infinitely more about a woman's love and resignation. Music conveys a depth of feeling and nuances of the soul that even the greatest poet cannot achieve. The Greek word for "music" is derived from the Greek *mousa* (muse).

In order to succeed, the operatic composer must not merely project his own personality into the main character of an opera, as Tchaikovsky did in *Eugene Onegin* or Hans Pfitzner in *Palestrina*. He must live *all* the characters, no matter how different they are from himself, because only that way can he bring them alive musically. Verdi and Bizet had this rare gift, and to a certain extent Strauss and Puccini. But, here Mozart reigned supreme; he was not only the greatest creator of "pure" (absolute) music, his "pure" musicianship was the ideal tool for the opera composer. In the summer of 1765, when he was nine years old, he performed in London for Daines Barrington, philosopher and jurist, who recalled the astonishing experience in his *Miscellanies* (1781),

> I said to the boy that I should be glad to hear an extemporary *Love Song*, such as his friend Manzoli might choose in an opera. The boy on this (who continued to sit at his harpsichord) looked back with much archness, and immediately began five or six lines of a jargon recitative proper to introduce a love song . . .
>
> Finding that he was in humour, and as it were inspired, I then desired him to compose a *Song of Rage,* such as might be proper for the opera stage. The boy again looked back with much archness, and began five or six lines of a jargon recitative proper to precede a *Song of Anger*. This lasted also about the same time with the *Song of Love*. And in the middle of it he had worked himself up to such a pitch, that he beat his harpsichord like a person possessed, rising sometimes in his chair. The word he pitched upon for this second extemporary composition was, *Perfido*.

A fascinating glance into the world of a child-genius. Quite a few successful operas have been written around the "Perfido" theme. Yet Mozart's early operas were not finished masterpieces. In *Bastien und Bastienne* there is lovely music but little dramatic insight as yet. But at the age of nineteen he composed *La Finta Giardiniera* which begins to show musical characterization, particularly in the ensembles. He was already able to musically "paint" his characters when they were on the stage, confronting each other.

Successful composers collaborate with their librettists, or write their own libretti, as Richard Wagner and Alban Berg did. *Figaro* is a first-rate libretto because da Ponte listened to Mozart's suggestions. Verdi found *his* da Ponte late in life when Arrigo Boito, a gifted composer, wrote the libretti of *Otello* and *Falstaff*, disinterestedly serving the greater genius of Verdi. The results are two of the greatest masterpieces of opera. Verdi's letters to his earlier librettists contain wishes, specifications, demands, complaints. Puccini had only Luigi Illica and Giuseppe Giacosa, no "true phoenixes", but *La Bohème* and *Tosca* came off in spite of the libretti, not because of them. Puccini was often enraged by his librettists. It took two years to produce the libretto of *La Bohème*. The last act was rewritten five times, though Puccini needed only eight months to write the score of the opera. Richard Strauss found his true phoenix in Hugo von Hofmannsthal, who wrote *Elektra, Der Rosenkavalier, Ariadne auf Naxos, Die Frau ohne Schatten, Die Ägyptische Helena, Arabella.* (In 1908, during their collaboration on *Elektra,* Strauss wrote to Hofmannsthal, "You are the born librettist, in my opinion the greatest compliment, because I believe it's much harder to write a good libretto than a beautiful play".) They collaborated long-distance, by letters. Their correspondence gives us an intimate analysis of the processes leading to the birth of an opera – the ideas, the arguments, the hopes, the doubts, the happiness and the sorrow.

The première of *Le Nozze di Figaro* in Vienna, on 1 May 1786, had been preceded by sinister intrigues that were as much a part of the operatic life in eighteenth-century Vienna as today. Three composers – Vincenzo Righini, Antonio Salieri and Mozart – had operas ready for production at the same time. Naturally, each wanted to have his opera produced first. Each also had his own *camarilla* at the Emperor's Court. The Irish tenor Michael Kelly, son of a Dublin wine merchant, who sang the part of Don Curzio, the stuttering notary in *Figaro,* later wrote about the cabals in his *Reminiscences* (he is better remembered for his book which was ghosted for him, than for his artistic achievements). He often played billiards in Mozart's house, admittedly coming off "second best". Later he retired to London, tried to compose music but eventually became a wine merchant. Sheridan called him "Composer of Wines and Importer of Music".

Kelly wasn't much of an authority on music. After an evening of string quartets in Mozart's home, he called the players "tolerable". The players happened to be Joseph Haydn, first violin; the composer Karl Ditters von Dittersdorf, second violin; Mozart, viola; and the composer Johann Baptist Vanhall, cello. But few contemporaries have written about Mozart as intimately as Kelly.

> Mozart . . . was remarkably fond of punch, of which beverage I've seen him take copious drafts. He was fond of billiards and had an excellent billiard table in his home. He gave Sunday concerts at which I never was missing . . .

Kelly also reported on the intrigues between the three opera composers in Vienna:

> Mozart was as touchy as gunpowder and swore he would put the score of his opera (*Figaro*) into the fire if it was not produced first, and his claim was backed by a strong party . . . Salieri was *maestro di*

cappella to the Court, a clever, shrewd man, possessed of what Bacon called crooked wisdom, and his claims were backed by three of the principal performers who formed a cabal not easily put down . . .

Kelly writes that he alone was "a stickler for Mozart" during the intrigues while Righini was "working like a mole in the dark to get precedence". Mozart himself conducted the rehearsals of *Figaro*. "All the original performers had the advantage of the instruction of the composer who transfused into their minds his inspired meaning". Kelly describes Mozart's "little animated countenance when lighted up with the glowing rays of genius". One evening when Kelly went to visit Mozart at home, the composer said, "I've just finished a little duet for my opera, you shall hear it". They sat down at the piano and sang together "the little duet", which was "Crudel! perchè finora", the beautiful duet sung in the third act by Susanna and Count Almaviva.

At "the first rehearsal of the full band", Mozart was on the stage "with his crimson pelisse and gold-laced cocked hat, giving the time of the music to the orchestra". While Benucci sang Figaro's aria, "Non più andrai", Kelly who stood close to Mozart heard the composer repeat sotto voce "Bravo! Bravo! Benucci".

. . . and when Benucci came to the fine passage, "Cherubino, all vittoria", the whole of the performers on the stage, and those in the orchestra, as if actuated by one feeling of delight, vociferated, "Bravo! Bravo! Maestro. Viva, viva, grande Mozart". Those in the orchestra I thought never would have ceased applauding, by beating the bows of their violins against the music desks. . . .

We must now forgive Kelly for writing mainly about himself:

In the *sestetto* (sextet) in the second act [which was Mozart's favourite piece in the whole opera] I had a very conspicuous part as the stuttering judge. All through the piece I was to stutter, but in the *sestetto* Mozart requested I would not, for if I did, I should spoil the music. I told him that although it might appear very presumptuous in a lad like me to differ with him on this point, I did, and I was sure that the way in which I intended to introduce the stuttering would not interfere with the other parts, but produce an effect . . . and I added (apologizing at the same time for my apparent want of deference and respect in placing my opinion in opposition to that of the great Mozart) that unless I was allowed to perform the part as I wished, I would not perform it at all . . . Mozart at last consented but doubted the success of the experiment.

Crowded houses proved that nothing ever on the stage produced a more powerful effect. The audiences were convulsed with laughter in which Mozart himself joined. The Emperor repeatedly called out "Bravo!" and the piece was loudly applauded and encored. When the opera was over, Mozart came on the stage to me, and shaking me by both hands, said, "Bravo, young man! I feel obliged to you and acknowledge you have been in the right and myself in the wrong. . . ."

Today Don Curzio does not stutter in the sextet because (as Mozart clearly felt) this would interfere with the music. But opera singers, being egocentric, haven't changed much. Not long ago, Lotte Lehmann told me in Vienna that she'd met an old colleague of her Vienna State Opera days who had often sung the part of Don Curzio. "Listening to him you would have thought that he had a leading part in *Figaro*", she said, smiling.

A persistent myth claims that *Le Nozze di Figaro* was a failure in Vienna. Actually the première was an enormous success, but then the Court *camarilla* of Messrs. Salieri and Righini went to work. After the ninth performance, *Figaro* was replaced by *Una Cosa Rara*, by the Spanish composer Vicente Martín y Soler. His opera is now remembered only because during the last supper scene in the final act of *Don Giovanni* the stage orchestra plays an excerpt from *Una Cosa Rara*, and Leporello comments on it approvingly: a fine touch of Mozart's sense of humour. Because almost every piece of *Figaro* was encored during the première, the performance had "the length of two operas", according to Kelly, which "induced the Emperor to issue an order on the second performance that no piece of music should be encored". Naturally, this was immediately interpreted as a victory of the anti-Mozart forces.

Oddly, *Le Nozze di Figaro*, the perfect *opera buffa*, never conquered the homeland of such operas. Perhaps the Italians believe that their own *opera buffa* is the best, or because *Figaro* is "different" from the "typical" *opera buffa*, such as *Le Barbiere di Siviglia* or *Don Pasquale*. The Italian indifference to Mozart has long baffled the world outside Italy. With few exceptions, Italians like drama, not comedy, at the opera house. The current Italian repertoire begins with *Norma* (1831) and ends with *Turandot* (1926). There should be drama, passions, tears – Bellini, Spontini, Verdi, Puccini wrote such drama. Wagner wrote super-drama and Italians love *Tristan und Isolde* but not *Meistersinger* which is "too funny". Even *Don Giovanni*, one of the greatest dramas of all, is considered a sort of *opera buffa* in disguise, and never conquered Italy. It's all very strange and paradoxical.

Figaro begins with the perfect comedy overture – light-hearted and gay, but with some serious undertones, indicating the mood of what is to come. Mozart didn't want his overtures to be a blueprint of the opera itself, whereas Weber's *Freischütz* overture or the prelude to Wagner's *Meistersinger* almost outline the plot. Mozart considered the overture literally "the opening" forming an inner unity with what comes afterwards. He achieved this by tonality, the overture "setting the key" (*Figaro* is a D-major opera). Incidentally, Mozart usually wrote his overtures after he'd finished his operas.

The *Figaro* overture ends with an exhilarating climax, that begins with the violins playing pianissimo and ends with the whole orchestra playing forte. (Later, Rossini made much use of the long crescendo which became known as the "Rossini crescendo".) When the curtain goes up, Figaro and Susanna are on the stage. He is measuring to see whether the bed will fit nicely in the room they were given by Count Almaviva. (Da Ponte, a man of taste, gets away with a mention of *quel letto* – the bed – in the recitative.) Meanwhile Susanna tries on a new hat in front of the mirror, becoming impatient with Figaro who fails to admire her. It is quite obvious who is running the show – certainly not Figaro.

Susanna has her misgivings about the room. Why? he wants to know. "Because I am Susanna and you are a fool", she replies. (Throughout the whole opera it will be shown that men are fools.) In the following *duettino* Susanna tells her fiancé her worries: the room is next to the room of the Count and the Countess. "Suppose one morning the Count rings and sends you three miles away (and she imitates the bell, "din-din, din-din"), and then, in one step, he could be at my door ..." There is an ominous rumbling in the orchestra, like faraway thunder preceding a thunderstorm. The drama is swiftly moving ahead. Susanna is already established as the key character around whom everything will revolve. She sings in all the ensembles and is on stage in most scenes. It is a perfect curtain raiser.

In his preface to the libretto, da Ponte made a polite bow to the Viennese, "a public of such refined taste and such assured understanding", but the Viennese displayed neither after the successful première. There were rumours that the Emperor had called *Figaro* "heavy". Heavy! The exhilarating comedy that has kept opera lovers happy for almost two centuries. In the second-act finale which brings together the Countess and Susanna, and later also Figaro and the Count, and finally also Bartolo, Marcellina and Basilio, there is confusion beautifully confounded.

Beaumarchais needed ten scenes to explain the complications. Mozart did it in less than a thousand bars of music. In his *Memoirs* da Ponte describes the principles of such a finale. It should be "a comedy within a comedy", must not be broken up by a recitative, and all singers must appear on the stage, even though dramatically they may not be needed. Da Ponte didn't manage to bring Cherubino into the second-act ensemble, but he did quite well with seven characters on the stage. Mozart did even better: the melancholy Countess, the angry Count, the slippery Figaro, the amusing Susanna, and the unpleasant trio of Bartolo, Basilio and Marcellina – each keeps his identity. Da Ponte said there must not be one dull moment in such a finale. There isn't.

Had he been alive, Beaumarchais might well have agreed with Stendhal, who didn't always understand Mozart's music but with a poet's intuition guessed the composer's intentions:

One could say that Mozart distorted the play as much as it is possible, but . . . he changed Beaumarchais' picture entirely . . . all the characters were turned towards the tender or the passionate. Mozart's opera is a sublime blend of wit and melancholy such as there is no other example.

"Every pause during the singers' natural breathing respite is filled with music as if an electric current were igniting the instruments into song", writes Paul Henry Lang. After Mozart's death, many imitations were written, by Johann Tost (*Figaro*, 1795); by Pietro Persechini (*Le Nozze di Figaro*); by Ferdinando Paer (*Il Nuovo Figaro*, 1797); and, in the same year, by Marcos Portugal (*Le Nozze di Figaro*). Henry Rowland Bishop, the noted nineteenth-century English musician, wrote an English adaptation, *The Marriage of Figaro* (1819). The latest addition is Giselher Klebe's modern version, *Figaro ässt sich scheiden* (Figaro Seeks a Divorce), with a psychiatrist in the cast, naturally.

On 13 January 1877, the *Prager Oberpostamtszeitung* reported,

Last night, our great and beloved composer, Herr Mozard [sic] arrived here from Vienna. We expect that in his honour Herr Bondini will schedule performances of *The Marriage of Figaro*, this popular work of his musical genius . . . We also wish to hear Herr Mozard play the piano.

Pasquale Bondini, the manager of an Italian opera company, had produced the Prague première of *Figaro* in December, 1786. It was an enormous success. The Prague public was not as Habsburg-minded as the Viennese. Or maybe they felt instinctively that *Figaro* was a great masterpiece. Mozart was delighted. On 14 January, he wrote to Gottfried von Jacquin, his friend in Vienna,

> . . . At six o'clock I drove with Count Canal to the so-called Bretfeld ball, where the cream of the beauties of Prague are wont to gather. That would have been something for you, my friend. I fancy, I see you running, or rather, limping after all those pretty women, married and unmarried! I neither danced nor flirted with any of them, the former, because I was too tired, and the latter owing to my natural bashfulness. (Blöde.) I looked on, however, with sheer delight while all these people flew about merrily to the music of my "Figaro", and arranged for quadrilles and waltzes. For here they talk about nothing but "Figaro". Nothing is played, sung, or whistled but "Figaro". No opera is drawing like "Figaro". Nothing, nothing but "Figaro". Certainly a great honour for me.

Mozart tells his friend that they all invented ridiculous nicknames for himself and his travel companions. "He delighted in this sort of familiar nonsense", wrote Eric Blom. There is no trace of solemnity in his private correspondence though there are often flashes of genius. Mozart wrote to Jacquin,

> Farewell, dearest friend, dearest Hinkity Honky! That is your name, as you must know. We all invented names for ourselves on the journey. Here they are. I am Punkititi. My wife is Schabla Pumfa. Hofer is Rozka-Pumpa. Stadler is Natschibinìtschibi. My servant Joseph is Sàgadaratà. My dog Gaukerl is Schamanuzky. Madame Quallenberg is Runzifunzi. Mademoiselle Crux Ramlo is Schurimuri. Freistädtler is Gaulimauli. Be so kind as to tell him his name. Well, adieu. . . .

Franz Xaver Niemetschek, the Mozart biographer, recalls in 1808 that Mozart had been cheered at the theatre, and later played the piano there in a "Big Musical Academy":

> We didn't know what to admire more, the extraordinary composition or the extraordinary performance: both created a total impression on our souls akin to sweet enchantment.
>
> At the end of the Academy, Mozart improvised alone on the pianoforte for half an hour and heightened our fascination to the highest degree, and there were overflowing ovations . . . **Mozart** counted this day among the best in his life . . .

A few weeks earlier in Vienna, Mozart had finished his D Major Symphony (K. 504), known as the "Prague" Symphony. It was performed in January 1787, and, according to Niemetschek, "remained a favourite piece to Prague audiences though it must have been heard a hundred times ... Mozart loved to be in Prague".

But the most important result of Mozart's happy journey to Prague was his decision to follow up his comic masterpiece with what was to become one of the greatest dramatic masterpieces of all times, *Don Giovanni*. Pasquale Bondini, the manager of the Italian opera company, cashing in on Mozart's local popularity, gave him a contract.

After his return to Vienna, Mozart discussed with da Ponte the libretto of the *Don Juan* theme that had interested him for some time, and da Ponte began to work on *Il Dissoluto Punito Ossie Il Don Giovanni*. In his *Memoirs* he writes, "For Mozart I chose *Don Giovanni*, a subject that pleased him mightily. And for Martini (as he called Martín y Soler, the composer of *Una Cosa Rara*) *L'Arbore di Diana* ... an attractive theme adaptable to sweet melodies ..." Da Ponte even helped Salieri to turn a French opera into an Italian one. Joseph II wondered how the librettist could do all these things. Da Ponte told the Emperor:

> I am going to try. I shall write evenings for Mozart, imagining that I am going to read Dante's *Inferno*. Mornings I shall work for Martini, pretending to study Petrarch. And afternoons will be for Salieri – he will be my Tasso.

Like his good friend Casanova, he seems to have had time for other diversions as well.

> I went to work on *Don Giovanni*. I sat down at my table and did not leave it for twelve hours continuous – a bottle of Tokay at my right, a box of Sevilla to my left, in the middle an inkwell. A beautiful girl of sixteen – I should have preferred to love her only as a daughter but alas ... – was living in the house with her mother. She took care of the family and came to my room at the sound of the bell. To tell the truth, the bell rang frequently, especially at moments when I found my inspiration waning ...

Many great librettists were scoundrels in their private life. Raniero de' Cazalbigi, Gluck's immensely gifted librettist and fellow reformer, was involved in many unsavoury deals in Vienna, "mismanaged" government lotteries, lent money at exorbitant rates to princes in distress. Da Ponte was always involved with politicians, debtors and the irate husbands of his numerous lady friends; his troubled affairs remind one of those of his great idol, Beaumarchais.

Mozart wrote *Don Giovanni* at a time of deep sorrow. His friend the physician Barisani had just died, and soon afterwards he lost his beloved father. In these dark days he conceived the unfathomably beautiful music of this opera, perhaps the greatest *dramma per musica* ever written, and one that projects the whole world onto the operatic stage. In the summer of 1787, he returned to Prague to finish the score which he dedicated to its people. The singers and the technical machinery in Bondini's theatre were not quite up to Mozart's exalted standards. (The theatre is still there, a beautiful baroque auditorium with frescoes and richly decorated boxes. It is now called the Tyl Theatre, Tylovo Divadlo, after the Czech playwright Josef Kajetán Tyl.)

The première of *Don Giovanni* had been scheduled for the wedding trip of Prince Anton of Saxony and Maria Theresia, the sister of Emperor Joseph II, but it had to be postponed. Instead *Figaro* was given as a gala performance. On 29 October 1787, Mozart conducted the first performance of *Don Giovanni*. Legend has it that he wrote the wonderful overture shortly before the performance, and the musicians played it from "pages still wet".

On 3 November, the *Oberpostamtszeitung* wrote,

> Connoisseurs and composers agree that such a work has never been given in Prague. Hr. Mozart conducted himself, and when he stepped into the orchestra pit, he received three ovations, and this happened again when he left. The opera is very hard to execute and everybody admires the good performance after a short rehearsal time.

That turned out to be an understatement. The success of *Don Giovanni* must have been extraordinary. Domenico Guardasoni, the stage manager, told Mozart and da Ponte that "as long as they lived there would never be any more bad seasons". *Don Giovanni* remained the most popular opera in Prague for the next hundred years, and was given 532 times during the century. One might say that it became the favourite opera of the nineteenth century, was forever adapted, often mutilated. Perhaps the first adapter was Casanova, then an old, ailing man, who had met Mozart at the Bretfeld Ball ("with all those pretty women, married and unmarried".) Casanova, truly an expert, may have contributed some substitutions and changes in the text. He must have watched the stage Don with mixed feelings.

Mozart was happy. He wrote to Jacquin, "I wished that my good friends were here for one night to take part in my happiness". And he asked, deeply worried, "Will my opera be given in Vienna?"

The days in Prague were the last happy days in Mozart's life. "A tender public and true friends carried him, so-to-speak, in their hands", Niemetschek wrote. When *Don Giovanni* was performed in Vienna, in May, 1788, the Viennese considered it "confused and dissonant". The only man there who understood the opera was Mozart's fatherly friend, Joseph Haydn, genius understanding genius. Three years later, Mozart was dead.

Opera: A Controversial Art

Opera is the most controversial art form. In fact, there is no complete agreement on whether it should be considered an art at all. Of the many thousands of operas written since 1600, few have survived: in the long run, quality breeds longevity. Popular taste may change, but the masterpieces seem to improve with age. Occasionally a work is "rediscovered" and enjoys a new vogue, but few become part of the permanent repertoire, which consists of perhaps one hundred works.

The etymology of the word "opera", which is the Italian word for "work", is uncertain. Originally, the expression was *opera per musica*, a musical work, and this came closest to defining it. Certainly, during the first hundred years of opera nobody was quite sure what "opera" was, though around 1800 it became synonymous with *dramma per musica*, which must not be confused with Richard Wagner's later *Musikdrama*. The difference between the terms *opera seria* and *opera buffa* can be very confusing as their meaning has changed over the centuries. The greatest masterpieces, such as Mozart's *Le Nozze di Figaro* and *Don Giovanni*, contain both serious and comic elements. The controversy about *Don Giovanni* persists; some call it a comic opera and others consider it a deeply tragic work. Da Ponte and Mozart called it a *dramma giocoso* which confounded the confusion. Had Mozart considered *Don Giovanni* pure tragedy, he wouldn't have written the ironic finale. He would have finished the opera with the catastrophic end of the Don.

Opera has been called artificial, a hybrid art form. Purists, who refuse to listen to it and whose admiration for Verdi is limited to his magnificent *Requiem Mass*, may not realize that the latter is in fact an opera in concert form.

Generations of writers have repeated Dr Samuel Johnson's statement that opera is "an exotic and irrational entertainment", without explaining that the quotation is out of context. In his *Lives of the Poets*, Dr Johnson refers to six cantatas with words by Hughes, which "seem intended to oppose or exclude the Italian opera, an exotick and irrational entertainment, which has always been combated . . ." Dr Johnson was referring to the Italian opera then given at the Haymarket by a company known in London as The Italian Opera. The audience didn't understand the words, chatted during the duller passages, and paid attention only to the tunes sung by one of the famous "canary birds", as the Doctor called the *divas*. He was delighted when *The Beggar's Opera* parodied the Italian opera, and "drove out of England the Italian opera which had carried all before it for ten years". He noted that Hughes' *Calypso and Telemachus* was "intended to shew that the English language might be very happily adapted to musick", starting an argument which is still going on.

Many people don't care much about painting or sculpture but they do not dislike or hate these art forms. Yet many people actually hate opera, and those who like it love it passionately. Very few can just take it or leave it. People have gone to hear opera for strange reasons. In 1782, Lord Shelburne wrote to Lord Thurlow, "My lord, I am going to the opera to cure a cold", because this was making him "incapable of doing anything else except conversing". Nowadays, people in London no longer go to the opera to converse. Many agree with Jonathan Griffin, the playwright, that "opera gives such a shot of vitality as the straight theatre seldom produces". At its best, opera is the most effective escape of all performing arts because of its *inner* reality. In *Journey towards Music*, Sir Victor Gollancz, a lifelong opera addict, wrote,

> It is opera that I find the more natural, and spoken plays the less closely connected with the reality of life; and if I am to see a play, then I prefer a poetic one, poetic in the narrower sense. Poetry provides the nearest approach possible, after music, to ultimate reality . . .

Sometimes opera has a shattering reality (the prisoners in *Fidelio*, singing their stirring hymn to freedom; the social and human tragedy of the poor soldier-hero in *Wozzeck;* and the deep problems underlying the light-hearted fun in *Figaro*). Peter Brook, the producer, calls it "alienation . . . the art of placing an action at a distance so that it can be judged objectively and seen in relation to the world". In opera, music "places the action at a distance" and may give it an inner truth. Not in *Tosca*, but in *Carmen;* not in *Lohengrin,* but in *Otello.*

Opera should be approached intellectually *and* emotionally. The confusing nonsense of the libretto of *Il Trovatore* or the improbable curse hovering over *Rigoletto* cannot be logically analysed. Nevertheless, the genius of Verdi makes these operas exciting (and unbelievable) experiences. The drama appeals to the mind, but the music touches the soul and the heart. No opera lover fails to be carried away by Manrico's "Di quella pira" in the third act of *Il Trovatore,* especially when the tenor interpolates the famous high C which is not in Verdi's score.

Owing to its complexities, opera poses enormous problems of performance. A soloist at the concert hall is judged for the way he feels and expresses the music. A symphony concert depends on the quality of the ensemble and the art of the conductor. Ideally, the music should be performed as the living expression of the composer's score. In opera, however, there are divergent elements. Music is one, action is another. There are things to be seen and to be heard, emotions to be sensed and felt. Aesthetically, it may be a mishmash but in the hands of a genius opera becomes a glorious experience, deeply satisfying. Wagner's *Gesamtkunstwerk,* or "total theatre", is a superb proof of the mixture-as-never-before. "His (Richard Wagner's) genius lies in the dramatic synthesis of the arts, which only as a whole, precisely as a synthesis, answers to our conception of a genuine and legitimate work of art", wrote Thomas Mann in his essay on Wagner, delivered on 10 February 1933, shortly after Hitler came to power. Wagner was Hitler's hero and favourite composer. Later on, Mann, in exile, changed his views about Wagner.

Because opera is such a demanding and complex art form, a performance rarely attains perfection – but then, "perfection" is a word that has no place in the vocabulary of the true artist because it can never be attained. Bruno Walter said that he'd never in his life conducted an opera performance which completely satisfied him. Many conductors admit that it is easier to come close to perfection in the concert hall than in the opera house.

Opera is dramatic entertainment, yet its singers rarely have the pre-requisites of dramatic actors. Until recently, acting on the opera stage was a ridiculous exhibition of stilted clichés. Of a great prima donna, Nellie Melba, her friend-biographer Percy Colson wrote that "to express a mild emotion, such as Juliette's love for Romeo, she would raise one arm, to express extreme passion or violent despair, she would raise two". Caruso, perhaps the most exciting tenor in recent history, was not a great actor. When the critics call an artist "a singing actor" they imply that he's better as an actor than as a singer. Even today, with imaginative producers, singers often depend on clichés, lifting their arms in moments of drama, and acting as no sensible person behaves in real life.

To be understood, opera must be lived. The audience doesn't have to be sympathetic – hostile audiences can be a challenge for the performers – but they must be involved in it. Unlike theatre-goers, most members of the opera audience go to hear the same popular masterpieces time and again; people who have attended thirty or forty performances of *Hamlet* or Goethe's *Faust* are the exception, but I know quite a few who have heard *Figaro* or *La Bohème* dozens of times and always discover something new and beautiful.

Opera needs an *active* audience. The relationship between stage, orchestra pit and auditorium has never been scientifically investigated, but everyone in the opera house knows its importance. Dull audiences stifle the most enthusiastic performers. Even a great artist resigns when his efforts are not appreciated, while a demanding audience may force a not-so-great performer to out-do himself. Today celebrated singing stars, who can choose their engagements, prefer houses known for their receptive audience – Milan's La Scala or Vienna's State Opera. New York and London audiences have improved considerably in the past few years.

Unlike architecture and painting which are expressed in terms of colour and space, music is dominated by the inexorable flow of time. A piece of music performed in the wrong tempo is like a building erected on shaky foundations. Setting and maintaining the right tempo and keeping up the flow of music is an important element of the conductor's task. Yet, paradoxically, it is this variable characteristic of opera that is so attractive to its habitués. Many prefer an imperfect live opera performance to an almost-perfect, recorded performance, where the touch of the master technician and acoustical cosmetics expert is apparent. The wonderful uniqueness about opera is that tonight's performance of *Figaro* will be different from last week's and from next week's. Unpredictability makes opera an exciting adventure.

HOW IT BEGAN

Opera has come a long way from its origins in sixteenth-century Florence. Conceived during the late Renaissance, it developed during the Baroque and matured during the Romantic Age. Created by aesthetes and theoreticians, not by dramatists and composers, it grew from the belief, widespread during the Renaissance, that music might revitalize the art of ancient Greek drama. The Renaissance expressed drama through poetry. To express the drama of the soul, another language was needed: music.

The early "music drama" was half drama and half music, which is what it remains to many critics today, who say that people in ordinary life do not sing when they express their thoughts and feelings. However, opera doesn't attempt credibility by expressing the conflicts of life through spoken words, it attempts to project the hidden emotions of the soul that mere words can never convey. As an art form, opera is an emotional phenomenon, not an analysable experience. Both Shakespeare's *Othello* and Verdi's *Otello* are timeless masterpieces. It remains a mystery of the creative spirit that Verdi was not intimidated by the greatness of Shakespeare's drama, but was stimulated to create his own expression of this human tragedy.

While the academicians were still mostly under the influence of the Renaissance, certain poets, artists and philosophers perceived the new, dynamic world of the Baroque, which Michelangelo and El Greco expressed in their paintings. In Florence, there emerged the *Camerata,* an artistic society of art-loving noblemen (Giovanni Bardi and Jacopo Corsi), poets (Ottavio Rinucini and Gabriello Chiabrera), singers (Jacopo Peri and Guilio Caccini), and musical theoreticians (Girolamo Mei and Vincenzo Galilei, the father of the great astronomer). Not a member, but in touch with the group was the gifted composer, Marco da Gagliano.

In 1581, Galilei had published his *Dialogo della Musica Antica e Moderna,* in which he attacked the musical system of the preceding age, the counterpoint and vocal polyphony of Palestrina and Orlando di Lasso that seemed to lead nowhere. He asked the artists to restore the simple, lucid, classic expression of the Greeks. The Florentine humanists based their theories on the assumption that the Greeks sang their tragedies on the stage. Actually, little was known about Greek music. The Greek drama was believed to have contained choruses, emotional outbursts and even arias sung throughout the play. The Florentines claimed that the Greeks had created the first operas. But no Greek scores exist. Galilei even composed several songs for voice accompanied by the lute which some historians consider a forerunner of the earliest opera. Unfortunately they are lost and we shall never know whether they combined drama with music.

Even before the *Camerata,* poets and musicians had attempted a new union of poetry and music. Torquato Tasso, the poet, had worked with Don Carlo Gesualdo, Prince of Venosa, whose new chords and modulations made him something of a radical member of a new "chromatic" school. Chiabrera collaborated with Caccini whose Preface to *Nuove Musiche* mentions "the idea of composing a harmonic speech ... music in which a noble restraint was placed on singing in favour of the words". Ever since, poets and composers have tried to find the balance between poetry and music, trying to divine whether "poetry must be altogether the obedient daughter of music", as Mozart wrote to his father. Richard Strauss wrote *Capriccio*, "a conversation piece with music", about whether the words or the music are more important in opera. Characteristically, he left the question open. At the very end of *Capriccio*, the Countess, whom both the poet and the composer adore, says that tomorrow she will announce which one of them she favours ...

From its earliest beginnings, opera depended on the support of aristocratic patrons. Towards the end of the sixteenth century, Ottavio Rinuccini, a noted member of the *Camerata,* skilled poet and much esteemed by the Medicis, wrote *Dafne, una favola pastorale* (a pastoral fable) to resurrect Greek tragedy. It was first performed some time in the 1590s, no one knows exactly when, in the palace of Jacopo Corsi. The music was written by Peri and Caccini. *Dafne* was a success, but Rinuccini was dissatisfied and continued to rewrite the libretto. In 1608, Marco da Gagliano set it anew to music (it was translated into German by Martin Opitz, and Heinrich Schütz wrote the music in 1627. Thus *Dafne* also became the first German opera).

The score of *Dafne* is lost but we have the libretto and the music of *Euridice,* which Rinuccini wrote later for the wedding celebration of Henry IV of France and Maria de' Medici. Again, Peri and Caccini wrote the music. On 16 October 1600, the world première of *Euridice* was given at the Palazzo Pitti in Florence under the direction of Jacopo Corsi. This event is generally looked upon as the first opera performance. Peri wrote most of the music; Caccini later added a few arias. Peri explained that he'd written the music to express various nuances of speech and feeling. Much of the work is written in the *recitar cantando* (recitative) style, a form that lies between words and music. A small orchestra supported the singers but it was not allowed to attract the attention of the audience. The text had to be clearly understood (a requirement that many later composers unfortunately did not consider important). The work, which consisted of classical-style choruses and tedious recitatives was called "a noble effort", and deserves interest rather than admiration. It was an academic effort by people whose intentions surpassed their abilities, reminiscent of earlier madrigal plays. Peri was an able musician but he knew little about drama while Caccini was mostly interested in the singing line and vocal *fioriture* (cadenzas, roulades, runs).

MONTEVERDI

Obviously, the stage was set for a genius who would understand what the *Camerata* was after and who wasn't afraid to break the rules of the game and create his own. Claudio Monteverdi had been born in Cremona in 1567. He was the first true genius in the history of opera, truly "the Aeschylos of music".

Monteverdi could have been a member of the small audience at the Palazzo Pitti in Florence that heard the first performance of *Euridice* in 1600. In nearby Mantua, Duke Vincenzo Gonzaga, who loved the "new" music drama, asked Monteverdi to set to music a drama which the Duke's Secretary of State, Alessandro Striggio, had written. Striggio's father had been a famous madrigalist and Striggio himself was no ordinary bureaucrat. It was Duke Vincenzo who financed the first performance, in February 1607, of *Orfeo*, Monteverdi's first opera.

Unlike most members of the *Camerata*, Monteverdi was not an esoteric aesthete and intellectual. He was a passionate, creative artist who sensed instinctively that music could express psychological conflicts, the passions of the soul. He used a small orchestra not only to accompany the singers but to express moods, conflict and passion and, above all, dramatic effect. Monteverdi created melodies that were not just 'graceful', as those of his predecessors had been, but sinister and often haunting. The protagonists were supported by special instruments. *Orfeo* is the first real opera in our sense of the word. One year later Monteverdi wrote *Arianna*, for the wedding of Francesco Gonzaga to Margaret of Savoy and Arianna's "lament" became a popular song. Of Monteverdi's late operas, two are now frequently performed: *L'Incoronazione di Poppea* and *Il Ritorno d'Ulisse in Patria*. *Poppea* has been successfully performed at many opera houses with a score that has been "modernized and enriched" by arrangers who seem to feel that Monteverdi's original may sound too "thin" to our ears. Unfortunately dead composers cannot defend themselves against their "arrangers".

Poppea is an astonishing work, very modern in its treatment of human emotions, with passionate music and beautiful melodies. It is timeless and powerful – a masterpiece. Monteverdi wrote it when he was seventy-five, a feat comparable only to Verdi's writing *Falstaff* at the age of eighty. Monteverdi has been compared to Wagner, because both created entirely new art forms; to Michelangelo, because of his titanic struggle for the expression of human emotions; to Rembrandt, because he unveiled the most secret depths of the soul. But when all is said, he is as incomparable as Haydn, who, single-handed, created the form of the string quartet, or as the inexplicable genius of Mozart.

Monteverdi, the creator of modern opera, also helped to develop the modern-style opera house. In 1612, after the death of the Duke of Mantua, Monteverdi, then famous all over Italy, became master of music to the Most Serene Republic of Venice, and conductor at St Marco's, one of the top musical jobs in Italy. There was no opera in Venice when he arrived there and he spent several years writing madrigals and church music, some of which were edited in 1927 by Francesco Malipiero, the modern Italian composer.

In 1630, Venice was swept by an epidemic of the plague. There was no audience for fun and artistic enjoyment. Two years later Monteverdi, who was then sixty-five, was ordained a Catholic priest and was ready for retirement. But five years later the first opera house was opened in Venice and he returned from retirement to become the world's first opera manager, at the Teatro San Cassiano. From Venice, the new performing art was exported to the courts of France and Vienna, where the early baroque opera became known as "Venetian opera".

In Vienna, the earliest operatic performances took place at the beginning of the seventeenth century. Opera was considered strictly an entertainment for the Emperor. Ferdinand III of Habsburg became the first patron of opera. His wife, Eleonora Gonzaga, had inherited her passion for opera from her father, the Duke of Mantua. The original score of Monteverdi's *Il Ritorno d'Ulisse* is now in the Austrian National Library. Local historians believe that Monteverdi was in direct contact with the Imperial Court though he never went to Vienna.

Two of his pupils, Pier Francesco Cavalli and Pietro Antonio Cesti (sometimes wrongly known as Marc 'Antonio from a contraction of his title, Marchese), wrote several works for Vienna. Cavalli, who went to Paris at the invitation of Cardinal Mazarin, wrote *L'Egisto* in 1643 for a Viennese production. The libretto is a Venetian "love chain", a comedy of error and intrigue: "Egisto loves Cloris who is enamoured of Lidio for whom Climene sighs" (Robert Haas). Cesti, formerly a Franciscan monk, was from 1666 until 1669 deputy *Kapellmeister* to the Emperor Leopold I, the most musical of the Habsburg rulers. Cesti's super-opera, *Il Pomo d'Oro*, was performed to celebrate in style the marriage of Leopold I to Margareta Teresa of Spain. The celebration, a gigantic pageant, lasted two years. Leopold I, who personified the idea of absolute monarchy during the baroque age, considered opera not only his personal hobby and private domain but also the expression of political power and Imperial patronage. He was a noted composer who wrote ninety-seven pieces of church music, nine "theatrical festivities", one hundred and two dances, and a requiem for his wife. When he thought he was going to die, he ordered his Imperial orchestra to perform his favourite compositions in an adjoining hall. A perfect way of dying for an Austrian emperor.

The Thirty Years War came to an end in 1648. The relief and gratitude to God is apparent in the exultant statues and buildings of the Viennese Baroque (that has shocked the very souls of many Puritan visitors). And there were super-pageants in which almost the whole population took part. Robert Haas writes that the celebrations included "Jesuit dramas, banquets and balls, Italian and Spanish comedies, a piece by Cesti called *Neptune and Flora*, a ballet performed by the nobility, introducing twelve Ethiopian beauties whose jewellery was of 'untold value', an overture by Draghi, two full-length equestrian ballets, one of which, the famous *Contesta dell'aria e dell' acqua,* was given in the Hofburg, conducted by the Florentine Cavaliere Alessandro Carducci, while another, *Germania Trionfante,* was staged at the Imperial Favorita." In addition there were three festival operas: Bertali's *Abele ed Atti,* Draghi's *Die siegprangende römische Monarchei,* and the *pièce de résistance,* Cesti's *Il Pomo d'Oro.*

Cesti's opera ran for a whole year and became the talk of Europe, an artistic *and* political event. The opera had five acts with sixty-seven scenes, fifty soloists and a cast of a thousand. A special theatre, Theater auf der Cortina, was constructed on the site, now known as Kaisergarten, by the famous Italian architects, Ludovico Burnacini and Jacopo Torelli, with seats for five thousand people (New York's Metropolitan has three thousand eight hundred seats). The total cost of the production was over 300,000 guilders. This presented no problem: the Emperor paid for it. Cesti's scene reaches from heaven to earth and the underworld. The story was written around the Judgement of Paris, with many liberties and distortions. In the end, Zeus makes a triumphal entry in *deus-ex-machina* style and rules that the apple shall be awarded not to one of three beautiful ladies but to the young Empress of Austria. The late Cecil B. De Mille would have been pleased with the production.

The opera house especially built for Cesti's opera was pulled down in 1683, during the Second Turkish Siege, for military reasons, but half a dozen other theatres and sites were requisitioned for opera performances. At the new Favorita, today the Theresianum, a large artificial pond was built for the presentation of "sea battles" on the stage. Once in a while a picture gallery was commandeered for stage-struck amateur players at the Court.

Having discovered their predilection for opera, the Italians never lost it. In Rome, opera flourished first as sacred opera, presented in the houses of cardinals and princes, and later as secular opera. The leading patrons were the Barberinis, three princes who built their own private opera house, the Teatro Barberini. It wasn't exactly an "intimate" house, having three thousand seats (about the size of La Scala in Milan). The opening performance, in 1632, was *Santo Alessio*, by Steffano Landi, a "noble, dramatic, melodic" work. Landi inserted comical and farcical elements, which may have been the beginnings of *opera buffa*. Five years later, the Barberinis produced *Il Falcone*, a musical comedy composed by Vergilio Mazzocchi, choirmaster of St Peter's. The libretto was by Cardinal Rospigliosi who later became Pope Clement IX. As papal envoy in Madrid, the Cardinal had studied the Spanish theatre. Thus a Pope was one of the originators of comic opera in Italy. In 1653, his *Dal Male il Bene*, a farcical comedy of errors, was performed, with many amusing situations which later residents of the Vatican City would probably prefer to forget.

The Roman school of opera influenced the various schools elsewhere in Italy. The late seventeenth century was the first "golden age" of opera. Around 1670, there were over sixty theatres performing opera in the city of Bologna. In 1678, one hundred and thirty different operas were performed in Rome, some of them in private houses. But the real opera addicts were in Venice, then a city of 150,000 people, where during the second half of the century over three hundred different works were performed in sixteen large opera houses.

Such operas were quickly composed, produced and forgotten, somewhat as films are today; few scores were printed, and when another theatre wanted to perform the work the composer sent his original manuscript there. If they didn't have all the necessary singers, the composer would adjust the score. The audience would read the libretto during the performance, often with the help of candles, which accounts for the burning down of a number of opera houses.

The "golden era" wasn't pure gold though. Owing to the continuous demand for new works, librettists and composers had to work rapidly. They had no time for such details as characterization or a convincing dramatic structure. The operas were rather short – Monteverdi's *Euridice* lasting only half an hour – and the emphasis was on favourite singers and elaborate staging. However, there were marvellous "transformation scenes" and other engineering triumphs of make-believe. Ballrooms were suspended over the permanent stage. To stretch their works, the composers would put in comical "intermezzi" and dances, such as occurred later in grand opera. Even Verdi felt compelled to insert ballets when he wrote *Aida*, the grandest of all grand operas, commissioned for the celebration of the opening of the Suez Canal. Unfortunately, the ballet usually interrupts the flow of the drama.

The Baroque is characterized by ornament – in buildings, sculpture, paintings, and in music. The baroque composers would sometimes merely outline the melodic line, leaving the ornamentation to the performers who were often masters in the art of singing, from simple *fioriture* to virtuoso coloratura passages. Singing became a matter of vocal pyrotechnics, unnatural for the human voice. Thus the castrato became the star of the opera. Emasculated before puberty, he kept his sexless, clear, boyhood timbre and, having attained the lung power and larynx of an adult, could do miracles of acrobatic singing. *Castrati* remained famous until the days of Gluck and Mozart, especially in Italy. In our own time their influence is still reflected in the "trouser roles" such as Cherubino in *Figaro*, Octavian in *Rosenkavalier,* the composer in *Ariadne auf Naxos.*

Foreigners in Italy were often shocked by the nationwide passion for opera that reached even into the churches. Divine services were held in the form of opera. At the time of the High Baroque, opera was the perfect expression of the arts: spectacular and overwhelming, beautiful and exciting ("Baroque" means grotesque and extravagant, bizarre and flamboyant). The famous composers and singers earned a great deal of money, the former receiving from two to four hundred ducats for a score, mostly from rich aristocrats. Later, boxes at the opera were leased to less aristocratic: rich people. Venice was the first city with regular operatic seasons, one after the beginning of the year, during carnival; an ascension season, from Easter to the middle of June; and an autumn season, from early September to late November. From Italy, the passion for opera spread over Europe, and finally to America, where the first Italian opera was given in 1824.

SCARLATTI, PERGOLESI, CIMAROSA

In the past decades, the genius of Monteverdi has been fully recognized. He was the first great creator of opera who injected life into opera and opera into life. (After him, only Gluck, Mozart, Verdi and Wagner deserve to be called innovators.) Monteverdi had the vision, the courage, the skill. He had studied the great polyphonic music written before him, and was a great polyphonist himself, but he was not satisfied with this music and the writing of madrigals, lyrical-poetic songs that were very popular. Monteverdi was a dramatic composer who sensed that he could express his dramatic ideas only through the medium of what *he* considered an opera. None of the operas written by his pupils, Cavalli and Cesti, have survived. The first really popular successes after Monteverdi's operas were Pergolesi's *La Serva Padrona* (1733), and Gluck's *Orfeo* (1762), another milestone in the evolution of opera. The great composers during the first century and a half of opera are better known to scholars than to the public: Lully, Purcell, Keiser, Telemann, Rameau.

Alessandro Scarlatti, who wrote one hundred and fifteen operas, cannot be omitted even from a short history of opera. A greater musician than his famous son, Domenico, a harpsichordist whose keyboard music is much admired, Alessandro Scarlatti was the most important influence between Monteverdi and Handel, yet his operas are forgotten for the same reason that Handel's operas are rarely performed: they were written for their own times.

Scarlatti wrote baroque operas for the baroque age. He was born, probably in 1660, in Palermo, and studied with Giovanni Giacomo Carissimi, an oratorio composer of repute. In Rome, Scarlatti attracted the attention of the former Swedish Queen, Christina, a strange and violent lady who had operas performed in her palace and who once shook hands with Pope Alexander VII so fervently that she broke some bones in his fingers.

For a while Scarlatti remained her protégé, but as the papal influence extended even to composing, he escaped to Naples where he became court conductor to the Spanish Viceroy. There he evolved a form of composition that later influenced Handel and many other composers. He developed the "modern" Italian opera, which means opera for singers, and he created the Italian overture in three movements, fast-slow-fast (Lully later created the French overture, which is slow-fast-slow). Scarlatti made the *da capo* aria the climax of the action: the aria is followed by a contrasting part and again ends *da capo*, as it began. Between such arias he wrote accompanied recitatives, which carried on the action. He knew a lot about singing and wrote beautiful melodies, and it is largely due to him that Italian opera remains synonymous with melody and the art of singing. Later, the focus of opera temporarily shifted to England, France, Germany and Austria, but it always returned to Italy, its home-land, and when Italian composers went elsewhere, they still wrote "Italianate" operas, for singers. Scarlatti's two best-known works, *Tigrano* and *Mitridate Eupatore*, deserve rediscovery. The latter, a five-act tragedy with two comic characters and a ballet, was composed for Ferdinando de' Medici in Florence. It has been called "a great classical masterpiece", because of the composer's genius for handling heroic figures in tragic predicaments.

His most famous pupil was Giovanni Battista Pergolesi who did almost as much for *opera buffa* as Monteverdi had done for *opera seria*. There is some academic dispute about whether *opera buffa* was created in Venice, or in Naples, where the *intermezzi* had become so popular that special houses were built for them around 1730. The *intermezzi* (the plural form of two one-act interludes, each called an *intermezzo*) were short, farcical plays accompanied by a small orchestra and were often added as comic relief to dull *opera seria* performances. *Opera seria* would transport the audience to the gods and their mythological doings. *Opera buffa* was strictly by and for the little people, low-brow and much more fun. They were domestic comedies about clever servants outwitting their dignified masters, or parodies of serious works and started as low-budget produc-tions, with only two or three characters that were well known to the audiences, almost like the characters of the older *commedia dell' arte*. The parts were sung by both men and women, except in Rome, where *castrati* sang the women's parts, because the Church wouldn't permit women on the stage. The men were usually bass voices, known ever since as *basso buffo*, and the women were soubrettes. This was something new. Until then the bass voice had expressed nobility and dignity, but *opera buffa* turned the bass voice into a comic. Could Verdi's *Falstaff* be anything but a bass?

It was no accident that Naples became the birthplace of *opera buffa*. Naples had been a part of Spain since 1505 and was administered by a Viceroy until it became a province of the Habsburg Empire in the early eighteenth century. The Spanish brought their own theatrical art to Naples. Their influence was strong in the libretti and in the comedies, which were reminiscent of the Spanish folk theatre. The music, however, was pure Italian. The gifted musicians of Naples had a talent for parody. The most gifted of them was Pergolesi. God knows what he might have accomplished had he not died in 1736, at the age of twenty-six.

Pergolesi used melody for the first time to express grotesque terror and musical realism. When Tracollo, in *La Serva Padrona*, is caught stealing and afraid to be hanged, he sings the aria, "Ecco il povero Tracollo" – the rope "chills me from head to foot". The accompaniment, a descending chromatic bass, is heard: he "shivers with fright", and there is a tremolo of fear. Pergolesi also used for the first time the art of the ensemble. In the *opera seria* it wasn't good manners to interrupt the solo aria of a singer. Pergolesi developed the art of the duet, in which two people argue, and he expressed their conflicting thoughts in his music. From the duet he progressed to the trio and a quintet. Sometimes he divided his ensembles into two groups of opposing forces. Pergolesi's technique was later brought to perfection by Mozart in *Le Nozze di Figaro*. There are other similarities in their masterpieces. The theme of both *La Serva Padrona* and *Figaro* is the clever servant who outwits the rather stupid aristocratic master and was one which remained prominent for half a century. Both Pergolesi and Mozart worked quickly, as though aware that there was little time, and both died young and poor. Mozart was overtaken by death before he could finish his *Requiem*, while, according to legend, Pergolesi completed his *Stabat Mater* on his deathbed (actually he wrote this work when he was nineteen and healthy).

Pergolesi was followed by Domenico Cimarosa, another Italian master of *opera buffa*. He was born in 1749, thirteen years after the death of Pergolesi, and wrote full-length comic operas. Unlike Pergolesi, a young man who protested against the "Establishment" and turned the sublime into the ridiculous, Cimarosa penetrated deeply into his characters, and was often tender and lyrical.

OPERA IN ENGLAND

English writers have tried long and hard to establish their country's position in the history of opera, but operatically England has never been an Empire. "Except for a rare sport, usually in some comic genre, no English operas have established themselves fully to this day", Brockway and Weinstock write in *The World of Opera*. A paradox, for England made great contributions to the development of church music and instrumental chamber music. In the days of Mozart and Beethoven, pompous German critics condescendingly called England "*Land ohne Musik*", a land without music, which was absurd. But England was often without opera. "The history of music shows us that up to the end of the sixteenth century the church was the only place in which music could be performed on an extended scale", Edward J.Dent wrote in *Opera*. "Instrumental chamber music ... like the English madrigals, was music for private houses ... English travellers like Milton and Evelyn went to Italy and saw the new entertainments that were called operas, but it was a long time before anything like a real opera could be put on the English stage."

Every nation gets the art it deserves. The Italians recognized themselves in opera. The Viennese wanted spectacles with music, and in their own manner reached the road to opera. The French loved the ballet, and for centuries accepted opera only when it contained some ballet. And the English public always wanted plays, with or without music, but the play was the thing; in this respect, they have outstripped any other nation.

But there are exceptions. Purcell was a genius, though his masterpiece, *Dido and Aeneas*, probably first performed in December 1689, was ignored for over two hundred years, until 1895, the bicentenary of Purcell's death. Handel remains immortal for his oratorios, not for his operas. He made the oratorio a specifically English art, a sort of opera on the concert stage, and the English loved it. Herr Georg Friedrich Händel (with umlaut) from Halle, Germany, who became more English than the English and tried so hard to establish opera in England, ruined opera there for centuries. He never understood the dramatic elements of opera as Gluck and Mozart did. It wasn't Handel's operas but *The Beggar's Opera* that became England's own form of vernacular opera, light and witty and amusing, like the later masterpieces of Gilbert and Sullivan. Professor Dent in 1949 tried to make up a list of native operas "which might be reasonably included in the repertory of a British opera house". He admits that Purcell's and Handel's operas belong in the category of "museum operas". *The Beggar's Opera*, naturally. But "after *The Beggar's Opera* we shall have to make a long jump". Weber's *Oberon*, undoubtedly (though some German *Professoren* will disagree), since "the libretto is as English as it can be in its absurdities ... it was composed for England and to us it belongs", as Dent says.

Passing over three popular favourites (*The Bohemian Girl*, *Maritana* and *The Lily of Killarney*) there is a long, long jump again until 1945, when Benjamin Britten's *Peter Grimes* was first produced at Sadler's Wells, and became a worldwide critical and box-office success. Many houses now perform *Peter Grimes*. "And even one permanent opera by a native composer, on an essentially native subject," could justifiably mean "a new chapter in English operatic history", Dent concludes somewhat wistfully. At any rate, the old notion that the English are not an opera-loving nation is gradually being broken down.

Opera in England is believed to go back to 1656 when Sir William Davenant's play, *The Siege of Rhodes*, was performed at Rutland House. Davenant (whose name is sometimes spelled D'Avenant) was then a poet laureate who amused himself by spreading the rumour that he was Shakespeare's illegitimate child. If he was – which is doubtful – he inherited nothing of his father's genius. Davenant had gone to Paris to visit Queen Henrietta Maria and her son, the future King Charles II, and became interested in the French drama and Italian opera. But his play was not influenced by foreign models. *The Siege* is about the capture of the island of Rhodes, defended by the Knights of St John against Sultan Suleiman the Magnificent, in 1522. The siege forms the background for fictional episodes that were "to advance the character of virtue in the shapes of valour and conjugal love". (Does that sound like Shakespeare Jr?) There was only one aria, the rest was dialogue-recitative. The music, by Matthew Locke and others, is lost. Davenant later wrote *The Cruelty of the Spaniards in Peru*, and *The History of Sir Francis Drake*. These scores, too, have disappeared.

Davenant's plays were successful but not because of the music. John Dryden expressed people's feelings in his preface to *Albion and Albanius*, "An Opera is a Poetical Tale, or Fiction, represented by Vocal and Instrumental Musick, adorn'd with Scenes, Machines and Dancing. The suppos'd Persons of this Musical Drama are generally Supernatural, as Gods, and Goddesses, and Heroes, which are at least descended from them, and are in due time to be adopted into their number." This isn't the proper climate for opera. A Frenchman, Louis Grabu, wrote the "musick" to Dryden's play. He didn't know much English, the music wasn't good – and the work was a failure. Little is known about the next English opera, *Venus and Adonis*, by John Blow, composed around 1685, except that the part of Venus was sung by Mrs Mary Davis, friend of the King. This work became the model for the first real English opera – Henry Purcell's *Dido and Aeneas*. It is now often compared to Lully's works because Purcell had as much influence on later composers in England as Lully had in France. Purcell was a church musician whose dramatic sense drove him to opera. In 1691, he collaborated with Dryden on

King Arthur, and later wrote the incidental music for Shakespeare's *Timon of Athens* and *The Tempest.*

Dido and Aeneas is a great operatic masterpiece, although it is short, less than an hour, with a simple story that was written for the youthful audience at Josias Priest's school for young ladies in Chelsea. Dido's moving lament, "When I am laid in earth", must have moved them to tears. It became one of the most famous songs of its time. The opera has no conventional happy end: Dido, jilted by Aeneas, commits suicide. Purcell's music has a wide range of emotions. The dances sound like Lully's (sometimes, indeed, Purcell would amuse himself by inserting a Lully composition).

Unfortunately, *Dido and Aeneas* is often treated almost like a ballet. False attempts are made to add instruments and to "orchestrate" the score for modern taste. Purcell's beautiful work should be performed as it was written, preferably in a small house. Purcell failed to win popular fame in his own epoch, perhaps because to some he seemed a late Elizabethan, to others a modern composer. Both the conservatives and the progressives saw his shortcomings rather than his great talent. If he had lived longer – he died in 1695, only thirty-seven years old – he might now be mentioned in the same breath as Handel.

After Purcell's death, Italian singers became the fashion. They brought Italian music to London. In 1708, Scarlatti's *Pyrrhus and Demetrius* was performed in London. At Vanbrugh's New Theatre in the Haymarket, later known as the King's Theatre, *Almahide* was performed, in Italian, in 1710. The composer is unknown; perhaps the work was a *pasticcio* (a work consisting of different elements) made by several composers. Dr Charles Burney, the eminent musical historian, wrote,

> The vocal Music of Italy can only be heard in perfection when sung to its own language and by its own natives, who give both the language and Music their true accents and expressions. There is as much reason for wishing to hear Italian Music in this genuine manner, as for the lovers of painting to prefer an original picture of Raphael to a copy.

Partisans of opera-must-be-sung-in-the-original-language will be pleased.

In 1710, Handel arrived in London. Ernest Walker writes, "It is a singular fact that the composer who has left the deepest impress on English music should have been a German who came to England as an upholder of a purely Italian art". The following year his opera *Rinaldo* was produced "to tremendous acclaim". In the previous year Handel had

had a great success in Venice with his opera *Agrippina,* which made him famous throughout Italy. He returned to London and decided to live there because he felt very much at home among the English. He came to look like John Bull, in 1726 was naturalized, dropped the umlaut in his name and became George Frideric Handel. Now he is English, no matter what people may say in Halle, Germany, or elsewhere.

For thirty years, Handel produced Italian opera in London. He was often in trouble – with his associates, his prima donnas, his public. A group of English aristocrats under the almost tone-deaf Duke of Marlborough favoured one of the Royal Academy's "associate composers", Giovanni Battista Buononcini. King George I, who loved music, was on Handel's side. In 1720, Handel had a sensational success with his *Radamisto,* and Buononcini with his *Astarto.* The opera lovers in London were divided into two factions. For some time Buononcini's tuneful operas were more popular than Handel's, who countered by importing famous prima donnas and expensive *castrati.* In 1721, he had much success with *Floridante* but Buononcini came up with *Griselda,* his best work, and when Buononcini was commissioned to write the music for the funeral of the Duke of Marlborough, Handel became desperate. He hired a famous Italian *diva,* Francesca Cuzzoni, who astounded everybody with a great performance in Handel's *Ottone.* Things got out of control though when the shareholders forced Handel to send for "la nuova sirena", Faustina Bordoni, a lovely mezzo-soprano. If anything is worse than one prima donna, it is two. The ladies actually fought each other on the stage, much to the enjoyment of their audiences. (The Callas-Tebaldi feud is dull, by comparison.) It may have been great fun for the public but not for Handel who was so angry with his two prima donnas that he threatened to throw them both out of his window. In the end, he was defeated not by them but by a new craze: *The Beggar's Opera,* first performed in 1728.

Handel's public had grown bored with mythological fables or stories about old Greece. The libretti's hellenistic characters or neo-Romans spoke a language no one understood. Suddenly, one John Gay, a talented poet with a gift for sharp satire and salacious innuendo, and Dr Johann Christoph Pepusch, an immigrant from Berlin, came up with a clever parody of Italian opera. Gay didn't like the Whigs; Pepusch hated his fellow-immigrant Handel – which didn't prevent his "borrowing" some of Handel's arias and Purcell's music. Pepusch also contributed two original numbers, an overture and a song. Gay's contribution was more important. *The Beggar's Opera* was an incredible success. Soon Gay was telling everybody how rich he was getting, and his leading lady Lavinia Fenton, who had created the part of Polly, did very well for herself, becoming the mistress and later the wife of the Duke of Bolton, finally inheriting his millions.

Handel failed to understand the success of *The Beggar's Opera,* thinking it was a passing fad and went on producing new operas and reviving old ones. In 1737, he suffered a paralytic stroke that immobilized his right arm. He went for a holiday to Aix-la-Chapelle, and after his return continued to produce operas until 1741 when *Deidamia,* his last opera, was performed. That year he began thinking about the oratorio that was to make him immortal: the *Messiah.* Afterwards, he wrote only oratorios, "shaking the dust of the stage from his feet ... and gave England a national substitute for opera" (Paul Henry Lang). Joseph Addison wrote in *The Spectator,*

> There is no Question but our Grand-children will be very curious to know the Reason why their Forefathers used to sit together like an audience of foreigners in their own Country, and to hear whole Plays acted before them in a Tongue which they did not understand ... There is nothing that has more startled our *English* audience than the *Italian Recitativo* at its first Entrance upon the Stage. ...

Despite Addison, after Purcell's death the English accepted Italian opera.

In 1706 Addison wrote a libretto about Henry II and Fair Rosamond which was set to music by Thomas Clayton. But *Rosamond* was a complete failure and Dr Burney made fun of it; he couldn't forgive Addison for his unkindness toward Handel.

Although Handel's operas are now being revived, they did not survive in the popular repertoire. He was a master of *bel canto* writing and created monumental *da capo* arias; but he knew that his audiences were mainly interested in artful singing and there is little drama in his operas. Even his great admirer, the incisive Dr Burney, only writes about Handel's arias and the singers, but never about the drama. Handel's vocal demands are too great for today's singers: a new generation of accomplished *bel canto* virtuosos would have to be especially trained to sing his arias. In 1960, Franco Zeffirelli's revival of Handel's *Alcina* at the Teatro Fenice in Venice occasioned the triumphal Italian debut of Joan Sutherland, who had sung the difficult part earlier in London.

After 1729, Handel changed from *opera seria* to the Neapolitan *opera buffa,* and failed again. His audience deserted him. First the people in the galleries, and later his aristocratic patrons went to hear *The Beggar's Opera,* with its popular English, Scottish, Irish, French and Italian folk songs. Its success was followed by many "ballad-operas" that travelled as far as Germany where they were followed by the German *Singspiel*, a spoken play with songs.

The French never accepted the fact that opera originated in Italy. They claim, with some justification, that around 1600 no one could really define what an opera was. However, the French had had their *ballet du cour* for half a century, the court ballet being the most sumptuous entertainment. In 1581, M. Balthasar de Beaujoyeulx – known around Paris as "the best violin-player of Christendom" – produced the *Ballet Comique de la Royne,* at a cost equivalent to at least half-a-million dollars at today's value. A ballet is not an opera, but when you add a little poetry and music, as Beaujoyeulx did, you might conceivably have something. The plot of the great ballet was insignificant: the King of France foils the evil sorceries of Circe. But so was the plot of Cesti's extravaganza, *Il Pomo d'Oro,* which was produced some eighty years later in Vienna, and which nevertheless everyone called an "opera".

In 1647, the French Court heard Luigi Rossi's *Orfeo.* The work had been commissioned by Louis XIV, probably at the behest of Cardinal Mazarin (who happened to be an Italian). Mazarin had the libretto translated into French; it was handed out among the audience, but they were bored. The music was pleasant, but had little relation to either the serious or light elements of the "plot". In 1660, Mazarin tried again; this time Cavalli's *Serse* was performed at the Louvre to celebrate the wedding of Louis XIV and Teresa of Spain. Again it was no success, perhaps because a *castrato* sang the part of Queen Amestris and the French never accepted the *castrati.* Two years later, Cavalli staged *Ercole Amante,* perhaps his finest work, but it failed. The French didn't like Italian opera; maybe, they just didn't like opera.

Ironically, the first successful composer of a French opera was a young man from Florence, Jean Baptiste Lulli, who later changed his name to Lully. He had been commissioned to revise *Ercole Amante* which meant that he added some of his own popular dance tunes. The dances were an immediate success and established Lully in Paris. A gifted and extremely ruthless man, he became the official *compositeur du roi,* and the master of all music in France. He then began a collaboration with Molière and they almost created something that might have become the first French opera.

But *Le Mariage Forcé, Le Bourgeois Gentilhomme* and *Pourceaugnac* were not so much operas as plays with some brilliant incidental music. In 1671, they worked together on *Psyche*, a *comedie ballet* that has many ingredients of opera.

The honour of having written the first French opera goes to two less gifted men, Pierre Perrin, the poet, and Robert Cambert, the musician. In 1659 they collaborated on *Pastorale*, and in 1671 on *Pomone*. Cambert wrote another opera but Lully prevented it being produced. Cambert had become too famous for Lully's taste, and had to flee to England, where he was later murdered by his valet, whether at the instigation of Lully remains one of opera's unsolved murder cases, like the alleged poisoning of Mozart by his rival Salieri.

Lully next joined forces with the poet Philippe Quinault. They started with a pastoral, *Les Fêtes de l'Amour et de Bacchus*, which wasn't an opera. But their next work, *Cadmus et Hermione*, certainly was. It was produced on 27 April 1673 – the birthday of French opera, according to some stubborn French. It was billed as a *tragédie-lyrique*, perhaps meaning that it was poetry with music rather than music with poetry, such as the Italian *opera seria*.

Louis XIV – who knew more about women than music, unlike his contemporary, Leopold I of Habsburg, who knew a great deal about music and nothing about women – liked *Cadmus et Hermione*. He liked Lully's next opera, *Alceste*, so much that he said he wanted to hear it every evening he spent in Paris. Lully became a prolific composer: fifteen operas, many ballets, pastorals, dances, church music. His operas were produced lavishly at the Court. Opera was (and still is) considered an extravaganza in France. The ballet should be in the middle of the opera when everybody has arrived and no one has yet left. (Richard Wagner made the mistake of placing the ballet in *Tannhäuser* at the beginning, when the *bon vivants* hadn't yet appeared, and there was a fine hullabaloo.) For the first time Lully used trained ballet dancers in his opera ballets. Occasionally the King and his courtiers would perform in Lully's operas (in Vienna, members of the Habsburg Court regularly appeared on the stage at that time). And he wrote very beautiful ballet music, with lovely melodies and fine orchestration. Even the Italians admitted that his accompanied recitatives had dramatic force. His choruses have been compared to Handel's, he learned the tricky problems of French enunciation, and created a French style of musical declamation. He could be superficial in his arias, but he could also be very good. He grew rich, his estate being worth over £350,000. He died in 1687, after hitting his foot sharply with his long baton while conducting a *Te Deum* to celebrate the King's recovery after an illness.

Four years earlier, Jean Philippe Rameau, one of the greatest French musicians, was born in Dijon. Rameau became an organist and composed sacred music. He is much revered as a great theoretician but he is also a great composer, though not of opera. He mistakenly boasted that the musician had the power to ignore the text; once he declared that "any newspaper could be set to music" (Rossini made the same remark about a laundry list: both were wrong). Consequently, most of Rameau's twenty-two operas are now forgotten. But he remains a great French master of orchestration, and his art was later continued and developed by Berlioz and Debussy. Rameau created haunting harmonies and strange rhythms that offended his listeners, and are now recognized as the work of a great innovator. In France, he is still known as "the enigma of French music". He was the first to make use of the clarinet in his scores and he also employed the full resources of horns and strings, with double stops and *pizzicati,* and created colours that now sound "modern". His great choruses influenced Gluck. No history on opera would be complete without him. He classified the chords and writes convincingly about abusing dissonances and the powers of harmony. "It is certain that harmony can arouse in us emotions corresponding to the chords . . . some are sad, others are languorous, tender, agreeable, surprising". A revival of *Les Indes Galantes,* written in 1735, was recently a great hit at the Paris Opéra: it is a series of spectacles, a prologue followed by three entrées – a musical dinner rather than an opera. Rameau called it a *ballet héroique.* His later opera *Dardanus* created one of the scandals that Parisians love more than opera. A critic wrote that "for three hours the musicians have no time to sneeze" (what would he have said of Wagner's *Götterdämmerung*?). Rameau was ahead of his time; he lent great power and excitement to French opera and became a very great composer. Among his few defenders was Voltaire who wrote, "In the long run it would be desirable that in the measure in which the nation's taste improves, Rameau's taste should dominate it".

Around 1740, Charles de Brosset, French historian, archaeologist and musicologist, wrote an essay about Italian opera that would have pleased Richard Wagner:

> By wanting to unite too many pleasures, opera weakens their enjoyment; in spite of many agreeable moments, opera for me has moments of tediousness, something the good French tragedy does not

know. . . . Partisans of opera will say that one does not go to the opera for the subject (the drama) but for the accessories of music and the spectacle which are preferable to comedy and tragedy. Some (Italian) librettos are admirable and interesting but the arias pinned to the end of every scene, not closely connected with the action . . . again create diversion. They enchant the ear but permit the interest to wane.

In the eighteenth century, the logical, brilliant French musicians and dramatists were the first to realize that there was no balance between action and music. In the preface to *Tarare*, Beaumarchais wrote, "*Il-y-a trop de musique dans la musique de théâtre*" (how very pleased he must have been with Mozart's economy in *Le Nozze di Figaro*). In the history of opera, the important contributions of the great eighteenth-century French thinkers are often forgotten. The French rarely understood their own masters – Rameau, Bizet and Debussy had their problems – however, it was the great French thinkers and musicians who created the conditions for the dramatic reform of opera. Gluck, Rossini, Wagner, and, later, Stravinsky, lived in Paris and were deeply influenced by French thought on music. The *cause célèbre* of the Parisian music world – the operas of Gluck, Wagner's *Tannhäuser* in 1861, the *Carmen* première, and Stravinsky's *Rite of Spring*, in 1913 – only served to enliven French music.

In 1752, Signor Bambini's Italian Opera Company presented Pergolesi's *La Serva Padrona* in Paris. The work had been given there six years earlier, causing no excitement. This time it became a *succès fou*, and the venerable professors of the Académie Royale de la Musique, as the Paris Opéra was called, considered Pergolesi's posthumous success a grave danger to their position. The professors wrote only *opera seria,* known in France as *tragédie lyrique*. The controversy between partisans of Pergolesi's wonderful *opera buffa* and the professors became a real war of the buffoons. Parisians were growing tired of sumptuous ballets and boring mythological fables. They were delighted with Pergolesi's ordinary-life characters. *Le tout Paris* was divided between the "King's Party" (musicians, academicians and abbés around Louis xv who were for Lully and Rameau) and the "Queen's Party" (Diderot, Rousseau and other radicals in favour of the Italian *opera buffa*). In his celebrated "Lettre sur la Musique Française", Rousseau wrote in 1753, "*Il faut que la musique se rapproche de la nature*". Three years earlier, Rousseau, a self-taught musical dilettante, had recognized both French and Italian opera. Now he murdered French opera in his ninety-two-page pamphlet:

I think I made it clear that there is neither rhythm nor melody in French music because the language is incapable of it; that French singing is nothing but a continual barking, intolerable to the ear; that French airs are not arias at all; nor is French recitative anything like real recitative. From which I conclude that the French have no music and are incapable of having any, or that if they should have any, so much the worse for them.

Obviously, Rousseau was exaggerating, unless he totally discounted the work of Couperin, Lully, Rameau. To demonstrate his ideas, Rousseau wrote *Devin du Village*, a rustic play set to music and performed in a rural setting. Peasants and simple people replaced the heroes of the ballet opera, creating a new form of lyric theatre, the French *opéra comique*, which became a typically French art form, often making fun of the *opera seria* with Gallic wit.

The war of the buffoons ended in perfect *buffo* style, by a defeat of the winners. The director of the Opéra-Comique, the headquarters of the *bouffons*, announced *Les Troqueurs*, a French comic opera, as "the work of a Viennese Italian". The "Italianists", sitting in a group underneath the Queen's box, cheered until they were hoarse. Then the director announced that the "Viennese Italian" was really a native Frenchman, M. Antoine d'Auvergne. He had composed *Les Troqueurs* after the libretto of a minor Parisian poet. The "Italianists" had been tricked into applauding and liking a genuine French *opera buffa*. That was the end of the war. The Italian company left Paris, having convinced the French that there was a future for comic opera in France. Paris was ready for the great reformer – Gluck.

THE GREAT REFORMER: GLUCK

The decline of *opera seria* occurred not only in Paris. In Italy, too, people became bored with the artificial, mannered baroque opera where passions were expressed through arias, and the drama was only in the voice. In the opera houses of Venice, the lethargy of such productions was brightened by the comical *intermezzi*. Paradoxically, the earliest reform (which for a while seriously threatened the development of opera) came from two Italian poets working at the Court in Vienna – Apostolo Zeno and Pietro Metastasio. They had studied Corneille and Racine, and tried to introduce the ideas of French classicism into their libretti. Their noble heroes were still rather rigid, and in Zeno's libretti there was the inevitable happy ending. Metastasio, however, dared end his libretti on a tragic note.

Metastasio, born in Rome as Pietro Trapassi, would himself have made a fine character in a libretto. He was famous for his wild love affairs, and grew old enough to reflect on life and love before he died at the age of eighty-four. His most famous love affair, strictly platonic, was with "the angelic, virtuous" Countess Althann in Vienna. No one is certain how many libretti Metastasio wrote; possibly a thousand, though the published statistics are confusing. His libretto of *Artaserse* was composed at least forty times. Hasse, Handel, Jommelli, Gluck, Paisiello, Piccinni and many forgotten composers used his verse; so did Haydn and Mozart. In 1819, Meyerbeer used Metastasio's *Semiramide riconosciuta,* that had already been set by Leonardo Vinci (no relation to the great painter), Hasse and Gluck. Metastasio wrote beautiful poetry – his finest libretti are considered classics in Italy, read for the beauty of their language – but he was more of a poet than a dramatist, his stories often seeming contrived.

Christoph Willibald Gluck (he was knighted in 1756 by Pope Benedict XIV) remains one of the genuine innovators in the history of opera. There was nothing in his early life to indicate his eventual fame. Born in 1714 in the Upper Palatinate (his name sounds more Bohemian than German), he studied the cello and composition with Bohuslav Czernohorsky in Prague, and then went to Vienna where a rich patron sent him to Italy (rich patrons play an important part in the history of opera). Gluck studied composition with Giovanni Battista Sammartini, one of the founding fathers of the symphony. In 1741, at the time that Handel was writing his last opera, Gluck wrote his first, using the libretto of Metastasio's *Artaserse.* He wrote eight other operas in the stylized form of the Italian *opera seria* and set to music almost twenty of Metastasio's libretti. He became successful and popular, but no one thought he might become great.

In 1745, Gluck went from Italy to Paris (where he was impressed by the works of Lully and Rameau) and then to London. He'd been invited by the Haymarket Theatre but found himself completely ignored, though Handel gave him some advice. Three years earlier the *Messiah* had been a triumph and Handel was now at the zenith of his fame. Gluck soon noticed that in London opera had "retired" into the oratorio. With his sound dramatic instinct he sensed that *opera seria* was getting nowhere. Something was wrong with the libretti of his admired Metastasio. Gluck left London and spent three years with Signor Mingotti's road company. He conducted opera in Dresden, Prague, Hamburg, Copenhagen, always keeping his eyes and ears open, and finally settled in Vienna in 1754. There he met Count Giacomo Durazzo, the director of the Imperial Court Opera and a dilettante librettist who wrote for Gluck *L'Innocenza Giustificata.*

Durazzo then performed a historic service to the evolution of opera: he introduced an Italian poet, Raniero de' Calzabigi, to Gluck. Calzabigi, probably born in Livorno in 1714 (the same year as Gluck), had recently arrived from Paris. He is another of the great librettists who led a fascinating life. His friend Casanova calls him "a great conniver, familiar with financial dealings, acquainted with the business of all countries, a *bel esprit*, a poet, a great lover of women". Quite a compliment, coming from Casanova. Calzabigi, who had enjoyed the "protection" of Madame de Pompadour, had been forced to leave Paris in a hurry. He continued his doubtful dealings in Vienna where he organized "lotteries" and lent money at exorbitant rates to financially distressed aristocrats. He was an intellectual adventurer – bold, cultivated, intelligent, witty. As a librettist, he borrowed much from Metastasio but later, when he knew the time for a change had come, he opposed him.

Metastasio knew that something was going on. In 1751, he wrote that Gluck "has surprising fire but he is mad". After Gluck composed *Il Re Pastore,* Metastasio wrote to the famous *castrato* Farinelli about "the Bohemian composer whose spirit, noise and extravagance have supplied the place of merit in many theatres of Europe ... " In 1761, the "mad" Gluck began to work on Calzabigi's libretto of *Orfeo ed Euridice.* The first performance at the Vienna Burgtheater, on 5 October 1762, is now considered by many historians as the beginning of the "modern" music drama. In Vienna, it is also arbitrarily known as the beginning of the great classical school of Viennese music which (they say) came to an end the day Beethoven died – 26 March 1827. Needless to say, cultures and civilizations do not begin and end on certain days.

Orfeo is not a flawless expression of reform. Gluck and Calzabigi had not yet eschewed the effects of *opera seria,* and the overture and much of the third act are stilted and dull. But there were moments of greatness in the opera – the Dance of the Furies, the scene in the Elysian Fields, the Dance of the Happy Shades, the incredibly beautiful and difficult aria "Che farò senza Euridice", of which Gluck himself said there must not be the least change in tempo or turn of expression, or "it will become an air for a puppet show".

Orfeo was not a success in Vienna. (The role of *Orfeo* was sung by the alto *castrato* Gaetano Guadagni; nowadays it is sung by a mezzo soprano.) After eight performances (one less than the original run of Mozart's *Figaro*) the revolutionary work was taken out of the repertory. During the next five years, Gluck had to go back to the bread-and-butter libretti of Metastasio and other, less gifted writers. But he kept in touch with Calzabigi and they now had some definite ideas about the "reform" of opera. Doubtless, it wasn't something that happened accidentally. Calzabigi and Gluck knew what they wanted and they brought it off. Gluck's fame as the "reformer" of opera has overshadowed Calzabigi's, but modern scholars agree that the Italian poet expressed his ideas before Gluck. Calzabigi was the senior partner in the reform movement, the intellectual inspiration which guided the composer towards his destiny. As early as 1755, Calzabigi had written his *Dissertatione su le poesie drammatiche del Sig. Abate Pietro Metastasio*, a brilliant criticism of Metastasio's technique.

Calzabigi's next collaboration with Gluck was *Alceste*, first produced in Vienna on 26 December 1767. Two years later, the score was published with a preface signed by Gluck which is without doubt the work of both men. In the form of a dedication to the future Emperor, Leopold II, Gluck writes,

> When I undertook to write the music for *Alceste*, I resolved to divest it entirely of all those abuses, introduced into it either by the mistaken vanity of singers or by the too great complaisance of composers, which have so long disfigured Italian opera and made of the most splendid and most beautiful of spectacles the most ridiculous and wearisome. I have striven to restrict music to its true function, that of seconding poetry by enforcing the expression of the sentiment, and the interest of the situations, without interrupting the action, or weakening it by superfluous ornament.... Furthermore, I believed that my greatest labour should be devoted to seeking beautiful simplicity, and I have avoided making displays of difficulty at the expense of clarity ... Such are my principles. By good fortune, my designs were wonderfully furthered by the libretto, in which the celebrated author, devising a new dramatic scheme, had substituted heartfelt language, strong passions, interesting situations, and an endlessly varied spectacle for florid descriptions and cold morality ...

This is, in a nutshell, a perfect analysis of musical drama, of what opera should be and must be in order to succeed; and it is the composer's honest tribute to his poet-librettist. It is also proof of their debt to

Monteverdi, Scarlatti, Handel, Rameau and all who had been there earlier.

Later, Calzabigi and Gluck quarrelled; Gluck's friends said that the poet claimed the credit for Gluck's inventions, and naturally Calzabigi's friends said the same thing about Gluck. Calzabigi himself set the record straight in 1784, when he wrote a letter published in *Mercure de France*,

> I hope that you will agree . . . that if Gluck created dramatic music, he didn't create it out of nothing. I furnished him with the material, the chaos, if you wish. The honour of this creation, then, belongs to both of us . . .

Alceste is better than *Orfeo* but it, too, was a failure in Vienna. The people were not ready for a *tragedia per musica,* as the poet called it. One critic wrote that it was "a dull requiem". No one was able to detect the complete unity of poetry and music that had never before been achieved to such a degree on the opera stage. The Viennese, never very perspicacious about their own geniuses, also disliked the third work written by Calzabigi and Gluck. *Paride ed Elena* was performed in 1770. Calzabigi amused himself with the ironic notion that Helena, not widely known as a virtuous woman, may have rejected the advances of Paris, that symbol of virility. The music is very beautiful. "O del mio dolce ardor" is Gluck's most beautiful love song.

Gluck stayed four more years in Vienna and then grew tired of the city that has always distrusted greatness. Calzabigi had disappeared after a scandal that couldn't be hushed up. Gluck found a new collaborator, the councillor at the French Embassy named Marie François Louis Grand-Leblanc Bailli du Roullet. He wrote for Gluck the French libretto of *Iphigénie en Aulide,* following Racine's version. The work was to be produced in Paris where Gluck's former pupil, the Austrian Archduchess Marie-Antoinette, was soon to be the Queen of France.

Paris was a logical choice. The war of the buffoons had cleared the air, and even the conservatives were on Gluck's side since he had written a *French* opera. The encyclopedists and progressive intellectuals were bound to applaud his reform ideas. And Marie-Antoinette promised her support.

The première of *Iphigénie en Aulide,* in 1774, was a stunning success. So realistic was the work that some people in the audience, forgetting this was an opera performance, had to be restrained from rushing on the stage to deliver poor Iphigénie. Gluck had created a new dramatic dimension with his music that went beyond du Roullet's libretto: he showed himself the precursor of Mozart's *Don Giovanni*, and he was suddenly the most famous composer in Europe.

"I was quite carried away by it," wrote the Dauphine to her sister Christine. "Nobody talks of anything else; you can't imagine what excitement there has been over this event; it is unbelievable; people take sides and attack one another as if it were some question of religion . . ." Abbé Arnaud, the director of the *Gazette de France*, said of one melody, "With that air one might found a religion". A few people said that Gluck's drama was great but would be the death of singing (similar accusations were later made after Wagner's *Tristan und Isolde* and Strauss' *Elektra*, because of their demands upon the singers).

Gluck reworked *Orfeo* and *Alceste* to French translations of the original libretti, making many changes. The French didn't like *castrati*, and Gluck rewrote the part of Orfeo for a tenor which somewhat upset the tonal relationship. When Hector Berlioz revived *Orfeo* in 1859, he combined the Vienna and the Paris versions and had Pauline Viardot, the great mezzo soprano, sing the title role. The success was incredible. Berlioz remembers:

> I shall not describe the excitement of the audience at this scene (Madame Viardot singing "J'ai perdu mon Eurydice"). Certain maladroit auditors so far forgot themselves as to cry "Bis!" before the sublime passage, "Entends ma voix qui t'appelle", and great difficulty was experienced in imposing silence upon them. . . . Some persons would even cry "Bis!" after Hamlet's "To be or not to be".

(When Toscanini conducted *Orfeo* at the Metropolitan Opera in 1909, the great purist added "Divinités du Styx" from *Alceste*, a trio from *Paride ed Elena*, and substituted for Gluck's own finale a chorus from Gluck's later opera, *Echo et Narcisse*. So much for purity.)

After the Paris première of *Alceste*, the Italian composer Nicola Piccinni arrived in Paris. He was a master of the Naples *opera buffa* and wrote with great facility; of his three hundred operas, about a hundred have survived, but few are performed. Piccinni, a mild-mannered, naïve man, was unaware that he'd been invited to Paris by Gluck's enemies. Once again, the traditionalists had started to attack him. They were joined by a "pro-Italian" party whose members couldn't stand the sight of "a German causing total revolution in France". Even Marie-Antoinette involuntarily became part of the intrigue when Jean-François Marmontel, writer and librettist, suggested that it might be great fun to ask both the German and the Italian composers to work simultaneously on the same libretto. Instead of the war of the buffoons there would now be a war of the composers.

Marmontel sent to Gluck and to Piccinni his libretto of *Roland*, the rewrite of a former text by Philippe Quinault that Lully had set in 1685. Half-way through the work, Gluck heard about the intrigue and became so furious that he threw his score into the fire. He wrote an indignant letter to his friend du Roullet which the poet published; now *le tout Paris* was divided into Gluckists and Piccinnists.

The first round ended in a draw. Gluck's *Armide* was produced in 1777. Five months later, Piccinni's *Roland* was performed. Both operas were successful. Marmontel's libretto of *Roland* was so good that even the Gluckists admitted it could have been written by Calzabigi. *Roland* is a mixture of *opera seria* and *opera buffa*, somewhat as *Don Giovanni*. The hero is also a demonic character.

The only men who took no part in the absurd conflict were Gluck and Piccinni who respected and liked each other. Piccinni, who was fourteen years the younger, tried in vain after Gluck's death to get subscribers for a memorial concert. He died in 1800, poor and forgotten.

The last episode in this absurd "war" occurred when the management of the Opéra commissioned Gluck to set an adaptation of Euripides' *Iphigénie en Tauride* – and then handed the same text to Piccinni. Gluck finished the work in time for the production in May 1779. It is his masterpiece. Baron Friedrich Melchior von Grimm, strictly an "Italianist", said, "I do not know whether this is song but perhaps it is much more than that. I forget the opera and find myself in Greek tragedy." Exactly what Gluck had set out to do. It is a great musical drama with wonderfully expressive music which later inspired Cherubini, Spontini, Méhul, Berlioz, Wagner and Strauss.

Gluck remained for a while in Paris, wrote his last opera, *Echo et Narcisse*, which was a failure when it was performed in 1779, and returned to Vienna where he lived quietly, widely admired. One day in 1782, he invited a twenty-six-year-old composer named Mozart to his house in the suburbs. The young man listened reverently to the great old master who had achieved the fusion of poetry and music into a music drama. Gluck died in 1787 – the year Mozart finished *his* greatest opera, *Don Giovanni*.

MOZART

The genius of Mozart cannot be analysed. Everything about him is enigmatic: the enormous range of expression which includes all human feelings, his awesome perfection in opera, chamber music, instrumental music, the symphony and other musical forms – as well as his versatility and the apparent (though not actual) facility with which he wrote. His output matches his quality and it is impossible to fathom how he could have written so much beautiful music during a life span of only thirty-five years. As an opera composer, Mozart is the greatest master of illuminating life through music and music through life. More than any other composer he understood life's complexities, the combination of tragedy and comedy, the mystical and the rational, passion and chastity, fear and serenity. It's all there, in his music, often in a synthesis which remains ambiguous. The mixture is there in his greatest operatic masterpieces: *Le Nozze di Figaro, Die Zauberflöte, Don Giovanni* and *Così fan Tutte*. Mozart's music is the very paradox of life. He remains the most timeless, most modern composer of all. Every age sees and hears him differently, finding in Mozart what it needs: love and irony, truth and duplicity, and always timeless beauty.

Because of his complexity, Mozart is the hardest to assess among all masters of classicism. Haydn systematically progressed from his early, almost naïve efforts to become the inventor of the string quartet (in our sense of the word), and of the modern symphony. Beethoven started in the classical tradition but in his final, "late" string quartets he reached the stratosphere of absolute music; he was always ahead of his time. Mozart, on the contrary, began almost as a mature artist. Gradually everything he attempted seemed to lead towards supreme simplicity and distilled clarity. His simplicity is the highest expression of his art. He, too, was ahead of his contemporaries, and not at all popular in Vienna when he died.

Mozart wrote his earliest operas, *Bastien und Bastienne* and *La Finta Giardiniera*, in 1775, when he was nineteen. The music is charming, but there is no dramatic structure. His early *opera seria, Idomeneo* (1781), is a fine work but never became a popular success. Neither did his last opera, *La Clemenza di Tito* (1791). Of his five masterpieces, two are written in the style of the German Singspiel, *Die Entführung aus dem Serail* (1782), and *Die Zauberflöte* (1791). The arias, duets and ensembles are connected by spoken German dialogue. In his Italian works, written in the style of the *opera buffa – Le Nozze di Figaro* (1786), *Don Giovanni* (1787), *Così fan Tutte* (1790) – Mozart uses recitatives instead of spoken dialogue. The recitative is either *secco*, with *continuo* (harpsichord) accompaniment, or *accompagnato* by orchestra. Mostly he used *secco* recitative which is as fast as normal speech. Almost all his operas are based on sound dramatic stories, further dramatized and deepened through music by "a good composer who understands the stage". Mozart wrote these words to his father in 1781, when he was only twenty-five years old. He had already learned the basic truth about the art of writing opera which many great composers never mastered. *Mozart understood the stage and its unwritten laws.* When he called poetry "the obedient daughter of the music", he didn't mean to downgrade the libretto but was simply stating that while he could express the drama though his music, drama must be there to begin with. His respect for the libretto is evident from the troubles he took when he collaborated actively with his librettist, from whom he expected a strong dramatic story, with real people, and real complications; he would do the rest.

Mozart even managed to inject life into the libretto of *Zauberflöte* and made the characters believable. "It takes more culture to perceive the virtues of *Die Zauberflöte* than to point out its defects", said Goethe. Emanuel Schikaneder, his librettist, had conceived the Queen of the Night as a good character and Sarastro as the force of evil. Mozart reversed this, and made the Queen in two virtuoso arias one of the most fascinatingly evil characters on the stage. In this opera alone his music ranges from solemn and dignified (Sarastro's arias and the choir of the priests, "O Isis und Osiris"), to melodies that became popular folk tunes, such as "Der Vogelfänger" and "Ein Mädchen oder Weibchen". The lofty story is enlivened by the nonsense of Papageno whose duet with Pamina – "Bei Männern welche Liebe fühlen" – is one of the most deeply human melodies ever written. Mozart even managed to give Sarastro the right dimension without making him ridiculous. G.B. Shaw wrote that Sarastro's music "would not sound out of place in the mouth of God". A fine performance of *Die Zauberflöte* is not only a play based on Masonic symbolism, of which there is plenty in the story, but a wonderful fairytale involving good and evil spirits, water and fire, men and animals, noble and silly human beings, singing boys and men in armour, mysterious ladies and somewhat boring priests, and a prince who loves a princess, loses his princess, and wins his princess. Goethe told Eckermann that most members of an audience will always be satisfied with what they see, whereas the initiated will not miss the more profound meanings, "as in the case of *Die Zauberflöte*". By "the initiated" he may have alluded to the fact that both Schikaneder and Mozart were members of the Grand Oriental Lodge of Freemasons. Although it is the music, certainly not the libretto, that makes the work a masterpiece, the first-performance programme in Vienna features Schikaneder's name in large letters, while Mozart's is way down, in very small print, mis-spelled as "Mozard".

The only Mozart opera based on a somewhat artificial libretto is *Così fan Tutte*, an amusing, ironic comedy, strictly caviar for the connoisseurs, and never as popular as his other masterpieces though many scholars agree with Donald Mitchell, who calls the first act "probably the most miraculous of Mozart's dramatic structures ... *Così* offers a whole truth, not the half-truth offered by much art and most of life, and the maximum of beauty ... he built a whole opera out of a world of ambiguity, dramatized that world and gave it unity."

Shakespeare allegedly wrote *The Merry Wives of Windsor* because Elizabeth I wanted to see Falstaff in love. Emperor Joseph II had at long last come to admire *Figaro* and *Don Giovanni*, and he wanted another *opera buffa* by da Ponte and Mozart. The Emperor told da Ponte the anecdote, based on a true story, which the poet turned into the amusing *quid-pro-quo* of *Così*. Two young men, after a bet with a cynical elderly philosopher, test their fiancées' fidelity by returning in disguise. The ladies fail the test but somehow all ends well, after tears mixed with laughter. It wasn't exactly a moral play but it suited da Ponte whose recitatives are witty and wise, and it suited Mozart's sense of irony and love of paradox. He laughs with, and at, his characters. In the last quintet of the first act, when the two girls cry and the two departing lovers seem heartbroken, cynical Don Alfonso says, "I don't know how to keep from laughing".

Mozart could express a whole personality with a little melody. A simple orchestration would characterize a person or a situation. The wonder is that even listeners who don't know much about music and cannot perceive how artfully his ensembles are built sense this instinctively. What he loved best was to write about love. *Don Giovanni*, for instance, has many facets of love, from the Don's Faustian passion to Don Ottavio's noble devotion (he can be almost embarrassingly virtuous), from the jealous fury of Donna Elvira to the coquettish flirtation of Zerlina. Mozart was able to express every nuance in his music. In his hands, opera, "the irrational art", becomes the most rational one. We understand Mozart's *Don Giovanni* better than Goethe's *Faust*.

No one knew this better than Goethe. Schiller wrote to Goethe, in 1797: "I had always placed a certain confidence in opera, hoping that from it will rise as from the choruses of ancient feasts of Bacchus the tragedy in a nobler form"; Goethe answered, "The hopes you placed in the opera you would find fulfilled to a high degree in the recent *Don Juan* (*Don Giovanni*)". Goethe was unmusical; when he heard some of his poems turned into *Lieder* by Schubert he thought only of the text. But the poet and dramatist understood the greatness of *Don Giovanni*. He regretted that no one had set his *Faust* to music, and said to his friend Eckermann, "Such music ought to be in the character of *Don Juan*. Mozart should have composed *Faust*". Absolutely right; Goethe sensed the affinity between Mozart's Faustian Don Giovanni and his own Dr Faust.

The wonder of Mozart is that he studied everything ("I am bathed in music", he once writes from Italy), adopted what he needed, yet always produced authentic Mozart. He knew that the Italian composers created character and action through music, that they had learned to express moods, feelings and passions in a manner that the spoken word could not convey. They could create musical miracles – allow people to quarrel, speak simultaneously, yet keep their individuality – all expressed through music. And the greatest master of this genre was Mozart. Sometimes he tells two different plots at the same time: one through his characters on the stage, and the other through his orchestra which refutes the stage, or comments on it, ironically. In Paris and Vienna, Mozart studied Gluck who once said that he was "trying to forget that he was a musician", because he thought the music must accompany the drama. Mozart never forgot that he was a musician. His "light" melodies are the pure expression of genius. Richard Strauss said in 1918 to Max Marschalk,

> The most perfect melodic shapes are found in Mozart; he has the lightness of touch which is the true objective. With Beethoven the melodies are heavier; one is clearly conscious of the labour. Listen to the remarkable expansion of a Mozart melody, to Cherubino's "Voi, che sapete", for instance. You think it is coming to an end, but it goes further, ever further.

During his work on *Die Entführung*, Mozart wrote to his father,

> . . . as passions, whether violent or not, must never be expressed in such a way as to excite disgust, so music, even the most terrible situations, must never offend the ear, but must please the hearer – or in other words must never cease to be music.

In *Die Entführung*, Selim Bassa, one of the six characters, never sings, only speaks. Some scholars believe that Mozart couldn't find a Turkish musical idiom that satisfied him, or that he didn't find the right singer for the part. The most interesting character in the Singspiel is Osmin, the first evidence of Mozart's virtuosity with comic characters, such as Figaro, Leporello, Papageno. During his short life, *Die Entführung* was given thirty-four times in Vienna, more often than any other of his masterpieces – one of the many ironies in the relationship between Mozart and Vienna, where he is now deified – and where his grave cannot be found. It doesn't matter. We have his music which will always live. Mozart didn't want to express God's wishes like Bach, or fight with fate like Beethoven, or become his nation's teacher-and-hero like Wagner. He wanted to say everything there was with music, which to him meant beautiful music. Trying to describe the music of Mozart one realizes the inadequacy of words.

BEETHOVEN'S *FIDELIO*

Fidelio, Beethoven's only opera, reflects the sad fate of its perennially tragic composer, remaining one of the most misunderstood master-pieces of an often misunderstood art form. It is not a perfect opera but it seems strange that even now so many people seem to agree with Wagner's arrogant opinion that the only good thing about the opera is the *Leonore* overture, though even nowadays some famous conductors conduct *Fidelio* mainly because of the great overture, which isn't really an overture since they play it between the last two scenes. It was placed there by Hans von Bülow, one of the earliest star conductors, and an early friend of Wagner. Gustav Mahler introduced the custom at the Metropolitan Opera, but at the Maggio Musicale in Florence, in 1969, Giorgio Strehler omitted the overture in his *Fidelio* production, thereby strengthening the dramatic structure, and proving that it doesn't belong there. Leonore and Florestan should walk directly from the dark dungeon into the sun-light of freedom. The third *Leonore* overture is a great piece of symphonic music, but it doesn't belong in the opera; Beethoven considered the overtures independent symphonic pieces.

Unlike Gluck or Mozart, Beethoven was not a musical dramatist. He was a musical genius who believed (like Schiller) in lofty ideals, humanity, liberty, the sublime victory of good over evil. Though he never married, he believed in the sanctity of marriage and in woman's fidelity – though no woman was ever faithful to him. (He was deeply shocked by the story of *Don Giovanni*. "*Il prétendait que Mozart ne devait pas prostituer son talent sur un sujet si scandaleux*", Madame d'Abrantes writes in her *Memoirs*.) When Beethoven began to think of writing an opera, he wanted a historic, moral story that would be close to the classic idealism of Schiller. Not primarily interested in character or plot or drama, he saw the characters as symbols of good or evil. Obviously, his noble aim should have been a failure because opera is a dramatic art.

Yet Beethoven almost succeeded because of his great genius. There are immensely moving moments in *Fidelio*. The scene of the prisoners, taken from their dungeons into the blinding sunlight and singing the incredibly moving ode to freedom, is one of the greatest moments in the entire operatic literature. And there is another exultant moment when Leonore and Florestan fall into each others' arms, in an apotheosis of love – love as Beethoven felt it.

The trouble with *Fidelio* begins at the beginning. Beethoven starts the opera as a Singspiel before he moves on to the heroic drama. The first scenes don't succeed because the composer was unable to convey the bourgeois nonsense of family life. But the mood changes when Beethoven, the idealist, expresses his ideas in the magnificent quartet scene. The appearance of the cardboard villain, Don Pizarro, is another lapse: Beethoven wrote less well about evil than about goodness. But the second act is a masterpiece, moving and intense, with great dramatic action. "Some day *Fidelio* will become to English music lovers what it is in Germany, the opera to which every right-thinking married couple goes on the anniversary of their wedding", writes Donald Francis Tovey. Beethoven's friend, Josef Ferdinand von Sonnleithner, had adapted the French original, Jean-Nicolas Bouilly's *Léonore, ou l'Amour conjugal*. Bouilly had written the true story of Florestan who is imprisoned by his political enemy and liberated by his faithful wife, but he set the story in Spain.

German critics call *Fidelio*, in their customary pompous style, *das hohe Lied* (the high ode) of married love. *Fidelio* is much more man's hymn to freedom, just as the Ninth Symphony is an Ode to Joy.

Beethoven had characteristically bad timing with his opera. On 13 November 1805, one week before the première at the Theater an der Wien, Napoleon's armies invaded Vienna. Napoleon let the people know that he'd come to "protect" them against the Russians (another "protector" told the Viennese the same thing in March 1938). *Fidelio* went through the final rehearsals in an atmosphere of widespread fear. The composer's friends had run away, or had other worries. The première took place before an auditorium filled mostly with French officers who had nothing better to do that night. A young English doctor, Henry P. Reeve, found the plot "a miserable mixture of low manners and romantic situations", but added that the music was "equal to any praise". After three performances, the opera was dropped. Beethoven's friends thought the beginning was too slow; he rewrote the overture, condensed the first two acts into one and shortened the last. This second version was tried out at the Theater an der Wien in 1806. Georg Friedrich Treitschke, an able dramatist, had expanded the finales of both acts and improved the text. This version was called *Fidelio* though Beethoven still liked the original title, *Leonore*, better. He wrote the *Leonore* overture No 3, but the audience was lukewarm. He complained to Baron Braun, the manager of the Theater an der Wien, one of Beethoven's ardent patrons. According-ing to a contemporary chronicler, Josef August Rockel, the Baron, ex-pressed the hope that the box office would improve during the following performances. On this occasion only the expensive seats had been sold. Perhaps the galleries would also be filled later on.

"I don't write for the galleries," Beethoven exclaimed.

Baron von Braun made the mistake of saying, "Even Mozart did not scorn to write for the galleries."

That did it. "I don't want my opera to be performed again," said Beethoven. "I want the score back."

Baron von Braun pulled the bell cord, gave orders that the score be returned to the composer, and thereafter *Fidelio* was forgotten for several years. Only the third version, performed at the Court Theatre in 1814, was a success, and it has been in the repertory of most German-speaking houses ever since, although non-German audiences still fail to appreciate this great work of art. Shortly before his death, Beethoven told his friend, Anton Felix Schindler, "Of all my children, that one (*Fidelio*) has brought me the most sorrows. And for that reason it is most dear to me".

For a long time *Fidelio* was reputed among artists to have "unsingable" parts. It is true that the parts of Leonore, Florestan and Don Pizarro contain enormous technical and musical difficulties. Usually the title role was given to a *hochdramatische* soprano but when Lotte Lehmann, a lyric-dramatic soprano, was given the part by Franz Schalk in Vienna, she brought it off with warmth and humanity rather than power and vir-tuosity. It became her favourite part though she became better known as the Marschallin in *Rosenkavalier*. In her autobiography she called Leonore "a strenuous task. It was almost beyond the limits of my power. I never had a highly dramatic voice, and the part made me feel that it demanded the utmost which I was capable of giving. But what a task it was! What joy to impersonate such a human role! I found in it the most exalted moments of my opera career and was shaken by it to the depths of my being ..." The vocal difficulties are enormous and there is the dramatic problem that Leonore, dressed as Fidelio, a man, must be convincing as a man (so that Marzelline falls in love with her) while she is actually the most feminine of women.

"My morning and evening prayer is for German opera", said Robert Schumann. He ignored *Die Zauberflöte* and *Fidelio* because he was thinking of German opera as a romantic symbol. He also ignored the Singspiel and had no use for Mozart's *Entführung*. The answer to Schumann's prayers came in 1821, when *Der Freischütz* was performed in Berlin. Neither the librettist, Friedrich Kind, nor the composer, Carl Maria von Weber, were well known. Weber had been the director of the Prague opera house at the age of twenty-six. In 1816, King Friedrich Augustus of Saxony made him Kapellmeister in Dresden, where he staged and conducted the works of Meyerbeer and Méhul's *Joseph*. He wrote an amusing Singspiel, *Abu Hassan*, which was fairly successful. Kind had written the libretto of *Der Freischütz* in ten days. Weber told his wife that it was "terribly exciting, super-extra, for there is the very devil in it".

In 1819, Spontini became Musikdirektor in Berlin and for a while Weber's career seemed to have ended. This changed with *Der Freischütz*, which became one of the most sensational successes in the history of opera. The première was attended by Felix Mendelssohn, Heinrich Heine and E.T.A. Hoffmann, now better known as the hero of Offenbach's opera *Les Contes d'Hoffmann* than as the composer of *Undine*, a precursor of *Freischütz*. In fact, all the German romantics were there that night. Within a few months, *Der Freischütz* was performed everywhere in Germany and also in Vienna, where the devil, as well as the guns and bullets, were removed by Imperial decree. New York heard the English version, *cum* devil, four years after Berlin.

Weber came to resent the libretto of *Freischütz*; most people loved his opera for Agathe, the sweet heroine, and the touch of *Gemütlichkeit*, whereas Weber had intended to write a *Musikdrama*. But he had great influence on Meyerbeer, Marschner, Spohr and even on Rossini, whose *Guillaume Tell* has some Weberian echoes. Above all, Richard Wagner admired Weber; without *Freischütz* he might never have written *Lohengrin*, the greatest work of the German romanticism. Weber had suddenly become the most famous composer in Germany. He never repeated his great success. *Euryanthe* (1825), commissioned by Vienna's Kärntnertortheater, has fine music, good arias, leitmotifs and almost psychological tone colours, but the libretto was bad and the action wasn't held together by the music. Schubert who never managed to write an opera said, "This is no music . . . it is all striving after effect".

A month later, when Weber was already quite ill, he accepted a commission from Charles Kemble, the manager of London's Covent Garden, to write an opera after an English libretto. Weber asked for a thousand pounds which, he knew, his family would soon need, and went to London. James Robinson Planché sent Weber the libretto of *Oberon* (written after Wieland's *Oberon*) in small batches, and Weber had to start composing without knowing the development of the plot. When Weber complained, Planché was "surprised". Weber consoled himself with the hope of having a better German version in the future. The London première of *Oberon* was successful. Weber conducted it and the few performances that followed, but it was too late. Several months later he died in his sleep in the house of an English friend.

Weber was a fine musician but a poor dramatist, and he was handicapped by bad libretti. Though he attempted a synthesis of the arts (which Wagner later achieved) he didn't understand dramatic continuity. But he did create new effects in musical characterization and orchestral colours, using clarinets, flutes and horns; no composer had ever made such effective use of the horns. His aim was to create human drama but he was more at home in the forests and meadows of Germany whose idiom he perfectly caught. *Der Freischütz* remains one of the most popular operas in Germany, owing to its beautiful melodies and tonal splendour, even though this German national opera is actually a Singspiel with spoken dialogue.

The other composers of the German romantic school are hardly known outside Germany. Ernst Theodor Amadeus Hoffmann was a fine poet but not a first-rate composer (he called Mozart "the inimitable creator of the romantic opera"). Heinrich Marschner's claim to fame is *Hans Heiling* (1833), which strongly influenced Wagner's *Der Fliegende Holländer*. Among unsophisticated German audiences, Gustav Lortzing remains popular with *Zar und Zimmerman, Der Wildschütz, Der Waffenschmied*, and there are people in Germany who would rather hear Otto Nicolai's *Die Lustigen Weiber von Windsor* than Verdi's *Falstaff*. Perhaps the best romantic composer after Weber was Friedrich Freiherr von Flotow. His *Martha* remains a perennial box office hit, and everybody knows the song "Letzte Rose" (The Last Rose of Summer) that Flotow (pronounced Floto) "interpolated" from an Irish folk song. However, the only great romantic German opera after *Freischütz* is *Lohengrin*.

OPERA IN PARIS

Although Luigi Cherubini, a Gallicized Italian from Florence, was long forgotten, he is now deservedly remembered and performed. He remains a composer's composer: even his competitors admired him. He terrified his peers because he knew so much, and had a lofty temper. Once he refused Liszt admission to the Paris Conservatoire because Liszt wasn't French; but neither was he. Beethoven often listened to Cherubini's works at the Theater an der Wien and was awed by Cherubini's great masterpiece, *Médée* (its overture probably inspired Beethoven to write his *Egmont* overture). Cherubini (1760–1842) had a long and interesting life, and became the musical czar of France when he headed the Paris Conservatoire. His Mass in F is considered a great work; to many he seems a latter-day Palestrina though most of his operas are rarely performed. *Lodoïska* (1791) was a great success in Paris and was repeated two hundred times that year, people comparing it to Gluck's *Iphigénie* and Mozart's *Don Giovanni*. His finest opera, *Les Deux Journées (The Water Carrier)* (1800), with a first-rate libretto by Jean-Nicolas Bouilly, deeply impressed Goethe. Beethoven so much admired this work that he always kept the score near his working table. Cherubini didn't respond in kind. About the *Leonore* overture No 3 he said haughtily, "I don't know what key it is in".

Today Cherubini's best known opera is *Médée* (1797). François-Benoît Hoffman wrote the libretto, using the text of Euripides. *Médée* is a masterpiece of classic nobility and dramatic horror. The title role of Medea is one of the most difficult of all, and Giuditta Pasta was right when she called it "that grand, fiendish part" for few sopranos have been able to sing it. Julie Scio, who created it in Paris, is said to have died after injuring her lungs fatally while singing it. A German singer, Clara Stöckl-Heinefetter, tried the part and died insane. Therese Tietjens sang it at Drury Lane in London and survived, but she gave up the part after a while. It was too much for her. Milan's La Scala performed *Médée* for the first time in 1909, one hundred and twelve years after the première.

In recent years, *Médée* was revived for three great modern singers. Maria Callas sang it in Florence in 1953, and at La Scala. Eileen Farrell performed it at a concert performance in New York in 1955, and three years later at the San Francisco Opera, the first performance of *Médée* staged in America. In 1972, Leonie Rysanek was a magnificent Medea at the Vienna Opera.

After the French Revolution, Madame Cherubini once said to Johann Adam Hiller, the German composer and director of the Gewandhauskonzerte in Leipzig, "In the morning the guillotine was busy, and in the evening one could not get a seat at the theatre". There were sixty theatres in Paris and they were always sold out. In times of terror people need escape more than ever. All the prominent composers in Paris – Cherubini, Nicolas Méhul, Jean François Le Sueur, and François Adrien Boïeldieu – wrote "revolutionary" music. (The most revolutionary music was written by a dilettante, Claude Joseph Rouget de l'Isle, a professional soldier, who created *La Marseillaise*, the most stirring national anthem of all.) A musical festival "celebrated" the execution of Louis XVI. Le Sueur composed a "terror opera", a great success in 1793, the year of terror, which is now thankfully forgotten.

Napoleon, who knew little about opera but was a good public relations man, wanted to revive the French "glorification opera", with the clear purpose of glorifying Napoleon. His first choice was Cherubini who, however, refused to become a "Court composer". Napoleon had better luck with Gasparo Spontini, a pupil of Piccinni, and himself a sort of musical Napoleon – arrogant, able, and convinced that he was of great importance. He'd come from his native Italy to Paris in 1803, and had a great success with *La Vestale*, written for Paris, a magnificent, classical Greek music drama in the Gluckian manner. Spontini had great dramatic talent, a sense of nobility and an ear for operatic effect; he was also a very great orchestrator. He himself considered *Olympie* (1819) his masterpiece but it wasn't a success. Spontini's temper and arrogance made him a megalomaniac. He told his admirer, Richard Wagner, that in *La Vestale* he had been the first to use the big drum in the orchestra. Wagner staged the first German performance, as Kapellmeister in Dresden, in 1844. Spontini conducted with an ebony baton "which he wielded like a field marshal". Wilhelmine Schröder-Devrient, who sang the title role, almost had a nervous breakdown, caused by Spontini's tyrannical attitude. The Metropolitan first performed *La Vestale* in 1925.

Spontini's second opera, *Fernand Cortez* (1809), made him even more famous, its greatest admirer being Napoleon. Wagner later used Spontini's blaring trumpets in *Rienzi* and *Lohengrin*. In 1819, Friedrich Wilhelm III of Prussia made Spontini chief Kapellmeister in Berlin, where he ruled like a musical monarch. With the exception of Gluck's *Armide* and Mozart's *Don Giovanni* he produced only his own operas there, and everybody was relieved when he was thrown out of Prussia by Friedrich Wilhelm IV. An unpleasant man, he was nevertheless a great composer, as most listeners will admit after hearing *La Vestale*.

After Cherubini and Spontini, no one could go farther in the direction taken by *Médée* and *La Vestale*. The inevitable reaction was towards the other extreme, the *opéra comique*, the genuine expression of what Richard Wagner later called "the Parisian style". The French themselves were not always sure what *opéra comique* was meant to be. Originally, an opera that had spoken dialogue was known as such, though it might be a drama; even *Carmen* was first known as an *opéra comique*. The first master of the genre which flourished during the Empire and the Restoration was Boïeldieu who wrote *La Calife de Bagdad* (1800), a great hit at Paris's second opera house, the Opéra-Comique, where it was performed for thirty-six years, and *La Dame Blanche* (1825), which became to the French what the *Freischütz* was to the Germans, except that its songs were sung as *chansons*, not as *Volkslieder*. It is the finest expression of French romanticism, and remained so popular – in 1862 the Opéra-Comique gave it for the thousandth time – that Bizet said he hated it, particularly when his own works got nowhere with the public. Then came Louis-Joseph-Ferdinand Hérold whose *Zampa* is still popular in France; and Daniel-Esprit Auber whose brilliant *Fra Diavolo* (1830), after a romantic libretto by Eugène Scribe, has survived to this day (Rossini said that "Auber produced light music but produced it like a great musician"). Two years earlier, Auber had created the first grand opera, *La Muette de Portici*. And then came Jacques Offenbach, the son of a cantor in a Cologne synagogue who went to Paris and became a completely French composer. Offenbach created the style of the French operetta, very different from the Viennese species: he had elegance, wit and irony, was often frivolous and sometimes moving. His works, among them *Orphée aux Enfers* (1858) and *La Belle Hélène* (1864), were often considered second-rate, but in the past fifty years there has been an Offenbach revival which started in Austria and Germany, where Offenbach is now famous as a genuine musical wit, a composer with depth and humour. Paradoxically he is best known for a work that has neither depth nor humour, *Les Contes d'Hoffmann*, written by Barbier and Carré from three episodes of E.T.A.Hoffmann's romantic fantasies. All over Europe, it is one of the most popular operas, and even tone-deaf people happily hum the *Barcarolle*. Yet the fantastic elements in the libretto seem to fascinate great producers, among them Walter Felsenstein whose sensational staging of *Hoffmann's Erzählungen* at East Berlin's Komische Oper was a great event in the history of modern opera production.

Voltaire's *aperçu*, "One goes to see a tragedy to be moved, to the

Opéra one goes either for want of any other interest or to facilitate digestion", could be disposed of as one of the master's lesser remarks; however, it became painfully true when the French discovered their passion for "grand opera", the mode that became the antithesis of Rameau, Gluck and Mozart. Instead of the lyric drama where the excitement came from within, from the characters, from drama or comedy, the grand opera became an extravaganza, a display of stunts and effects (in Auber's *La Muette*, there was even an eruption of Vesuvius). Stage technique, always popular in France, became *la science des planches*, the science of the boards. Its great master was Eugène Scribe, the author, alone or in collaboration with others, of over four hundred plays. Scribe created *la pièce bien faite* (the well-made play); he was a master craftsman whom Hollywood would have loved and who influenced the stage technique of all who came after him because of his unfailing instinct for what could be done on the stage. The younger Dumas once said that a dramatic author who had Balzac's knowledge of the human soul and Scribe's stage technique would be the greatest dramatist of all. Scribe and his melodramatic pupils constructed the self-acting plot that could be used in any language. He managed to insert arias and ballets in such a way that they didn't even momentarily hinder the plot.

After the Revolution and the Napoleonic wars, the French were ready for "law and order", and there was certainly a semblance of law and order in Scribe's neatly constructed plays and libretti. The great days were over, and *la grande nation* was eager to remember *la gloire* – at least on the stage. This was the era of the pseudo-classical drama of Victor Hugo and Alexandre Dumas. And the greatest master of the new style in opera, a *genre éminemment français*, was a Prussian Jew, named Jacob Liebman Beer, from Berlin. He became Giacomo Meyerbeer. He is not fashionable now, and often misunderstood, but he was a cultivated, intelligent man and a very gifted composer. He worked with Scribe and came to understand the French so well that they became infatuated with him. Balzac called *Les Huguenots* "as true as history itself". Georges Sand thought the opera's hero was "one of the greatest dramatic figures". Mendelssohn disagreed (once again, two incompatible German Jews): he called the ballet of the nuns in *Robert le Diable* "a veritable scandal" (at midnight, the nuns come out of their graves and dance a ballet in the ruins of a monastery). Schumann called it "a conglomeration of monstrosities". But the man who hated Meyerbeer more than anyone else and helped to destroy him was Wagner. ("Some have suggested that Wagner hated Meyerbeer primarily because he was a Jew but a chronological analysis of Wagner's anti-Semitic sayings and writings suggests that it was the other way around: Wagner hated Jews primarily because Meyerbeer was one", write Brockway and Weinstock. Paul Henry Lang says that "Berlioz and Wagner owed much more to Meyerbeer than they were willing to acknowledge".)

Meyerbeer was an immensely gifted musical dramatist, his craftsmanship superb. It is true that he made opera a super-spectacle, often substituting effect for beauty, but he wrote wonderful melodies and powerful ensembles. In his major operas, *Les Huguenots*, *Le Prophète*, *L'Africaine*, there are moments of great beauty. That also applies to *La Juive*, the passionate work written by Jacques Fromental Halévy, seven years younger than Meyerbeer. *La Juive*'s libretto was written by Scribe. The part of Eléazar, the heroine's father, remains one of the greatest tenor parts. Of Caruso's first performance (it was his thirty-sixth role at the Metropolitan), Irving Kolodin writes, "It was without doubt the most striking artistic triumph of his career". It was also, in December 1920, his farewell performance to the Metropolitan, and to opera.

The work of Meyerbeer and Halévy will undoubtedly be revived because there is much beauty and dramatic excitement in them.

ROSSINI: A LAZY GENIUS

Gioacchino Rossini was seldom performed around the turn of the century. Certain ponderous but influential German critics had decided that next to the *Meister* from Bayreuth, the giant of giants, the composer of *Il Barbiere di Siviglia* was insignificant. His opera was called an "isolated" masterpiece, a stroke of luck. And today another group of music critics and writers tries hard to convince us that at his best Rossini was as good as Mozart, and maybe better. Francis Toye, his biographer, writes about "A la faveur de cette nuit obscure", the second-act trio from *Le Comte Ory*: "For loveliness of melody, originality of harmony, charm of part writing, it is beyond praise, worthy of Mozart at his best". Such comparisons sometimes sound better when they are written, than later when they are read. Mozart is the genius of musical comedy and tragedy. Rossini remains the genius of musical farce. In 1837, the National Theater in New York performed a mixture of Mozart's *Figaro* and Rossini's *Barbiere*, billed as *The Two Figaros*.

Rossini's *Barbiere* alone would have made him immortal, but he wrote thirty-five other operas – having had eleven produced by the age of twenty-one. He was twenty-four when he wrote the masterpiece which excited such men as Beethoven, Schubert, Brahms, Berlioz and Wagner. Even the gloomy Schopenhauer loved it. When Rossini went to Vienna in 1822, the local composers, Beethoven and Schubert, were ignored and *il grande Mozart* ,was completely forgotten. Beethoven, not always an astute critic of other people's music, gave Rossini valuable advice when he told him, "Give us more Barbers". Rossini wrote his *Barbiere* in thirteen days. Beethoven, who had spent painful years revising *Fidelio* and writing three different overtures for his opera, must have envied Rossini, who fitted one overture to three of his operas. Rossini, a singer himself since childhood, understood the magic of the human voice as only a gifted Italian could. He did a great deal for singers, although later in life he grew weary of their problems.

Rossini had a magnificent instinct for music. Music – sounds and voices – meant everything to him. He also had wit, esprit, an impeccable technique and great, perhaps excessive, facility. He might have become one of the greatest opera composers, like Gluck, Mozart, Wagner, Verdi, had he taken as much interest and care in his libretti as they did. Francis Toye calls Rossini's career "a tragedy of bad libretti". Rossini hated to work hard. In his famous letter to an unknown young composer, Rossini tells him:

> ... Wait until the eve of the performance. Nothing stimulates the inspiration more than sheer necessity ... and the insistence of a frantic impresario who is tearing out his hair by the handful. At my time all the impresarios in Italy were bald at the age of thirty. I wrote the overture to *Otello* in a small room in the Barbaja Palace, where the baldest and fiercest of all impresarios locked me into my room, alone with a plate of spaghetti, and under the threat not to let me out until I had finished to my last note ... With the *Barber*, I had a much easier time: I did not compose an overture at all but took the one intended for the opera *Elisabetta*. The public was quite satisfied ...

Rossini was a lazy genius. When he didn't feel like working hard, which happened often, he would borrow from himself: a Rossini festival, featuring several of his works in the same week, might give the listeners the uncomfortable feeling of where-did-I-hear-this-before? The overture now used for *Il Barbiere* (which is not the overture originally written by Rossini for the première) had been used by Rossini earlier in two operas, *Aureliano in Palmira* and *Elisabetta, Regina d'Inghilterra,* which belonged to the *opera seria*. That the same overture should fit an *opera seria* and an *opera buffa* is indicative of Rossini's genius.

Mozart's creativity ended abruptly; he died at the age of thirty-five. Rossini was thirty-seven when, from one day to the next, he stopped composing. Musicians, artists and theorists have failed to understand this. Admittedly, he was successful, rich and famous. But whatever the reason he lived another thirty-nine years and only once did he turn back to music – when he wrote his beautiful *Stabat Mater*. He never wrote another opera. Possibly, after the success of Meyerbeer's *Huguenots* in Paris, Rossini realized that his art, particularly the art of *opera buffa*, was no longer in demand. In Frankfurt, he met Mendelssohn, and spoke about his grave concern for the future of opera – opera, as he knew it. Rossini always took a pessimistic view of the durability of his works. He thought that only his *Barbiere*, the third act of his *Otello* and the second of *Guillaume Tell* would survive. He turned out to be wrong: much more of his work remains first-rate opera.

He became a professional wit, bon vivant, raconteur and gourmet. *Tournedos à la Rossini*, like the peaches called after Nellie Melba, were creations of the great Escoffier. Unfortunately, more people know Rossini and Melba for these dishes than for what they achieved.

Rossini began as a nineteenth-century composer of *opera buffa*, continuing the great tradition of Pergolesi, Cimarosa, and Paisiello. Like Mozart, he too was "bathed in music", absorbing everything that was good and turning it with unerring instinct and suave genius into authentic Rossini. He wrote his one-act opera *La Cambiale di Matrimonio* when he was sixteen. Afterwards, maybe too quickly, he wrote more than a dozen other operas before *Il Barbiere*. Two of them, *L'Italiana in Algeri* (1813), an amusing two-act *opera buffa*, and *Il Turco in Italia* (1814), have been revived in the past years. *Il Turco* was a great success in 1955 at La Scala with Maria Callas.

Rossini was famous and admired when he decided to set to music the first play of Beaumarchais' *Figaro* trilogy. It was an audacious undertaking. There would be comparisons with Mozart's earlier *Le Nozze di Figaro*. And there would be resentment among the partisans of Paisiello, the revered old master who had set *Le Barbier de Séville* in 1782 under the title *Il Barbiere di Siviglia*.

Giovanni Paisiello was a pupil of Piccinni, and of the Neapolitan Conservatorio di Sant' Onofrio. He wrote successful operas when he was very young, and became so famous that Empress Catherina II of

Russia invited him to become the director of the Italian opera in St Petersburg. There he wrote *Il Barbiere di Siviglia* (in 1782, when Mozart wrote *Die Entführung*) which became widely admired. Returning from Russia, Paisiello stayed for a while in Vienna, dedicated several works to Emperor Joseph II, and finally settled in Naples, where he became the great old man of *opera buffa*. His best works – *La Bella Molinara, Nina, Pazza per Amore* – combine wit with dramatic force, fine humour and excellent craftsmanship. Mozart much admired Paisiello who is in line for "rediscovery".

His successor in St Petersburg was Domenico Cimarosa whose *Il Matrimonio Segreto*, written in Vienna in 1792, was performed everywhere, and is still performed by chamber music ensembles and at festivals. There is great affinity between Mozart and Cimarosa, who also wanted to be a musician first and foremost. (Unlike Gluck who considered himself "more a painter and a poet than a musician".) His masterpiece belongs with the finest of the comic operas – *La Serva Padrona*, Paisiello's *Barbiere*, Mozart's operas, and Rossini's *Barbiere*.

Rossini and his librettist, Cesare Sterbini, anticipated trouble from the Paisiello camp, while they worked on their *Barbiere*. Cautiously, they entitled their opera *Almaviva, o sia l'Inutile Precauzione*. But alas even this turned out to be a useless precaution. The première of Rossini's *Barbiere*, at the Teatro Argentina in Rome, on 20 February 1816, was often interrupted by the Paisiellan forces, and there was an uproar when Manuel del Pópolo Vicente García, who sang the part of Almaviva, tuned his guitar on the stage before accompanying himself on it. (Wagner later used this device effectively and amusingly in the second act of *Meistersinger*, when Beckmesser begins to serenade Eva.) Rossini became convinced that his new opera was a failure. He took to his bed and stayed there until his friends came the following night to tell him that the second performance had been a great success.

Il Barbiere is a great "singers' opera" (when Rossini was asked what was needed to make a career in opera, he said, "Voice, voice and again voice"). The greatest moments in *Il Barbiere* are demonstrations of vocal virtuosity: the "Largo al factotum", the magnificent aria "Una voce poco fa" (which created the initial successes of several prima donnas) and the "calumny" song. Unfortunately, Rossini's Italian predecessors had paid no attention to one of Gluck's main reforms – the composer himself must write the complete vocal part with all embellishments. They often left the vocal ornamentation to the ingenuity, skill – and vanity – of the singers. Today it is the accepted practice that the singer sings only what the composer wrote, although *Werktreue* is not so closely adhered to as in instrumental music where no serious artist would dare ignore the score. Some singers still take liberties when their vocal ability is not up to the composer's demands, trying to make it easier for themselves by transposing arias and omitting difficult passages. That is known as "taking the music down", and it is done everywhere. "Whether it is honourable, admirable or even defensible, is quite another matter", writes Irving Kolodin. ". . . Unlike programmes for athletic events, in which deviations from a norm will be faithfully noted, programmes in the opera house are notoriously noncommittal about what is actually going on". Such practices are detected only by people who know the score well or, even better, are endowed with absolute pitch.

Still, things are better now than at the time of Rossini, whose contract for *Il Barbiere* contained this clause: "Maestro Rossini obliges himself to make, if necessary, all the changes to suit the capabilities or exigencies of the singers". Rossini wrote the part of Rosina for a mezzo-soprano; the first Rosina in Rome was Geltrude Giorgi-Righetti, a mezzo. Soon, however, the famous soprano *divas* wouldn't leave such a fine part to a mezzo (for similar reasons, they later requisitioned the part of Carmen). They had it transposed, "taking the music up", and Rosina became a coloratura. Recently, some coloratura contraltos or mezzos, of whom there are few, have sung the part in the original key. At La Scala, Giulietta Simionato sang Rosina in 1952 under Victor de Sabata. It has been the favourite role of many singers who chose it for débuts – from Giulia Grisi, Maria Malibran, Adelina Patti, Luisa Tetrazzini, Nellie Melba to Amelita Galli-Curci, Toti dal Monte, Bidu Sayão, Victoria de los Angeles and Roberta Peters.

The worst absurdities committed against Rossini's score have occurred during the scene of Rosina's music lesson. Although he composed such beautiful music, 'Contro un cor che accende amore', famous sopranos have sometimes preferred to substitute their own choice. Both Patti and Melba weren't ashamed to sing 'Home, Sweet Home'; and Melba often sang *Mattinata* by her friend Tosti, composed a hundred years after Rossini's death; some rather eccentric ladies have even used the Mad Scene from *Lucia di Lammermoor*.

Yet Rossini's *Il Barbiere* survived; it was so good that nothing could destroy it. Following this success, Rossini, during a six-month period from December, 1816, to May, 1817, wrote three more superb operas. *Otello* has much beauty and was an international success for a long time (though today most opera lovers favour Verdi's *Otello*). *La Cenerentola* (Cinderella) is a brilliant tour de force which demands elaborately ornate singing from the mezzo coloratura – which is fine, provided she is as good as Fedora Barbieri or Giulietta Simionato. *La Gazza Ladra,* a fabulous success in the nineteenth century, has also been revived since World War II, when people once again became interested in Rossini.

In 1822 Rossini wrote his last Italian opera, *Semiramide,* which he called a "tragic melodrama". Three years later, he went to Paris and became, so far as the French were concerned, a French composer. For the Italians he remains an Italian composer. Nevertheless, *Le Comte Ory*, one of Rossini's later masterpieces, never became a success in Italy because it was set to a French text. The most famous of Rossini's "French" operas were *Le Siège de Corinthe* (brilliantly revived in 1969 at La Scala by a team of American artists under Thomas Schippers) and *Moïse et Pharaon.* Rossini had rewritten his earlier Italian *Mosè in Egitto*; to please the French, he had added a ballet which he "borrowed" from his own *Armida.* Even Cherubini, not a man who was easy to please, said he was "pleasantly surprised", and Balzac called it "a tremendous poem in music" though in fact he didn't know much about music. Then came *Le Comte Ory*, after a Scribe libretto, which became a great success in Paris. No one discovered that much of the score was borrowed from Rossini's *Il Viaggio a Reims,* which had been a failure. But there were twelve new numbers; audiences thought then that it was graceful and elegant, and they still do.

Rossini's last and grandest opera is *Guillaume Tell,* his bow to the French grand opera. It took him six months, a very long time, to finish the score. The opera lasted six hours (as long as *Götterdämmerung* or *Parsifal*) and is a mixture of brilliance and boredom. The critics liked it, and it was given fifty-six times during the season following its première. It was Rossini's answer to Meyerbeer; he wanted to prove that he too could write grand opera. Seven years after the première of *Guillaume Tell,* Meyerbeer had a triumphal success with *Les Huguenots.* Rossini became very bitter about the younger composer whom he'd helped. Meyerbeer always spoke with great admiration about Rossini. As a swan song, *Tell* was a failure. Beethoven had been right when he told Rossini to give us more *Barbers.*

BELLINI AND DONIZETTI

Rossini sponsored two younger Italians who became the greatest composers of *bel canto*: Gaetano Donizetti and Vincenzo Bellini. They understood the possibilities of the human voice, its range and power, its beauty and mystery, and wrote melodious arias for beautiful voices. They understood melody, which is the soul of music (no matter what contemporary composers may think and say about this), and they knew that there could be no opera without sung melody.

Bellini, long ignored, is now considered a very great composer. Since Maria Callas made her Metropolitan début in 1956 at the opening-season performance of *Norma*, which she'd sung earlier at both La Scala and Covent Garden, there has been a Bellini renaissance all over the world. Verdi, the incorruptible old master, called Bellini "one of the greatest masters of melody". Bellini's melodies exude feelings, memories, passions; they are the very soul of his operas. Unlike Schubert, who often woke up with a wonderful tune in his head, Bellini would declaim the words of the different parts before setting them to music, observing the inflexion of his own voice, and "the degree of haste or languor in the delivery". He did it almost scientifically, and impressed both Verdi and Wagner as a superb composer.

Bellini's image in musical history has oscillated between extremes. In the 1830s he was very famous. Forty years later, when Wagner's influence was spreading, he was completely ignored. In the past thirty years he was first rediscovered by the musical historians and later by the public. Our age understands this "romanticist with a penchant for melancholy, his softly elegaic melodies" (Paul Henry Lang). He is a very modern composer; his dramatic, haunting style is sometimes heard in the nocturnes and ballads of Chopin, in Massenet and Tchaikovsky, and perhaps even in Brahms, Debussy and Puccini. Musical analysts have described Bellini's arias and melodies as "neurotic ecstasy", and some compare them to Verlaine's poetry. Such comparisons are always dangerous: Bellini's long melodious passages, followed by a display of vocal fireworks, are strictly his own.

Bellini's greatest successes were *La Sonnambula* and *Norma*, premièred in March and December, 1831. *La Sonnambula*, with its absurdly romantic libretto, offered black-and-white emotions, which Bellini turned into melody. It made Bellini famous and established his style. Typical is Amina's aria, "Ah! non credea", where the tense emotion of the first part erupts into the *bel canto* embellishments(*fioriture*) at the end. This remained the great "double aria" of *bel canto* – a melodious *cavatina* followed by a brilliant *cabaletta*. Such operas need great singing stars, and Bellini had two of the greatest when *La Sonnambula* was first performed at Milan's Teatro Carcao: Giuditta Pasta and Giovanni Battista Rubini.

After the success of *La Sonnambula* La Scala commissioned Bellini to write a new opera. His able librettist, Felice Romani, wrote *Norma* (which Schopenhauer called a masterpiece) and Bellini demanded and got a formidable cast for the Scala première: Pasta sang Norma, Giulia Grisi was Adalgisa, and Domenico Donzelli sang the part of Pollione. The première was a failure, but La Scala continued to perform the opera until success came; it has remained Bellini's most successful masterpiece. *Norma*'s dramatic libretto was a handicap for Bellini who was better in writing elegaic arias than dramatic situations (it has been said that *Norma* would have been a great libretto for Verdi). Yet *Norma* also has "Casta diva", one of the greatest, most difficult virtuoso arias written in the lyric *bel canto* style, which becomes flowing and magical when performed by a truly great singer like Callas.

Rossini persuaded the management of the Théâtre-Italien in Paris to give his young friend Bellini a commission, and there Bellini wrote *I Puritani*, in which he came close to merging the styles of both Italian and French opera. Rossini helped with advice and criticism. The protagonists of *I Puritani* (after a good libretto written by Count Carlo Pepoli) are real human beings who suffer and exult through the melodies of their arias. The première, in 1835, with a sensational cast (Grisi, Rubini, Tamburini, Lablache) was such a success that the four artists became known as "the *Puritani* Quartet", as they toured Europe in Bellini's most mature work. Eight months after the première of *I Puritani* Bellini died, at the age of thirty-four. Cherubini and Rossini attended his funeral where three members of the *Puritani* Quartet sang a melody from *I Puritani*.

After the death of Bellini, the ruling Italian composer was Gaetano Donizetti, last of the great *bel canto* masters. He didn't work as hard and thoroughly as Bellini; his facility outdid even Rossini's. When he was told that *Il Barbiere* had been written in thirteen days, he said, with a shrug, "Yes – but then Rossini was always a lazy man". Donizetti, even lazier by his own standards, composed the last act of *La Favorita* in five hours – yet managed to produce some very fine music in the last act. Bellini once asked his publisher, Giovanni Ricordi, four times the usual fee for an opera; he explained that he composed one opera while "other men" (Donizetti?) wrote four. It took Donizetti eleven days to write *Don Pasquale,* his *opera buffa* masterpiece, and the most likely to survive.

Donizetti was a virtuoso composer who possessed both the strength and weakness of that virtuosity. He might compose fine arias, but he would dash off the music between them and write flimsy, dull accompaniments. He composed seventy-five operas in twenty-nine years. Much of his work is done too easily, but at his best Donizetti wrote beautiful melodies and graceful stretches of music.

He seemed to like libretti with exotic settings: *La Regina di Golconda* (India), *Emilia di Liverpool*, *Otto Mesi in due Ore* ("Eight Months in Two Hours") set in Siberia. His best operas survive – *L'Elisir d'Amore* (1832), *Lucia di Lammermoor* (1835), *La Favorita* (1840), *La Fille du Régiment* (1840), and, of course, *Don Pasquale* (1843). *Lucia*, a great hit at the première in San Carlo, Naples, remains a popular success in spite of the libretto which, written by Salvatore Commarano (eighteen years later he was to write the immortal nonsense of Verdi's *Il Trovatore*), is a triumph of confusion. The music is not exactly distinguished. But *Lucia* has the Mad Scene, a *ne plus ultra* tour de force for prima donnas, and the great sextet "Chi mi frena in tal momento", which remains one of the finest ensembles in opera. It is splendid music, and very effective. The Mad Scene, almost completely unrelated to the dramatic action, displays the virtuosity of a great prima donna. Afterwards, nineteen other composers wrote "mad scenes", giving their prima donnas such murderous *fioriture* that only a "mad" woman would be expected to sing them. Anna in Donizetti's *Anna Bolena* and Imogene in Bellini's *Il Pirata* seem also afflicted by the same madness. Verdi had the courage to create a coloratura heroine, Gilda in *Rigoletto*, who does not become mad: she gets murdered instead, and has to sing her final aria sewn up in a sack!

Donizetti's tenth opera was *La Fille du Régiment*. One of its great admirers was Mendelssohn (who nevertheless knew little about opera). But we must be eternally grateful to Donizetti for *Don Pasquale*, a sparkling *opera buffa* gem and a superb farce. While *Don Pasquale* was being rehearsed, Donizetti felt that "something was missing", he went home, searched among his manuscripts, found an aria and sent it to the great tenor, Giovanni Mario, asking him to sing it to Norina in the garden scene. "Com'è gentil" was a very great success at the sensational première. So also was the great bass Luigi Lablache in the title role.

Donizetti was a gifted musician and a nice man. When one of his friends, an opera manager, complained that he was going to be bankrupt and asked the composer for help, Donizetti said he had an "idea". He enlarged it into a libretto, wrote the score, and nine days later *La Favorita* was ready for rehearsal. It saved his friend from bankruptcy.

It remains a phenomenon to many historians that four great Italians of the early nineteenth century – Spontini, Rossini, Bellini, Donizetti –

produced their best works in Paris. "The style of the Paris school is still the dominating influence of the taste of almost every nation", wrote Richard Wagner, no great admirer of the French, as late as 1865 to King Ludwig II of Bavaria.

A PERFECT OPERA

Opera lovers, who rarely agree on anything, almost without exception consider *Carmen* a perfect opera. It has a dramatic story, believable characters, strong atmosphere, wonderful melodies, brilliant orchestration. A good *Carmen* performance has excitement from beginning to end; one can hear the opera repeatedly yet each time it seems to improve. Because *Carmen* is so good, it is almost impossible to stage it. I've heard *Carmen* over fifty times, all over the world, but have never seen a completely satisfying *mise-en-scène*. (*Don Giovanni*, another near-perfect work, poses a similar problem.)

Carmen is surrounded by many legends. The failure of its première, at the Opéra-Comique, on 3 March 1875, is said to have broken the heart of its composer, Georges Bizet. A touching story but not quite true. Actually, the opera was fairly well received, and the press was not hostile. Bizet left the Opéra-Comique in a state of disappointment but certainly not a heart-broken man. He died on 3 June. Later it was confirmed that he'd been suffering from angina. On the night he died *Carmen* was performed for the twenty-third time and during the following season it was repeated twenty-seven times.

The lukewarm reception of *Carmen* was mostly due to the libretto. The Opéra-Comique was a family theatre, and the French bourgeois (who are often the most bourgeois of all) were shocked by the tragic story that ends in death. They were used to pleasant operas with happy endings. And the more conservative critics accused Bizet of having written a "Wagnerian" score, while the French Wagnerians said he hadn't gone far enough. The libretto was based on Prosper Mérimée's scandalous bestseller *Carmen*, written in 1845. The librettists, Henri Meilhac and Ludovic Halévy, a cousin of Bizet's wife, had somewhat cleaned up the Mérimée original and made Carmen, the rather vicious gypsy whore, into a woman of doubtful character, but still one who would be acceptable – and certainly attractive – to the bourgeois. In this they succeeded admirably: doubtless, more women than men were shocked by *Carmen*. Halévy and Meilhac understood that bad women are more interesting than good ones; it has been so since Madame Potiphar. They made Carmen an unmarried woman (the real Carmen was an unfaithful wife), allowed her only one lover besides Don José, and created her antagonist, the pure, lovely Micaëla, so good that Don José looks twice as bad when he deserts her for the gypsy. The place of action is Seville, always a popular locale with librettists (*Il Barbiere di Siviglia, Le Nozze di Figaro, Fidelio, Don Giovanni*). The librettists did a superb job, supplying Bizet with the sort of libretto that must at once be set to music. And indeed it took him only just over two months to write the score.

Bizet put all he had and knew into *Carmen*: the brilliant sunshine and black shadows of the Spanish landscape, the folk-song melodies and exciting rhythms, great arias and brilliant orchestration (Spaniards consider the music pseudo-Spanish, yet some of them admit it reflects the very soul of Spain). Bizet had never been to Spain, but with the vision and imagination of the true lyric poet he created his own Spain. The music of *Carmen* needs a first-rate conductor who "hears" lights and shadows, who senses its rhythm and flow; otherwise it can only too easily sound like kitsch.

Bizet was often misunderstood during his short life. He is another great composer who died, much too early, at the age of thirty-seven. Although his first important opera, *Les Pêcheurs de Perles,* already showed his excellent orchestration and sense of exotic colours, a critic called the première at the Théâtre-Lyrique in 1863 "a fortissimo in three acts", the sort of "witty" remark characteristic of music criticism in France during the Second Empire, and not only then and there.★

The French critics never really tried to understand *Carmen*. They had reluctantly accepted naturalism in their novels and dramas but refused to accept it on the opera stage. They called Carmen "bizarre" and "incoherent". One critic wrote, "The vulgarities and the realism of the libretto are unbecoming to a lyric work". Sensuous passions were acceptable in a novel and a spoken drama, but in the opera house everything must be *"joli, claire, bien ordonné"*, perhaps as it was in Gounod's *Faust* or *Roméo et Juliette*.

Nothing is *bien ordonné* in *Carmen*. The passions are not well ordered and the melodies are not "charming". The difference between Bizet and

★ The only man in Paris who understood music and music criticism was considered an eccentric: Hector Berlioz. In the past thirty years, a growing number of people in France and elsewhere, are beginning to have second thoughts about Berlioz. He is hard to understand because he doesn't fit into any category, but he emerges as an unusually gifted composer. His operatic masterpiece, *Les Troyens*, is a powerful music drama. Sir Donald Tovey calls it "one of the most gigantic and convincing masterpieces".

Gounod is that between genius and talent. No one could call *Carmen* elegant or lovely – on the contrary, it is vicious, brutal, painful – as life often is. The characters behave as people do in real life, and Bizet wanted no compromise. No one understood this better than Wagner's erstwhile close friend and later arch-enemy, Friedrich Nietzsche, who wrote, with an obvious allusion to his ex-friend, who had just finished his *Tristan und Isolde*,

> Yesterday – would you believe it? – I heard Bizet's masterpiece for the twentieth time. Once more I attended with the same gentle reverence. How such a work completes one! ... This music is wicked, refined, fantastic ... it possesses the refinement of a race, not of an individual. And how are they obtained? Without grimaces! Without counterfeiting of any kind! Free from the life of the grand style! ... Fate hangs over this work, its happiness is short, sudden, without reprieve ... I envy Bizet for having had the courage of this sensitiveness, which hitherto in the cultured music of Europe has found no means of expression – of this southern, tawny, sunburnt sensitiveness. And finally, love, love translated back into nature! ... Love as a fate, as a fatality, cynical, innocent, cruel, and precisely in its way *Nature* ... I know no case in which the tragic irony which constitutes the kernel of love is expressed with such severity, or in so terrible a formula, as in the last cry of Don José with which the work ends: "Yes, it is I who killed her, I – my adored Carmen!"

Carmen was too good to be misunderstood for long. It became a real success half a year after its première – too late for Bizet. In Vienna, the spoken dialogues were replaced by accompanied recitatives by Bizet's friend, Ernest Guiraud. The Viennese are proud of *their* first *Carmen* to this day, and well they might be. When *Carmen* was revived in 1883 at the Opéra-Comique, the critics and the public cheered it as a masterpiece, and by 1904 one thousand performances had been given. In 1959, it moved from the Opéra-Comique to the Opéra, approaching its three thousandth performance. Today it is in the repertory of all opera companies.

The part of Carmen is one of the most coveted operatic roles. It is sung by mezzos (as intended by Bizet) and by sopranos who were attracted by the psychological, musical and dramatic challenge of the part. There are four great singing roles, and many people feel that Don José, rather than Carmen, is the central figure in the tragedy because Carmen remains the same person from the beginning to the end while he changes. Nietzsche called *Carmen* "the most penetrating masterpiece of the nineteenth century". It so impressed other composers that no one has since tried to write another *Carmen*, perhaps the greatest of all marks of respect.

Paradoxically, while Bizet the genius was ridiculed, his much less gifted contemporary, Charles Gounod, was almost deified in France. (Gounod's noble, godlike appearance, and his long white beard, helped to create the image.) Gounod's *Faust* remains one of the most popular works in the repertory but compared to *Carmen* it is second-rate salon music, and the Faustian ideas cannot be taken seriously. The critics hate *Faust* and the public loves it. Everything is wrong about the "adaptation" of Goethe's greatest drama, by two hacks, Jules Barbier and Michel Carré. The characters are as artificial as Madame Tussaud's wax figures, and the story of Sin-Doesn't-Pay is glorified kitsch. But Gounod was a good musician, and he wrote easily remembered melodies, though they rarely have any relation to the libretto or the characters. *Faust* remains the most popular opera in Paris. In 1883, the Metropolitan Opera opened in New York, and the "six most important opera composers" were to be engraved on the proscenium arch. The millionaire experts decided to place Gluck, Mozart and Verdi on the left side, and Wagner, Beethoven and – Gounod on the right. Perhaps they'd never heard of Bizet; or were puritanically shocked by *Carmen*?

Gounod remains apparently indestructible. His *Roméo et Juliette* is still quite popular. The Romeo and Juliet story has attracted many composers; the finest version is Bellini's *I Capuletti ed i Montecchi*, which has been revived in Italy in the past years. Messrs Barbier and Carré wrote the libretto for Gounod, treating Shakespeare as shabbily as Goethe. The immortal love story is reduced to a series of sentimental love duets. The two librettists delivered their concoctions also to Ambroise Thomas who is famous in France as the composer of *Mignon* and *Hamlet*. Any resemblance between Shakespeare's and Gounod's *Hamlet* is not coincidental, but idiotic. Americans and the British have been either amused or infuriated by the Barbier-Carré version. Another much esteemed French composer of the era, Camille Saint-Saëns, had better luck with *Samson et Dalila*, based on a libretto by Ferdinand Lemaire. Saint-Saëns had taste and melodic invention, and it is always pleasing to hear his beautiful music.

But the French like *Faust* best, and there is rarely a week in Paris without a performance of Gounod's opera.

Goethe sensed the deeper truth when he told his friend Eckermann, "Mozart should have composed *Faust*". Lorenzo da Ponte might have been able to create the libretto, preserving as much as possible from the First Part of Goethe's great drama. Beethoven admired Goethe but he couldn't have done it because unlike Mozart he did not understand the stage. Richard Wagner, who considered it, might have succeeded; his *Faust Overture* was to be a section of a later *Faust Symphony* (there is a deep affinity between Faust's Gretchen, the *ewig-weibliche* symbol of Goethe's drama, and Wagner's Brünnhilde, the only human and believable character in his *Ring*). Only Schumann, in his *Faust*, came close to Goethe's poetic fantasy. There have been dozens of other musical treatments of *Faust*. Arrigo Boito, who wrote the great libretti of Verdi's *Otello* and *Falstaff*, attempted the subject in his own opera, *Mefistofele*. Even Meyerbeer, approached by Jules Barbier to do a *Faust* opera, said in a rare moment of modesty, "*Faust* . . . is a sanctuary, not to be approached with profane music". And so it remains a strange fact of opera life that when people talk of *Faust*, they mean Gounod, whose opera has nothing to do with Goethe. Ernest Newman admitted there was lovely music in Gounod's *Faust*, ". . . if you do not attempt to see the characters as Goethe has drawn them. Once you begin to think of these matters, you can only smile at Gounod and his fellow criminals who concocted the libretto."

When Gounod died in 1893, he was the most famous composer in France. Yet Jules Massenet's *Manon* – much finer than anything Gounod ever wrote – was already eight years old. It is often said that Massenet is "too charming" to be great. He had taste and elegance and he wrote beautiful, French music; he didn't make the mistake of attempting such subjects as Goethe's *Faust* or Shakespeare's *Hamlet*. Instead he went back to a great French love story, Abbé Prévost's *L'Histoire de Manon Lescaut et du Chevalier des Grieux*. Henri Meilhac, of *Carmen* fame, and Philippe Gille wrote the libretto. *Manon* was first performed in 1884 at the Opéra-Comique, becoming an instant – and abiding – success. Massenet has been accused of being workmanlike and clever, "an imitator", but *Manon* is the work of an artist and aesthete, containing beautiful melodies, and two great singing parts. Musically less dramatic than Puccini's (later) *Manon Lescaut*, Massenet's opera has the better libretto, is more poetic, and seems more enduring of the two works. Indeed, none of his other operas has had the durability of *Manon*. *Thaïs* is sometimes revived for famous sopranos such as Mary Garden or Maria Jeritza, while the *Méditation* from *Thaïs* has become as famous, and as much overplayed, as the *Intermezzo* from *Cavalleria Rusticana*. *Werther*, adapted from Goethe's novel, was less successful, and remains known as a "tenor's opera". Massenet was not successful at portraying virtuous women. They bored him. He was the musical poet of beautiful sinners. Towards the end of his life he wrote *Don Quichotte* which became a personal success for Feodor Chaliapin, and remains the goal of a great bass, though the libretto is bad and the music is often boring. Of Massenet's competitors only Gustave Charpentier had success with *Louise*, a woman of "total amorality", in the sense of the fin-de-siècle. Mary Garden sang the part at Oscar Hammerstein's Manhattan Opera House and Geraldine Farrar at the Metropolitan, but now the success of the opera is restricted to France.

WAGNER: GENIUS OR MONSTER?

Richard Wagner remains the most controversial genius in music, perhaps in all the arts. The controversy began during his life – over ten thousand books about him were published before Wagner's death in 1883 – and continues still. The musical world is divided into Wagnerians (sometimes called Wagnerites) and anti-Wagnerians. Many have switched positions as they discover more about their genius, or their monster. In the case of most artists, knowledge of their private lives is not essential to an understanding of the nature of their work. Bach, the allegedly philistine family man who lived a humdrum existence, and Haydn, who patiently carried out his duties for his princely masters and lived in a small house with a nagging wife, expressed the heights and depths of their passions in their music. Mozart, often (falsely) remembered as a *wunderkind* and darling of the gods, who can be naïve, almost childish in his letters, knew more about the dark abysses of the soul than any other musician. Beethoven might have had a terrible row with his landlady because he poured two pitchers of water over himself on a hot day, in the middle of his room, but he could then sit down and work on one of the later string quartets, the greatest absolute music ever written. The mystery of the creative spirit is unfathomable, and should remain so.

Although Wagner's private life doesn't explain his work, it cannot be ignored in an analysis of his work, because it is often the direct antithesis of his creative spirit. Furthermore, bad people are generally more interesting than good ones. Wagner is fascinating: an incredible music-dramatical genius who was an undiluted monster. He talked endlessly, nearly always about himself; he had a mania for always being right; he pretended to know everything; he wrote hundreds of pages about politics and music, against the Jews and vegetarianism, and had them published, at somebody else's expense. He was most hostile towards those from whom he borrowed (ideas, trends, money). Allardyce Nicoll says that Wagner,

> ... despite all his grandiloquent protestations of originality and despite all the mystic mumbo-jumbo with which he invests his inventions, shows himself the inheritor of earlier traditions. Nietzsche was intuitively right when he averred that the Master of Bayreuth was, in essence, a French romanticist. From the tensions of Victor Hugo and Dumas he freely imbibed, and his structural power he derived from that most despised of popular playwrights, Eugène Scribe.

Wagner is that enigmatic blend of good and evil, great and cruel, that sporadically appears in Germany, the country of Kant and Himmler, of Bach and Walter Ulbricht, of Goethe and Goebbels. Wagner's conceit was almost pathological. He read everything aloud to his relatives and friends. He didn't expect criticism, only applause. Deems Taylor writes in *Of Men and Music*,

> (Wagner) had the emotional stability of a six-year-old child. When he felt out of sorts, he would rave and stamp, or sink into suicidal gloom ... He was almost innocent of any sense of responsibility. He was convinced that the world owed him a living ... He was equally unscrupulous in other ways. His second wife had been the wife of his most devoted friend, from whom he stole her. And even while he was trying to persuade her to leave her first husband he was writing to a friend to inquire whether he could suggest some wealthy woman, any wealthy woman, whom he could marry for her money ... He had a genius for making enemies. He would insult a man who disagreed with him about the weather ...

But Taylor also concludes that "this undersized, sickly, disagreeable, fascinating little man was right all the time ... What if he was faithless to his friends and to his wives? There is greatness about his worst mistakes ... The miracle is that what he did in the space of seventy years could have been done at all, even by a great genius, is it any wonder that he had not time to be a man?"

He was a complex monster. Financially, he cheated his best friends. In *Richard Wagner, The Man, His Mind and His Music*, Robert Gutman writes,

> Otto Wesendonck (with whose wife Wagner later ran away) who bought the publishing rights to *Rheingold* and *Walküre* in 1859, had wide experience with Wagner's character and was perhaps not too startled to learn that *Rheingold* was sold again to Schott of Mainz without any intention on Wagner's part of repaying the original advance. As requital Otto was granted the rights to *Götterdämmerung* – an unwritten work! But in 1865 Wagner demanded that Otto without reimbursement give up all claims to the *Ring* (he had also paid for the incomplete *Siegfried*) and even surrender – "amiably and generously" – the autographed orchestral score of *Rheingold*, his only remaining asset of these transactions, to the *Ring*'s newest proprietor, the Bavarian King. The climax of double dealings came, when King Ludwig's ownership rights, for which he had paid untold thousands of marks, were ignored by Wagner, who proceeded to sell the *Ring* to individual theatres for his own profit.

Obviously Wagner was a crook on a scale befitting his musical genius. His duplicity extends to almost everything else he did. He extolled the virtue of chastity in his early operas while having numerous affairs. Working in his study in Haus Wahnfried in Bayreuth on the first act of his Bühnenweihfestspiel *Parsifal*, allegedly a religious work, he wrote to his "*douce amie*", Judith, to send him amber and powdered scents which he spread in his bathroom, located underneath the study, so that he could breathe in "the aromatic fumes rising from below and with them memories of Judith's glowing embraces", while working on the pious admonitions of good, old Gurnemanz. Yet he had the audacity to refer contemptuously to Rossini as "Italia's voluptuous son, smiling away in luxury's most luxurious lap".

Wagner's pathological hatred of the French and the Jews is a matter of record, and made him the idol of Adolf Hitler. Wagner had "the incredibly bad taste", writes Thomas Mann, to write *Capitulation*, a satire on the agony of Paris in 1871. "Most nineteenth-century anti-Semites would have been genuinely horrified by Auschwitz, but one has the uncomfortable suspicion that Wagner would have wholeheartedly approved", writes W. H. Auden. In "Know Thyself", Wagner wrote, in 1881, about the great solution (*die grosse Lösung*) concerning the Jews, urging his fellow Germans to "conquer false shame and not shrink from ultimate knowledge" (*nach der Überwindung aller falschen Scham die letzte Erkenntnis nicht zu scheuen*). A terrifying sentence. Wagner's *letzte Erkenntnis*, the ultimate knowledge, later became the *Endlösung* (final solution) of Himmler and Eichmann.

Wagner hated nearly all fellow composers, and he hated most those from whom he learned most. He hated Mendelssohn and was deeply influenced by Mendelssohn's Scottish Symphony. He hated Meyerbeer and ridiculed the grand opera – and wrote his own grand opera, *Rienzi*. He hated Scribe and wrote his structurally derivative *Meistersinger* libretto. The difference between Wagner's aesthetic, polemical writings and his musical and dramatic practices is bewildering. In *Oper und Drama*, his most important treatise about opera as an art form, published in 1851, he severely condemned Mozart:

> Nothing seems more characteristic to me concerning Mozart's career as an opera composer than the careless indiscrimination with which he approached his task; it did not occur to him to ponder over the aesthetic scruples underlying the opera; on the contrary, he proceeded with the composition of any text submitted to him with the greatest lack of self-consciousness.

One wonders whether to be infuriated by Wagner's impertinence or amused by his stupidity and ignorance. The amazing thing is how long people were fooled by him, and how many are fooled by him to this day.

Theoretically, Wagner condemned duets and ensembles because they make the words difficult to hear; according to his writings, the words are as important as the music, maybe more important. Whereupon he wrote *Tristan und Isolde,* with its great and wonderful love duet in the second act, in which the words were made nearly unintelligible by the overwhelming power of the passionate music. In *Meistersinger* there are not only arias, choruses and a ballet (all that Wagner hated so much about the despised Meyerbeer), but even a quintet! And because Wagner was such a genius, it happens to be the greatest quintet ever written for the operatic stage. About the book of *Götterdämmerung,* with its "poisoned drinks, conspirators' ensembles, massed choruses, and Scribe-inspired *coups de théâtre*", Bernard Shaw wrote quite correctly that it has much in common with Verdi's *Un Ballo in Maschera*.

In his writings Wagner demanded that conventional arias linked by recitatives are to be replaced by what he called "continuous *melos*" (preferring the Greek word *melos* to melody which he considered vulgar). He argued strongly against "the singers' opera" where plot and orchestra are subordinated to vocal display, as in the works of Rossini and Bellini. Wagner carried this out in *Rheingold* and parts of *Die Walküre*. But in *Götterdämmerung, Meistersinger* and *Parsifal*, with their powerful choruses, he wrote post-Meyerbeer super-grand opera, and in *Der fliegende Holländer* and *Tannhäuser* he often stops the action by giving the singers beautiful arias.

Wagner's main problem was not his enemies but his friends. The closest friend was young Friedrich Nietzsche, the greatest thinker of the late-nineteenth century, who considered Wagner his ideal "superman", the emanation of the eternal, who would bring about the regeneration of all the arts in the spirit of ancient Greece. As a young philosopher, Nietzsche was overpowered by Richard Wagner, the man and the artist. "He saw in Wagner the herald of the new Dionysian man" (Lang). The break came when Nietzsche's romantic admiration was challenged by his critical powers. He began, deeply shocked, to sense Wagner's insincerity. He must have had his first doubts when he was privileged, among Wagner's closest friends, to read the manuscript of his autobiography. He later wrote,

> That which is circulated as Wagner's autobiography is fiction, if not worse, intended for public use. I must confess that every point we know from Wagner's description I regard with the greatest suspicion. He was not proud enough to utter the truth . . . even in biography he remained true to himself – he remained an actor.

In 1873, Nietzsche wrote regarding Wagner that "he who believes in himself only is no longer honest toward himself". The final break came nine years later when Nietzsche heard *Parsifal*, which he called "Christianity arranged for Wagnerians". Nietzsche had known Wagner was a cynical atheist, and that what seemed like a conversion was due to Wagner's wife, Cosima. Nietzsche also knew that among close friends Wagner was still cynical about his wife's beliefs. It is no secret that the editors of his letters deleted many of Wagner's anti-Christian polemics. Nietzsche who knew the Master better than anyone else rightly sensed opportunistic and materialistic beliefs behind *Parsifal*. Wagner was keenly aware of the bourgeois sanctimonious mentality of the Germans, "for God, Kaiser and Reich"; Nietzsche knew this and was ashamed of Wagner for pandering to the public and "der Psychologie der Masse". It was the end of a beautiful friendship. Wagner survived easily, but Nietzsche brooded about the disappointment and some believe it may have contributed to his later insanity.

"Wagner," writes Victor Gollancz in *Journey towards Music, A Memoir*, "was a man ... of fascist mentality, coloured by something essentially, if not exclusively Teutonic, and it is above all in the *Ring* that this side of his nature emerges. By a fascist mentality I mean a preference for war against peace, for violence against gentleness, for retaliation against forgiveness; a glorification of strength and a contempt for weakness; an exaltation of health and a disdain for suffering. And by Teutonism (not for a moment to be thought as the mark of all or even of most Germans) I mean a predilection for vastness as against proportion, for cloudiness as against precision, for an inflated romanticism and a vague nobility ..."

Wagner began by writing poetry and philosophical studies. In 1831, at the age of eighteen, he began to study counterpoint. Two years later, he wrote *Die Feen* (The Fairies), and a historical grand opera, *Rienzi*. He was under the influence of his predecessors (Meyerbeer, Halévy, Spontini, Spohr, Méhul, Marschner) and borrowed freely from them. Hanslick described the first-act finale as a mixture of Donizetti and Meyerbeer, and an anticipation of Verdi. Wagner was furious but then he calmed down and wrote *Der fliegende Holländer* where the master's hand becomes visible, and audible (journeying from Riga, in 1839, Wagner had experienced violent storms between Pillan and Gravesend which made his trip, according to his own description, more terrifying than "the first voyage of Columbus"). There are already great moments in the *Holländer*, such as the Dutchman's appearance in the first act, Senta's ballad and her meeting with the Dutchman, and the ghost chorus in the last act. The opera was a failure in Dresden, in 1843; the audience was bored and after only four performances the work was dropped for twenty-two years. *Tannhäuser* (1845) and *Lohengrin* (1847) are romantic operas; but again, there are long flashes of Wagnerian genius. No romantic composer had yet written anything as exciting as the Venusberg music. And there is drama and excitement in the schizophrenic female characters, Elisabeth and Venus, whom Wagner, with blinding clarity, saw as *the* woman. *Lohengrin* remains *the* German fairytale opera, in which Wagner used orchestral colours that had never been heard before.

Tannhäuser did quite well in Dresden in 1845 but Wagner's real troubles with the work began in 1861, at the Paris Opéra. During the second performance members of the local Jockey Club, who used to arrive late at the opera house, started a riot because they had missed the splendours of the ballet at the beginning of the first act; they were joined by a large group who were opposed to Wagner. After the third performance, he withdrew the work.

Lohengrin too had a mixed reception. Wagner wrote it backwards, beginning with the third act, and ending with the prelude. Liszt (Wagner's future father-in-law) presented the opera at his small Hoftheater in Weimar. The orchestra had only thirty-eight members and the singers were second-rate. Gradually, however, *Lohengrin* was accepted and remains one of the composer's most popular works. Weber's influence is obvious but Wagner surpasses his predecessor; no one before him had created orchestral effects that might almost be called impressionistic.

In 1849, Wagner joined the revolutionary movement in Dresden, went on the barricades, had to flee from Germany into Switzerland (he didn't hear *Lohengrin* performed in Germany until 1861). As a refugee in Zurich, he wrote his theoretical essays, *Das Kunstwerk der Zukunft,* and *Oper und Drama.* He had become acquainted with the pessimistic philosophy of Arthur Schopenhauer and saw the answer to many questions in Schopenhauer's romantic interpretation of the cosmic nature of music ("music is the melody whose text is the world"). This sounded great to the impressionable mind of Wagner. But Schopenhauer also said, "Music is more powerful than words, music and words is the marriage of a prince and a beggar". German romanticists always considered music supreme among the arts, but Wagner wrote that the poetry must derive from the myth, that the musician must be the servant of the poet.

Gradually, Wagner evolved his grandiose concept of the *Gesamtkunstwerk* (total theatre) where drama, music, scenery, lights are welded into a powerful unity.

Wagner worked long and hard on his librettos. In a letter to Richard Strauss, Hugo von Hofmannsthal, the librettist, praises Wagner's dramatic structures "and the inimitable excellence with which the way is prepared for the music". A good libretto must be a good play which also "prepares the way for the music". Great librettists are rarer even than great playwrights.

Wagner's poetry is dominated by alliteration. The third accented syllable alliterates with the first or second, or both. Sometimes Wagner overdoes this, sacrificing sense and lucidity, as in Isolde's *Liebestod,*

In des Wonnenmeeres wogenden Schwall,
In des Welt-Atems wehendem All.

At the first Bayreuth Festival, in 1876, Lilli Lehmann, the Woglinde in *Rheingold,* had the doubtful pleasure of singing the first words in the *Ring,*

Weia! Waga! Woge, du Welle, walle zur Wiege!
Wagala weia! Wallala, weiala weia.

Pretty meaningless, in German or any other language – but all criticism is suspended when one listens to the music. Wagner's wonderful orchestra always reflects on, or interprets, never just accompanies, the events on the stage. It delivers a running commentary on the psychology of the characters. This is not Wagner's invention – Monteverdi did it in his *stile recitative* much earlier – but Wagner brought it to unprecedented perfection. Yet even in his great orchestral passages in the *Ring*, there are sometimes grand opera moments that impress adolescents of all ages – thunder and lightning in *Rheingold*, the gods' entry into Valhalla – in between moments of great beauty.

Much academic nonsense has been written about Wagner's use of the *leitmotif*. Wagner didn't invent it – Monteverdi had already used recurrent themes, and so did Grétry and Gluck – but he developed the principle and used it with astonishing freedom. His leitmotifs are not musical clichés; he never used them rigidly or mechanically, as one would assume after studying some German guidebooks and commentaries. Wagner uses leitmotifs to express psychological happenings, using them to build up his amazing symphonic technique. Debussy called the leitmotifs "visiting cards", and it is true that sometimes Wagner used them absurdly. When Brünnhilde is torn by wild passion in the third act of *Siegfried*, one suddenly hears the dragon motif. Some people think it might have been a private joke, but Wagner's humour wasn't very subtle, except in *Meistersinger*, when he suddenly impresses us with wonderful nuances of humour (but everything about Wagner is unpredictable – for every one of his rules, there are many exceptions). In the prelude to *Götterdämmerung*, Siegmund's and Sieglinde's love theme is used skilfully and concurrently with Brünnhilde's devotion to Grane, the horse. Such inconsistencies prove that it would be absurd to interpret Wagner's creative genius literally, through mathematically used leitmotifs. Wagner was no book-keeper but a genius.

When he is carried away by inspiration on a magnificent scale, which happens often in his late works, he writes wonderful symphonic music of such sensuous beauty and passionate power that one should close one's eyes and surrender. The problem of listening to Wagner is that total theatre demands total immersion. "If we are to get the full benefit from Wagner's operas, we have simultaneously to identify ourselves with what we hear and see on the stage . . . and to distance ourselves from it." writes Auden.

In 1854, having evolved his aesthetic principles, Wagner began to write *Götterdämmerung*, the "last day" of his tetralogy, *Der Ring des Nibelungen*, which he tackled first. When he found that too many things remained unexplained, he went backwards, and wrote *Siegfried* (which happens earlier than *Götterdämmerung*). After the second act of *Siegfried*, he became involved in the conflict between the principles he'd written and the music he was inspired to write. He gave up *Siegfried*, and resumed work on it only twelve years later, after he'd written *Tristan und Isolde* and *Meistersinger*, two totally different masterpieces, each unsurpassed in its own way. *Tristan* remains the greatest orgy of love ever written for the stage, and *Meistersinger* is a wonderful romantic comedy – and the only work of Wagner's whose characters are not artificial heroes, gods and dwarves, but real human beings (Wagner called it, rightly, his "perfectest masterpiece").

And suddenly he went back to the interrupted *Siegfried*, and when he'd finished and there were more things to say, he went farther backwards, and wrote *Die Walküre*, and finally *Rheingold,* which opens the tetralogy. Such achievements imply hard work. In his working habits, Wagner was a bourgeois – pedantic, writing clean pages, keeping regular hours; but in his conception he was entirely the opposite.

Tristan und Isolde completely reverses Wagner's lofty theories on the poet ruling the musician. *Tristan* is a *musical* masterpiece. The music – the orchestra – always comes first. The words often retard the plot or, at worst, create boredom. No one goes to *Tristan* to listen to the poetry. It's the music that matters.

Meistersinger is Wagner's finest work. The libretto has genuine humour and great poetic beauty and the music both drama and charm. It is everything a comic opera should be, though not according to Wagner's theories – but fortunately he didn't bother about those when writing the work. Compared to the hallucinations of the suffering, feverish Tristan, who is an artificial creation and a bore, Hans Sachs is real and human, and proof that Wagner was a poet. Ironically, Sachs reaches greatness not when he is alone on the stage, during the *Fliedermonolog* or *Wahnmonolog*, but when he is talking to Eva, or to Stolzing, or in the quintet of the third act.

All composers are glad to be performed; Wagner, however, the incurable egomaniac – Thomas Mann calls him a "theatromaniac" – demanded to be performed in his own shrine, a monument to his *Musikdrama*, and – as he later saw it – a Valhalla to the German Empire that had emerged in

1870. Wagner, the former revolutionary, had come full circle. He had been in Bayreuth as an impecunious twenty-two-year-old conductor one summer evening in 1835, and exclaimed, "Ten horses couldn't pull me away from here"; he was given to extravagent statements even at that early age. Within a day or so he set out for Nuremberg, to conduct a concert, and he didn't return for thirty-five years. In 1870, when he was trying to finish the *Ring,* he revisited Bayreuth. He'd for some time wanted a theatre of his own. "I'm going to build my own house and educate my own artists," he wrote. "I don't care how long it takes".

He went to Bayreuth to see whether its baroque Margravian Opera House, which then had the largest opera stage in Germany, would answer his requirements. He immediately decided it wouldn't. The auditorium was too small and the acoustics were nothing special. Then he walked up the nearby Green Hill, a wooded slope a mile north of the town, and concluded that its summit would make a splendid setting for his theatre. "Nowhere else! Only here!" he said. The city fathers of Bayreuth, overwhelmed by his enthusiasm, made him a present of the site. On 22 March 1872, the cornerstone was laid. Wagner composed his own Imperial March for the occasion, and afterwards he conducted Beethoven's Ninth Symphony, his favourite. He was convinced he had a "mandate" from Beethoven.

The Festspielhaus was opened on 13 August 1876. On opening day there was a formal procession of notables and musicians from the centre of Bayreuth to the top of the Green Hill. Peter Ilich Tchaikovsky, who was a visitor, later wrote, "I watched the arrival of Kaiser Wilhelm from a window of a neighbouring house. Then came into view a number of brilliant uniforms, then the instrumentalists from the Wagner Theatre, with Hans Richter (the conductor) at their head, then the tall figure and the well-known features of the Abbé Liszt, and finally, in a fashionable carriage, a man with an aquiline nose and thin, derisive lips – Richard Wagner."

The first festival was an artistic success but a financial failure (the deficit was 150,000 marks), and Wagner couldn't afford to put on another until 1882, the year before his death. On July 26, *Parsifal* was first performed. Wagner had assembled a great cast; Hermann Winkelmann (Parsifal), Amalie Materna (Kundry), Emil Scaria (Gurnemanz), Theodor Reichmann (Amfortas). The honour of conducting this Christian *Bühnenweihfestspiel* was given to Hermann Levi, a Jew. *Parsifal* is really two things, depending on whether one is exposed to it in the mysterious

dimness of the Festspielhaus or analyses it in the cool light of next morning. As a spectacle, it is an emotional experience with moments of indes-
cribable beauty. It is impossible not to be moved by the Transformation
Scene, the scene of the flower maidens, the divine beauty of the Good
Friday music. But afterwards one has second thoughts. There are times
when it becomes a children's play for retarded adults. The mumbo-
jumbo around the Holy Grail is strictly late Cecil B. De Mille. "*Parsifal*",
writes Paul Henry Lang, "is sincere only in the passages where the
composer's imagination triumphed over the self-imposed religious-
metaphysical bonds, where the irrepressible creative force of the musician
overcame the calculating preoccupations of the thinker: everywhere else
Parsifal is false and mere theatralism". Wagner is a better magician than
Klingsor, the magician in *Parsifal*. Klingsor remains a parody. Wagner
hypnotizes us with beautiful music.

Perhaps he isn't the composer for logical-thinking people – and thus
will always be assured of a worldwide audience and perennial popularity,
though he will have his ups and downs. Richard Wagner raises the
philosophical, ethical question whether genius makes badness permissible
in man.

At the time of Wagner, there was little contemporary German opera.
His influence was too strong. His imitators never succeeded; and few
dared oppose him. There are some happy exceptions. Engelbert
Humperdinck wrote *Hänsel und Gretel* (1893) and *Die Königskinder*. He
was a solid craftsman of pronounced originality who knew the stage,
possessed humour, and used folk songs advantageously. Unfortunately
Hänsel und Gretel, a jewel, is often considered "a children's opera", and is
usually performed with a second-rate cast in the afternoon, whereas
Eugene d'Albert's *Tiefland*, which is unmitigated kitsch, is given at night,
with a first-rate cast. But Humperdinck is making his way: in America,
and nowadays also in Europe, *Hänsel und Gretel* is one of the most
performed works in the repertoire.

Another exception was Johann Strauss (Son), the genius of the Viennese
waltz. His finest operetta, *Die Fledermaus*, is now performed at the Vienna
State Opera and the Metropolitan. Some German houses present *Die
Fledermaus* as a "comic opera", as though ashamed to get involved in
operetta. But *Die Fledermaus* needs no excuse. It is sparkling and ingenious
from the first to the last note, with great melodies, wonderful orchestration, charm and wit; as an operetta *Fledermaus* is as perfect as *Carmen* is as
an opera Among the admirers of Johann Strauss was Richard Wagner

who once conducted a Strauss waltz on the stage of the Bayreuth Festspielhaus.

To his own nation Verdi is more than a great musician: he symbolizes Italy's national spirit and its musical soul. No other composer ever achieved this (though Sibelius is almost deified in Finland) and no one but Verdi could have survived it. "Wagner was admired but Verdi was loved", Carlo Gatti, Verdi's biographer, once said to me. Italians love Verdi's patriotism, his flair for drama, his gift of melody, his knowledge of the vocal art. During the *Risorgimento*, when the Italian patriots fought against Habsburg Austria for their independence, the letters v.e.r.d.i. chalked on house walls were a political anagram for "Viva Emanuele Re d'Italia." Today in Italy, Verdi remains a living presence; he belongs to the family.

1813 was a blessed year in the history of music. Wagner was born in Leipzig, and Giuseppe Verdi, who outlived him by 18 years, was born in Roncole, a small village in Parma. (Another blessed year was 1685 which gave us Johann Sebastian Bach and Georg Friedrich Händel.) The distinction is important: Wagner was always a bourgeois, a city man, while Verdi remained a peasant, with a peasant's shrewdness and pride. Inevitably the two great composers, against their own will, became the anti-poles of leading musical movements. They were constantly compared to each other by people who misunderstood them both. Many writers in Germany, Great Britain and America accused the young Verdi of writing "hurdy-gurdy" melodies, and later condemned him for "imitating" Wagner. After the première of *Aida*. Verdi exclaimed bitterly, *"Bella glora, dopo tanti anni di carriere finire imitatore"* (nice glory, to end up as an imitator after so many years of work). Verdi never imitated Wagner. His art was diametrically opposed to Wagner's, yet Verdi admired him. When he heard that Wagner had died in Venice, in 1883, he wrote his publisher, "Sad, very sad . . . A name has gone that will leave a powerful impress on the history of art". Rereading this letter, Verdi, an honest man, crossed out the word *"potente"* (powerful) and wrote on top *"potentissima"* (most powerful).

Verdi understood the difference between their respective geniuses. "Do you think that under this (Italian) sun I could have composed *Tristan* and the *Ring*?" he once asked. He wrote dramatic music and melody, not *Weltanschauung* and metaphysics. His music made even the most improbable librettos acceptable though not believable. No one understands what happens in *Il Trovatore*, but everyone appreciates the characters and their motivations. His heroes and villains wear costumes of the past but their emotions and conflicts are timeless, for Verdi understood and created human beings on the stage. Modest, decent, retiring, he knew the difference between himself and Wagner, and between their work. Once he said, "Opera is opera, and symphony is symphony". *Otello* is opera. *Tristan* is symphony.

Verdi had a passion for privacy. Little was known about his private life before the publication of biographies by Gatti, Toye and Abbiati. There is much lore and legend about him in Parma where he is revered as a saint. He was a quiet, reticent man with a fine sense of humour: for only a man blessed with this virtue could have written the music to *Falstaff*. When one Bertani Prospero, having disliked *Aida*, wrote asking for a refund, Verdi obliged, but demanded a written statement that Bertani would not attend any other Verdi opera. Gatti (who met Verdi in 1892) remembered him as "frail and elegant, with a wonderful bearing. He had a fine head, long white hair, and a proud nose, and there was a hidden fire in his eyes though his face was serene. His manner was never intimate. Even his close friends wouldn't put an arm around his shoulder, and we Italians are usually quite informal. He refused to write his memories. He said, 'Isn't it enough that people have to listen to my music? Why should they be forced to read my prose?' "

In his younger days he would work from morning until late night, with nothing but a cup of black coffee. *Rigoletto* was finished in forty days. Verdi was in such creative haste that he didn't bother to write out the accompaniment in the score, leaving the details for later. The handwriting of the miraculous aria "La donna è mobile" gives the impression of having been written in great haste. Verdi gave it to the tenor only two hours prior to the first performance at the Teatro Fenice in Venice: certain that it would become a popular success, he feared the whole town might whistle the melody before it was even sung. Though he was accused by some critics of "killing off the art of *bel canto*", he understood the human voice and singing. He never strained the voice beyond its natural range. He wrote each singer's part in the singer's own key – tenor key for the tenor, alto key for the mezzo-soprano, and so on.

Verdi's beginnings were unspectacular. He cautiously felt his way and worked out things by trial and error. After writing *Oberto*, a nineteenth-century *opera seria* betraying the influence of Bellini, and *Un giorno di regno*, an experiment in *opera buffa*, he became famous overnight after La Scala's première of *Nabucco*, in 1842. Ostensibly this is the story of the Jews under Babylonian domination but audiences in Italy understood the real meaning: their nationalistic movement had been glorified by Alessandro Manzoni and Silvio Pellico. Austrian censorship was unable to interfere with the passionate chorus of the Jewish prisoners, "*Va pensiero sill'ali dorate*" (Fly, thought, on golden wings), which became a sort of underground anthem. After the enormous success of *Nabucco*, La Scala gave Verdi a contract with a blank space for his fee. Giuseppina Strepponi, a well-known soprano who had sung the part of Leonora and later became Verdi's second wife, advised him to ask for the fee which Bellini had received for *Norma*.

Verdi was only slowly finding his way and of several operas after *Nabucco*, only *Macbeth* (1847) is interesting. He was fascinated by Shakespeare and Schiller, his favourite playwrights, but his two operas based on works of Schiller (*I Masnadieri*, Francesco Maria Piave's libretto of *Die Räuber*, and *Luisa Miller*, Salvatore Cammarano's version of *Kabale und Liebe*) were not successful. Neither were *I due Foscari*, *Giovanna d'Arco*, *Alzira*, *Attila*. Even Verdi's greatest admirers admit his failures and though some of his early works are sporadically revived they are never successful. By 1849, Verdi was unable to overcome these disappointments, and he retired to his country estate in Sant' Agata, not far from his native Roncole, and looked after his fields. At night he read Shakespeare and Schiller, and studied the chamber music of Haydn, Mozart, Beethoven. One can still see the books and scores in his house there.

In 1851, however, the retired landowner surprised the world with *Rigoletto*. Piave's libretto, from Victor Hugo's *Le Roi s'Amuse*, was originally called *La Maledizione*, but the Austrian censors objected. They also forced Piave and Verdi to change the character of the libertine Francis I (Hugo's play had been banned in Paris after the first night), and thus the French King became the anonymous "Duke of Mantua". This didn't harm *Rigoletto*, which has beautiful melodies, great ensembles, dramatic situations, continuous excitement and the wonderful last-act quartet, "Bella figlia dell'amore", in which Verdi brilliantly expressed the individual characters by melodic lines, and blended four psychologically different parts into a dramatic ensemble. No one since Mozart had been able to write with such a skill. *Rigoletto* was a great success. Even Victor Hugo who had hated Piave's libretto loved the opera. Only a few incorrigible critics deplored the end of the *bel canto* era that had produced *Médée* and *Lucia di Lammermoor*.

Two years after *Rigoletto*, Verdi wrote two different works that are now among the most popular of all extant operas: *Il Trovatore*, premièred on 19 January 1853, at the Teatro Apollo in Rome, and *La Traviata*, first given in Venice forty-six days later. Cammarano had used a Spanish tragedy, *El Trovador*, by Antonio García Gutiérrez and made a complete mess of it. Whether Verdi knew what was going on in this mystifying tale remains an enigma, but he set the text in a few weeks, and created a masterpiece of drama, melody and lyrical beauty. Popularity has vulgarized the great melodies, but "D'amor sull'ali rosee", "Il balen", and "Di quella pira" are stirring arias when they are well sung. Azucena, the gypsy, is one of Verdi's most memorable characters, one of the greatest mezzo parts – and, incidentally, the only character in the opera who seems to know what it is all about.

After the great success of *Il Trovatore*, *La Traviata* was a dismal failure at the Teatro Fenice in Venice. Today many people love it best of Verdi's three early successful operas. Musically, *La Traviata* is more beautiful than *Rigoletto* or *Trovatore*, intense and subtle from beginning to end, as delicate as the heroine. Violetta's great aria, "Sempre libera", is Verdi's immortal contribution to the double aria, a melancholy *cavatina* followed by an exciting, vocally very difficult *cabaletta*. Verdi uses the music the way a great dramatist uses words, in order to carry the story forward. In the last act, the tragedy is both in the drama and in the music. However, the first-night audience in Venice laughed during the saddest moments. Piave's libretto from the younger Alexandre Dumas' *La Dame aux Camélias* had been staged in street clothes which amused the people. Unfortunately, the leading lady was plump and healthy-looking, not the sort of woman who dies of consumption in the last act. After the failure, Verdi said philosophically, "Time will decide". A year later, when the opera was restaged in Venice, with costumes of the Louis XIII period and Maria Spezia, a slim soprano, *La Traviata* was a success. (Nowadays it is staged in the style of the Dumas era.) Again, the critics panned Verdi for using leitmotifs and "imitating" Wagner. But in fact Verdi uses recurrent themes and melodies, more as Beethoven did, to build up dramatic continuity.

His next two operas, *Les Vêpres Siciliennes* (1855) and *Simone Boccanegra* (1857) never became very popular (Verdi's case proving once again that a composer's most popular works are often his best, though there are exceptions). *Un Ballo in Maschera* (1859) has a bad libretto and exciting music. Antonio Somma had done an almost literal translation of Scribe's libretto for Auber's *Gustave* III but the censors forced the librettist to change the King of Sweden into a character called "Riccardo, Conte di Warwick". An interesting character is Oscar, the page, clearly a colleague of Cherubino. Verdi's next opera, *La Forza del Destino,* which also suffered from a weak libretto, is too long and confusing, with both solemn and comic elements, but it has some marvellous music, and is still often performed.

The next work, *Don Carlos* (1867), was a big step forward in the composer's evolution. There are not many set numbers and it is Verdi's first attempt to write a music drama. The orchestra speaks with its own voice and the music is often dramatic, haunting and very beautiful. In his quiet way, Verdi was as much a revolutionary as Wagner. Joseph Méry and Camille du Locle had skilfully condensed Schiller's *Don Carlos* into their libretto. Written for Paris, *Don Carlos* emerges with many grand opera traits, from the unspectacular ballet to the spectacular auto-da-fé. What saves this work is the dramatic music and its great arias, Philip's "Ella giammai m'amo", and Eboli's "O don fatale", Rodrigo's "O Carlo, ascolta", and Elizabeth's "Tu che la vanita". Generations of Verdi-lovers have sat unhappily through much of *Don Carlos*, awaiting the great arias.

Aida (1871) had been commissioned by Ismail Pasha, Khedive of Egypt, to celebrate the opening of the Suez Canal. This unlikely premise led to one of the all-time hits in the repertory. Many managers call *Aida* the most popular work of all. It is apparently the perfect mixture for this absurd art form having a tender love story, violent passions, exotic colouring, great climaxes. There are spectacular ballets; the triumphal entry of Radames is the excuse for bringing in everything from elephants to companies of soldiers. *Aida* fits the Metropolitan matinée as well as a night at Verona's Arena. It is the grandest of grand operas, but it also has moments of wonderful intimacy. It is alternatively low-, high-, and middle-brow. The "Nile" scene is one of the finest and most dramatic ever set to music. Nothing is ambiguous: the protagonists – kings, high priests, princesses – behave entirely in character. Tenors are terrified of their great aria, "Celeste Aida", sung shortly after the curtain rises, and often turning beauty into banality by shouting the B flat at the end *fortissimo*, instead of singing it *pianissimo*, as Verdi wrote in the score (which is, of course, much more difficult). There are many other problems in *Aida* – but Verdi solved them all, and created an immensely popular masterpiece.

Verdi was already immortal – but his greatest time was yet to come. During the sixteen years following *Aida* he composed a beautiful string quartet (a foretaste of the yet unborn *Otello* and *Falstaff*), and his moving *Requiem* for Alessandro Manzoni, which is really an opera in the form of a dramatic requiem. Verdi loved to conduct it, considering it a sacred duty. At the age of seventy-three, the great old man wrote his tragic masterpiece, *Otello*, and at eighty, he wrote *Falstaff*, his comic masterpiece. Though these works don't surpass the popularity of *Aida*, they are immeasurably greater and are perhaps the exception to the rule that the greatest works are always the most popular.

Both *Otello* and *Falstaff* were written by Verdi's last and finest librettist, Arrigo Boito. It was another great climax in the history of opera, the meeting of a poet and of a composer who understood each other. Monteverdi found Rinuccini, Gluck had Cazalbigi, and Mozart was blessed with da Ponte; much later, the co-operation of Hofmannsthal and Richard Strauss created some great operas. But the case of Boito and Verdi is the most interesting. Boito was already a world-famous composer; he'd worked for over fifty years on his masterpiece, *Mefistofele*. As a young music critic he had attacked and angered Verdi. Later Boito came to admire him (even music critics sometimes change their minds) and suffered from Verdi's aloofness. But when he concluded that Verdi needed a congenial librettist, he sacrificed composing and devoted the rest of his life to the collaboration with the great old man from Sant' Agata. Yet Boito reached a measure of immortality by virtue of being associated with the greatest tragedy and the greatest comedy in the history of Italian opera. In La Scala's museum there is the framed letter in which Verdi tells Boito that he has finished the score of *Otello*. Just two words – "*E finito*". Boito cried when he read the message.

Boito did the impossible by turning two of Shakespeare's plays, *Othello* and *The Merry Wives of Windsor*, into operatic libretti without ruining Shakespeare – and producing two of the best libretti ever written. Verdi loved Shakespeare and called him "the greatest authority on the heart of man". He couldn't read the English original, and thus couldn't fully appreciate Shakespeare's poetry, but this was rather an advantage because, in opera, music takes the place of poetry. Among his earlier libretti, Verdi liked *Macbeth* best; he'd drafted the whole libretto himself, before calling in Piave, and he'd taken endless trouble with detail. He was happy with Boito's *Otello* and asked for the comic opera which he'd wanted to write for forty years. When he wrote it, at last, it was the greatest Italian work of its genre.

Verdi's characters remain eternally human. Paul Henry Lang writes,

Verdi's men and women can be divested of their exterior, of the sixteenth-century ruffs, Egyptian tunics, Venetian armour, and Gypsy robes, for Rigoletto's pathetic impotence, Aida's unflinching love, Iago's diabolic cunning, Othello's senseless jealousy, and Azucena's vengefulness will always remain. These constant elements in man Verdi has given us in music, in opera, which exemplifies the essence of the lyric drama . . .

It is difficult to describe *Otello* or *Falstaff*. *Otello* has the "endless melody", that Wagner talked so much about; like *Tristan*, it is a great love story, with the orchestra providing dramatic continuity and psychological insight. Verdi knew more about the human voice than Wagner who ruined many good singers (and still ruins them) with his atrocious demands. In his treatment of Iago, Verdi showed "the shrewd exploit of the psychological quality of the baritone voice" (Brockway and Weinstock).

After the enormous success of *Otello* in 1887, with Francesco Tamagno and Victor Maurel, Verdi spoke of retiring but Boito, his publisher Tito Ricordi, and, most of all, his wife Giuseppina, urged him to go on with *Falstaff*. He was attracted by Boito's libretto, which was even better than *Otello*, because it is much harder to write a comic opera than a serious one. Verdi pretended that this was an intimate enterprise, and that he worked on *Falstaff* "to amuse himself", and might produce it once in Sant'Agata. He had always been very tough with his librettists, but this time he didn't ask Boito for a single change. He worked only two hours a day – he was almost eighty – and needed two years for *Falstaff*.

Verdi had wisdom and was immensely practical. He had trouble with Victor Maurel, the first Iago, who had begun to suffer from megalomania. Maurel wanted "exclusive rights" to the part of Falstaff. Verdi was irritated, but he considered Maurel the best Falstaff, and made him sing it, with no exclusive rights. Prior to the première he wrote him two letters which Maurel later published in *La Revue de Paris*:

I admire your research on *Falstaff*. But be careful . . . When art becomes science, something baroque results that is neither art nor science. To do well, yes! To do too well, no! Don't try too hard to adjust your voice. With your great talent as a singing actor, with your accent and pronunciation, the role of Falstaff, once learned, will emerge already created, without your searching your brain and without your studying to obtain different vocal effects – studies which might even be injurious to you. Study little. Au revoir, a bientôt.

Verdi

But the problem worried Verdi, and he later wrote,

You already have the *Falstaff* libretto. As soon as it is printed, you will have the score. Study, examine as much as you like the verses and the words of the libretto but don't bother *too* much with the music. Don't think it strange that I tell you that. If the music is sufficiently characteristic, if the character of the person is well understood, if the emphasis of the dialogue is correct, the music flows by itself and resolves itself.

Verdi

The première of *Falstaff*, the event of the year, took place on 9 February 1893. Puccini, Mascagni and many other musical celebrities were in the audience. At Verdi's request, Edoardo Mascheroni conducted. The critics were in a state of rapture. No longer was Verdi accused of "imitating" Wagner or "ruining" *bel canto*. They recognized *Falstaff* as an almost perfect work of art, beauty and truth. *Falstaff* will never attain the popular success of *La Traviata* or *Aida*; it remains caviar for the connoisseurs. However, latter-day productions – from Toscanini, Karajan and Bernstein, among others – show that even a caviar opera has a chance of being accepted by a large and grateful public.

The late Carlo Gatti once told me, "Verdi was loved wherever he went. On the street, men would take off their hats, when he walked by. When he was sick, the police had straw mats placed in Via Manzoni, underneath his room at the Grand Hotel Milan, to mute the sound of the horses' hoofs. His funeral took place on a dark, damp day. Verdi had left instructions that there must be neither music nor singing. Half the people of Milan were there. No one was permitted to approach the grave, and we all stood at a distance, silently crying. Verdi couldn't decree that there should be no weeping. Then, suddenly, there rose from among the crowd a chorale – soft at first, then louder and louder as it swept through the throng, the heart-stirring 'Va, pensiero' from *Nabucco*. A month later, the coffin was carried from the city cemetery to be buried at the crypt of the Casa Verdi in Piazza Buonarroti, while Toscanini conducted nine hundred voices in the 'Va, pensiero'. The people of Italy had done as Verdi wished, but now they did what they felt they had to do."

PELLÉAS ET MÉLISANDE

Claude Achille Debussy, born in 1862 in Saint-Germain-en-Laye, began his musical career under the influence of Massenet's lyricism and Wagner's "endless melody", but found his artistic identity in his early twenties, when he began to invent a new harmonic system which later led to "impressionism" in music. He studied the sixteenth-century music of Orlando di Lasso and Palestrina; he was not interested in Italian opera. He went to Bayreuth in 1888 and the following year, and was particularly impressed by *Parsifal*, "one of the most beautiful monuments ever raised to the imperturbable glory of music". Later, he changed his mind about Wagner (as so many others before and after him). While attending four consecutive days of *Der Ring des Nibelungen* in London, he visited the Empire Music Hall, to enjoy vaudeville, "a reward for good behaviour". Unfortunately, there is no musical hall in Bayreuth today.

Many Frenchmen since Wagner have suffered from a Wagnerian trauma and *Tristan und Isolde* was not performed in French until 1914. The French oscillated between adoration and hatred. Their leading composers went to Bayreuth and admired the orchestration of *Tristan* and *Parsifal*. In 1889, Guillaume Lekeu, a pupil of César Franck, was carried out of the Festspielhaus unconscious. Emanuel Chabrier often broke into tears during Wagner performances, and remained all his life under Wagner's influence. So did Edouard Lalo and Vincent d'Indy. Paul Dukas, in *Ariane et Barbe-Bleue*, made skilful use of Wagner's technique of leitmotif but like Debussy he later broke away from Wagner's devastating influence. The wisest comment was made by Camille Saint-Saëns who said, "*La Wagneromanie est un ridicule excusable. La Wagnerophobie est une maladie*".

After his Wagnerian period Debussy became impressed by the drama and the music of the Far East, during the Paris Exhibition of 1889. He read Verlaine and Mallarmé, attended Mallarmé's Tuesday "at-home" gatherings, was a popular figure in the artistic circles and the night life of Montmartre. Fastidious and elegant, with his dark beard, his soft, melodious voice, and a slight touch of melancholy, he was very much a fin-de-siècle character. He was predictably unpredictable. When young Marcel Proust wanted to give a party for him, Debussy begged off. "It would be best if we went on meeting casually". He liked the company of the symbolist poets and impressionist painters, but at that time had no artistic doctrine himself. His favourite hangout was Reynold's Irish and American Bar, in the Rue Royale, where Debussy and Toulouse-Lautrec felt at home among the English jockeys and trainers in their garish tweed-jackets. Debussy called them *les gens à carreaux* (checks). He sat at the long bar with the polished mahogany rail, which Toulouse-Lautrec, known as Monsieur le Vicomte Marquis, called "the colour of Rembrandt". The circus drawings of Lautrec, and later the clown studies of Picasso and Rouault can be traced in Debussy's music to the circus and the music-hall.

Debussy, Frenchman through and through (he called himself *musicien français*), became convinced that French music must emancipate itself from the influence of Beethoven (Beethoven the romantic, not the classicist), Schumann and Wagner, and go back to the eighteenth-century French classics, Couperin and Rameau. Somehow he overcame the influence of post-romanticism, and created his own new, "modern" music. "Debussy's influence since the dawn of the present century has been no less decisive than that exercised in the past by Monteverdi and Wagner", writes Marc Pincherle. Both Stravinsky and Schönberg, the totally different masters of modern music, have come under Debussy's influence. Edward Lockspeiser, Debussy's biographer, rightly explains Debussy not as a reflection of his period but as *the* period. "Music was at that time regarded as a quintessential, privileged art, and I see no other composer who so closely realized the musical ideals to which the writers and painters of his time openly aspired".

Debussy never liked the term "impressionism" in connection with the new music that he'd invented. But he couldn't help his shifting harmonies being compared to the beautiful sounds of the language used by the symbolist poets, and to the colours and lights of the Impressionist painters (Rimbaud even associated colours with vowels – A was black, E was white, I was red, O was blue, U was green). Debussy's music is atmospheric. His only opera, *Pelléas et Mélisande*, is a unique work of art, a perfect masterpiece in its own way, resembling no other work in the lyric theatre; for here was a composer able to express the subtlest moods of the soul. Its influence on later composers has been very strong. Debussy worked ten years on the play by Maurice Maeterlinck, "an opera libretto in search of a composer" (Lockspeiser). The plot is deceptively simple. Mélisande, a young princess, is found by Golaud in the forest near his castle; Golaud marries her. His younger brother, Pelléas, falls in love with Mélisande. Does she love Pelléas? One is never quite sure. Motivations are vague, feelings remain unspoken. Golaud kills Pelléas and Mélisande dies of sorrow, but her death does not explain the enigma.

Everything in *Pelléas et Mélisande* depends on mood and impression rather than action and statement. It is a drama of fleeting sounds, delicate harmonies, subtle nuances. The lovers seem drawn to each other by inner compulsion rather than erotic passion. They never reach the paroxysm of the lovers in *Tristan und Isolde* – but then they are human, never heroic. There are no arias. The voices go on and on in a sort of speech-song, almost like spoken language. The orchestra follows the text, weaving motifs about the voices in such a delicate, tender way that one rarely becomes aware of it. The leitmotifs are not used in the musical structure, as in Wagner's operas, but to delineate character and enhance impression and mood. Debussy's work has a great if somewhat unreal beauty. Loud dissonances are used only once, when Pelléas is murdered. The opera needs patience, understanding and complete immersion from the listener; one must hear it again and again to feel the transparent beauty of Debussy's music. *Pelléas et Mélisande* will never be "popular", as *Carmen* is: the libretto lacks action, the characters are indecisive, the drama is only in the emotions. But in a true, deep sense the characters are real and human, and listeners trying to understand Debussy will be rewarded by a new, beautiful kind of music.

The première at the Opéra-Comique in 1893 (a vintage opera year that also gave us *Falstaff*) was enlivened by a wonderful Parisian scandal. Two weeks earlier Maeterlinck had announced in *Le Figaro* that Debussy's *Pelléas et Mélisande* "is a work which is now strange and hostile to me . . . I wish for its immediate and emphatic failure". Maeterlinck also challenged Debussy to a duel and threatened to beat him up with his walking stick. Maeterlinck was enraged because his lady friend, Georgette Leblanc, the French *diva*, had been promised the part of Mélisande, and then Debussy decided to give it to Mary Garden, a young Scottish soprano. Debussy said, "When it comes to music, Maeterlinck is like a blind man in a museum". Two years after Debussy's death, Maeterlinck heard the opera for the first time. Afterwards he wrote to Mary Garden, "I had sworn to myself never to see the lyric drama *Pelléas et Mélisande*. Yesterday I violated my vow, and now I am a happy man. For the first time I have completely understood my own play, because of you." He should have added, "and mainly because of Debussy". Later, Maeterlinck told Henry Russell, the impresario, "I was completely wrong in this matter and he (Debussy) was a thousand times right". He realized that Debussy's music gave his play a depth of soul that mere words can never reach.

Pelléas et Mélisande is performed everywhere, and remains an outstanding *succès d'estime*, the perfect synthesis of poetry and music, of sights and sounds, the most beautiful expression of the French total theatre. Romain Rolland, one of the few music critics in Paris who understood

Debussy, called *Pelléas et Mélisande* "one of the three or four outstanding achievements in French musical history".

RICHARD STRAUSS

Richard Strauss was born in Munich, in 1864, two years after Debussy. They met once, in Paris, and Strauss talked mostly about money, his favourite subject, which distressed Debussy, the aristocrat, who cared little about business and royalties. It is possible that Strauss, a shrewd musician, sensed that Debussy, hardly known at that time outside his small circle, might one day outrank him as one of the early masters of what is now known as modern music. When Strauss heard a performance of *Pelléas et Mélisande* at the Opéra-Comique in 1907, in the company of Romain Rolland, he complained of the "monotony" and commented on the "Wagnerian elements". Rolland later wrote, "Strauss didn't let a single Wagnerian imitation pass without remarking on it, and not in praise. 'But that's the whole of *Parsifal*', he said of one passage." The following year, there was the première of Strauss's *Elektra,* with the orchestra playing in a post-Wagnerian manner, in the style of "endless melody", with recurrent leitmotifs. All his life, Richard Strauss tried to get away from Wagner's influence, attempting to approach his "god", Mozart, but he didn't succeed. "I cannot write about Mozart, I can only adore him", he once said. He liked to think of his *Rosenkavalier,* "a comedy with music", in connection with Mozart's *Figaro,* and of *Die Frau ohne Schatten* as his *Zauberflöte,* but few people share this extravagant assessment.

Richard Strauss is a very popular opera composer, and also a controversial one. He was an accomplished musician at the age of fifteen. His father, the first horn player of the Munich Opera, was said to be one of the few men whom Richard Wagner feared. His mother, a member of the wealthy Munich brewing dynasty of Pschorr, assured the family of money and comfort. Strauss was always fond of beer, and of *Skat,* a German card game. After conducting a stunning *Tristan* performance that left the audience limp with emotion, Strauss would relax drinking beer and playing *Skat.* A robust Bavarian, he is the only *fin-de-siècle* composer who remained totally unaffected by the morbid melancholy of his period. Some critics now dismiss him as a "virtuoso composer". Strauss never apologized for his virtuosity, but wisely enjoyed it.

He began his musical career in Meiningen, as an assistant conductor of Hans von Bülow, Wagner's friend. His early works show the influence of Berlioz, Liszt and of course Wagner; it seems only natural since a young man from Munich could hardly avoid the overpowering influence of the *Meister* in nearby Bayreuth.

Strauss wrote his masterpieces in his younger years and outlived his greatness: this is his tragedy. In the 1890s, after the success of his tone poems *Till Eulenspiegel's Merry Pranks* and *Don Quixote*, Strauss was the most talked-about composer in the world. The première in Dresden of his opera *Salome* (1905), was a terrific success, and also a shock, especially for Americans. Brockway and Weinstock wrote, "Strauss' *Salome* is more decadent than Oscar Wilde's play because it takes itself more seriously". This clinical study of sensual perversion and sexual aberration ends in an astonishing climax with Salome's *Schlussgesang* before she kisses the severed head of John the Baptist, and is brutally killed by Herod's soldiers. There was also the notorious Dance of the Seven Veils, the first striptease on the opera stage. At the première in Dresden, Marie Wittich who sang the part of Salome refused to strip ("I won't do it, I am a decent woman") and let a ballerina perform the dance, though later on she distressed Strauss by doing the dance herself. Strauss explained how the parts in *Salome* should be done, writing, "The acting must be restrained, as simple as possible, in contrast to the wild, excited music". Unfortunately, his advice is not always followed. Strauss's old father said after *Salome*, "It sounds like nothing but ants crawling up and down your trousers". Cosima Wagner, feeling at the moment like a decent woman (perhaps trying to forget how she'd run away from her husband, Hans von Bülow, and had a child by Wagner), called it "pure insanity". In Berlin, Kaiser Wilhelm permitted the performance only after Intendant Hülsen had the idea of showing the Star of Bethlehem in the sky, perhaps to announce the Coming of the Three Kings. His Majesty said, ". . . this thing will do Strauss no end of harm". In his *Reminiscences* Strauss says, "From this harm I was able to build my villa in Garmisch". It was the sort of remark that the German critics didn't forgive. They would take it for granted that a famous *diva* owns a castle, or that a great conductor now flies his own jet, but a "serious" composer shouldn't be thinking of money.

In Vienna, Gustav Mahler was refused permission to stage *Salome* at the august Court Opera. The opera was given at the plebeian Volksoper and introduced a beautiful, gifted soprano from Moravia, Maria Jeritza. At the Metropolitan Opera, *Salome* had to be withdrawn by Heinrich Conried, the general manager, after the first performance, "at the insistence of a certain Mr Morgan", according to Strauss. The New York newspapers had joined J.P. Morgan in their demand that *Salome* be suppressed. The first London performance under Sir Thomas Beecham was badly mutilated by the censors. "No head of the dead prophet was allowed for the final scene, only a dish of blood – which all agreed looked like pink blancmange", writes Harold Rosenthal. Another London scandal was caused in 1949 by Salvador Dali's macabre settings. The scandals that surround *Salome* would fill a nice, gossipy volume.

Three years after *Salome*, Strauss topped the furore with his *Elektra*, a dramatic poem in which the orchestra dominates. Hugo von Hofmannsthal had written the libretto after the great tragedy of Sophocles, Elektra and Orest avenging their father's murder by killing their own mother and her lover. Though never as popular as *Rosenkavalier*, *Elektra* is the most powerful expression of Strauss's genius. Strauss did not follow the motto of his adored Mozart who wrote that "passions, whether violent or not, must never be expressed in such a way as to excite disgust". The passions in *Elektra* are brutal, ugly, shocking. But they are interrupted by some of the most tender lyrical moments in modern opera. The scene between Elektra and Orest is deeply moving. And there are grandiose moments of terror too; Strauss's version successfully matches the Greek tragedy of Sophocles which is no mean achievement. Few people understood the music in 1909. The critics called Strauss "degenerate" and "insane". Ernestine Schumann-Heink relinquished the role of Klytämnestra after the première, when Strauss allegedly asked Ernst von Schuch, the conductor, to make the orchestra play louder ("I can still hear the voice of Frau Heink"). Strauss employed an orchestra of one hundred and five men in *Elektra*, but he always demanded that the orchestral symphony must not overpower the singer. For an hour the stage is dominated by three demented women. Only a master conductor (Strauss himself, or his pupil Karl Böhm) can interpret the score so that the voices can be understood clearly. *Elektra* is a shocker, but it still emerges as a masterpiece – powerful and very timely in this neurotic era.

Elektra was the first co-operation between Hugo von Hofmannsthal, the sensitive Austrian poet, and the tough-minded Bavarian composer, two totally different artists. Hofmannsthal was concerned with aesthetics, and the meaning of art. Strauss understood the stage; he asked, "Will the audience get the idea?", and actively collaborated long-distance on the libretto. His suggestions, expressed in his letters, show how much he knew about the theatre.

Some operas have become successful in spite of their libretti (*Il Trovatore*,

Madame Butterfly) but they are the exception. Nearly all successful opera composers have worked hard with their librettists. Wagner said, "While listening to a good, rational opera, people should, so-to-speak, not think of the music at all, but only feel it unconsciously while their fullest sympathy should be occupied by the action represented". Gluck knew this; and so did Mozart, Strauss and Puccini, and, above all, Verdi. Charles Burney wrote about Gluck,

> He studies a poem a long time before he thinks of setting it. He considers well the relation which each part bears to the whole; the general cast of each character; and he aspires more at satisfying the mind than flattering the ear ... It seldom happens that a single air of his operas can be taken out of its niche and sung singly with much effect; the whole is a chain of which a detached single link is but of small importance.

One would think that modern producers and performers would have learned the importance of the organic unity of drama and music, of "the relation which each part bears to the whole", but many haven't. There are producers of opera (usually they come from another medium) who don't bother to study the drama and the score, and instead try to *épater* their audiences by gimmicks. There are singers who don't care what happens in an opera as long as they can show their vocal supremacy. "A Scarpia who never bothered to find out what happens after his demise, or a Wotan who does not know *Götterdämmerung* (in which he doesn't appear) is hardly going to be an ideal representative of his role", writes Rudolf Bing.

Ideally, the librettist must have a strong sense of drama. More than the poet, he must be able to compress action and feelings so that they will fit the cadence of the music, which is different from that of the spoken language. (Thus the ideal librettist was Boito because he was a first-rate dramatist and also a good composer). Calzabigi, Metastasio and da Ponte were masters of dramatic compression; so were Meyerbeer's Scribe and Verdi's Piave. Wagner, a great dramatist, was reluctant to condense his alliterated wisdom, and there are some very boring half-hours in the *Ring* (Wotan's interminable tale in the second act of *Walküre*, the often un-intelligible question-and-answer game between Mime and the Wanderer in the first act of *Siegfried*) and in *Parsifal*, where Gurnemanz talks much too much and says far too little. The librettist must aim at straight diction. Elaborate metaphors, abstract phrases, complex and obscure sentiments are dangerous in opera where the words are often swallowed up by the music. (All this is demonstrated in the Hofmannsthal-Strauss *Frau ohne Schatten* which never became a real success, owing to the libretto.)

Music should explain straight emotions, not metaphysic metaphors. The librettist must also have a sense of the language, using words that can be easily sung, avoiding others that cannot. He should be direct, unafraid to make such simple, strong statements as "I love you", or *"C'est moi qui l'ai tué! Ah! Carmen! ma Carmen adorée!"* Which means that he should be a good poet, but not necessarily a great one. He must have humility; he should listen to the wishes and suggestions of the composer. Great poets don't need someone else's music; they create their own.

The correspondence between Strauss and Hofmannsthal gives a fascinating insight into the working of a realistic composer, and a poet given to mysticism and always bothered by aesthetic problems. Yet Hofmannsthal who had a high regard for his own poetry was always ready to change words and alter phrases, to rewrite sentences and scenes, to stimulate the composer's imagination. He knew that Strauss was the better dramatist. In 1907, Strauss asked Hofmannsthal to end the first act of *Semiramis* (a project that was never finished) with a solo scene "because monologues always end an act effectively". Strauss later proved it in *Rosenkavalier*, *Arabella*, *Daphne*, *Capriccio*. But Hofmannsthal was firm about subject matter, sets, costumes and technical detail, where he considered himself superior to Strauss.

Their most successful collaboration was *Der Rosenkavalier*, which was often panned by the critics and always loved by the public (Cecil Gray called the opera "a worn out, dissipated *demi-mondaine,* with powdered face, rouged lips, false hair and a hideous leer"). Puritanical critics objected to seeing the Marschallin "in bed", at the beginning of the opera, after the orchestral prelude gives a pretty good idea of what has been going on there, before the curtain rises. Some people fail to understand that Hofmannsthal wrote a comedy of manners in Maria Theresa's Vienna, slightly risqué, but always in perfect taste. (What would Hofmannsthal say to the things which we are exposed to nowadays on the stage?) He created the wonderful character of the Marschallin who loses her young lover to a silly girl and learns the meaning of resignation. The Marschallin is one of the most feminine, charming, real women in the whole literature, and one of the most sought-after parts in opera. It is also one of the most demanding; it proves whether a singer performs only with her voice or also with her heart as well. Unless a soprano is able to identify herself completely with the part, she shouldn't attempt it. A good test is to see whether the eyes of the women in the audience remain completely dry after the first act. If no one shows the trace of tears, the Marschallin was a failure. The trio in the third act, "Hab'mir's gelobt", ranks with the ensembles of Mozart, Verdi and the quintet in *Meistersinger*. In fact, the libretto of *Rosenkavalier* is so good that it has been successfully performed without music; but after listening to the opera, one realizes that Strauss added another dimension. The monologue of the Marschallin is good poetry, but the orchestra unveils some of her secret feelings.

Hofmannsthal and Strauss never re-created the magic of *Rosenkavalier*. *Arabella*, a sort of poor man's *Rosenkavalier*, has charm and some beautiful music, but there are too many half-hours when inspiration is replaced by facility, and facility by banality. *Ariadne auf Naxos* has some of Strauss's finest music, but even he and Hofmannsthal failed to blend elements of Gluck's *opera seria* with the *commedia dell'arte* around Molière's *Le bourgeois gentilhomme*. It is a virtuoso intellectual *tour de force*, caviar for the connoisseur. Strauss achieves sublime beauty with a chamber orchestra of thirty-seven players.

The most ambitious project of Hofmannsthal and Strauss, *Die Frau ohne Schatten*, has a mystical, ambiguous libretto, burdened with enigmatic symbols, and some wonderful music. This is the story of a woman who cannot bear children and wants another woman's "shadow" (symbol of fertility). Even the sweep of the Straussian climaxes cannot conceal the lack of real drama. The qualities of the score are mixed: Strauss writes beautifully about people's feelings (the music he gave Barak, the simple, suffering man) but sometimes he slips into pretentious virtuosity.

After the death of Hofmannsthal in 1929, Strauss created *Die schweigsame Frau*, with Stefan Zweig, a brilliant comedy based on Ben Jonson's *Epicoene or The Silent Woman*, bound to become a popular success one day. The première in Dresden in 1935 was conducted by Karl Böhm, the great Maria Cebotari singing the title role. The name of Stefan Zweig, a Jew, disappeared soon from the programme and the following year Strauss resigned as head of the Nazi Reichsmusikkammer.

Strauss wrote three operas with Joseph Gregor, a pedestrian librettist. He also wrote both the libretto and the music of *Intermezzo*, a charming, autobiographical comedy, in which he pokes fun at himself. During the rehearsals in Vienna, Strauss was pleased with Alfred Jerger, who performed the part of Hofkapellmeister Storch (Strauss), and who, during a scene with the wife, asserted strongly that he was the head of the house. "Excellent!" Strauss said. Then his wife, the former Pauline de Ahna, a singer, told Jerger that his performance was idiotic, "Don't dare to play it that way!" He didn't.

At the age of seventy-seven, Strauss wrote with the help of Clemens Krauss, the great conductor, a "conversation piece with music", *Capriccio*, around the problem that has plagued opera for four hundred years: which is more important, the words or the music? Strauss was too shrewd to give an unequivocal answer; an undramatic work with beautiful music, it should be given in the more intimate frame of a smaller house.

Strauss heard his penultimate opera, *Die Liebe der Danae*, only during the dress rehearsal at the Salzburg Festival, on 14 August 1944. Afterwards he thanked the performers with tears in his eyes, "Auf Wiedersehn in a better world". The Festival lasted only two days. Writing Strauss's obituary in 1949, Ernest Newman wrote, "Strauss left music a different thing in many ways from what he found it. He enlarged enormously the scope of psychological and characteristic expression ... his Baron Ochs, Octavian, Marschallin, Salome, Elektra, Orest and Klytämnestra are as alive as any characters in music ... Yes, he was of the royal line, even if some queer kink of indolence and cynicism in him made him often content to play the part of the Old Pretender."

PUCCINI

Bloodless esoterics take a dim view of Giacomo Puccini, of his "effects" and "tricks". But the fact is that Puccini remains (with Mozart, Wagner, Verdi, Strauss) one of the most successful opera composers anywhere. *La Bohème* and *Madame Butterfly* are all-time box office hits, with *Carmen*, *Aida*, *La Traviata*. Italian opera is the only one that is not ruined by travel and translation. Translations of Wagner and Strauss remain problematical. With Verdi and Puccini the melodic line is so strong that they cannot be spoiled. Antonio Ghislanzoni, who wrote the libretto of *Aida*, once said in humorous verse, "Our music reigned supreme in the universe as long as it was Italian music. The moment it became cosmopolitan music, it never got out of Italy."

In his early days, Puccini was accused by Italy's avant-garde critics of "internationalism", because he sounded more French (Massenet) than Italian, and wrote "exotic" music. But Puccini remains completely Italian even when he takes his listeners to Japan (*Madame Butterfly*), the American West (*La Fanciulla del West*), or China (*Turandot*). Italian opera flowed in his bloodstream; he instinctively understood the secret of writing for the lyric theatre, and for singers. They love him for his melodious, effective arias. Once he said, "God touched me with His little finger and said, 'Write for the theatre, only for the theatre'." Even more revealing is another Puccini remark, "I have more heart than mind". Millions of opera-goers love Puccini because they feel his heart-beat in his music, at a time when it has become very unfashionable to write with one's heart. He also became a master of dramatic, brutal effects which he learned from the *verismo* school in Italy.

Verismo, the realistic way of treating violence, began in the 1890s, but can be traced to Amilcare Ponchielli's most famous opera, *La Gioconda*, after a libretto by Arrigo Boito (using the pen name, an anagram, Tobio Gorria), performed at La Scala in 1876. It is a violent melodrama with effective bravura climaxes, in which Maria Callas made her international début in the title role at the Arena of Verona in 1947. The immediate birth of *verismo* was a prize contest for one-act operas sponsored by Edoardo Sonzogno, the Milan music publisher. Both Pietro Mascagni's *Cavalleria Rusticana*, which won the prize in 1890, and Ruggiero Leoncavallo's two-act opera *Pagliacci*, also commissioned by Sonzogno, are now considered the pillars of *verismo*. Toscanini conducted the première of *Pagliacci* at the Teatro dal Verme in Milan, in 1892. Both works are now given on the same evening. Both have a realistic libretto, passion and murder; both have fine tunes and great arias. Caruso was the most famous Canio of all, always breaking the audience's heart (and a little, his own) when he sang "Vesti la giubba". Both Mascagni and Leoncavallo are remembered as one-opera composers, though both have written other works.

Verismo started out as an Italian reaction against Wagner. (It would be interesting to ascertain whether Wagner did more for the musicians he influenced or those who reacted against him.) *Verismo* paid a compliment to Wagner by accepting some of his idiosyncrasies – the use of motives, his musical characterization – but Italianized and assimilated his technique. There is no symphonic development in the orchestration, the melo-drama is expressed through arias and duets, and the dénouement is always violent – murder and death. (Yet even the strongest *verismo* ending wasn't as shocking as those of Strauss's *Salome* and *Elektra*.)

Puccini soon overcame the influence of *verismo*, of Bizet's dramatic power and Massenet's lyricism. He had his first success in 1884, when he was twenty-six. His one-act opera, *Le Villi*, failed to win a prize at the Sonzogno contest, but his friends Boito and Ponchielli helped to produce the work at Milan's Teatro dal Verme. It was a success – the only success he had for almost ten years. His next work, *Edgar,* was a dismal failure but the house of Ricordi (Milan's greatest music-publishing firm) continued to support him. It was *Manon Lescaut,* in 1893, that made him famous. Overnight he replaced Mascagni and Leoncavallo in Italy as the best-liked contemporary composer. In London, only G. B. Shaw predicted that Puccini would eventually become the successor to Verdi.

Manon Lescaut had much of the mature Puccini – strong drama, interesting harmonies, beautiful melodies. (It remains somewhat inferior to Massenet's treatment of the same story.) Then came *La Bohème*, his fourth opera. Toscanini conducted the première at the Teatro Regio in Turin. The story of *La Bohème* has a stormy history. His friend Leoncavallo had sent Puccini a libretto, based on Henri Mürger's *Scènes de la Vie de Bohème*, which Puccini turned down. This didn't prevent him from announcing later that his own librettists, Giuseppe Giacosa and Luigi Illica, had written their version based on Mürger's book. In the meantime, Leoncavallo had started work on his own libretto. His opera was performed a year after Puccini's and was no success. That was the end of another beautiful friendship.

La Bohème is the first opera in which Puccini completely identified himself with his characters, and became infatuated by them. He fell in love with Mimi; later, he fell in love with the heroine of *Madame Butterfly*. In *La Bohème* he created his very personal lyrical style, characterized by dramatic concentration, exciting musical colours and melodious invention. Puccini's harmony and orchestration were much admired by Ravel and Schönberg. When his operas are well interpreted, they reveal tender beauty and subtle detail. Little has been written for the opera stage since 1896 that is as beautiful as the love duet in the first act of *La Bohème* and the magnificent quartet, or rather double-duet, in the third act, when the two couples break up, one in sorrow and one in anger.

In his photographs Puccini seems the archetype of the *fin-de-siècle bon vivant*, the dapper *boulevardier* wearing his hat at a rakish angle, always looking at pretty women, driving fast cars and motorboats. But there was another Puccini few people knew: lonely, insecure, self-critical, often miserably unhappy. He came from four generations of gifted Italian musicians. His great-great-grandfather had been organist and choirmaster at San Martino in Lucca, where Puccini was born in 1858. As a boy, he once walked all the way to Pisa, ten miles away, to hear *Aida*. He never forgot it, and was so excited by Verdi's music that he decided to become a composer. He studied at the Conservatory in Milan, where he attracted the attention of Giulio Ricordi, Verdi's publisher, who commissioned Puccini to write an opera. While Puccini worked on *Edgar*, his private life was extremely complicated. He was living with Elvira Gemignani, the wife of a school friend in Lucca. He was always involved with women. After the success of *La Bohème*, he had fame and wealth.

His instinct for the stage always made him select a libretto that was right for him. When he wasn't satisfied, he would drive his librettists until he had what he wanted. The history of his next opera, *Tosca*, is not a nice one. Puccini had seen Sarah Bernhardt in Victorien Sardou's *La Tosca*, and didn't like the play. Later, Puccini was told that Verdi had said he would compose *Tosca* if he weren't so old. (Fortunately, Verdi became more interested in Shakespeare and Boito than in Sardou.) Puccini began to think about Sardou's play. He had been able to follow the story, though he didn't understand French, which indicated that here were the seeds of an effective libretto. He asked Illica to write it, but he had already started work on a libretto for Alberto Franchetti, a composer now forgotten. In no time, Messrs Illica and Ricordi persuaded Franchetti to release the libretto to Puccini, "the only man able to write the music for such a vile and vicious story". Then Illica and Giacosa wrote the libretto, assisted by Puccini, Ricordi and Sardou, who supplied useless suggestions.

The premiere of *Tosca*, in January, 1900, at Rome's Costanzi Theatre was almost as dramatic as the plot. It was rumoured that Puccini's enemies were after him. Some latecomers created a disturbance, and the curtain was dropped. Later, the opera proceeded. The critics didn't like the torture scene, among other things, and the newspapers accused Illica and Ricordi of dishonest dealings with Franchetti. But *Tosca* became a success despite its story which includes, chronologically, torture, attempted rape, suicide, murder, execution, and more suicide. It is strictly a black-and-white story. The corrupt police chief of Rome, Scarpia, is a sardonic villain, Cavaradossi a hero. But *Tosca* has a few great arias, Tosca's "Vissi d'arte", and Cavaradossi's "E lucevan le stelle". Puccini had learned to create character and atmosphere with a few bold chords. Even in moments of passion he never made impossible demands on his singers, as did Wagner and Strauss. As an Italian he instinctively loved the human voice and knew its limitations.

During a visit to London, Puccini saw a performance of a play, *Madame Butterfly*, by the American writer David Belasco. He understood little English but was moved by the love story of a sweet Japanese girl, rushed backstage and asked Belasco to let him use the play for his next opera.

Belasco later explained that he'd said yes, without going into any business detail: "It is not possible to discuss business arrangements with an impulsive Italian who has tears in his eyes and both arms around your neck".

Madame Butterfly became Puccini's most beloved child, the only one of his operas he could bear to hear from beginning to end in later years, because it had caused him more heartbreak than any other of his works. Giacosa and Illica had written the libretto. At the première at La Scala in 1904 people hissed and booed, and the papers wrote about "the fiasco at La Scala". The critics said that Puccini's Japan was unbelievable and his heroine a cardboard figure. Opera audiences have disagreed since 1904. The great love duet in the first act, and Cio-Cio-San's aria, "Un bel dì, vedremo", have an almost hypnotic effect. After the Scala failure, Puccini withdrew the opera, divided the too-long second act into two parts, and made other revisions. Three months later, the new version was a phenomenal success in Brescia, and soon all over the world.

The Metropolitan Opera, at this time engaged in a fierce war with Oscar Hammerstein's Manhattan Opera House, seized the chance to score off their enemy and invited Puccini, who was visiting New York, to "supervise" new productions of *Manon Lescaut* and *Madame Butterfly*, for a fee of $8,000. Puccini bought a new motorboat – and saw a new Belasco play, *The Girl of the Golden West*. Inspired, he wrote *La Fanciulla del West*, after a libretto by Guelfo Civinini and Carlo Zangarini, and at its gala première at the Metropolitan in 1910, Caruso, Emmy Destinn and Antonio Scotti sang and Toscanini conducted. It had no success and was dropped. The libretto was as ridiculous as the characters, and Puccini's inspiration seemed to have gone. Yet he made an astonishing comeback with *Il Trittico* (trilogy), three very different one-act operas: *Il Tabarro, Suor Angelica* and *Gianni Schicchi*. The world première at the Metropolitan in 1918 was a failure, but the following year the first Italian performance in Rome of *Il Trittico*, under Toscanini, was a triumph. *Il Tabarro* is a powerful thriller; *Suor Angelica* is impressionistic and melodious, and remained the composer's favourite. But the finest of the three short works is *Gianni Schicchi*, a humorous masterpiece with a brilliant score that has been called "the spiritual child of Falstaff", but remains completely Puccini.

And then Puccini started work on his greatest, most interesting opera, and musically his finest score. *Turandot* is a modern grand opera with endless melody, sweeping choruses, colourful orchestration, great climaxes, and beautiful arias. Writing from his heart, Puccini gave the two most melodious arias not to the heroine, but to Liù, the little Chinese girl who dies because she loves. Puccini's version of the old Chinese fairytale by Carlo Gozzi is a triumph of the composer's genius, accepted even by highbrows who take a dim view of *La Bohème et al*. While Puccini worked on the last act, he suffered from a throat complaint that turned out to be cancer. He worked feverishly, and took the score with him to the hospital in Brussels, where he died. His friend Franco Alfano finished the third act, using Puccini's notes. But the abyss between genius and talent is quite audible, and there is a sudden let-down where Puccini's orchestration ends. Toscanini knew it when he conducted the première at La Scala in 1926. He stopped the orchestra, turned towards the audience with tears in his eyes, and said, "Here ... Maestro Puccini lay down his pen". Then he continued Puccini's swan song, making the composer's place secure in the history of opera.

Next to Puccini, the other post-Verdian composers in Italy are not important. Francesco Cilea's *Adriana Lecouvreur* (1902) is still performed in Italy and elsewhere, and has great parts which singers love. Umberto Giordano's *Andrea Chénier* (1898) seems to be getting younger and more exciting as time goes on. The story of a poet during the French Revolution, skilfully written by Illica, is an effective mixture of love and horror, passion and poetry, and Giordano wrote some great arias. In a class by itself is Ferruccio Busoni's *Doktor Faust* which Dent called "a drama on a spiritual plane far removed from the operatic level", comparing it to Berlioz' *Les Troyens*. But Busoni will remain more admired than performed. Italo Montemezzi remains performed with *L'Amore dei Tre Re*, after an original libretto by Sem Benelli; he is a composer of taste and discernment. Ermanno Wolf-Ferrari, half German and half Italian, combines German technique with Italian wit, not a bad combination. He is a master of the twentieth-century *opera buffa*: *Le Donne Curiose* (1903), *Il Segreto di Susanna* (1909), *I Gioielli della Madonna* (1911) have all had brief careers. But, after all is said, Puccini's *Turandot* – finished in 1924 – remains Italy's last great and successful contribution to opera.

OPERA IN AMERICA

Opera in the United States goes back to 1735, when a one-act ballad opera, *Flora, or the Hob in the Well*, was produced in the courtroom at Charleston, South Carolina. In the North, opposition to music was strong among the Quakers and the Presbyterians, and the Church of England took a dim view of music outside the church. *Flora* was imported from London where it had been performed two hundred times in twenty years. The earliest recorded opera performances in New York were around 1750, *The Mock Doctor*, and, naturally, *The Beggar's Opera*. Some libretti have survived, though not the music. Among the first opera-like compositions is *The Temple of Minerva*, by Francis Hopkinson, a signer of the Declaration of Independence. In 1781 (when Mozart wote *Idomeneo*) his historical allegory was performed in Philadelphia, in the presence of George and Martha Washington. The music is lost. Then came James Hewitt's *Tammany* (1794), and Benjamin Carr's *The Archers, or Mountaineers of Switzerland*, an adaptation of Schiller's *Wilhelm Tell*. Not much happened until 1845, when William Henry Fry's *Leonora* was performed at the Chestnut Street Theatre in Philadelphia. When some excerpts were presented in New York in a concert version in 1929, Wallace Brockway and Herbert Weinstock report: "The audience found it excruciatingly funny, much to the annoyance of certain critics with a sense of history".

In 1855, George Frederick Bristow's *Rip van Winkle*, based on a text drawn from Washington Irving by Jonathan Howard Wainwright, was performed at Niblo's Garden in New York. No operas of any importance were performed after this until the Boston première, in 1906, of Frederick Shepherd Converse's *The Pipe of Desire*. In 1910, the Metropolitan gave it twice, once with *Pagliacci*, and then with *Cavalleria Rusticana*. The following year, Victor Herbert's first opera, *Natoma,* an early-California story by Joseph Deign Redding, was given at the Metropolitan. Mary Garden and John McCormack sang the main parts. H.T. Parker described the opera as "a dull text set to mediocre music". Victor Herbert's second opera, *Madeleine,* was performed four times.

When the co-managers of the Metropolitan, Giulio Gatti-Casazza and Andreas Dippel, offered a prize of $10,000 for the best opera composed by an American, Horatio W. Parker, professor of music at Yale, won it with his opera, *Mona*, after a libretto by Brian Hooker ("Mona, a princess of Britain, brings about the death of Gwynn, her lover, by insisting on playing a man's part in the world", according to Messrs Brockway & Weinstock). It was a success.

Walter Damrosch's *Cyrano de Bergerac*, after a libretto by the *Sun*'s critic, W.J. Henderson, was produced at the Metropolitan in 1913. H. E. Krehbiel, Henderson's colleague, wrote, "It offers nothing which points even remotely to a solution of the problem of English or American opera". The critics liked Damrosch's *The Man Without a Country* (1937) rather better and nineteen performances of it were given at the Metropolitan. Not long afterwards Hamilton Forrest composed *Camille*, his own version of Dumas' *La Dame aux camélias*. Mary Garden sang the title role in Chicago at the première and remembers it as "a pretty dismal failure".

Deems Taylor had a real success with *The King's Henchman* (1927) and *Peter Ibbetson* (1931). Edna St. Vincent Millay wrote the libretto of *The King's Henchman*, and Tullio Serafin conducted the Metropolitan première. Pitts Sanborn concluded that "for the most part, *The King's Henchman* is based firmly upon Wagner". *Peter Ibbetson* was a smash hit, and in 1933 became the first American opera that ever opened the season at the Met.

More recently, Louis Gruenberg's *The Emperor Jones* (with Kathleen de Jaffa's libretto after Eugene O'Neill's melodrama) became a success, both for the composer and for Lawrence Tibbett as Jones; it was later revived in Italy and Holland. Richard Hageman's *Caponsacchi* had only two performances at the Metropolitan. In 1937 at Philadelphia's Academy of Music, Fritz Reiner conducted Gian Carlo Menotti's *opera buffa*, *Amelia Goes to the Ball*. The Metropolitan produced it the following year as a curtain raiser for Richard Strauss's *Elektra* (which must have been something of a handicap). Pitts Sanborn called it merry and delightful though "American it is not, except through geographical accident". *Amelia* has often been performed since. Menotti showed his talent later with *The Medium* (1946), *The Telephone* (1947), *The Consul* (1950), which was widely performed all over Europe; *The Saint of Bleecker Street* (1954), *The Old Maid and the Thief*, and *Amahl and the Night Visitors*. The critics were not kind to Menotti because he tried various media, wrote "radio-television semi-operas", was said to sound like "watered-down Puccini", and to be "publicity-conscious". Obviously, it is not easy to be a composer in America. Menotti has great talent, and despite a bad press *Amahl and the Night Visitors* has remained the most frequently performed opera in the United States for the past fifteen years and is often given by high school and church groups.

In 1958, the Metropolitan produced Samuel Barber's *Vanessa*. It was not a great success but did better at the Spoleto Festival in 1961. Barber's *Antony and Cleopatra* was commissioned for the opening of the new Metropolitan Opera House in Lincoln Center, and was "respectfully received", which is a polite way of saying that it was not exactly a success. The Met. gave it a fine production; the cast was headed by Leontyne Price. More enduring seems the success of two works by Virgil Thomson, the eminent critic: *Four Saints in Three Acts* (1934), based on a Gertrude Stein libretto, is rather oddly called "an opera to be sung"; *The Mother of Us All*, also based on a Stein text (1947), is a mixture of American legend and history. Among the cast of characters are Ulysses S. Grant, Lillian Russell, "Virgil T.", Jo the Loiterer, and Gertrude Stein. One of the best contemporary American composers, Aaron Copland, wrote two operas: *The Second Hurricane*, produced in New York under Orson Welles in 1937, and *The Tender Land*, performed in 1954 at the New York City Center, with no great success.

The New York City Opera has done much to further the development of American opera, some composers being subsidized by Ford Foundation grants. Among the new works produced in New York in the recent past were Douglas Moore's *The Ballad of Baby Doe*, *The Devil and Daniel Webster*, and *The Wings of the Dove*; Robert Ward's *He Who Gets Slapped*, and *The Crucible* (after Arthur Miller's play); Marc Blitzstein's *Regina*; Hugo Weisgall's *Six Characters in Search of an Author*; Carlisle Floyd's *Wuthering Heights* and *Susannah*; Kurt Weill's *Street Scene*. The San Francisco Opera presented Norman Dello Joio's *Blood Moon*, and the Chicago Lyric Opera staged Vittorio Giannini's *The Harvest*. None of these works seems to have won a place in the history of opera. American music critics, somewhat like their British colleagues, are often frustrated by their country's insignificant contributions to the evolution of opera. The fact remains, however, that almost all good operas are the product of what the British call "the continent of Europe". Operatically, the United States is not a super-power.

It would be a sad story except for George Gershwin's *Porgy and Bess*, the best-known and certainly the best American opera. Though it is close to being a musical and some stuffy critics reject it (as they rejected the works of Offenbach, Johann Strauss and Kurt Weill), *Porgy and Bess* is beautiful, true, melodious, a genuine masterpiece. First produced in Boston in 1935, its songs ("It ain't necessarily so", "Summertime", "I got plenty o'nuttin") have become part of America's folk music. No higher honour could be bestowed on Gershwin.

CZECHS AND RUSSIANS

Some operas become worldwide successes – *Figaro, Lohengrin, Carmen, Aida, La Bohème, Rosenkavalier* – and others become very popular in their own country. The musicologists call them "national" or "folk" operas, for no plausible reason whatsoever. In Italy, France and the German-speaking countries, operas are registered into their epoch and become part of the pre-classic, classic, romantic or modern schools. Yet in a wider sense both Mozart and Verdi wrote "folk" operas, and so did Weber and Bizet. (Is *Carmen* a "French" or a "Spanish" opera?) Nationalistic distinctions should have no place in music, the most universal of the arts.

Thus Bedřich Smetana's *Prodaná nevěsta* (*The Bartered Bride*) is not a Czech "national" opera but a masterpiece in its own right. It meets all prerequisites: an excellent libretto by a gifted Czech writer, Karel Sabina; real protagonists; beautiful melodies, great arias, fine ensembles. It has one of the finest comedy overtures, a wonderful mixture of melancholy and humour (which is the test of a great comic opera), and it evokes people's love of their homeland and its superb landscape. After the première in Prague, in 1866, Smetana revised the opera twice, from a two-act Singspiel with spoken dialogues to a three-act opera with accompanied recitative. In Prague it is performed as often as *Faust* in Paris, or *Die Zauberflöte* in Vienna, or Verdi's most popular operas in Italy.

Smetana's other works are less known abroad. *Dalibor* (1868), mistakenly labelled a Czech *Fidelio* because of certain superficial similarities, is slowly emerging as a work of great, though somewhat static beauty. *Hubička* (*The Kiss*) is a charming comedy. Smetana worked on this gay, lyrically beautiful peasant-life opera while he wrote the often tragic, autobiographical string quartet *Z mého života* (From My Life). After the first performance of *The Kiss* in 1876, Smetana became totally deaf, and wrote to a friend, "Unfortunately, I was the only man in the packed house who did not hear a single note of the music – my own music". (Beethoven too was totally deaf, when he attended a performance of his *Missa Solemnis*. Yet each perhaps sensed the music with his inner ear and knew exactly how it sounded.) Smetana was dedicated to his country and to the beauty of nature; in this respect, he resembled Schubert. In his comic operas, he escaped the influence of Wagner which can be traced in *Dalibor* and *Libuše*, the latter perhaps his finest opera. It was written for the opening of the National Theatre in Prague, in 1881. The building burned down soon afterwards, and a new building was reopened in 1883, with *Libuše*. The heroine is the mythical ancestress of the Czech nation and this opera is performed in moments of national greatness or tragedy. The libretto is epic rather than dramatic – even Smetana's power and coloration couldn't overcome this defect.

Czech folklore is even stronger in the operas of Antonín Dvořák. He remains best known as a composer of chamber music, instrumental music and symphonies, and of religious music. Dvořák loved to write operas, but he had no sense of drama and most of his works don't hold the audience's attention. His best-known opera is *Rusalka*, Jaroslav Kvapil's libretto based on Gerhart Hauptmann's play, *Die versunkene Glocke* – Ottorino Respighi also used it for his opera, *La Campana sommersa* – about a girl who becomes a water sprite. The theme was also used in Adam's ballet *Giselle*, Lortzing's *Undine*, Tchaikovsky's *Swan Lake*, Puccini's *Le Villi*. The music of *Rusalka* is very beautiful and very Czech, lyrical and melodious. It was his ninth opera.

Leos Janáček is now emerging as the greatest Czechoslovak opera composer since Smetana; some day he may be called his country's greatest musician. Janáček comes from Moravia, where he was known only to a small group of friends. His masterpiece, *Její pastorkyňa* (known abroad as *Jenůfa*) was not performed in Prague until 1916, twelve years after the première in Brno, the capital of Moravia. Max Brod, the Jewish poet (and Kafka's closest friend), translated *Jenůfa* into German, for its performance at the Vienna Opera. Maria Jeritza created the part at the Metropolitan in 1924. Ernest Newman called it "the work of a man who is ... only a cut above the amateur". *Jenůfa* is now considered a great, modern masterpiece.

Life for Janáček began at sixty-two, when other composers retire. Stimulated by late success, he wrote *Kata Kabanová* (1921), the story of a Moravian Madame Bovary; *The Cunning Little Vixen* (1924); *Věc Makropulos* (1926), his own libretto based on Karel Čapek's exciting play, *The Makropulos Affair*; and *Z mrtvého domu* (1930), adapted by Janáček from Dostoievski's *From the House of the Dead*. At the beginning of the score it says, "In every human being there is a divine spark", the credo of the great Moravian humanist who expressed his love of life, people and nature in his own idiom, opera. It was performed two years after Janáček had died in 1928.

Ever since, the composer's stature has grown rapidly. Janáček was able to translate the rhythm of the Czech language into music, and he wrote subtle changes in rhythm and melody. His orchestration is never "luxurious" but rather sparse; he was afraid of "varnishing his works with instrumentation", as Strauss had often done. Janáček ceased using lined paper, drawing the lines of the stave himself, so that he would remain conscious of every little bit of space. Like Béla Bartók, he started out as a nationally known composer who later won universal admiration. Bartók went back to the almost lost folk melodies of Hungary. Janáček discovered the melodies of nature and translated them into his music. In *The Cunning Little Vixen* he wonderfully paints the Moravian forests in a neo-impressionistic manner, and invents the language of the animals. Janáček is a very great composer, well on his way to immortality.

So is Béla Bartók, who didn't contribute much to opera. His one-act treatment of the old Bluebeard legend, *A Kékszakállú Herceg Vára* (Duke Bluebeard's Castle), was first performed in Budapest. The libretto is rather sombre and undramatic; the music is great. Bartók's contemporary, Zoltán Kodály, wrote a folk ballad, *Háry János*, which is now being performed abroad; it has an amusing story, good characters, fine Hungarian melodies. Earlier, Karl Goldmark had become known in Europe, and later in America, with his first and most successful opera, *Die Königin von Saba* (1875). Among his later works are *Das Heimchen am Herd*, after Dickens (1896), and *Ein Wintermärchen*, after Shakespeare (1908). A splendid and inventive craftsman, who was much esteemed by his friend Brahms, Goldmark is due for a comeback. The most popular Hungarian "folk" opera though is Ferenc Erkel's *Hunyadi László*, a rousing, patriotic work immensely popular in Budapest since its première in 1844. (Erkel indirectly created one of the most famous Hungarian pieces written by a non-Hungarian, when he introduced Hector Berlioz to the *Rákoczy March* in 1846.)

The Poles, too, have their Erkel. He was Stanislaw Moniuszko, a contemporary of Frédéric Chopin (whose name is pronounced *Chop*-pen in Poland, with the accent on the first syllable.) Moniuszko's *Halka* was first given by a professional company in Vilna, in 1854. (Vilna is now in the Soviet Union; this tells the whole tragedy of Poland.) *Halka*, a sad story of peasant life, modelled after Glinka's *A Life for the Czar*, is rarely performed outside Poland, but is still extremely popular there.

The Russian composers are no longer mentioned in the folk-opera group; perhaps their political and space prominence has elevated them to a higher status. Non-Russians still hear "folklore" in *Boris Godunov*; Russians just hear great music in it. Mussorgsky didn't intend to write a folklore opera. He wrote a musical tragedy about the people of his homeland. He identified himself with his characters, as Mozart did, or Verdi when he wrote *Falstaff*, which isn't about a drunken English aristocrat but about a wise old man (like Verdi) with a wonderful sense of humour. In *Boris Godunov*, modest Petrovich Mussorgsky caught the very soul of Russia and the Russian people – tragic and humorous, sombre and guilt-ridden, warm and brutal. He wrote the great score in a year. He felt there was something in

Pushkin's *Boris Godunov* that he wanted to express in music, and he did it. One of the absurd legends around opera claims that he was a "dilettante". The truth is that he was a great genius. Everything was "wrong" with *Boris*, in the opinion of his non-dilettante contemporaries: there was no heroine, too many chorus scenes, "scandalous" harmonies, and so on. As a result of such idiocy, Mussorgsky's original score was not heard until 1928, forty-seven years after his death in 1881! Even today, most people know only the "revision" done by Mussorgsky's friend, Nikolai Andreievich Rimsky-Korsakov. He was a great orchestrator, but Mussorgsky's bold musical ideas were covered by Rimsky's "luxurious" orchestration. He did to the austere, uncompromising Mussorgsky what later arrangers have done to Monteverdi. Even great conductors, who should know better, don't conduct the original version. Both Toscanini, who introduced the work at the Metropolitan in 1913, and Karajan, who made it a super-extravaganza at the Salzburg Festival in 1966, used Rimsky-Korsakov's version (which Karajan's critics called *Holiday on Ice*.) Olin Downes, not a revolutionary, wrote, "The music is far more dramatically truthful and modern in texture in Mussorgsky's original version than in the Rimsky-Korsakov editing". Mussorgsky has been compared to Mozart, for the way he outlines his characters in music, and to Wagner, for his handling of the choruses. All nonsense: Mussorgsky is incomparable, and he created a great work of art. A "modern" version by Shostakovich was given by the Metropolitan in 1960. Mussorgsky also wrote *Khovanshchina,* which he called "another heavyweight", and a comic opera, *The Fair at Sorochintzy.* Both were unfinished when he died; they are undramatic and somewhat confused, but the touch of genius is there in the bold characterizations, the forceful music.

Russian opera began long before *Boris.* The date usually given is 9 December 1836, when Mikhail Ivanovich Glinka's *A Life for the Czar* was first performed in St Petersburg. Italian opera had been popular there before; Paisiello, Cimarosa and Martín y Solar had worked in St Petersburg. Glinka's work was well orchestrated and people liked the music, but the story was undramatic; so was his second opera, *Ruslan and Lyudmila.* Grand Duke Mikhael Pavlovich once told Liszt that when he wanted to punish his officers, he ordered them to listen to a performance of *Ruslan.* Liszt didn't agree; he said Glinka was a genius.

Alexander Porfirievich Borodin left his opera *Prince Igor* unfinished, when he died in 1887. He had worked eighteen years on it, but sometimes he was more interested in chemistry than in music. In wintertime, he would compose only when he was too sick to give his chemistry lessons.

Prince Igor was orchestrated by Alexander Glazunow and Rimsky-Korsakov. It is a fascinating work, with "Oriental" colouring (Borodin came from Georgia), and strange rhythms. Debussy and Stravinsky (a pupil of Rimsky-Korsakov) greatly admired Borodin's opera.

Rimsky-Korsakov, who helped to polish and finish the masterpieces of his more gifted friends, and almost ruined them, never wrote a masterpiece himself. *Sadko*, after his own libretto, is best known for *Song of India*. His only opera that won real success outside Russia is *Le Coq d'Or*. The amusing libretto is by Vladimir I. Byelsky, after a satirical fairytale by Pushkin. Beecham introduced the work at the Covent Garden Royal Opera House, and Monteux at the Metropolitan. It has a great coloratura part, the Queen of Shemakha, and the music is beautiful. Rimsky also composed *Mozart and Salieri* (1897), based on Pushkin's story of Mozart's being poisoned by his jealous competitor. Rimsky-Korsakov shouldn't have written operas since he always claimed that "opera is essentially a false artistic genre".

Piotr Ilyich Tchaikovsky is usually kept apart from the Russian "nationalist" fellow composers, as though he'd never been a member of the party. His critics, in Russia and elsewhere, said he was too "cosmopolitan", long before the word became a dangerous invective in Moscow. His finest opera, *Eugene Onegin,* has much beautiful music but somehow fails because Tchaikovsky just didn't understand the stage. It is, perhaps, an autobiographical work, or a projection of various moods, based on a poem by Pushkin, who inspired most of the Russian composers. The hero is a passive character in true Russian tradition. The best aria is written for Lenski, the hero's antagonist. *Eugene Onegin* has beautiful lyrical passages and its sadness ought to make people cry – but it doesn't. His second opera, *Pique Dame,* has been more successful, though musically it is not as good as *Onegin.* But somehow Tchaikovsky managed to combine drama and song, situation and music, much better than before. Tchaikovsky's operas are performed, but they never create genuine excitement. Only *Boris Godunov* succeeds in this.

THE MODERNS

Modern opera, in the sense it is used here, is an opera written in a musical idiom that goes beyond Wagner's romanticism and Debussy's impressionism. The borderlines are blurred. Richard Strauss's *Elektra* (1909) is modern in its intellectual and musical treatment, but his *Arabella* (1929) is not. Puccini's *Turandot,* composed in 1924, is less modern than Schönberg's Mimodrama *Erwartung,* composed in 1909, and performed the year Puccini wrote his last work. "Modern" is not necessarily synonymous with the twentieth century. Some works of our century are neo-classic, going back in form and content to the eighteenth century. It is too early to make valid judgements about many works written in the past fifty years; operas, like good wines, need time to develop and mature. Some that were sensational first-night successes are already forgotten; others, originally ignored, are getting attention. Modern composers have a tendency to be condescending about box office figures, speaking of "art for art's sake". Giuseppe Verdi, who knew more about opera than most other composers, was always more interested in the box office returns than in the opinions of the critics. He knew that in the long run the judgement of the box office was often more accurate!

Igor Stravinsky, perhaps the greatest modern composer, was more interested in ballet than in opera when he wrote for the stage. *Petrouchka* and *Le Sacre du Printemps* may survive his operas. *Le Rossignol (The Nightingale),* written in 1914, still betrays the influence of his teacher, Rimsky-Korsakov. *Mavra,* a modern *opera buffa* written as a conscious reaction against "Wagner's inflated arrogance", is rarely performed. But *Oedipus Rex* (1927) has had a successful career, though the libretto is in Latin; the music is remarkable for its expressive power. *The Rake's Progress* (1951), based on a libretto by Wystan Hugh Auden and Chester Kallman, from the old Hogarth moral tale, already has a large following. The final scene among the lunatics of Bedlam has great emotional force. Stravinsky conducted the world première at the Teatro Fenice in Venice.

Serge Prokofiev, the great Russian composer, had a popular success with *The Love of Three Oranges* (1921), a brilliant, witty treatment of Carlo Gozzi's fantastic comedy. The composer wrote his own libretto. The opera's charm and exotic colouring reminds one of Rimsky-Korsakov. *The Fiery Angel* (1922-25), which Prokofiev considered his best work, was condemned "for its parody and expressionism" by the Soviet critics. Under political pressure, Prokofiev composed *War and Peace* (who would dare set Tolstoy's immense novel to music?), but there is no inner conviction in it. He was more successful with *Betrothal in a Monastery,* after Richard Brinsley Sheridan's *The Duenna* (and known under this title in America). In this work Prokofiev shows imagination and virtuosity.

Dmitri Shostakovich's *Lady Macbeth of Mzensk* was an immediate and somewhat scandalous success, because at one point the orchestra realistically imitates the sound of sexual intercourse. (Compared to Shostakovich's rather crude treatment, Richard Strauss was more elegant and subtle in his *Rosenkavalier* prelude.) Nothing is subtle about *Katerina Ismailova*, as the opera is sometimes called. Repeated hearing proves that the score is banal and third-rate.

Italy has offered little in the field of modern opera; the French contribution is more important. Paul Dukas' *Ariane et Barbe-Bleue* is witty, brilliant and occasionally moving. Maurice Ravel's *L'Heure Espagnole* (1907) and *L'Enfant et les Sortilèges* (1925) are masterpieces, in spite of their miniature form, that show the wide range of the great master of impressionism. The first work is a brilliant, farcical tale, while *L'Enfant* deals movingly with the theme of innocence. The orchestration is shimmering in wonderful colours. The art of miniature also appears in Manuel de Falla's works, *La Vida Breve* (1905) and *El Retablo de Maese Pedro* (1923), after an incident from *Don Quixote*. De Falla expresses the true Spanish idiom with imagination and refinement. *La Vida Breve* is now performed in many languages.

The members of a modern school of composing, known as Les Six, sponsored by a brilliant manifesto of Jean Cocteau, made significant contributions to opera. Darius Milhaud's *Christophe Colomb* (1930) impresses and often confuses audiences who are not sure whether this work, after a libretto by Paul Claudel, is a mystery play, a late-Greek drama, or an expression of symbolism. (Even modern newsreel methods are employed on the stage.) Arthur Honegger wrote several operas but only two are now regularly performed: *Antigone*, a continuous recitative after a text by Cocteau, and *Jeanne d'Arc au Bûcher*, a dramatic oratorio by Claudel. Honegger goes back to Lully; he is severe and uncompromising in his music. The most successful of Les Six is Francis Poulenc. His religious opera, *Les Dialogues des Carmelites*, has been much performed since its première at La Scala in 1957. The story – about a group of Carmelite nuns driven from their convent by the French Revolution and suffering martyrdom – is dramatic, and the music more "conservative" than that of his fellow composers, and it has lyrical power and great charm.

In Germany, Paul Hindemith is much respected as the composer of *Mathis der Maler*. After the Zurich première in 1938, Hindemith was accused of "*Kulturbolschewismus*" by the Nazis, and went to America. In 1957 his opera *Die Harmonie der Welt* was given in Munich; an impressive, though static work. He was more successful with his earlier *Cardillac* (1926), with a libretto by Ferdinand Lion based on E.T.A. Hoffmann's

Das Fraulein von Scuderi. Ernst Křenek's most important serious work is *Karl V* (1938) but his greatest success was the jazz opera *Jonny spielt auf* which was a sensation in 1927, for its staging and music. It was a stunning show: in one scene a full-size steam locomotive appears on the stage, and in the end Jonny, the Negro musician, dances on the globe. Late revivals, however, have not been successful.

Another composer who had a sensational success and is now forgotten was Erich Wolfgang Korngold. When *Die tote Stadt* was performed in Vienna in 1921, Korngold, twenty-four years old, was hailed as "the Viennese Puccini". The opera's double role of Marie-Marietta became one of Maria Jeritza's greatest triumphs. It has an effective libretto with the bizarre background of Bruges ("the dead city"), beautiful melodies and lush orchestration, but a recent revival in Vienna was not successful; Korngold's musical idiom seems hopelessly dated. His second work, *Das Wunder der Heliane* (1927) was never a great success, though it had a fine role for Lotte Lehmann.

Hans Pfitzner, the contemporary and bitter personal enemy of Richard Strauss, who never got over his competitor's popular success, is much overestimated between Vienna and Munich, and perhaps too much underestimated elsewhere. His epic work, *Palestrina*, first conducted in 1917 by Bruno Walter, is almost as much admired there as *Parsifal*. It has some great music, but Pfitzner's own libretto is a hopeless jumble of contrasting elements; the noisy second act doesn't belong to the opera. None of his other works, *Der Arme Heinrich, Die Rose vom Liebesgarten, Das Herz,* was successful outside Germany. Pfitzner, a violent Nazi follower during the Second World War, died in Salzburg in 1949, a bitter, disappointed man.

The collaboration of two immensely gifted artists, Bertolt Brecht and Kurt Weill, gave us two masterpieces: *Aufstieg und Fall der Stadt Mahagonny,* and *Die Dreigroschenoper* (The Threepenny Opera), a new version of *The Beggar's Opera*. The libretti are excellent; Weill was a composer of taste and imagination, with a fine sense of satire. Possibly because he later wrote musical comedies in America, he isn't taken "seriously" in some quarters; just as Johann Strauss remains an "operetta" and "waltz" composer.

Carl Orff, born in 1895, became internationally known only after the Second World War. His *Carmina Burana*, "a scenic oratorio", has strong rhythms, arresting harmonies and an apparently new sort of orchestration. His *Catulli Carmina* (1943) and *Il Trionfo d'Afrodite* (1953) created some excitement, and so did *Die Bernauerin* (1947), and *Antigonae,*

Oedipus, der Tyrann and *Prometheus*. Orff has been much performed during the past two decades. Other moderately successful modern composers are Werner Egk (*Columbus, Irische Legende, Der Revisor, Die Zaubergeige, Peer Gynt*); Gottfried von Einem (*Dantons Tod*, his most powerful work to a libretto which Boris Blacher wrote from the great play by Georg Büchner; *Der Prozess*, after Kafka's *The Trial*); and his latest work (1971), *Der Besuch der alten Dame*, after the brilliant Friedrich Dürrenmatt play. Boris Blacher (a distinguished musician and teacher, who wrote *Die Nachtschwalbe, Abstract Opera No 1*, and *200,000 Taler*); and Rolf Liebermann (*Penelope, Leonore 40/45, The School for Wives*). Frank Martin, a French-Swiss from Geneva, was successful with *Der Sturm*, based on Shakespeare's *The Tempest*.

The modern composers are great craftsmen and experimenters, but few of them are born dramatists. There is no critical agreement about them and their works. Hans Werner Henze (*Die Bassariden, Boulevard Solitude, Elegy for Young Lovers, Der Prinz von Homburg*) is admired by some critics and avant-garde experts, and very much disliked by others (Pierre Boulez, for instance, has severely attacked Henze). There is much argument about Wolfgang Fortner (*Bluthochzeit, Maria Stuart*); Krzysztof Penderecki (*The Devils of Loudun*); Karl-Birger Blomdahl (*Aniara*); Bruno Maderna (*Von A bis Z*); Giselher Klebe (*Der Räuber*); Günther Schuller (*The Visitation*); Isa Krejzi (*Antigone*); Paul Dessau (*Herr Puntila und sein Knecht Matti*); Siegfried Matthus (*Der letzte Schuss*). None of these works seems to have made a deep enough impression to warrant re-staging in a number of houses. The list is not complete. In the early 1970s, it appears that the modern composers who have made important and possibly permanent contributions to modern opera are few: Stravinsky, Schönberg, Berg. Their works are already considered "classics".

Vienna's golden musical age, the classical era that began with Gluck's *Orfeo* in 1762 and ended sixty-five years later with the death of Beethoven, made the city a citadel of Western civilization, comparable only with Athens at the time of Pericles and Phidias, and with Florence at the time of Leonardo da Vinci, Raphael and Michelangelo. Actually, Vienna's dominating position as a city of music didn't end with classicism. Towards the end of the nineteenth century, Brahms, Bruckner, Mahler, Johann Strauss and Hugo Wolf lived there, all of them at the climax of their creative powers. (Wolf's *Der Corregidor*, musically a beautiful work, suffers from the usual lack of drama but still delights dedicated Wolf admirers.) And around the beginning of our century three young men lived in Vienna who later were to create an entirely new kind of music: Arnold Schönberg, Alban Berg, Anton von Webern.

Musically, the Viennese are conservative people – the complete works of Mahler, and of Schönberg, Berg and Webern were first performed in Vienna in the late 1960s – but the city has often stimulated composers who wrote for the future. In 1805, the violinist Radicati who, at Beethoven's request, worked out the fingering for Beethoven's three Rasumovsky string quartets, opus 59, wrote, "I told him that surely he did not consider these works to be music. Beethoven replied, 'Oh, they are not for you, but for a later age.'" During the Vienna Festival of 1969, Schönberg's works, and those of Berg and Webern, were performed in an atmosphere of understanding and enthusiasm. Perhaps the "later age" is already here for the creator of the twelve-tone system who made a break when he dispensed with the system of harmonic relations that had been in force since Johann Sebastian Bach.

Schönberg's earlier works are still influenced by the chromaticism of Wagner's *Tristan* and the impressionism of Debussy's *Pelléas*, but in *Erwartung* (1909) and *Die glückliche Hand* (composed in 1913, first performed in 1924 at Vienna's Volksoper), he no longer recognized the principle of key in music – where a piece written in the key of C-major is based on the fixed relationship of tones in the C-major scale. Schönberg arranged the twelve half-tones of the scale in fixed, almost geometric sequence, occasionally turning it upside down, and reading it backwards, somewhat reminiscent of the "learned" art of medieval music, and Bach. Schönberg's enemies called the result "tonal anarchy". His admirers said it was the beginning of a new kind of music. The ultimate truth may be somewhere between the extremes. Repeated hearing of the music of the masters of the New Viennese School raises the question whether they are not, perhaps subconsciously, very late post-romanticists, with one foot in the nineteenth century, the other in the twentieth.

Neither the one-act monodrama *Erwartung, Die glückliche Hand*, nor *Pierrot Lunaire* (1912), a marvellously beautiful song cycle, are conventional operas. *Von Heute auf Morgen* (1929), written after the success of Hindemith's "Gebrauchsoper" *Neues vom Tage*, is a one-act comic opera with arias and recitatives, but the story is banal and undramatic, and the music almost impenetrable. But Schönberg left us a powerful, unfinished opera when he died. Two acts of *Moses und Aron* are finished, but not the third act of this Biblical drama. The première was in Zurich, six years after Schönberg's death. Schönberg wrote his own libretto, which has the simple structure of a Biblical story: the exodus of the Israelites from Egypt is told in a few scenes. The drama is between Moses, the philosopher, and Aron, the man of action. Moses gives the people the tables of the law; Aron gives them the golden calf. The leaders are opposed by the choruses that form a super-protagonist, as in *Boris Godunov*, and are divided in half-choruses. Speaking choruses are blended organically with the singers. The speech is done with rhythmical precision. Moses speaks in a *Sprechstimme*, the voice rising and falling relative to the indicated tone intervals (Schönberg wrote that "everything is bound together with the time and rhythm of the music"). He claimed the voice was capable of subtle modulation, *bel parlare*, quite different from, yet comparable to, *bel canto*. Aron sings his part; he is a *Heldentenor*. *Moses und Aron* has elements of the oratorio and of opera (Schönberg had much admired Puccini's *Turandot*) and he blends contrasting elements. It is a powerful work – Schönberg left elaborate stage instructions – and productions of this masterpiece in Zurich, Berlin, Boston, London – were greeted with admiration and enthusiasm. The day may come when *Moses und Aron* is in the repertory of many great opera houses.

The day has already come for Alban Berg's *Wozzeck* and *Lulu*. *Wozzeck* (1921), based on Büchner's drama about the execution of Christian Woyzeck, is the only opera since Puccini and Strauss that sells out at the opera house. Berg, a great dramatist, skilfully condensed Büchner's twenty-six scenes to fifteen, tightened the drama and deepened the characterization. He connected the scenes, as Wagner and Debussy had done, by short orchestral interludes. Repeated hearing will establish harmonies, even melodies, expressing emotions and associations. Everything becomes astonishingly clear. Berg, using eighteenth-century musical forms (fugue, sarabande, gavotte, passacaglia), illuminates psychological sensations and synchronizes emotions and actions on the stage. His *Gesangs-sprache* (song-speech), is different from Schönberg's *Sprechstimme* (speech voice). Berg developed his own musical idiom, expressing powerful emotions with extreme economy. *Wozzeck* is a great masterpiece, a song of humanity.

Berg's second opera, *Lulu*, develops and refines his ideas even further, combining action on the stage with strong emotion, but it is not helped by the libretto. *Lulu* became a great success in Stuttgart, where Wieland Wagner produced and Anja Silja, a great singing actress, made Lulu her most brilliant part; and it was successful even at the conservative Vienna Staatsoper.

Singing and Singers

THE ART OF SINGING

Opera projects the human voice. The first opera performance – Jacopo Peri's *Euridice*, on 9 February 1600, in Florence – was the beginning of singing as a modern art. Giulio Caccini, his fellow composer, wrote a few arias with florid passages for his daughter Francesca, a member of the cast, an early prima donna.

In 1602, Caccini published an essay, *Le nuove musiche*, about solo singing with accompaniment in which emotions would be expressed and the text clearly enunciated – a revolutionary thought. Until then, "singing" had been an almost monotonous declamation with no relation between the text and the contrapuntal music. Caccini's ideas were developed by Vincenzo Giustiniani, a Roman nobleman who published in 1628 *Discorso sopra la musica*. He analysed the singing of some ladies in Mantua and Ferrara, admiring "the design of exquisite passages delivered at opportune points, but not in excess". The singers, he said,

> ... moderated or increased their voices, loud or soft ... now slow, breaking off with a gentle sigh ... now with long trills, now with short and with sweet running passages sung softly ... They accompanied the music and the sentiment with appropriate facial expressions, glances and gestures ... They made the words clear in such a way that one could hear even the last syllable of every word which was never interrupted or suppressed by passages and embellishments.

Since then, the vocal art has evolved from the early age of *bel canto* (beautiful song) to the romantic era of the nineteenth century. It is still with us, though contemporary music demands a new type of singer, able to perform the *Sprechstimme* in Schönberg's *Moses und Aron* or the song-speech in Berg's *Wozzeck*. And that is just the beginning. Yet opera is often erroneously called a static art. The *bel canto* had its golden age, and so had nineteenth-century singing; some day historians may discuss a golden age of twentieth-century singing.

It is not true, as is often claimed, that today's great singers don't really know the art of singing. There is no Caruso or Tauber or Lotte Lehmann; nevertheless, our era has its own great singers able to express dramatic power and psychological insight – one thinks of Callas's Norma, Sutherland's Lucia, Nilsson's Isolde, Gobbi's Falstaff, Fischer-Dieskau's Wozzeck, London's Don Giovanni, Ghiaurov's Mephistophélès, to name just a very few. Under the guidance of great conductors – Toscanini, Walter, Furtwängler, Szell, Karajan, Krips, Böhm, Boulez, Bernstein, Solti – the leading singers display sounder musicality than the self-indulgent prima donnas and star tenors of the past. The style, taste and musicianship which some singers in Vienna, after 1945, developed in their singing of Mozart might well have aroused the envy of singers of the golden age.

Under the influence of the German school, which demands a fusion of all artistic elements at the opera house, many people now take a dim view of the "singer's era". Today the works of Bellini, Spontini and Donizetti are presented in a "modern" way: the score must be followed, and all elements – drama, continuity, orchestral playing, staging, lighting, acting and singing – must form a unity. People forget that these operas were written to demonstrate the glory of the human voice, the most beautiful and expressive musical instrument of all.

The seventeenth and eighteenth centuries in the lyric theatre were dominated by the *opera seria*. The libretti were limited to mythological or Hellenistic subjects, the drama was stilted, and good invariably triumphed over evil. The characters would express their emotions in the artful arias – *aria cantabile, aria di bravura,* and so on – that were allotted to the protagonists. The artists were ranked as strictly as members of the military establishment. First came the *primo uomo*, followed by the *prima donna*, the tenor, *secondo uomo, seconda donna,* and *basso*; each were allotted their arias according to their rank in the hierarchy of the opera house. There was no inner relation between plot and drama; the librettists were having a tough time. Even the exact position of the singers on the stage was regulated by protocol. Front and centre was reserved for the primo uomo and the prima donna. The left side was considered superior to the right side. Metastasio sometimes wrote exactly where and how the singers should be placed.

Opera seria was an extremely serious business. In 1720, the composer Benedetto Marcello wrote in *Il Teatro all Moda*,

> The singers, male and female, are to keep their dignity above all things, never listening to any other actor; saluting the people in the boxes, joking with the orchestra, so that people may clearly understand that he or she is not Prince Zoroaster but Signor Forconi ... If the singer plays the part of prisoner or slave, he must take care always to appear well powdered, with many jewels on his dress ... the prima donna must always raise one arm, then the other, constantly changing her fan from one hand to another ...

There would be a small orchestra: strings, oboes, bassoon, horns, trumpets, percussion, harpsichord. There was no conductor; the harpsichordist (*maestro al cembalo*) would supervise the accompaniment. Sometimes there was a chorus. The *opera seria* was a spectacle rather than dramatic entertainment. The stage machinery had been developed in Venice, by the middle of the seventeenth century. There might be earthquakes and sea battles on the stage, floods and thunderstorms, birds would be released, and there would be a lavish ballet. Between the monotonous scenes, a few *buffo* scenes (*intermezzi*) would be sandwiched as comic relief.

No one liked to sit in a dark auditorium. In Italy, opera was performed mostly in public theatres; in Austria, Germany and France, mostly in court theatres, where the general public was often admitted. Singers would talk to one another on the stage, while a colleague was singing an aria. Some talked to their admirers in the boxes. No one seemed to mind. Good singers were applauded and bad ones hissed. The opera house was a social gathering place. There might be gay parties in the boxes (called *Logen* in Austria), which were owned by important families and passed on from father to son. During the boring recitatives, the people in the boxes would gossip and gamble, flirt and fight, drink and make love, talk politics and business. Simon Towneley Worsthone, in *Venetian Opera in the Seventeenth Century*, calls the box "the boudoir from which the world of politics and fashion could be discussed and plans for future policies laid". Charles Burney remembers an opera performance in Milan, in 1770, when "the noise was abominable, except while two or three airs and a duet were sung".

The famous singers were respectfully listened to while they displayed technique and imagination. The singers considered the composer's score as a blueprint, providing interpretations, somewhat as jazz soloists do now.

They were expected to provide the artistic excitement. Their vocal art saved the evening. In 1723, Pier Francesco Tosi, the author of *Observations on the Florid Song,* discussed the singer's approach to the *da capo aria,*

> In the first part, they require nothing but the simplest ornaments of good taste, and few, that the composition may remain simple, plain and pure. In the second part, they expect that to their purity some artful graces be added, by which the judicious may hear that the ability of the singers is greater; and in repeating the air, he that does not vary it for the better is no great master . . . Let a student, therefore, accustom himself to repeat them always differently, for . . . one that abounds in invention though a moderate singer, deserves more esteem than a better singer who is barren of it.
>
> Let him who studied under the disadvantage of an ungrateful genius remember for his comfort that singing in tune, expression, *messa di voce*, the appoggiaturas, trills, divisions, and accompanying himself are the principal qualifications . . . I know they are not . . . sufficient to enable one to sing in perfection . . . but embellishments must be called to their aid . . .

Tosi consoled his readers that "study will do the business". He defined the *appoggiatura* as a note inserted between two other notes to give "grace and elegance". He called the trill at the end of the cadence "very essential . . . one who has it imperfectly will never be a great singer, let his know-ledge be ever so great". In an *aria di bravura* there had to be roulades and divisions, which were either "gliding" (*legato*) or "marked" (*non-legato*). A *messa di voce* "from a singer using it sparingly and only on the open vowels, can never fail of having an exquisite effect". The singer would begin in pianissimo, increase the tone to fortissimo, and go back to pianissimo, ending with a *bravura* cadence.

Today such virtuoso devices might often be artistically inexcusable but not in the eighteenth century. Mozart often used roulades to express rage and vengeance (Donna Elvira in *Don Giovanni*), or harmony and jubilation. Many *bel canto* devices were not primarily used to display the singer's virtuosity, but for a deeper purpose. They belonged in the score though the early composers hadn't written them in (Rossini, Bellini and Donizetti wrote their own cadenzas). During the first half of the nine-teenth century, beautiful singing was the most important element in the opera house. The Italians, the French, Mozart and Beethoven wrote difficult, often rewarding singing parts. They understood that good singing created dramatic excitement.

Today, prominent singers are said to travel too much. But even the singers of earlier centuries travelled a lot. In Italy, the opera season lasted from 26 December to the beginning of Lent. Short seasons might be given between Easter and 15 June, and from September to November. Singers would commute between the important opera houses. Composers would also move around, delivering scores, supervising rehearsals, perhaps "conducting" the première from the harpsichord. In Austria, Germany, Spain, Russia, and the Italian states, singers and composers became members of court establishments and would spend much of their time there. Some had contracts permitting them to go elsewhere for stipulated periods of time. When such singers sang *cantatas* (vocal chamber music), they were known as *virtuosi di camera,* or *Kammersänger* (in Austria and Germany, the latter title is now given by the government as a special honour). There was much argument among audiences whether singers should indulge in *bravura* singing. Tosi praises the "ancient" singers for their artistic restraint and denounces "modern" singers for their athletic feats and vulgar manners. Such modern singers, he said,

> terminate the cadence of the first part with an overflowing of passages and divisions at pleasure, and the orchestra waits; in that of the second, the dose is increased, and the orchestra grows tired; and on the last cadence, the throat is going like a weather cock in a whirlwind, and the orchestra yawns.

Surprisingly little has changed since Tosi wrote this in 1723. There will always be "modern" singers and they will always have their public. Actually, the material often needed some jazzing up. The librettists wrote situations rather than plots, and ambitious singers were tempted to "embellish" the libretto, particularly if a certain aria didn't fit a singer's voice. Even Mozart didn't hesitate to delete "Il mio tesoro" from the Vienna production of *Don Giovanni* when the tenor couldn't sing it, and to replace it with the easier "Dalla sua pace".

In the late nineteenth century, a discussion began between the admirers and enemies of Wagner as to whether it was "artistically" sufficient of itself to sing *bel canto* beautifully. The Meister had written loftily about the "higher purpose" of art, which was also "educational". Today it is agreed that the singer should not only sing beautifully but that he must also know the meaning of the music he performs. A distinction is made between a good "singer" and an "artist". Technically, beautiful singing always meant a beautiful natural timbre of the voice, an even scale through various registers, an unbroken legato, precise intonation, clear elocution.

There must be no harsh sounds, no audible "breaks" between the registers, no nasal tones, no shouting.

These principles remain valid. Good singing today is basically what it was two hundred years ago though Verdi's and Wagner's dramatic requirements, the *parlando* of Strauss, and the modern idioms have created new demands. There is an increasing need for good voices in a growing market; in certain categories, especially the Wagnerian *Heldentenor* or the *hochdramatische* soprano, the supply is so limited that a few singers virtually have a monopoly. But most singers expect their careers to be shorter than their famous predecessors' careers (Melba, Slezak, Battistini were singing beautifully in their late sixties). Jet travel, hectic rehearsal conditions, sudden changes in climate create physical and nervous strain. Famous singers cannot afford to stay in one place, to study and grow artistically. They must be heard in many places, although not too frequently; on the international singers' exchange everybody has his price. Competition was always brutal; no one could, or can, afford to relax if determined to get ahead or stay at the top. Radio and television appearances are difficult – the microphone is pitiless – and recording sessions can be nerveracking. A bad record hurts the singer's prestige. A good record puts him up against his own public image. He must compete with himself at his best. Record buyers don't always realize that a singer's exceptional recording performance may be the result of several "takes" and refined vocal-cosmetic operations in the studio. People are disappointed when they hear the singer in person, thinking he isn't as good as on his recordings in comparison with which he can only lose.

His most serious challenge today is the problem of repertoire. Some singers are content to sing a number of parts in popular operas. But what if they want to do more than Mozart, Wagner, Verdi, Strauss, Puccini, and a few special roles? They may go forward, if they are able to sing Berg, Schönberg, Henze, Britten; they will sing these parts rarely, for a small group of people. Or they may turn backwards to the long-forgotten works of the eighteenth and early-nineteenth centuries. This isn't easy either. The greatest singing stars of the past centuries combined technical virtuosity with an almost hypnotic presence (Pasta and Malibran fascinated their audiences though they often sang wrong notes). Florid singing must be understood to be mastered. Not many singers today are trained for it. They must sing correctly and at the same time must project conviction and emotion, sometimes violently (Norma and Medea, for instance, are studies in passion). The singers must study the old parts thoroughly, perhaps with the help of a musicologist. They must transfer

themselves into the style of a past epoch and make the old music acceptable to modern taste without diluting it. Hard work and thorough
musicality are needed, and the rewards are not always adequate. After a
few laborious experiments the artist may regretfully conclude that it is
more gratifying to sing yet another Tosca or Rigoletto.

One often hears the complaint that "there are not enough great singers
around". There were never more than half a dozen superstars at any
time, artists whose names automatically sold out the house. Caruso, Patti,
Melba, Chaliapin, Gigli, Jeritza, Melchior, Flagstad were some of the
members of that exclusive club; more recently Callas, Tebaldi, Sutherland,
Corelli, Ghiaurov. Opera lovers have deplored the bad state of singing and
talked wistfully of "golden" epochs ever since Tosi wrote in 1723, "the
profession is suffering from a precipitous decline". Our grandparents
spoke longingly of Malibran, Lilli Lehmann, Schumann-Heink, the de
Reszkes, Scotti, Caruso. Our generation remembers nostalgically the
"golden" age of the 1920s, Lotte Lehmann, Jeritza, Mayr, Schmedes,
Gigli, Pertile, Fleta, Lauri-Volpi, Tauber, Pinza. But one tends to forget
the second-rate singers and evaluates the epoch only in terms of the very
best.

The post-World War II generation of outstanding vocal artists is as rich
as any previous "golden" era. Geographically, the scene has shifted from
Europe, where two wars, lack of food, nervous unrest and postwar havoc
have decimated generations of promising young singers. Nowadays the
United States has become the reservoir of healthy voices. In the past
seasons, Bayreuth (where powerful voices are needed) has increasingly
relied on the contributions of American artists. La Scala's first revival in a
century of Rossini's *Le Siège de Corinthe*, in 1969, was sung by Beverly
Sills, Marilyn Horne, Justino Díaz. Many Italian critics agreed, reluctantly,
that a new era had begun in the history of singing. America could no
longer be kept out.

Mozart, Rossini, Bellini wrote many parts in their operas especially for
certain singers. They knew what to expect from their stars. Verdi,
Wagner and Strauss wrote mostly without such considerations; the
German composers were attacked for their demands on the human voice.
There are also managers, impresarios and celebrated conductors who don't
always understand vocal problems. They tempt singers to sing the wrong
parts, to sing the right parts too early, to sing too much. A famous
conductor needs a new Isolde, and ruins a promising artist.

The constantly increasing size of the orchestra encourages composers to write exposed high notes that will be heard above the orchestra. Musical pitch was lower at the time of Mozart and Rossini. Today's A=440 is almost half a tone higher than the A=422 in Vienna around 1800. (The Vienna Philharmoniker now play A=444 which makes violinists sound more brilliant, but it is hard on the horn players.) At the time of Mozart, the Queen of the Night in *Die Zauberflöte* had fewer problems with her devilish arias, which were then half a tone lower.

"High notes are at once the opera singer's glory and the opera singer's scourge", writes Henry Pleasants. But the composers should not always be blamed. Verdi did not put in the high Cs in Manrico's "Di quella pira" in *Trovatore*. The celebrated nineteenth-century tenor Enrico Tamberlik did, because he knew that the high Cs were where the glory, the action (and the money) were. He asked Verdi for permission. The Sage from Sant' Agata told Tamberlik it wasn't the composer's business to quarrel with the public. But the high Cs had better be good. He wasn't always as tolerant. Shortly after the première of *Aida*, he wrote to Giulio Ricordi,

> Nicolini always cuts his part !!! ... A mediocre Aida!! A soprano singing Amneris! And on top of all that, a conductor who dares to change the tempi !!! ... I hardly think we need to have conductors and singers discover new effects; and for my part I vow that no one has ever, ever, ever even succeeded in bringing out all the effects I intended ... Neither singers nor conductors ... But now it is the style to applaud conductors too, and I deplore it not only in the interest of the few I admire, but still more because I see that the bad habits of one theatre spread to others, without ever stopping. Once we had to bear the tyranny of the prima donnas, now comes that of conductors as well ... I close with the request that you tell the House of Ricordi that I cannot tolerate the above mentioned state of affairs, that the House of Ricordi, if it pleases, withdraw my last three scores from circulation (and I should be very glad of it) but that I will not tolerate any changes being made. Whatever may happen, I repeat: I cannot tolerate it.

In 1887, Ferruccio Busoni wrote, "As an Italian, I must substantiate the sad fact of the disappearance of *Don Giovanni* from the Italian repertoire ... How much is there in *Don Giovanni* that we are still not able to grasp, and of which only a new genius will inform us?" The same year, the twenty-three-year-old Richard Strauss wrote to his former teacher Hans von Bülow that he regretted being unable to join in celebrating the

Don Giovanni jubilee in the Hamburg Theatre, and added that he made "a new, very attractive acquaintance in Herr Mahler who appeared to me a highly intelligent musician and conductor ... one of the few modern conductors who knows about tempo modification".

In 1891, the hundredth anniversary of Mozart's death, G.B.Shaw, after a *Don Giovanni* performance, wrote about Victor Maurel, a famous Mozart singer (and Verdi's choice of Iago),

> I am sorry to add that alterations of Mozart's text were the order of the evening, every one of the singers lacking Mozart's exquisite sense of form and artistic dignity. Maurel, though he stopped short of reviving the traditional atrocity of going up to F sharp in the serenade, did worse things by dragging an F natural into the end of "Finch han dal vino" and two unpardonable G's into the finale of the first ballroom scene ...

And in New York at that time, the critics noted that the three stage-orchestras were often omitted from the ballroom scene because they were unable to play together. It was common practice for the two *divas*, Emma Eames and Marcella Sembrich, to force "repetition" on the Letter Scene in *Figaro* by showing the audience that the ink had spilled, "and the letter would have to be rewritten".

And in 1958, Irving Kolodin wrote in New York that "unlike programmes for athletic events in which deviations from a norm will be faithfully noted ... programmes in the opera house are notoriously noncommittal about what is actually going on". Not many people in the audience notice the liberties which some singers take with their parts, even today. Verdi wanted the end of the "Celeste Aida" aria sung pianissimo and *morendo* (dying away), but few tenors are able to do this, and many refuse because the audience might feel that the singer let them down. Instead, the last tone is bellowed out, fortissimo; if it comes off, the house erupts in applause. Many tenors transpose down "Che gelida manina" in the first act of *La Bohème*, but at the end of the act, after they walk off with Mimi, they add a top note which is not in Puccini's score.

Years ago, there was some excitement when Tebaldi sang "Sempre libera" in *La Traviata* one tone lower than written; an argument ensued between enraged purists and Tebaldi's defenders, who claimed that such things were always done. In this instance, the transposition affected the whole tonal structure. Alfredo Germont later joins Violetta off stage; as he too had to sing his supporting line one tone lower than written, he didn't sound like a youthful lover (and lyrical tenor). Some high tones are more essential than others. A Butterfly unable to sing a D flat as the climax of her entrance shouldn't sing the part at all. The D flat was intended by Puccini as a melodious and dramatic climax. Another very important entrance is made by Brünnhilde at the beginning of the second act of *Walküre* when she greets Wotan with "Ho-jo-to-ho!" ending with a ringing high C. This is a test of breath control, vocal chords and steady nerves. Some singers are unable to reach the exposed high C, or to hold it. If that happens, there is a let-down in the house which Brünhilde cannot overcome no matter how well she sings later. In *Tristan und Isolde*, Isolde sings a high C in her first narrative, and another in the second act. Both reflect the terrific emotional tension and are very important. A singer unable to produce these two top notes shouldn't attempt to sing the part of Isolde.

Opera singers rarely talk about their art, but often about themselves. Few are interested in discussing style, technique, and the future of opera. This is not merely vanity or lack of intellect. As a group they are no more conceited than, say, surgeons or scientists. Their egotism is the result of their fiercely competitive life. Most of them sing too much, travel too much, often get tense and tired; they begin to force their high notes and strain their voices. After a bad performance – and everybody has them – they are open to all sorts of doubts and anxieties. If they have first-rate vocal equipment, a mind capable of grasping their predicament, and enough will power they manage, after a vocal crisis, to come through intact. Many prominent singers go through such a crisis once in a while, using up not only the interest of their voices but also – their capital.

Surprisingly few singers understand the mystifying nature of their chosen instrument. The human voice – that converts breath into sound – is a combination wind-and-string instrument, the most expressive of all instruments and the most difficult to master. It consists of the vocal cords and certain bony cavities in the mouth, throat or nose, called resonators. The cords are comparable to the strings of a violin, the resonators to its body. But the singer – and this is one of the difficulties – has nothing tangible that is comparable to the violinist's bow. It is only his breath, controlled by various sets of muscles, that can produce sound from his instrument.

Unlike the violinist, the singer cannot see his instrument, and thus he cannot manipulate it as easily. Furthermore, not even the most skilful laryngologist can tell, by examining the vocal cords, whether the patient has the equipment of a good singer.

And here the mystery of the voice deepens. Apparently, everyone is born with similar vocal cords, and all can sing, though some better than others. Only very few, however, can sing beautifully. No matter how superior a voice may be, its owner will never become a truly great artist without acquiring a thorough knowledge of technique. (In the 1920s, Margit Schenker-Angerer, the handsome wife of a rich man, made a sensational début under Franz Schalk at the Vienna State Opera. She had a beautiful "natural" voice and some technique, but it didn't prove solid enough, and after a few years she had to give up singing on the stage).

Anyone endowed with average intelligence and a willingness to persevere can learn the technique of singing. But then another elusive element enters the picture – the singer's ability to employ the technique of using his voice with maximum effectiveness. The combination may seem natural, yet in any one era only a handful of men and women in all the world possess it. Theirs will be fame and wealth – before taxes. Thousands of singing teachers spend their lives instructing tens of thousands of pupils in the art of accomplishing this feat, but it is almost freakishly rare for a pupil to find a teacher who understands his special problems and who can make him understand how to go about solving them. There are few singers who stay with the first teacher they had.

Much of the trouble lies, no doubt, in the peculiar nature of the voice as a musical instrument. Although the singing teacher's own technique may be above reproach, there is little that even an intelligent pupil can learn by watching him sing. Nor can the teacher always perceive precisely what is physically wrong with the way a pupil is handling his voice and make specific suggestions for correcting it. It will never become known how many aspiring young singers have been ruined by their singing teachers, and it is just as well, for the number must be large and would deter anyone who feels he could become a singer from seeking out a teacher.

No one can say who is the best teacher for a pupil. The teacher's task is to find where the shortcomings originate. Some advertise a *bel canto* method yet the best assert that no such method exists. A singing technique rarely comes naturally. The singer must learn how to use, not to abuse, the muscles that are involved, directly and indirectly, in the production of sound. He must learn to control his vocal mechanism, lungs, abdomen, and diaphragm; the technique of relaxation, contraction, resonance; and there is breath control, which is fundamental. When an otherwise good voice produces certain flat notes, or there is a certain "break", is it the tightness of the muscles, false breathing, a psychological block? What may help one singer may damage another. It is sometimes said that male singers shouldn't study with women teachers, that a soprano shouldn't work with a bass, that no one should try to imitate a famous singer, that one shouldn't try to change the character of a voice, that famous singers are not necessarily good teachers. But there have been successful exceptions to the rules.

Every singer is said to have "three different voices". Of course, nobody has more than one voice. But as the singer progresses from his (or her) lowest to the highest tone, there must be smooth transition and uniform quality, which also eliminates a good deal of wear and tear of the voice. This sounds easy, yet only a few contemporary singers have attained this goal. That doesn't mean that the others were rejected by the public. Some very highly paid singers are unable to negotiate the transition with perfect smoothness. Chances are that their voices won't last as long as those who have learned to shift their vocal gears properly.

Still another baffling aspect of singing is the act of breathing. Italian opera singers long ago came up with two pointers on the subject: "To breathe well is to open up the bottom of one's throat", and "Sing *above*, not with, your breath". The meaning of the first rule may be readily apparent to anyone. The second makes immediate sense to a singer, and may even disclose its meaning to the layman who ponders it for a while. But what the Italians neglected to explain was exactly *how* to open the bottom of one's throat, and *how* to sing *above* the breath. Some singers whose technique is excellent explain that you should take the fullest amount of breath with a minimum of effort, and expend it with the greatest economy to achieve a maximum of effect, or resonance. Some take in air through the mouth, sometimes visibly and audibly. Some are able to inhale deeply but inaudibly through the nose, with no resultant swelling of stomach or abdomen or even the upper part of the chest. If a long passage doesn't allow them time for a deep breath, they take what the Italians call *mezzo fiatto* (a half breath), through the mouth, replenishing the stock of air just enough to get them through to the end. Those who master the technique can sing both *legato* and fast staccato phrases, as well as exhausting *prestissimi*, without having to draw a breath. Ideally, the audience should never become aware of the singer's breathing. A singer who sings well should never consciously think of his vocal cords; neither should he be concerned with the resonators in his head (the hard part, such as teeth and bones), or with the resonating effect of his chest. A singer who doesn't co-ordinate these resonators, or who uses only his head resonators, may sound disembodied. The principle of economy remains essential: to achieve maximum effect with minimum effort.

A singer cannot go on the stage without adequate preparation. He must vocalize, warm up his voice. No two singers vocalize in the same way, though all consider it a ritual. Each involves his own technique and sequence. Usually a singer begins warming up the middle register and then runs through the entire range. Thoughtful singers listen attentively to their own voice trying to determine what condition it is in after a night's rest, or not enough rest. The voice may also be affected by food and drink, cigarette smoke, the weather, the singer's general physical condition, and other intangibles. He sings a few long passages in a tentative fashion until confident that his voice is in good shape, responsive to his demands. Even a very great singer's voice is no great delight during his vocalizing exercises, but they are essential. The ritual may last from twenty minutes to an hour, and usually keeps the singer's singing mechanism warmed up all day. Some take a nap in the afternoon, others a walk; they may need another short period of vocalizing to regain full control of the voice before going onstage. All singers hate to be interrupted when vocalizing. Many don't like to speak afterwards, not even on the telephone, because the speaking voice often interferes with the singing voice. Some carry a scarf, even in balmy weather, and some expose themselves to the open air. Contrary to popular belief, rain and wet air are not as bad as wind, and dry air that is polluted with dust particles.

Nowadays singers, both male and female, are expected to sing beautifully and to *look* beautiful. Even in Bayreuth, today's audiences will no longer accept the ladies and *Heldentenöre* of Wagnerian proportions. The theory was that as long as they produced volume and high notes, they were permitted to look as they pleased. Today some authorities contend that a singer benefits from a moderate degree of plumpness; others adhere to the lean-and-muscular school. Too much dieting is dangerous. Sometimes the voice of a conspicuously lean singer is likely to lack opulence, though conspicuous stoutness has its drawbacks too because it may interfere with breathing. Many modern singers exercise a lot. Singing is, after all, a form of athletics, and good breathing means developing a variety of strong muscles and co-ordinating their use.

Ideally, a singer should find it almost as easy to sing as to speak; singing should be no strain at all. Only singers with a very solid technique attain this enviable state. It is believed that a well-trained singer whose technique is sound should be able to stay at the top of his profession for at least twenty years, provided he doesn't let himself in for too much wear and tear. This, of course, accounts largely for the disturbingly large turnover among first-rate singers in the recent past. Fifty years ago, although there was no radio, or television, successful singers became financially secure after ten years. Income taxes were low, and in spite of exhausting concert tours they travelled by boat or Pullman, and so were forced to give their voices a respite between engagements. They might have been tempted to let down a little on the road, far from the eyes and ears of the demanding critics and discriminating audiences in the big cities.

Modern recordings, radio and television have changed all that. Present-day concertgoers, even in remote towns, expect the very best, and why shouldn't they? Concerts are the most taxing engagements of all. Few opera singers sing more than thirty minutes during the whole evening. A concert means singing for more than an hour, in a variety of languages and vocal styles. The concert singer is the centre of attraction from start to finish, with no chorus or fellow soloists to relieve him, and only a piano by way of accompaniment, instead of the orchestral passages that mercifully help carry the opera singer along. He gets little assistance from lights, make-up, costumes or sets. And at the end of the recital the exhausted artist must accept an invitation to the house of a leading local art patron, and may even be asked to sing "just one little number".

The undeniable appeal of high notes has been explained in many ways. It is associated with virility in tenors, and with perfection where women are concerned. High notes present an element of risk and danger, like the moment at the circus when the music stops, and the acrobat starts his precarious flight through space while the drums are rolling ominously. A tenor's high C from the chest is as demanding as a soprano's pin-pointed high C as Isolde or Turandot. It should be done naturally but it isn't natural, for a woman's head voice naturally ends at the F or F-sharp.

Singers like their high notes where they are most effective and can be reached without too much difficulty. Composers often place them where they are hard to reach and not effective. "One may complain that high notes have nothing to do with music, that they represent athletic or acrobatic rather than melodic or lyrical achievement," writes Henry Pleasants. "All this is true. But argument is no avail. And many of us would be secretly sorry if this were not so."

Few singers of the past attempted to visually convey the emotions of the characters they were representing on the stage. Celebrated *divas* got away with their beautiful and impeccable vocal technique. They had some standard gestures expressing love, hatred, jealousy, scorn, and so on. Since the end of the Second World War, there has been a marked change. Some prominent singers now attempt the Stanislavski approach – that facial expression and gestures must reflect true inner feelings. The creative producers of the opera stage – the late Wieland Wagner, Felsenstein, Rennert, Schenk, Strehler, Visconti, Zeffirelli – demand complete integration of their singers. The smallest detail of the portrayal of a character must be true. This is not always easy since many operatic libretti contain artificial situations. But accuracy and realism even in minor matters improve a performance. The best singers prefer to sing their parts in the language they were originally written in, though this means studying several languages. Even in sensitive translations, many words and phrases that convey the meaning accurately enough are often incompatible with the score because of inflexion or because of the number of syllables. It is impossible to translate Wagner's *Stabreim* without sacrificing either the tonal values or the meaning of the words. But to sing Wagner in the original language is not easy for foreigners, and to sing well is not enough; the part must be convincingly performed. Undoubtedly, modern audiences demand a great deal from the artists.

THE CASTRATI

The earliest *bel canto* singers were the *castrati*, boys emasculated by surgery between the ages of seven and twelve. They kept their boyish treble voices, but acquired the lungs and chest, and thus the breath and power, of adult males.

After rigid training a *castrato* could sustain the emission of breath up to one minute or more, holding out a tone, or singing virtuoso passages. Eighteenth-century audiences went wild over such an athletic feat. The greatest *castrati* were more famous in Italy than the leading prima donnas.

When St Paul wrote to the Corinthians, "Let your women keep silence in the churches" (I Corinthians 14:34), he unintentionally created a deplorable practice that lasted for centuries. The Church forbade women to sing in church, and later in the lyric theatre. In Rome, women were not permitted to appear in opera until the middle of the eighteenth century. The first famous *castrati*, Pietro Paolo Folignato and Girolamo Rossini, were admitted as full-fledged members of the choir of the Sistine Chapel in 1599. Earlier, Orlando di Lasso had six in his choir in Munich around 1560. The last great opera *castrato*, Giovanni-Battista Velluti, died in 1861.

The famous church *castrato*, Domenico Mustafà, retired as director of the papal music in 1902. Emma Calvé described his "fourth voice", probably a falsetto, as "strange, sexless, superhuman, uncanny".

The Church, although indirectly responsible, never sanctioned the practice of emasculation. The operation was considered a crime, punishable by death. However, the famous *castrati* earned a great deal of money, and greedy parents continued to take their boys to a doctor. During the heyday of these singers, over four thousand boys were castrated every year in Italy.

An aura of scandal surrounds the sex life of the famous *castrati*. Castration doesn't limit sexual activity. There were many stories about their alleged sexual power, their love affairs with women in very high circles. Perhaps women were attracted to them just *because* they were different! In his *Memoirs*, Casanova describes a *castrato* at the Alberti Theatre in Rome, in 1762: "In a well-made corset, he had the waist of a nymph and, what was almost incredible, his breast was in no way inferior, either in form or beauty, to any woman's; and it was above all by this means that the monster made such ravages ... When he walked about the stage during the *ritornello* of the aria he was to sing, his step was majestic and at the same time voluptuous".

Castrati were like other famous artists: some were kind and some were vicious. Farinelli was a famous singer and also an accomplished statesman, decent and humble. Caffarelli was arrogant and vain. Michael Kelly, the Mozart "biographer", writes about the perils of Nancy Storace, Mozart's first Susanna. In the early 1780s, she had appeared in Florence, as second woman with Luigi Marchesi, a famous *castrato*. In an opera by Francesco Bianchi, Marchesi "in one passage ran up a flight of semitone octaves, the last note of which he gave with such exquisite power and strength that it was ever after called *la bomba di Marchesi*. Immediately after this song, Storace had to sing, and was determined to show the audience that she could bring a *bomba* into the field also. She attempted and executed it, to the admiration and astonishment of the audience, but to the dismay of the poor Marchesi." When the manager asked Nancy to stop, she refused "saying that she had as good a right to show the power of her *bomba* as anyone else". Marchesi issued an ultimatum: if Storace wouldn't leave the theatre, he would. He was the star. Nancy was fired.

The education of a *castrato* was brutal. Many were trained at the Conservatorio Sant'Onofrio in Naples. Charles Burney was there in 1770. He reports that "during the winter the boys rise two hours before it is light, from which time they continue their exercise, an hour and a half

at dinner excepted, till eight o'clock at night; and this constant per-
severance, for a number of years, with genius and good teaching, must
produce great musicians." Ten years later, Kelly visited there and "left
the place in disgust". Angus Heriot, the author of *The Castrati in Opera,*
writes that young Caffarelli had to start with one hour of singing exercises
before the mirror; in the afternoon there was theory, counterpoint,
harpsichord playing, composition. They were also trained to become
composers, to write their own ornamentations and cadences. At the age
of sixteen, they would make their operatic début, usually in a female role.
If they were lucky, they might be offered a position in some court, where
they were tactfully called "*musico*". They had long careers, and quite a
few of them lived to be seventy or eighty. The only *castrato* voice on
records is Alessandro Moreschi's, who retired in 1913 from the Sistine
Chapel Choir, though he was not a great singer.

The *castrati* were much admired in Italy where the people have a
predilection for high voices: tenors there are always more popular than
basses, just as sopranos outshine mezzos. In eighteenth-century opera,
castrati and female sopranos were often cast as heroic males. Gluck's
Orpheus was originally sung by a *castrato*. Today it is cast with a mezzo-
soprano. Handel wrote mezzo arias for the *castrato* Senesino with whom
he had almost as many problems in London as with his famous prima
donnas.

Castrati always had a pseudonym, taken from their birthplace or their
teacher. The most famous were Farinelli, né Carlo Broschi, and Caffarelli,
né Gaetano Majorano. Farinelli spent ten years as an important member
of the Court of King Philip v of Spain. Every night he would sing four
songs, always the same, to the melancholy monarch, to alleviate the
King's grave depression. Under Philip's successor, Ferdinand vi, Farinelli
acquired so much power that it was reported, "Farinelli drills tenors and
sopranos one day and ambassadors and ministers the next". He'd been a
pupil of Niccolò Porpora, the greatest singing teacher of his time.
Porpora was brutal but he got results. The young Joseph Haydn met
Porpora in Vienna in 1753, and remembers, as quoted by Georg August
Griesinger, "There was no lack of *asino* [fooling about] and pokes in the
ribs, but I put up with it all, for I profited greatly with Porpora in singing,
in composition and in the Italian language."

After Farinelli's début in Naples, when he was fifteen, he went to Rome
where he won a competition against a trumpet player, which remains a
great *bel canto* legend. Burney reported,

During the run of an opera [probably by Porpora] there was a struggle every night between Farinelli and a famous player on the trumpet in a song accompanied by that instrument: this at first seemed amicable and merely sportive, till the audience began to interest themselves in the contest, and to take different sides. After severally swelling a note in which each manifested the power of his lungs and tried to rival the other in brilliancy and force, they had both a swell and shake together, by thirds, which was continued so long, while the audience eagerly awaited the event, that both seemed exhausted; and in fact, the trumpeter, wholly spent, gave it up . . . when Farinelli, with a smile on his countenance, showing he had only been sporting with him all that time, broke out all at once in the same breath, with fresh vigour, and not only swelled and shook the note, but ran the most rapid and difficult decisions and was at last silenced only by the acclamations of the audience.

Some authorities call Farinelli "the greatest singer who ever lived". His scales, trills and "nightingale imitations" in "Quell' usignuolo", by Geminiano Giacomelli, were incredible. The nightingale song was one of the four he had to sing every midnight for poor King Philip v. Afterwards, he had to stay up with the King until five in the morning. No wonder he became a powerful influence. Later, he produced opera for the court, brought fine singers to Spain, commissioned libretti from Metastasio and had them set by various composers. In 1750, he won a well-deserved knighthood in Spain. Burney writes, "His talents had effects upon his hearers beyond those of any musical performer in modern times".

The other great *castrato*, Caffarelli, five years younger than Farinelli, was quite different. (Handel wrote for him the famous "Largo" from *Serse*; "Ombra mai fù".) He was vain and arrogant, always involved with irate husbands (once he had to spend most of the night hiding in a cistern), and sometimes didn't care when he was in bad voice. Metastasio wrote to Farinelli about Caffarelli's appearance in Vienna, in 1749, noting "a ridiculous tone of lamentation which can turn the most cheerful allegro sour". Yet Caffarelli was so admired in Italy that he could do no wrong even when he was "disturbing the other performers, acting in a manner bordering on lasciviousness with one of the female singers". Occasionally he spent a few days in prison, and was often involved in duels. Once he had to leave France within seventy-two hours, after insulting Louis xv about the size of a snuff box that happened to be a personal gift from the

King. In the end, he built himself a nouveau-riche palace in Calabria, bought a dukedom with it, and had an inscription put up over the portal, "Amphion Thebas, Ego Domum" (Amphion built Thebes, I this house). The Neapolitans laughed and said, "Ille cum, tu sine" (He with, you without).

Another famous *castrato* was Luigi Marchesi, the creator of the *bomba*, who insisted on making his first entrance "descending a hill, his arrival heralded by a fanfare". A German contemporary described his voice as "perfectly pure and silvery, extending from the low C to D above C. With the loveliest declamation and deportment, he combines much musical insight. In the execution of passages and the so-called hammer stroke (*il martello*) he is commonly reckoned superior to Farinelli." The last famous *castrato* was Giovanni-Battista Velluti. He met Rossini in 1813 when he appeared in the first performance of Rossini's *Aureliano in Palmira* in Milan. In his *Life of Rossini*, Stendhal writes,

> At the first rehearsal with orchestra, Velluti sang the aria straight through, and Rossini was dazzled with admiration; at the second rehearsal, Velluti began to embroider the melody, and Rossini, finding the result both exquisite in performance and well in keeping with his own intentions as composer, approved, but at the third rehearsal, the original pattern of the melody had almost disappeared beneath a marvellous filigree-work of embroidery and arabesque.
>
> At last there dawned the great day of the première. The *cavatina* itself and Velluti's whole performance created a furore; but Rossini found himself confronted with insuperable difficulties in trying to identify what Velluti was supposed to be singing; his own music had grown completely unrecognizable ... The young composer's vanity was deeply wounded: his opera was a failure and all the applause had gone to Velluti, his soprano.

Rossini instantly "drew the inevitable conclusions from this humiliating experience". Henceforth, he would write the singers' embellishments himself. A few years later, Beethoven brusquely refused to change the *tessitura* of some difficult passages in the Ninth Symphony and the *Missa solemnis*, which Henriette Sontag and Caroline Unger, both very young at that time, had requested. He told them, "to learn it and it will come". Handel and Mozart were wiser, substituting an aria that was too difficult for a singer. Wagner and the composers after him wouldn't do it either.

THE PRIMA DONNA

The prima donna remains the most fascinating person in opera. Often declared dead and buried, as opera itself, she remains indestructible. Let us hope she will always be with us, for she puts the bubbles into the operatic vintage champagne.

The prima donna is a phenomenon that transcends the world of opera. She is a semi-public figure, the object of ardent admiration and violent dislike, the centre of galas and scandals. She need not have a beautiful voice or a beautiful figure, but she must have that certain magic that makes her, for one evening, the centre of her universe. Hated or loved, she leaves no one indifferent. Both her admirers and detractors agree that she is unique. The prima donna is surpassed only by another phenomenon: two prima donnas. Happily, there has always been more than one at the same time. Pasta had Malibran, Grisi had Lind, Melba had Eames and Sembrich, Lotte Lehmann had Jeritza, and Callas had Tebaldi.

The prima donna is adored by her public, hated by her colleagues, and feared by her employers, the managers of the great opera houses. A great tenor can be murder, but a great *diva* is worse. The only people today who are not afraid of her are the leading star conductors and producers. The royal battle between a Karajan and a Callas is the supreme spectacle of the operatic world.

Vittoria Archilei was an early prima donna but her primacy was soon threatened by Adriana Basile from Naples who appeared in Florence around 1610, a few years after the "birth" of opera. The title "prima donna" was not yet known. Madame Basile, "bell' Adriana", was beautiful and blonde, with black eyes and a voluptuous figure. She married a Neapolitan named Muzio Baroni and went from Florence to Mantua where Duke Vincenzo Gonzaga was an early-baroque patron of music and opera. As the ruler of a small state which was often threatened by its more powerful neighbours, especially Parma, the Duke shrewdly aimed for artistic prestige rather than political power. (In Austria today, the Vienna State Opera and the Salzburg Festival have done more for their country's image than the politicians.) The Duke composed madrigals and played the cembalo. He appointed Monteverdi court composer, Torquato Tasso court poet, and Rubens court painter. A handsome man, he was always involved with women. (He was once said to have spent a night with a complaisant lady in a brothel and was almost killed by a hired assassin, not unlike his namesake, the Duke of Mantua in Verdi's *Rigoletto*.)

Great *divas* appeared at his Court and were expected to sing and engage in extra-curricular activities. Adriana Baroni, "Sirena del Posillipo", was no exception. Then the Duke's younger brother, twenty years old and already a cardinal in Rome, fell in love with Adriana who sang the title role in Monteverdi's *Arianna*. Her great monologue, the "lament of Arianna", became very famous and was later often imitated. A special theatre costing two million scudi was built for the première. Baroni earned 200 scudi a month, Monteverdi not more than fifty. Ever since, prima donnas have made more money than celebrated composers.

After the death of Duke Vincenzo in 1612, Mantua was invaded by the mercenaries of General Aldringen, who burned down the palace, destroying Monteverdi's manuscripts. Later, Monteverdi went to Venice. There Baroni became the star of his operas, and those of his pupils, Cesti and Cavalli. After her retirement, a book, *Il Teatro della Glorie della Sign. Adriana Basile*, contained all the articles and reviews praising her. Her daughter, Leonora, became more famous even than Baroni. Cardinal Respigliosi, later Pope Clemens IX, admired her; Milton dedicated a poem to her; and Cardinal Mazarin invited her to sing in Paris. The prima donna had become an international institution.

An early-baroque prima donna was Georgina who made her career in Rome, and later went to Sweden where Queen Christina gave her asylum. Georgina next showed up in Naples where the Viceroy Medinacoeli fell in love with her. When he was exiled to Spain, the *diva* surprised everybody by attending him. Later she was permitted to return to Rome. In France, Marthe le Rochois was the first great prima donna. She was ugly, "with thin arms . . . she always wore long gloves", but a great actress. Her Armide (in Lully's opera) was famous for her regal bearing and excellent song. At the age of forty-eight she retired with a state pension of a thousand francs. Her successors were two *femmes fatales*. Madame Desmatins once planned to have the opera director assassinated. An anonymous chronicler reports that she managed to have the archbishop of Paris poisoned because he'd left her for another lady. Worse even was the notorious Maupin who wore men's clothes, called herself "Monsieur d'Aubigny," and kept the company of pretty women. She was much cheered in Lully's *Cadmus et Hermione*. After getting involved in duels with several men and killing one, she had to leave Paris. She went to Spain, but later returned again. She died in her thirties.

In London, Handel, as manager of the Haymarket Theatre, imported Francesca Cuzzoni from Parma. The critics compared the range and power of her voice to that of the famous *castrati*. Then Handel made the mistake of hiring another *diva*, Faustina Bordoni, and offering her twenty-five hundred pounds a year, five hundred more than he was paying Cuzzoni. He hoped that the rivalry between the two prima donnas would stimulate interest in opera. He was right: soon there were duels, affairs, pamphlets, fist fights between the fans of Cuzzoni and Faustina. Burney wrote that the rivalry destroyed "theatrical tranquillity". Lady Pembroke commanded the Cuzzoni fans, Lady Burlington the Faustina forces. Handel tried to appease both *divas* by giving them good parts. In his opera *Alessandro* (1726) he composed roles of equal importance. They behaved well, and eleven performances were given. The following year, during Buononcini's last London opera, *Astianatte*, a fight broke out in the pit, and spread to the stage where Cuzzoni and Faustina began to pull each other's hair. (The following year, *The Beggar's Opera* parodied the Italian opera.) Faustina went to Italy and Cuzzoni to Vienna where she was paid 24,000 guilder a year. According to the *London Daily Post*, she killed her husband, the composer Pietro Giuseppe Sandoni, and escaped to Holland, where she was jailed for her debts. The sensible Dutchmen let her out of jail in the evening so she could perform and pay her creditors; afterwards she was taken back to jail. She retired to Bologna where she died in abject poverty in 1770.

Faustina went on to become the first lady of European opera. She married the German composer, Johann Adolf Hasse, and went with him to Dresden, where the couple got a large salary from Duke August the Strong. Dresden became a centre of Italian opera in Germany. For some time Hasse was more famous than Handel, not to mention the modest St Thomas cantor in Leipzig, Johann Sebastian Bach. The Dresden opera reflected the philosophy of the baroque: no one cared about the drama as long as sets and costumes were sumptuous. The best boxes were reserved for the aristocracy. Burney praised the clarity and the speed of the "allegro singing" of Hasse-Bordoni, as she called herself. She could sing "accented legato", virtuoso runs and was praised for her recitative and elocution. When the Seven Years War finished off the Dresden opera, Hasse and his wife went to Vienna and later to Venice.

When Fräulein Gertrud Elisabeth Schmeling, in 1765, gave a concert in her home town, Kassel, a certain Carlo Morelli, *primo uomo* of the Landgrave of Hesse, reported, "Ella canta come una tedesca", she sings like a German. In Berlin, Frederick the Great once said that he would rather have his horse neigh than hear a German *diva* sing. Elisabeth took the name of her husband, Giovanni-Battista Mara, a cellist in the orchestra of Frederick's brother, Prince Henry of Prussia. When the King had problems with Mme Mara, he would imprison her husband until his wife gave in. When Grand Duke Paul of Russia went to Berlin on a state visit, in 1776, Frederick celebrated the event with an opera by his Court Kapellmeister, Johann Friedrich Reichardt. Mara refused to sing one of the arias which she didn't like, and the King sent her husband to jail again. Mara sang the opera, but so softly that no one could hear her. The Grand Duke complimented her, "presumably out of politeness or ignorance, for he certainly didn't hear me". She was a real prima donna. Four years later she and her husband escaped to Bohemia.

Mara sang only in Italian or English, never in German. There was no need: Handel and Hasse wrote their operas in Italian, Gluck in French. Mara's voice reached from the low B to the three-staff F, and her cadenzas, trills and fioriture were said to be fantastic. In London she often sang in concerts, and appeared with Haydn. Burney called her "a divinity among mortals". But she refused to act saying, "Why should I sing with arms and legs? I have my voice". In Paris, the ladies said that Mara wasn't very chic. Goethe called her *höchst vollendet* (most perfect) and wrote a poem for her eighty-second birthday.

Angelica Catalani, born in Sinigaglia in 1780, was known as *prima cantatrice del mondo*. Stendhal wrote, "Her voice is filling the soul with a kind of astonished wonder, as though she beheld a miracle". Queen Charlotte, however, said that she wanted cotton wool in her ears when Catalani sang. The age of florid song was coming to an end. Catalani was too late, for a new era had discovered a different kind of singing. She sang the part of Susanna in Mozart's *Figaro*, "embellishing" the music, and incidentally appropriating the Cherubino aria, "Voi che sapete". She sang Paisiello's aria, "Nel cor più non mi sento", to which Pierre Rode, the famous violinist, and Giacomo Gotifredo Ferrari had written variations, and she embellished the variations, by way of fighting a duel, which she won, against the violin. Napoleon heard of her fame and offered her 100,000 francs if she would stay in Paris. Catalani later called the audience with Napoleon "the most terrible hour of my life". She refused, and went to London where her benefits netted 90,000 guineas, including a payment of 200 guineas for singing *God Save the King*. All prima donnas love money, and like their earnings well publicized. Catalani developed other whims that remain the characteristics of many prima donnas. In Leipzig, she had the rug on the podium removed because it wasn't "worthy" of her;

instead, she placed an Indian scarf on the ground and stepped on it. The public gave her an ovation. More recently, Maria Jeritza and Maria Callas have shown a similar fancy for elegant trappings.

Catalani was a social climber and married a French diplomat named Valabrègue, who was expensive and lost her earnings playing cards. But she always made money; at the Teatro Fiorentino in Naples she arranged a concert, with the tickets seven times the normal price, and sold out. Even when she had to sing "against" Giuditta Pasta, Henriette Sontag and Maria Malibran, Mme Catalani remained *la prima donna assoluta*. Goethe met her in Marienbad and immediately wrote a poem for her. She asked him "what instrument he was playing". Goethe said he wasn't a musician, he was the author of the *Werther* novel. Catalani said, yes, she remembered it, "a very amusing book".

The age of *bel canto* was ending though two great tenors still practised the art: Manuel del Pópolo Vincente García and Giovanni-Battista Rubini. García, the original Almaviva in Rossini's *Barbiere*, is now remembered as the father of two famous prima donnas, Maria Malibran and Pauline Viardot. He was the most famous singing teacher of the nineteenth century; in 1825, he introduced Italian opera to New York. One of his favourite parts was Don Giovanni, written by Mozart for bass-baritone. His son, Manuel García, was the teacher of Jenny Lind and Mathilde Marchesi, who taught Melba, and thus the art of *bel canto* was handed down to some singers of the twentieth century. García's son died in 1906, at the age of one hundred and one.

Giovanni-Battista Rubini was the great tenor of Donizetti and Bellini. He was not good-looking and was an indifferent actor, but all that was forgotten when he began to sing. After the première of *Lucia di Lammermoor* in Paris, in 1837, when Rubini sang Edgardo, the critic Pierre Scudo wrote about "the sob of fury which Rubini emitted from his trembling mouth". Bellini much admired the tenor. While he composed *Il Pirata*, Rubini would sing each song for him after Bellini wrote it down. Anton Rubinstein said that he formed his ideas about "noble and eloquent phrasing" from the example of Rubini. Liszt who toured with the great tenor also admitted that he'd learned to phrase on the piano after listening to Rubini. The tenor retired to his birthplace, as so many Italian singers do. In Romano di Lombardia, near Bergamo, he built himself a palazzo which is now a museum. When he died, in 1854, Henry F. Chorley wrote in *Thirty Years' Musical Recollections* that "the tradition of his method died with Rubini". It was the end of *bel canto*.

The end of florid singing coincides with the end of the *opera seria*. The reforms of Gluck, the *buffo* operas of Mozart, the works of Cherubini and Beethoven had imperceptibly changed people's taste. The *opera buffa* masterpieces of Paisiello, Mozart, Cimarosa, and Rossini were becoming popular. The orchestra became more important, and the singers had to be more than mere vocal virtuosi. Gluck and Mozart had created their *dramma per musica*. It wasn't enough to make a spectacular entrance and sing florid arias.

The first prima donna of the new era was Pasta, née Giuditta Negri, born of Jewish parents, in Saronno, near Milan. She studied in Milan and became famous in 1822, when she was twenty-four. She remained *the diva* for the next ten years. Coins were minted showing "the incomparable Pasta". She must have been a "modern" singer, with a pronounced flair for dramatic parts. She might sing badly but (as Callas in our day) would always excite her audience. When she sang Paisiello's *Nina* in Paris, the *Allgemeine Musikalische Zeitung* reported, "Not only did this enchantress hold her listeners spellbound, she was herself so seized and carried away that she collapsed before the end". Brava! We need more women like Pasta to keep opera alive. Stendhal regretted that Rossini never composed a work for her:

> If ... Rossini were to discover a voice which never fails to thrill our very souls with the passionate exaltation which we used, long ago, to capture from the masters of the golden age; a voice which can weave a spell of magic about the plainest word in the plainest recitative; ... if Rossini were to discover such a world of wonder, who doubts that the miraculous would happen, that he would shed his laziness like a garment, settle down unreservedly to a study of Madame Pasta's voice, and soon start composing within the special range of her abilities?

Pasta created the part of Amina in *La Sonnambula* and of Norma in 1831, which makes her part of musical history. Stendhal compared her to "the mood over a lovely landscape". Chorley, who knew more about music, wrote that "Pasta never changed her readings, nor her effects, or her ornaments; what was to her true, once arrived at, remained with her true forever". She never spared herself; but she may have been a mezzo, as Stendhal indicated, who forced her high tones, and later she paid for it. She didn't last long on the stage, and died in 1865.

Her competitor was Maria Malibran, the elder daughter of the great Manuel del Pópolo Vicente García. She was a mezzo soprano, and, above all, a very great actress, often performing in a very dramatic manner, and straining her voice. Malibran would identify herself with her parts. Around 1830, Malibran and Pasta often appeared in the same repertoire in Paris and London. There were the inevitable comparisons. Ernest Legouvé, the French critic, saw Pasta as the daughter of Sophocles, Corneille, Racine; and Malibran as the daughter of Shakespeare, Victor Hugo, Lamartine. The real opera lovers were happy with both of them. Liszt wrote in 1838 to his publisher, Maurice Schlesinger, about "those divine secrets of a Malibran or Pasta who gave a single note or a single phrase an irresistible inflexion". Later Schumann said that Liszt's art was close to that of Paganini and Malibran.

Malibran studied singing with her famous father. According to a story that, I hope, is apocryphal, the composer Ferdinando Paër and a friend passed Manuel García's house in Paris, and heard terrible screams from a window. Paër said, "It's nothing serious – just García beating trills into his daughter". She first sang in Paris when she was sixteen, and made her début a year later in London as Rosina in *Barbiere*. In 1825, she sang in Meyerbeer's *Il Crociato in Egitto* opposite the *castrato* Velluti. That year the García family went to New York. Maria Malibran was heard in *Barbiere, Otello* (Rossini), *La Cenerentola, Romeo and Juliet, Il Turco in Italia, Don Giovanni*. The company performed at the Park Theatre. Rossini's *Barbiere*, the first Italian opera heard in America, was so successful that it was often given during the following months.

Years later, Lorenzo da Ponte wrote about the first American performance of "his" *Don Giovanni*. He was then an old, broken man who had failed in the grocery and liquor business and was teaching Italian. Public opinion was divided between admirers of Rossini's *Barbiere* and partisans of *Don Giovanni*. Da Ponte writes about an American gentleman, "a great lover of music", who usually went to the opera to sleep, asking his friends to wake him up for the main arias (the type still exists in present-day opera houses). Da Ponte sat next to him during a *Don Giovanni* performance and was surprised: his neighbour didn't fall asleep. Later he told da Ponte, "You don't go to sleep at a performance of an opera like this, and you don't sleep after it all night". The American gentleman really understood opera.

Maria Malibran sang the part of Zerlina. Richard G. White, the American music critic, called her "the most accomplished vocalist, the most dramatic singer, in all respects the most gifted musical artist of modern days ... She had such beauty of person and charm of manner that she became the most supreme of prima donnas – the sort of woman who from her first appearance has been accustomed to see the world at her feet". Malibran was both "the idol of society" and "admired by the general public". She was not only "fascinating", but "as good as an angel". She married François-Eugène Malibran, a French merchant in New York. He was fifty and she was seventeen. Her father didn't like it and he turned out to be right. A few months after the wedding, M. Malibran was bankrupt, in jail, "a prisoner for debt". He admitted that he'd married Malibran for her money. She paid his debts and left him. Nine years later she met the man she really loved, Charles de Bériot, the great Belgian violin virtuoso. She was a nice woman who, on Sundays, between performances in *The Devil's Bridge* at the Bowery Theatre, would join the choir in Grace Church, at the corner of Broadway and Rector Street.

Opera manners were different then. During a performance of Rossini's *Otello*, people got bored and asked Desdemona to sing "Home, Sweet Home". Malibran had to oblige, then continued to suffer as Desdemona. (Melba later fulfilled similar requests but at least she waited until the end of the opera.) Malibran went back to Paris, and performed in Rossini's *Tancredi*, for the benefit of her rival Henriette Sontag. Perhaps she was really "as good as an angel". Bellini became so excited when he heard her that he went backstage to embrace her. One day, the great bass, Luigi Lablache, asked her why she didn't sing in Italy. (Lablache was in Vienna in 1827, when Beethoven died, and sang in the memorial performance of Mozart's *Requiem* and paid the other singers out of his own pocket.) Malibran went to Milan and created such excitement at La Scala that the police had to clear the house. In Venice a convoy of gondolas received her "like an empress". She died shortly after a fall from a horse in London. Sir George Smart, the conductor, recalls that she collapsed in Manchester after singing a duet with Maria Caterina Caradori-Allan: "I'll sing it again but it will kill me", she said, when people asked for an encore. It did kill her. "She passed over the stage like a meteor", wrote Chorley. She was twenty-eight when she died, in 1836. One year later, on the same day – 23 September – Bellini, who had liked her so much, died also.

In 1828, when Malibran returned to London from America, she often sang with (and against) Henriette Sontag. There began another "war of the prima donnas" that delights impresarios, box-office managers and fans. In Paris they appeared together in *Don Giovanni*, Sontag as Donna Anna, Malibran as Zerlina. Malibran had the more famous admirers (Rossini, Bellini, Chopin, de Musset, Lamartine) but Sontag had the more beautiful voice – and Malibran admitted it. "My God!", she exclaimed once, "why does she sing so beautifully?" In Paris, the two *divas* disappointed their admirers when they embraced each other on the stage and broke into laughter.

Henriette Sontag, born Gertrud Walburga Sonntag, in Koblenz, in 1806, came from a theatrical family. Her mother was an actress. At the age of nine, the *Wunderkind* made her début in Prague, and next she appeared in Vienna. Weber liked her so much that he offered her the title role in *Euryanthe*. After her first performance in Berlin, in 1825, in *L'Italiana in Algeri*, the actress Karoline Bauer wrote,

> There appeared on the deck of the ship a slight, youthful girl in a sky-blue skirt and a tiny feathered hat framing a charming, forget-me-not face ... The voice was neither full nor strong but pure as a bell, clear as a pearl, silver-bright, mellifluous, particularly in the middle, flexible and of seductive sweetness. And how beautifully she trilled – like the bright jubilation of a soaring lark. Incomparably enchanting was her *sotto* voice ...

No wonder that Berlin, "normally so cold, so businesslike, so sober, was a madhouse, full of instant rapture and enthusiastic, pure madness". Karl von Holtei, the librettist, wrote, "I've seen more beautiful women, greater actresses ... but never have I experienced such an intimate communion of charm, fascination, loveliness of sound".

In 1827, Sontag married Count Carlo Rossi, a diplomat at the Sardinian legation. The Sardinian Court in Turin refused to sanction the marriage. The social standing of a prima donna was not what it is today. This would have ended the career of Count Rossi. The Court finally agreed to the marriage, but Henriette Sontag had to retire from the stage. King Friedrich Wilhelm III named her a Freifrau (Baroness) von Lauenstein. She accompanied her husband whose career took him to The Hague, Frankfurt and St Petersburg where Czar Nicholas I asked her to appear in *La Sonnambula* and *Lucia* at the Court Opera. Turin reacted angrily but the Czar wrote, "What Countess Rossi does at my court, in accordance with my wishes, may never in any way be called unfitting". In 1848, Count Rossi retired. For a while the Rossis lived in Berlin in genteel poverty. Sontag's fortune had been wiped out by inflation and her husband's gambling (indeed the husbands of several prima donnas were incurable gamblers). Then Benjamin Lumley, the London impresario, offered Sontag a six-month contract. In 1849, she appeared at Her Majesty's Theatre in the title role of Donizetti's *Linda di Chamounix*.

Chorley wrote, "The first notes were sufficient to reassure everybody that the artist was in her place again ... All went wondrously well". Later, Sontag went to America where she sang too much. She died of cholera in 1854, in Mexico City.

Maria Malibran's younger sister, Pauline Viardot, was the greatest mezzo-soprano around the middle of the nineteenth century. (The García dynasty did for singing almost what the Bach family did for composition. When Pauline's father was born, in 1775, Mozart was writing his violin concertos. Pauline's son, a good violinist, died in 1941.) As a girl, Pauline sometimes accompanied her celebrated sister on the piano but never appeared with her on the stage. The sisters were quite different. Viardot began as a gifted pianist, studied with Liszt, and performed with Clara Schumann. In 1839, she made her début in Paris and London as Desdemona in Rossini's *Otello*, reminding many people of Malibran in the same part. She became famous at once, sang Donna Anna, Norma, Rosina. In 1840, she married Louis Viardot, the director of the Théâtre-Italien in Paris. Pauline Viardot was the first "intellectual" prima donna: a great musician, a great actress, a great woman. She wasn't satisfied just to sing well; she would completely identify herself with the parts she was singing. Musset said she was able "to get tragic inspiration from her musical inspiration". Though she would sing some bravura pieces, such as a version of Tartini's *Devil's Trill* sonata, she was not satisfied with vocal acrobatics. Heinrich Heine said, "She is no nightingale who has only talent to weep and trill, and she is no rose for she is ugly, of a sort of noble ugliness". A picture shows a matinée at the Villa Viardot. Pauline plays the organ. Anton Rubinstein is at the piano. Among the guests are the German poet Theodor Storm, King Wilhelm I of Prussia, Bismarck, and Ivan Turgenev.

The love story between the great Russian poet and Pauline Viardot is an authentic legend in prima donna history. Though she was deeply in love with Turgenev for forty years, she never divorced her husband. Books have been written about the fascinating and touching *ménage à trois* (April Fitzlyon, *The Price of Genius*), and the poet himself wrote what he felt, in his famous play *A Month in the Country*. In her youth Pauline had seen much unhappiness in her parents' home when her sister Maria, still legally married to M. Malibran, had a child by Charles de Bériot. Later, Pauline accepted in her own home Turgenev's illegitimate daughter. She must have been a very unusual woman, and it is no accident that so many unusual men adored her: de Musset, Heine, Berlioz. Among her friends were Chopin and George Sand, Delacroix, Rossini, Schumann, Liszt. She admired Mozart more than any other composer (she owned the original score of *Don Giovanni*) and loved the oratorios of Handel and Mendelssohn.

Her closest "musical" friend was Meyerbeer who would not allow any new work of his to be performed in Paris unless Pauline had a part in it. He'd originally written *Le Prophète* as a vehicle for Gilbert-Louis Duprez as John of Leyden; as the great dramatic tenor was no longer in top form, Meyerbeer rewrote his opera around the role of Fidès – the mother who denounces her own son, the first great "mother role" of the century. As Fidès, Pauline Viardot became one of the great artists of the century, and firmly established the mezzo-soprano on the opera stage. Fidès probably later influenced Verdi when he created Azucena, the gypsy mother, in *Trovatore*. Pauline Viardot inspired Gounod to write *Sapho*, his first opera, with a great mezzo part, and Saint-Saëns to write *Samson et Dalila*. No one wanted to perform the opera, which was said to be too serious, but Pauline gave the second act privately at her summer place, singing the part of Dalila. The best was still to come. Brahms wrote his *Alto Rhapsody* for her and she sang the solo part in Jena, on 3 March 1870.

Mezzo-sopranos remain the Cinderellas of opera. No mezzo-soprano, alto or contralto (as she is called when her voice has a darker, deeper timbre such as Marian Anderson's) attains the fame or earns the money of a great soprano or coloratura, the ladies with the thrilling high tones. Pasta and Malibran never reached prima donna status although Malibran sang Leonore in Beethoven's *Fidelio*, an exposed soprano part, and Pasta was the first Norma. Perhaps they were not genuine mezzo-sopranos (Ernest Newman called them "messy sopranos").

Exponents of the lower range must study hard, have sonorous low tones and should be able to sing a high C. They are also expected to tactfully blend into the background as gypsies, duennas, old maids, mothers, witches (*Frau ohne Schatten*), a blind woman (*La Gioconda*), a teen-ager (*Hänsel und Gretel*). If Bizet, Verdi, Saint-Saëns, Wagner and Strauss hadn't intervened, the poor mezzos would have long jumped into the orchestra pit. And even Verdi wasn't always helpful. In *Aida*, Amneris has some beautiful arias and the more elegant costumes, but every opera novice knows that she isn't going to get her Radames, though she has the last word in the opera. No wonder that many mezzo-sopranos attempt the more spectacular soprano parts. It takes wisdom and fortitude

The Opera

to go the opposite way as Regina Resnik did who began as Aida and later switched to Amneris. Even Carmen, the greatest mezzo part of all, is no longer exclusive, since the higher-range ladies now give their own, "sophisticated" versions of the great seductress. Rarely is the mezzo permitted to look seductive and glamorous. In *Elektra*, her mother, Klytämnestra, is a subject for advanced students of Professor Freud. In *Il Trovatore* and *Un Ballo in Maschera*, the mezzo should look as disgusting as possible. Even Mozart, who called all women singers soprano, treated her shabbily: Marcellina in *Figaro* whom no one wants, and Dritte Dame in *Zauberflöte*. If she is a borderline mezzo, she may be Dorabella in *Così*.

Verdi developed the mezzo character when he gave her the splendid part of Princess Eboli in *Don Carlos*; her great aria "O don fatale" usually brings down the house. And the great old man lavished his subtle irony on a mezzo in *Falstaff*. Dame Quickly, of "Reverenza" fame, the only one of the three merry wives of Windsor who doesn't interest Falstaff is the one who gets him, though quickly and briefly, in the last act. A wonderful joke for a mezzo with a sense of humour.

And there is Wagner, who also called all women sopranos, until he wrote the *Ring*, but created parts that are now in the mezzo domain. In *Tannhäuser,* Venus (who should look the part) is seen dimly and rejected by the tenor; in *Lohengrin*, poor Ortrud spends the whole first act standing on the stage, singing only a few lines in an ensemble; in *Walküre*, Fricka is *the* nagging wife; and in *Meistersinger*, Magdalena always looks a little ridiculous next to David, the apprentice, who could be her son. No, the mezzo's lot is not an easy one.

"When I look back on my life as a whole", Richard Wagner wrote with customary overstatement in *My Life*, "I can find no event that produced so profound an impression upon me. Anyone who can remember that wonderful woman at this period of her life must to some extent have experienced the almost satanic ardour which the intensely human art of this incomparable actress poured into his veins." The incomparable actress was Wilhelmine Schröder-Devrient who sang Leonore in Beethoven's *Fidelio* in Dresden in 1823, when she was nineteen, and helped Beethoven to make his opera a success, after two tragically false starts (Wagner himself was only sixteen when he heard her in *Fidelio* in 1829 in Leipzig). Yet the less excitable Chorley agrees with Wagner. "There was a life's love in the intense and trembling eagerness with which she passed in review the prisoners . . ." Exactly what I felt when Lotte Lehmann, the greatest Leonore of my life, performed the scene. Schröder-Devrient (and Lotte Lehmann) began her career at the Hamburg Theatre. She started out as a dancer, became an actress, and made her début at the Burgtheater in Vienna in 1819 as Aricia in Schiller's *Phädra;* her mother played Phädra. Two years later, she made her opera début as Pamina in *Zauberflöte*, and later sang Agathe in *Freischütz*. Weber conducted and called her "the best Agathe in the world". She was also the first Senta in *Der Fliegende Holländer*, and the first Venus in *Tannhäuser*.

Her record in history is established though she never tried to sing the Italian parts. Italian composers want melodious singing while many German composers, especially since Wagner, prefer declamatory song (Strauss's *parlando*, Schönberg's *Sprechstimme* and Berg's idiom all go back to it). The German language, with its many consonants, is not an ideal singing language as is the mellifluous Italian, rich in vowels. Towards the end of her singing life, when Schröder-Devrient sang the German *lieder* repertoire, the critics often complained that she would declaim rather than sing.

Privately, Wilhelmine was not a German *Hausfrau*; on the contrary, she transposed the passions of her operatic parts into her personal life. She had three husbands and many lovers. She shocked the good burghers of Dresden when she declared that their dull life was "no grist for my art". In the end, she was not certain that she had accomplished anything. "Unfortunately, I can point to no results, and only throat-clearing and spitting succeed from time to time", she wrote to Clara Schumann in 1850, ten years before her death.

Labels and clichés survive certain people and their achievement. Jenny Lind remains the "Swedish nightingale". The "nightingales" were several nineteenth-century coloratura prima donnas. Not just sopranos who managed to sing high tones, but genuine coloraturas, carefully trained, who could reach the high E or high F with no difficulty, and could always – this is important – sing lyrically and beautifully. A true coloratura uses no tricks, has the full scale, and sings the delicate staccato runs that have been the despair of would-be coloraturas ever since Mozart created the "fiendish part" of the Queen of the Night. The coloratura's repertoire is charming rather than exciting. Besides Mozart, Rossini, Donizetti, Bellini, Meyerbeer and Verdi also wrote for her. Verdi gave the coloratura a new, dramatic dimension with the title role in *La Traviata* and Gilda in *Rigoletto*. Richard Strauss, no friend of the coloratura ladies, created the ultimate test of virtuosity and musicality with Zerbinetta's "Grossmächtige Prinzessin" aria in *Ariadne auf Naxos*.

Coloraturas often start young. Their voices retain a sweet purity. Because they must be technically correct, they rarely experience vocal crises, and continue to sing over a long period. Giulia Grisi, Henriette Sontag and Jenny Lind all sang well at the age of fifty, Melba until her sixties, and Patti still sang in public when she was seventy. They are rarely dramatic actresses but their vocal virtuosity often delights opera lovers.

Even among coloraturas, Jenny Lind remains a phenomenon. She had more admiration, and made more money, than any other nineteenth-century prima donna except Adelina Patti, yet she acted completely unlike a *diva*. For a while, she was managed by the improbable and inimitable Phineas T. Barnum. She would earn ten thousand dollars for a concert. Even today she remains an enigma. She was never involved in a scandal. Her alleged attraction to Hans Christian Andersen is almost an Andersen fairytale. He admired her, but died a bachelor. She married her able accompanist, Otto Goldschmidt, and lived a dull, domestic life. Her favourite part was Norma, and she was often called "the *casta diva* among prima donnas", which has a Barnumesque flavour. She also sang Giulia in Spontini's *La Vestale*, and Lucia, but she refused to sing Donna Anna, unless the original recitatives were used, and Mozart's finale was included when she sang in *Don Giovanni*; she permitted no changes in the oratorios of Handel and Mendelssohn, although in other works she would sing her own cadenzas and *fioriture*.

At the age of twenty-nine she retired from the opera stage because "opera wasn't worthy" of her. She sang only *lieder* recitals or in oratorios, which were "more religious". She also talked a great deal about "devoting myself to charity". Present-day historians of opera take an uncharitable view of her. "Her whole life was a series of pious, sanctimonious attitudes, relieved, when she chose to turn it on, by compelling charm", Henry Pleasants writes in *The Great Singers*. "More astonishing than any of her vocal miracles is the plain fact that she could put these attitudes over. On the stage she may have been less than a great actress, although she certainly was a good one. Off stage she was supreme".

Many of her letters show her as a cold, often calculating woman who cleverly promoted her saintly image, the ugly duckling who became famous, sweet and so good! Born in Stockholm in 1820, she was the child of a bigoted schoolteacher. Her own mother didn't want her and put her into foster homes until she was nine; then she studied as an actress-pupil. At sixteen she was a full-fledged actress. She never had a real home, and no one ever gave her emotional warmth. One can easily see the connection between the "nightingale" and the "*casta diva*".

She studied with the younger García in Paris who later said that he never had to explain anything twice to Jenny. García had many famous pupils, yet he kept only her picture in his studio. She left Paris with a violent and irrational dislike of the French, "a nation shut out from the common portion of God's blessing upon men, and deservedly so". The true Jenny was beginning to show. She never sang in France, and never in Italy, another "immoral" country. She was a sensation in such "moral" cities as Vienna, Berlin, London. She sang well, and her image – innocent and pure and "spiritual" – enchanted her audiences and the critics. Heine recalls that during her concert tour in England the church bells were rung for her, as though she had just descended from heaven (after one of her early performances, Hans Andersen said, "It showed art in its sanctity"). Even Mendelssohn and Clara Schumann agreed; and Eduard Hanslick, the tough Viennese critic, wrote about "her warbling and piping ... a thing of the most enchanting beauty in the mouth of Jenny Lind".

What made her accept Barnum's offer to go to America? She needed little money for herself. She'd started a Mendelssohn Foundation in Leipzig, and in England she gave "ten thousand pounds in six months" to various charities. Her Barnum-managed American concert tour is remembered as a promotion miracle in the annals of American music. Ten thousand people heard her concerts in New York. Tickets would fetch several hundred dollars on the black market. "It is a gift of God to make so much money and be able to help people," dear Jenny wrote from Boston. Her programme always included some Swedish songs and the ever-popular "The Last Rose of Summer". At the end of her American tour, she bought up the remainder of her contract with Barnum; she thought he made too much money from her. That was a mistake. "His showmanship had been exactly right for her", Joan Bulman writes in *Jenny Lind*. "They formed the perfect partnership. When she worked alone, she had to bear the limelight as the 'woman without fault', while at the same time those faults she had began to show – and they were not of a kind that Americans found endearing". When she left America in May, 1852, her image had faded. But elsewhere she remained the much admired "Swedish nightingale" until her death in 1887.

Eduard Hanslick, who had no use for Richard Wagner (whereupon Wagner made him immortal as the prototype of Beckmesser in *Meistersinger*), called Adelina Patti "a musical genius". He wrote, "Patti's Zerlina creates the illusion of a beautiful natural phenomenon, perfect, artless, inexplicable". George Bernard Shaw called her "the spoiled child with the adorable voice", and that her "offences against artistic propriety are mighty ones and many". Who was right? Perhaps both. Patti's first recording – one of the earliest, made in 1905 – is Cherubini's "Voi, che sapete". Her voice is bird-like, light and graceful (one must, of course, discount the primitive technique of the recording). She pays not too much attention to phrasing and rhythm, yet somehow the recording, which she made at the age of sixty-two, has a truly Mozartean flavour.

She had a beautiful, though rather cool voice, a "white" voice, which ranged from C to high F and she used it perfectly. She was the *prima donna assoluta* of her time, from 1860 to 1900, an epoch of golden voices. Patti fascinated her public with her voice and manners, and her rags-to-riches story. The daughter of a Sicilian tenor and a Roman soprano, she became famous and rich, and lived in a castle. She consented to sing for emperors, czars and queens. Nellie Melba, who later inherited Patti's crown, wrote in her *Melodies and Memories*, ". . . the most golden voice to which I have ever listened. The timbre was exquisite, the diction crystalline. I took my lesson from her for she had much to teach".

Patti had no doubts about herself. After she became famous, her contract stipulated that she didn't have to attend rehearsals, and that her name must be printed "at least one third larger" than the names of other artists (though the larger-print clause was not unknown in Hollywood in the 1930s). She gave "farewell performances" for years, and eventually retired to a castle in Wales.

Most prima donnas, rather than ask for a certain amount of money, demand "just a little more than anyone else". Patti was possibly the most avaricious *and* prodigal of all prima donnas. As soon as she'd earned "a little more than anyone else", she would throw the money away. In St Petersburg she stayed in a hotel suite of twelve rooms where exotic plants had been placed, and "gilded cages in which nightingales sang for their great rival". After her performance, she appeared on the stage with the Czar and the Czarina, while a rain of flowers came down on them from above, six thousand dollars worth of flowers, paid for by the members of the wealthy Jockey Club. After another Patti performance, six Russian generals waited for her in the lobby of her hotel, placed her in a "flower chair" and carried her to her suite while an orchestra played.

Were Patti alive today, she would be the darling of gossip columnists and illustrated magazines. Avarice is not a virtue, but it may become a legend when practised by a great prima donna. After a soirée in the house of a Parisian aristocrat, her host sent Patti a magnificent diamond ring in lieu of the customary cheque. Instead of a thank-you note, she sent word back to her host that he may have forgotten to add her salary. For once though she'd taken on more than she'd bargained for. The aristocrat sent her a ring with a much smaller stone, and his apologies. He had indeed made a mistake, he wrote: the smaller ring was Madame Patti's salary. Would she please return the large stone which was "for another great *diva*".

She liked luxury and comfort even on the operatic stage, where sopranos are often expected to die in misery. The American baritone David Bispham writes in *A Quaker Singer's Recollections*,

> I shall never forget her closing scene in *Aida*, where she and the tenor are supposed to be immured in a tomb of stone. At the close of the duet, Patti, who had instructed the stage manager to make her comfortable, would carefully adjust a sofa cushion which had been placed conveniently at hand. She would kick with one high-heeled Parisian slipper a train behind her, and, assisted by the tenor, would compose herself in a graceful position – and die.

One of the most amusing Patti stories is told by Colonel J.H. Mapleson, the flamboyant English nineteenth-century impresario, in *The Mapleson Memoirs*. At two in the afternoon, shortly before a performance of *La Traviata* in Boston, Signor Franchi, Patti's agent, went to collect her contractual fee, five thousand dollars. Mapleson was "at low water just then" and could offer "only the trifle of eight hundred pounds [then four thousand dollars] as a payment on account". The agent declined the money and went to talk to his client. He then informed Mapleson that the Colonel was a "fortunate" man. Mme Patti would take the four thousand dollars and would be at the theatre in good time for the beginning, "dressed in the costume of Violetta, with the exception only of the shoes". As soon as she received the balance of one thousand dollars, she would put on her shoes, and make her appearance on the stage.

After the opening of the box office, Mapleson had another eight hundred dollars which he gave to Patti's agent who informed him that the great prima donna already had one shoe on. "Ultimately", writes Mapleson, "the other shoe was got on, but not, of course, until the last forty pounds [two hundred dollars] had been paid".

Yet even her great admirer, Hanslick, had to admit that Patti "is no Traviata, no *dame aux camélias* . . . the piquant *haut-goût* of the demimonde is completely wanting". Hanslick considered this "a fault which I would rather praise than condemn", and hastily added that "such delicate shading from piano to expiring pianissimo . . . I have never heard before". The prima donna may often be wrong, but she can do no wrong, so far as her public is concerned.

Shaw was exasperated because Patti would often end her opera performances (a piano having been pushed through the curtain) with "Comin' thro' the Rye", or "Home, Sweet Home". Shaw wrote, "Will not some sincere friend of Madame Patti's tell her frankly that she is growing too big a girl for that sort of thing?" Yet Henry Krehbiel in the New York *Tribune* wrote, "Mme Patti has every reason to feel glad and grateful at the admiring esteem which is awarded to her by the public in New York".

Adelina was Italian, born in Madrid, brought up in New York, and her first language was American-English, a combination worthy of a Nabokov character. She started her career at the age of seven in New York. Her father let her sing Rosina's aria "Una voce poco fa", from Rossini's *Barbiere*. It remained her most famous achievement. At fifteen she sang the terribly difficult part of Lucia. At sixteen, in 1861, she made her début in Covent Garden as Amina in *La Sonnambula*; that day, 14 May, was the beginning of "Patti's reign" in England. Three years later she sang the part in Vienna. Hanslick, totally bewitched, wrote, "When she begins to sing and act, both eye and ear are happy to say yes to the rash judgement of the heart. What a youthful fresh voice, ranging evenly and effortlessly from C to the F above the staff. A silver-clear, genuine soprano, it is wonderfully pure and distinct, particularly in the higher tones. The middle register has a suspicion of sharpness but the impression is rather of brisk morning freshness. The lower register still lacks force. Her bravura is considerable, more brilliant in leaps and staccati than in legato. Over all is immeasurable charm."

Later, even Verdi wrote to Patti, after her performance in *Rigoletto*, "alla mia unica è vera Gilda". Her greatest roles were Rosina, Norina, Amina, Lucia, Zerlina, Violetta and Aida. Her rivals never surpassed her. Christine Nilsson (no relation to today's Birgit) was another "Swedish nightingale", who became famous and rich in America and lost her money, which she'd invested in real estate, after the fires in Chicago and Boston. Pauline Lucca, a Viennese, was an interesting *diva*, on as well as off stage, where she broke batons and contracts, was three times married and had herself photographed in Bad Ischl with Bismarck, which created some excitement. Towards the end, Patti had to contend with Marcella Sembrich, Emma Calvé, Emma Nevada, and Nellie Melba. But until her death, in 1919, she remained "the Queen of Song".

CARUSO

Caruso was unique. He remains the most fascinating, and most dearly remembered singer of the twentieth century. Fifty years after his death, his records sell at a brisk pace. Best of all, Caruso is still very much with us – at the Metropolitan, at La Scala, in Covent Garden, in the studios of voice teachers, and in the minds and hearts of singers all over the world. He is a living presence, comparable only to Toscanini. Tenors are often, and unfairly, measured against him. If one of them has a trace of Caruso's metallic timbre, people say wistfully, "He's wonderful but he is no Caruso". In America John McCormack was known as the "Irish Caruso", but after Caruso's death, McCormack said, "The greatest tenor is dead, and the next one has not arrived".

Many singers have attained fame in a role with which they remain associated: Tamagno as Otello, Lotte Lehmann as Marschallin, Callas as Norma, Chaliapin as Boris Godunov, Jeritza as Tosca, Richard Mayr as Ochs von Lerchenau. Caruso remains identified with a large repertoire ranging from Rossini to Puccini. He was the greatest tenor of his time: his closest rivals, Allessandro Bonci and Giovanni Zenatello, couldn't touch him. Among Caruso's successors were some outstanding tenors: Leo Slezak from Moravia who sang both the German and Italian reper- toire, a great Lohengrin and a great Otello; Giovanni Martinelli, strong and brilliant; Beniamino Gigli, a sweet, lyrical tenor, singing with extra- ordinary ease (he could sing an impeccable high C sitting on a chair); Giacomo Lauri-Volpi, a great Andrea Chénier and Calaf (in *Turandot*); Aureliano Pertile, a sensuous, full voice; Tito Schipa and Miguel Fleta (the original Calaf) who specialized in pianissimo singing; the great Richard Tauber, a famous Mozart tenor with an incredibly sweet timbre who later sang the operettas of his friend, Franz Lehár, which the critics didn't forgive; in Vienna, Alfred Piccaver from England was almost as famous as Caruso was elsewhere. Each of them would have been the *primo tenore* except that there was Caruso.

The legend of Caruso, the greatest tenor, often conceals the story of Enrico Caruso, a lovable man with no star allure. Francis Robinson, his admiring biographer, writes that Caruso sang 607 times in eighteen seasons at the Metropolitan. "His record of cancellation is almost zero. Once he was announced to sing, he sang". Caruso's deep sense of responsibility, to his public and his management, made him sing even when he should have called off a performance. This noble attitude hastened his death.

He died, in 1921, at the age of forty-eight, of cancer of the throat (exactly as Puccini died, three years later, he who had always admired Caruso). Could Caruso have lived much longer had he spared himself? The doctors later thought he might have kept his great voice, but possibly not the breath to control it.

Caruso was born in Naples, in 1873, and grew up in poverty, the eighteenth of twenty-one children. As a teenager, he began to sing the Neapolitan folk songs that we now love so much on his recordings. He sang them everywhere, in the street and on the beach. He might never have learned to sing if his mother hadn't helped. Somehow she scraped together the money for his lessons and encouraged Enrico who was a sensitive, shy boy. His début in Naples, in Morelli's *L'Amico Francesco*, was no sensation. But when he sang at Milan's Teatro Lirico (not at La Scala), in Giordano's *Fedora*, he was successful, and as Nemorino in Donizetti's *L'Elisir d'Amore*, he created "a sensation in the annals of the Teatro alla Scala", writes Giulio Gatti-Casazza. (*L'Elisir* was known as a "Caruso opera" and it was in the part of Nemorino that he broke down at the Brooklyn Academy of Music, on 11 December 1920, when, coughing blood, he couldn't finish the performance.) But his home town rejected him in the part of Nemorino. Caruso learned the bitter truth that a prophet is not without honour save in his own country. He sang the tenor solo in Verdi's *Requiem* which Toscanini conducted one week after Verdi's death, in January, 1904. Verdi-Toscanini-Caruso: the apotheosis of opera, which remains an Italian art.

Caruso took good care of his voice, wearing a fur coat and woollen muffler even when he walked only a few steps to a car. He would never tell the driver where to take him; a friend or attendant would do all the talking. He would walk the two short blocks from the Hotel Knickerbocker to the Metropolitan Opera House between two men who protected him against autograph hunters and admirers, so he wouldn't have to talk to anyone in the street. If he was asked a direct question, he wouldn't answer, pointing regretfully at his throat. He wouldn't go into a room where other people were smoking; however, he might smoke a cigarette when he was especially nervous during a performance. Even then he would never inhale. On the day of the performance he wouldn't speak on the telephone or receive a visitor.

Much has been written about his voice but each Caruso recording is better than a thousand words. It wasn't an ideal tenor voice, with its metallic, almost baritonal timbre, but the combination of his voice, beautiful singing and personality created a glorious impression; people sensed instinctively that this great tenor was also a fine human being. He had to work hard to make his voice the magnificent instrument which it later became. His classmates in singing class called it a "glass voice" because it would break in the high tones. When he came to the B-flat in Don José's "La fleur que tu m'avais jetée" (*Carmen*), he would crack the high note. But slowly and carefully he built up the top. It was a virile tenor's voice and it affected people because there was something mysterious and deeply moving in it, an exhilarating quality that very few singers are ever blessed with. Caruso's voice evokes passion. Intensely human, it expresses and magnifies man's joy and suffering.

His wife, Dorothy, writes in *Enrico Caruso, His Life and Death*, "His humanity was deep, his humour was broad, his faith was high ... His consciousness of being his own source was the force which spurred him towards perfection ... He didn't preach tolerance, kindness, generosity, justice, resourcefulness – these requisites of wisdom were the elements of which he was made". When young people asked him what a great singer needed, Caruso said, "A big chest, a big mouth, ninety per cent memory, ten per cent intelligence, lots of hard work, and something in the heart". (Two hundred years earlier, Pier Francesco Tosi wrote in his observations on the florid song, "Oh, how great a master is the heart! Confess it, my beloved singers, and gratefully own that you would not have arrived at the highest rank of the profession if you had not been its scholars ... ")

Caruso never spoke ill of his rivals, and almost all of them loved him though his colleagues occasionally wearied of his predilection for practical jokes on the stage. Nellie Melba called him "a simple, lovable creature", loved his generous heart and was touched "by his complete lack of snobbishness"; she was always afraid, when she appeared with him, that he would try to brighten up the lachrymose scenes in opera, of which there are many. In the last act of *La Bohème*, when poor Mimí is dying in an iron bed in the middle of the stage, surrounded by beautiful melodies and tearful listeners, Caruso often felt he had to cheer people up. Once Melba staggered onstage as the dying Mimi, and when the Bohemians pushed the bed from the wall to the centre of the stage, a collective gasp went through the auditorium of Covent Garden. Caruso had secretly placed a chamber pot under the bed which stood revealed in splendid isolation.

An uncomplicated man who loved to eat spaghetti, drink Tuscan wine, and smoke terrible cigars, Caruso made no compromise where his art was concerned. In a touching letter to his wife he writes about a performance as Radames in *Aida*,

I mounted myself and taked my public. There were many calls and
people were crazy ... Heats, umbrellas, hendekacifs, canes all in the
aria, a shouts that arrived in heaven. I think many people will have no
voice for many days ... I must give my soul to take the public.

The confession and the secret of Caruso's art: he gave his soul to take his
public. He never stopped working. At the Metropolitan alone he sang
thirty-seven different parts.

The recording industry never paid off its everlasting debt to Caruso.
In the days of the phonograph, many artists were ashamed to have their
voices recorded. Caruso brought dignity to the new medium. One day in
1906, he was approached in Milan by F. W. Gaisberg of the Gramophone
and Typewriter Company in London. Caruso agreed to sing ten arias in
one afternoon, for a hundred pounds (about fifty dollars for one record).
In London, the executives considered this an "exorbitant" demand, and
forbade Gaisberg to record. Fortunately, he ignored them. Caruso sang
ten arias in two hours. According to Gaisberg, he made no mistake, took
his hundred pounds and left. It was probably the most profitable deal in
the history of the Gramophone and Typewriter Company. Caruso made
his last recordings in 1920. His lifetime royalties were estimated to be
between four and five hundred thousand pounds.

Caruso was not a very great actor, but he trained himself to do everything right. He would adjust his gloves as he made his entrance in the first
act of *Rigoletto*, and he would play with a pack of cards while singing
"La donna è mobile", one of his favourite parts. He had his disappointments. He was depressed when Puccini refused to give him the part of
Cavaradossi in the world première of *Tosca* (which went to Emilio de
Marchi). Caruso was in the Covent Garden première of *Madame
Butterfly*, with Emmy Destinn and his friend Antonio Scotti. Puccini
later said, "He's singing like a god".

THE LAST GOLDEN AGE

The last golden age of singing – the end of the nineteenth century, and
the early years of the twentieth – is dominated by the towering influence
of Richard Wagner who was not the singers' best friend. Wagner put the
German repertoire, and German singers, into the great opera houses of
the world. He wasn't, of course, the first German opera composer.
Gluck, Beethoven, Weber, and Mozart (with *Entführung* and *Zauberflöte*)

had come before him. But their singing requirements were modelled after the Italians. Wagner's were his own. He created his super-orchestra, and compelled the singers to sing forcefully. Some people said he made them scream. Furthermore, they had to scream in German, a language rich in consonants. Only healthy voices using correct techniques could withstand such demands, without getting prematurely damaged.

Yet Wagner understood the relation between language and music. He knew that the German language, essentially dramatic, needed its own musical idiom, and he created the declamatory style. Older singers, brought up on Rossini, Donizetti, Bellini, even on Bizet and Gounod, couldn't cope with Wagner's demands. This didn't bother Wagner at all. Having developed his own instruments and his orchestra, he went on to educate his Wagnerian singers. Among the early ones were Ludwig Schnorr von Carolsfeld who died at the age of twenty-nine, possibly because Wagner had overtaxed him with his demands for atrociously long rehearsals. His last words were, "Farewell, Siegfried! Console my Richard!" Schnorr expired in true Wagnerian style and Wagner, usually cold-blooded about his artists, was moved. "My King!", he wrote to Ludwig of Bavaria, "He was ... consecrated to me, faithful to me ... In this singer I have lost much". Other prominent Wagnerian singers were Amalie Materna, the first Kundry; Albert Niemann, the first Siegmund (*Walküre*); Hermann Winkelmann, the first Parsifal; Emil Scaria, the original Gurnemanz.

And there was Lilli Lehmann (no relation to Lotte) who sang a hundred and seventy roles in a hundred and nineteen operas, in German, Italian, and French. She was an intellectual artist who would not compromise in artistic matters. Her book, *Mein Weg*, is still much admired. She made her début at seventeen at the Prague German Theatre as First Lady in *Zauberflöte* and later replaced an indisposed soprano as Pamina. In Prague, she met Richard Wagner and was impressed by "his yellow damask dressing gown, red tie, a black coat lined with pink atlas". She reached stardom slowly. At the first Bayreuth Festival, in 1876, when she was twenty-eight, she was one of the Rhine Maidens. Wagner wrote, "Oh, Lilli, Lilli – you were the best of all and – you, child, were right – that will never be again. That was the greatest magic, my Rhine Maiden ... " Twenty years later, she was in Bayreuth again, singing Brünnhilde, but it was no longer the same. She couldn't get along with Frau Cosima's direction and dared to antagonize her; it took real courage to do that.

The Wagnerian repertoire was only one side of her art. She could sing almost anything. Hanslick called her creations "products of a superior mind". She wasn't modest, and she was tough, though she was self-disciplined, thorough, idealistic – very German. One night she attended a *Tristan und Isolde* performance under Gustav Mahler at the Vienna Court Opera. A few minutes before the last act, Anna Bahr-Mildenburg, who had sung Isolde, became indisposed. Lilli Lehmann was sixty and hadn't sung Isolde for four years. She put on Bahr-Mildenburg's costume and finished the part. Another time, at the Metropolitan, she took over, at four in the afternoon, the part of Fricka in *Rheingold*, which she had never studied. David Bispham, who sang Alberich, later wrote, "Let me say that there is not one artist in a thousand, perhaps not another in the world, physically, nervously, mentally and musically able to perform such a feat".

She was the first German singer who sang a universal repertoire. Later, Ernestine Schumann-Heink, Emmy Destinn, Maria Jeritza, Lotte Lehmann also showed unusual scope in their choice of parts. (Two pupils of Lilli Lehmann were Olive Fremstad and Geraldine Farrar. Today many Americans have shown similar adaptability, singing the German, Italian and French repertoire.) As an old lady, Lilli Lehmann produced *Don Giovanni* in Salzburg; she sang Donna Anna. The great baritone, Francesco d'Andrade, was Don Giovanni. Later, in her production of *Die Zauberflöte*, Lilli Lehmann sang the First Lady – the part in which she'd started her career half a century before. She died in 1929 at the age of eighty-one, a great artist.

The last golden age of singing was a golden time for opera lovers. The nineteenth-century Italian repertoire was sung, Meyerbeer was still popular, the French operas of Bizet, Gounod, Massenet were given, and there were Verdi and Wagner. The era was particularly rich in male voices, and for the first time, the lower voices – baritones and basses – became popular. The earlier Italian composers had preferred tenors; Rossini wrote three tenor parts in his *Otello*. Verdi created great lower register parts: Rigoletto, Macbeth, Count Luna in *Trovatore*, King Philip in *Don Carlos*, Iago and Falstaff; he shared the Italian fascination for high voices but he understood that the baritone voice is the normal male voice. The French composers contributed Méphistophélès in *Faust*, Escamillo, Don Quichotte, and Wagner created the great parts of the Dutchman, Hans Sachs and Wotan.

Victor Maurel remains famous as Verdi's first Iago and Falstaff. He was an intellectual artist, who considered the voice a means of dramatic characterization, and was very sure of himself. When Verdi, having admired him as Simon Boccanegra, said he would write Iago for him, Maurel expected the opera to be called *Iago*; he even demanded it. Verdi was irritated, ignored the demand, but gave him the part since he was the best singer at that time. Verdi was a practical man.

Francesco Tamagno remains identified with Verdi's first Otello, but there the similarity with Maurel ends. Tamagno looked like the son of a simple Piedmontese restaurateur, which he was. He could sing a glorious high C – some said he shouted it – and he knew the value of his high C (he once added five extra high Cs to the *stretta* in the last act of Rossini's *Guillaume Tell*). After the glorious *Otello* première in Milan, Tamagno stepped out on a balcony of the hotel, and sang "Esultate!" The people in the street had come to cheer Verdi, not him. Verdi was not pleased, but he had learned to understand tenors.

Jean de Reszke was a great tenor, and a great artist. Born in Poland in 1850, he was elegant and aristocratic. He sang the great Italian and French parts (Radames, Don José) and also Tristan and Walther (*Meistersinger*). (His brother, Edouard, was a famous bass.) The critics agreed that no one had sung Tristan and young Siegfried as beautifully, but Jean de Reszke's career ended six years after his first Tristan; many people said he'd shortened his career by singing Wagner's demanding *heldentenor* parts. P. G. Hurst (*The Age of Jean de Reszke*) wrote that he'd committed vocal suicide. Perhaps he just sang too much; once he sang the parts of Roméo, Faust, Don José and Siegfried within six days. To the Wagnerians he proved that Wagner's great parts should be sung by singers who know the art of beautiful singing. A lyrically sung Tristan is finer than a shouted Tristan. But few non-German tenors of the Italian-French repertoire have dared follow de Reszke's example; most of them leave Tristan and Siegfried to the German and Scandinavian Wagnerian tenors.

The golden age was not limited to the singers of Europe. The first American stars appeared in European opera houses and at the Metropolitan. Minnie Hauk, a famous Carmen, and Emma Albani sang in Germany. Lillian Nordica, born in Farmington, Maine, sang Isolde opposite Jean de Reszke's Tristan. (An American and a Pole in Wagner's holy love epos; some Ur-Wagnerians must have wondered what the world was coming to.)

American singers around the turn of the century had the same problems as today. There were no small opera houses in their country where they could learn by experience. They had to go to Europe and sing in several foreign languages. If they wanted to succeed, they had to be better than the European singers. They had to be genuine, European-made stars if they aspired to sing at the Metropolitan. Nordica had talent, ambition and a wide range of roles. Once she sang Violetta the night after her Brünnhilde (*Walküre*). It is not true, as is often claimed now, that "in the old days" the stars sang less, only that they moved around less. (Hans Hotter, the great bass-baritone, once appeared in Aspen, Colorado, between two performances in Bayreuth within ten days.) Nordica could sing a thrilling high C but some people said she had a certain coolness. Shaw praised her vocal skill but noted her "inability to fill up with expressive action the long period left in *Lohengrin* by Wagner for that purpose" and called her "Elsa of Bond Street". Philip Hale, the Boston critic, wrote after *Les Huguenots* that "Nordica ... did not touch the heart". This is a common complaint by European critics today about some noted American singers. Their voices and technique are admired but "they don't touch the heart". But Americans usually work hard to overcome that handicap, and many succeed. Nordica did. Towards the end of her career, she was praised by Philip Hale for "moments of vocally emotional beauty" as Marguérite in *Les Huguenots*.

The last golden age had its *prima donna assoluta*: Nellie Melba, born Helen Porter, near Melbourne, Australia, in 1859. For almost forty years after 1888, she was the "Queen of Covent Garden", where her appearances were known as "Melba nights". Everybody was there who was anybody, including the Royal Family. Melba was also the great *diva* in Paris, Milan, New York, Chicago. At the height of her career she would get ten thousand dollars for one concert. The Prince of Wales, later King Edward VII, was her admirer, and the Duc d'Orléans was the great romance of her life – a prima donna storybook life. Melba even had the (reluctant) admiration of her competitors, which happens rarely among prima donnas. Mary Garden, in *Mary Garden's Story*, writes about the high C which Melba sang, already off stage, at the end of the first act of *La Bohème*,

> ... The way Melba sang that high C was the strangest and weirdest thing I have experienced in my life. The note came floating over the auditorium of Covent Garden; it left Melba's throat, it left Melba's body, it left everything, and came like a star and passed us in our box and went out into the infinite ... My God, how beautiful it was.

Melba's intonation was impeccable, and her technique was almost perfect. She had studied with Mathilde Marchesi who was a pupil of the great *bel canto* teacher, Manuel García the Younger. Shaw wrote admiringly that "she sings really and truly in tune". Her repertoire was small, and as she became famous, it got smaller. People wanted to hear Melba only in her best parts: Lucia, Gilda, Juliette, Desdemona, Mimi. A recording she made with Caruso in 1910, in America, of the love duet of *La Bohème*, is beautifully done. Her voice glows with an inner fire and emotion; at the end, the two great voices blend in a heavenly pianissimo. "When I sing with Caruso in *La Bohème*, I always feel as if our voices had merged into one", she once said. John Pitts Sanborn Jr, the American critic, called Melba's voice "sculptural – it has the quality of physical form". Massenet called her "Madame Stradivarius", and Joseph Joachim, the great violinist, compared Melba's voice to his Stradivari violin ("A Stradivari," he explained to her, "sounds small in a small room and swells as the room increases, always retaining its beautiful quality"). The critics discussed where nature ended and art began with Melba, which was perhaps the highest tribute paid to her art. Her sustained notes were perfectly even, with no trace of tremolo; she had no mannerisms, no vocal tricks. A coloratura (like a violinist) must never give the impression of labouring under technical difficulties. A great coloratura *diva* must give her audience the impression that she enjoys bringing off a formidable *tour de force*, making it a *tour de joie*. Her trill alone would have made her famous; it was facile, pure, brilliant – the trill of a bird.

She was never a great dramatic actress. After her first Manon, at the Metropolitan, *The New York Times* critic wrote, "Madame Melba has the voice of a lark and, so far as her acting is evidence, the soul of one also". She kept both her voice and her emotions under control, and thus saved her vocal cords. This and her impeccable technique enabled her to sing in opera in her late sixties. "The secret of her clarity of tone is her ideal looseness", *The Times* critic in London wrote after her farewell concert at the Albert Hall, when she was sixty-seven. "Last night it was very noticeable how she slipped away from the consonants, giving them the least possible value, to get the musical part of the word, the vowel".

There is a peculiar fascination in a pure, beautiful "white" voice that soars to dizzy heights with complete facility. Melba could sing a high D, a high E, and a high F, two and a half tones on top of the high C, and there was not the smallest change in the quality of tones from bottom to top. There was no suspicion of throatiness. The critics admired "the Melba attack". "The term 'attack' is not a good one," wrote W. J. Henderson. "Melba indeed had no attack. She opened her mouth and a tone was in existence. It began without any betrayal of breathing; it simply was there."

When Verdi heard Melba as Desdemona in his *Otello*, he was enchanted. Desdemona is a musically difficult part; no unmusical singer could do it well, certainly not to the satisfaction of the old maestro. When Arthur Nikisch heard her sing her entrance phrase in *Faust*, "Non, monsieur! Je ne suis ni demoiselle, ni belle", he rushed backstage to tell her what an artist she was, and invited her to sing with his Leipzig Gewandhaus Orchestra. In her famous essay "On the Science of Singing" Melba wrote, "The singer's mission is to interpret the message of the composer, and not to mutilate or embellish it with extraneous ideas", but she didn't always practise what she preached. As Rosina, in Rossini's *Barbiere*, she would sometimes sing "Stille Nacht", an Austrian song, in an eighteenth-century Spanish setting!

Her sang-froid was famous. While singing the Mad Scene in *Lucia* at the San Francisco Opera House, she saw flames break out in the gallery, and there were shouts of "fire!". Melba calmly stepped to the footlights and asked everybody to file out in order. When the frightened conductor began to scramble up from his platform to the stage, Melba gave him an imperious look and shouted, "Stay where you are, Bimboni!", and when he continued his hazardous climb, she gave him "a resounding crack on the head". Her melodramatic début at La Scala had been preceded by threatening anonymous letters: she would be poisoned, the lift in her hotel would crash, and if she dared venture out into the street "a stiletto would be waiting for her". But by the time she was halfway through the Mad Scene in *Lucia*, the audience was under her spell, and afterwards the ovation lasted for ten minutes. The critic of the *Corriere della Sera* wrote, "Many are the stars who have fallen on the stage of La Scala. Madame Melba won a great battle yesterday". After her farewell in 1926, she went home to Australia where she died in 1931.

Melba never had real competition. Marcella Sembrich and Emma Eames were not in her league. Luisa Tetrazzini and Amelita Galli-Curci sang only coloratura parts, thrilling their audiences with virtuoso *fioriture*, crowned by E's and F's at the end of a cadenza. When Tetrazzini sang at Oscar Hammerstein's Manhattan Opera House in 1908, she was hailed as "a new Melba". The real Melba left no doubt in her memoirs as to what she thought of *that*.

Emma Calvé, born one year before Melba, never had Melba's fame though she was the better actress. Shaw found her Santuzza (*Cavalleria Rusticana*) "irresistibly moving and beautiful", and compared her to Eleanora Duse. She was a versatile artist. In *Figaro* she sang three parts –

Cherubino, Susanna and the Countess. She said she had "three voices" and later acquired a disembodied "fourth voice" after studying with Mustafà, one of the last *castrati* at the Sistine Chapel, who advised her "to practise with your mouth shut tight for two hours a day for ten years". Calvé did it in three years, and proved it in Massenet's *Sapho*. She became a very great Carmen. Shaw wrote about her "power of seduction which she exercises without sense or decency", and he was so shocked by her death scene, "horribly real", that "nothing would induce me to go again: to me it was a desecration of a great talent. I felt furious with Calvé". What would Shaw have felt about some latter-day Carmens?

Two other contemporaries of Melba were Mary Garden from Scotland and Geraldine Farrar from Massachusetts. The centre of prima donna gravity was moving towards the Anglo-Saxon countries. Garden remains unforgotten as Debussy's beloved Mélisande. "Just that one little phrase, 'il fait froid ici', came from her lips, and you shivered under the chill winds that blow between the worlds of the real and the unreal", Frances Alda wrote in *Men, Women and Tenors*. She was a great singing actress. "Every one of these women I sang had a special quality of her own, and in every one of them I had a different singing voice", she remembered. ". . . Salome was vice personified; Louise was *l'amour libre;* Mélisande was mystery, secrecy; Sapho was the common cocotte of Paris, and I made my voice that."

Geraldine Farrar was, like Mary Garden, a glamorous woman, small, slender and very pretty. She studied with Lilli Lehmann, "a hard task-master who demanded the ultimate". Elderly Metropolitan *aficionados* remember her as Tosca, Butterfly, Carmen, Mimi, Manon. She was an artist with a fine sense of phrase and pace, and she had a celebrated argument with Toscanini who went to the Metropolitan during the 1908–9 season. She told him, "Maestro, I am a star", and the Maestro observed that the stars are in heaven. She didn't repent and she was right when she pointed out that "the box office" was on her side. She was, next to Caruso, the most popular singer at the Metropolitan ·she sang Butterfly ninety-five times in sixteen seasons. She retired in 1922 from the Metropolitan. When she died in Connecticut, in 1967, many old subscribers remembered her with warmth and sadness.

After the turn of the century, the operatic stage was dominated by non-Italian singers. The great stars were Marcella Sembrich (Polish), Melba (Australian), Garden (Scottish), Eames and Nordica (American), Emmy Destinn (Czech), Lilli Lehmann (German). And there were the brothers de

Reszke (Polish), Maurel (French), Ernest Van Dyck (Belgian), whom Beecham called the best Tristan. When *verismo* swept the opera houses with the works of Mascagni, Leoncavallo, Giordano and Puccini, a new generation of great Italian singers appeared: many of them are already familiar to record collectors. They sang the difficult parts in the new operas with dramatic tension and much realism. Antonio Scotti is remembered as Maurel's successor; many thought he was a greater Scarpia, Iago and Falstaff than Maurel (the greatest Falstaff of our generation was Mariano Stabile). Another baritone super-star was Titta Ruffo, one of the "grandest" voices of all time. Even his colleagues were unable to describe his voice. Giuseppe de Luca, a great baritone, called Ruffo "a miracle", which in itself is a miracle. Maurel called Ruffo's top notes "the most glorious baritone sounds he ever heard" and Ruffo's recording of "Nemico della patria" from *Andrea Chénier* proves it. Caruso and Ruffo recorded together "Sì, pel ciel" from *Otello* in 1914, one of the finest recordings ever made. They never appeared together in the opera, because Caruso never sang Otello.

Another super-star of the era was Boris Chaliapin, born in Kazan in 1873, one of the greatest basses of all time. He became *the* Boris Godunov, but he was also unique as Méphistophélès in Gounod's *Faust*, Don Quichotte, Leporello, Don Basilio. He was a big singer, big in anything he did, even in his excesses. He would instruct conductors about *tempi*, his fellow singers about interpretations, the chorus where to stand. He is not the only temperamental bass. Michael Bohnen also liked to conduct the orchestra from the stage, while he was singing. At the Rome Opera, Boris Christoff, during a *Don Carlos* rehearsal in which he sang the part of King Philip, got into an argument with Franco Corelli, the tenor who sang Don Carlos, and both drew their stage swords. Not long ago, two famous Italian singers, Cesare Siepi and Vladimiro Ganzarolli, had a violent argument during *Don Giovanni* at the Vienna State Opera. As a result, only three singers were on the stage during the final sextet, an ironical twist to Mozart's ironical finale.

The critics were often shocked by Chaliapin's personal characterizations, though they always forgave him after hearing his Boris. Chaliapin became so angry with the critics in New York that he didn't sing there from 1907 to 1921; in retrospect, he admitted that he had been "no doubt bizarre and uncouth". Farrar called him "a fascinating barbarian". Chaliapin was not just a singer, even a great singer, but a great actor who brought enormous power and gusto to whatever he was doing – eating caviar, drinking vodka, or singing the "Song of the Flea". He was interested in painting and – like Caruso and Maurel – was a talented graphic artist, and was the first modern master of what he called "psychological make-up". Once, when his costume had not arrived, he gave a stunning performance in street clothes at a dress rehearsal of *Boris Godunov* in Paris, which gave him great and well-deserved satisfaction. Chaliapin understood that dramatic illusion is not a matter of costumes and cosmetics. He remained a great artist and a great individualist until his death, in Paris, in 1938.

THERE'LL ALWAYS BE SINGERS

My first memorable opera performance was *Le Nozze di Figaro*, at the Vienna State Opera, with Lotte Lehmann, Elisabeth Schumann and Richard Mayr as the Countess, Susanna and Figaro; I've forgotten who sang Count Almaviva and Cherubino. Franz Schalk conducted. It must have been in the early 1920s. I was still a student at the *Gymnasium*, in my hometown Ostrava, in Moravia, and I'd been invited to Vienna by Uncle Alfred, my "rich" uncle. The *Figaro* performance remains the highlight of this visit; later I also heard *Don Giovanni*, the famous Roller production with the two towers, and very fast changes of scene – better than any other staging I've seen since.

In the fifty years since then I've heard all the great singers of our time. Each of us has his favourites. Ask a dozen fellow opera *aficionados* about their memories, their favourite singers and you will get a dozen different answers. This is one of the attractions of opera: we never agree.

Rather than enumerate the great singers I've heard I prefer to sit back and think of the great moments certain singers have given me; I think of Richard Mayr as Leporello and Ochs; of Alfred Piccaver singing "Le Rêve" in Massenet's *Manon*, often appearing with Lotte Lehmann, the most feminine singing lady of my memory, a complete artist who later wrote, "It has always been my highest goal to make every opera as humanly convincing as possible. Gestures, even if they must be stylized when borne by the music, must nevertheless arise from genuine human feeling". This conviction made Lotte Lehmann the greatest Leonore in Beethoven's *Fidelio*, the greatest Sieglinde, and the most human Marschallin (*Rosenkavalier*) of all. Her Octavian was often Maria Jeritza, also a great Tosca and Turandot. There are others. Lawrence Tibbett, a great actor with a sonorous voice; Kirsten Flagstad, perhaps the greatest Isolde until Birgit Nilsson developed her immensely human concept of

Isolde. Nilsson is that phenomenon, a *hochdramatische* soprano who is also very feminine, and sings the enormous emotional range from Brünnhilde, "die Ewig-Weibliche," to Turandot. There were the great *Heldentenöre*: Erik Schmedes, Lauritz Melchior, Leo Slezak, Richard Schubert, and, more recently, Max Lorenz and Wolfgang Windgassen.

Our time expects an artist to be a complete person – singer and man (or woman) projecting, above all, a personality. I remember Paul Schöffler, the greatest Hans Sachs of my memory, a wonderful blend of humanity and humour; Hans Hotter whom I'll always think of as Wotan, even when I meet him in the street; George London, the suffering Dutchman and the suffering Amfortas in *Parsifal*, whom Wieland Wagner called "the Jewish Christ" (which wouldn't have pleased Wieland's grandfather very much); and for similar reasons I remember Callas's Norma, Maria Reining's Marschallin, Leontyne Price as Leonora (in *Trovatore*), Sena Jurinac as Octavian and Cherubino; Helene Wildbrunn's Brünnhilde; Ljuba Welitsch, the greatest Salome of my life; three great lyrical tenors, Jan Peerce, Richard Tucker, and Jussi Björling who sometimes sounded more Italian than the Italians; the great altos – Marian Anderson, "a voice that one hears once in a hundred years", as Toscanini told her; Giuletta Simionato, with her regal bearing even when she played a gypsy; Regina Resnik, the intellectual member of the mezzo team; and there are singers who are less spectacular as vocalists than as all-round artists – Fischer-Dieskau, Seefried, Mödl, Christa Ludwig, Eileen Farrell, Patzak, Maggie Teyte, Leonie Rysanek, Wilma Lipp, Anja Silja, Joan Sutherland, Montserrat Caballé, Beverly Sills, Nicolai Ghiaurov, Geraint Evans.

There are many I haven't mentioned – and many that are yet to come, for there will always be singers.

People in Opera

THE MANAGER

Opera is the most ambitious, the most difficult of theatre arts. The managing of a modern opera house requires not only artistic judgement, but a high degree of executive skill and familiarity with the complex economic problems that now beset all performing arts. Furthermore, in a medium with so many imponderables, the opera manager needs a great deal of luck. A couple of productions may not come off; stars may become ill and cancel; poor judgement or the whimsicality of popular taste may turn success into failure. After weeks of painstaking preparations and countless rehearsals, an opera's incredibly intricate machinery can be thrown into confusion by the slightest mistake – a spotlight in the wrong place, a premature entrance, a late cue, a momentary lapse of memory, a sudden misunderstanding, a false note.

Ideally, the manager of an opera house should be a skilled diplomat and experienced lion-tamer, combining charm with authority, artistic integrity with a flair for the current public taste. He must persuade his artists to perform at their best, and persuade somebody else to pay for it; he should induce as many people as possible to buy tickets, and ask others to make up the inevitable deficit. The manager is forever compelled to compromise between his artistic conscience and his sense of economic guilt, between what *should* be done and what *can* be done. He usually finds himself pitted against his artists (except the few he may mollify temporarily with much-coveted parts), against his board of directors or bureaucrats (hostile to the steadily mounting deficit), against union officials (who want more money for their unions' members), and against his public and the critics (who rarely agree with what he is doing).

Opera lovers are an enthusiastic, vociferous and frankly prejudiced tribe. Nearly everybody has his own ideas as to how to run an opera house, and is sure he could do it much better than the manager. In Vienna which once was, and still pretends to be, "the world capital of opera" (a local claim based more on memories of the past than on achievements of the present), the *Operndirektor* holds the most controversial job in the country. No one has held it very long. The average artistic lifetime expectancy of Vienna's *Operndirektor,* based on the record of the past hundred years, is seven years.

The Vienna Opera is known as a "conductor's house", because during its greatest years it was run by prominent conductors: Hans Richter, Gustav Mahler, Richard Strauss, Franz Schalk, Clemens Krauss, Karl Böhm, Herbert von Karajan. They were more popular in Vienna than statesmen, film stars or soccer players, and they were also more vulnerable. All Viennese consider themselves co-directors of their *Oper*, and all feel entitled to criticize it violently, especially those who never go there. Karajan once admitted to me that he was resigned to run the Opera with the help of an administrative staff and the unsolicited advice of 1,700,000 Viennese. When he resigned in 1962, and then returned, after he'd publicly insulted several members of the Austrian Cabinet, having at last won artistic autonomy for his house, he became one of his country's great heroes, not unlike Prince Eugene of Savoy who saved Austria against the Turks. Having saved the *Oper* against the bureaucrats, Karajan celebrated by conducting a gala performance of *Aida*, during which he, and not Radames, was the great victor.

Even earlier, strong conductors like Gustav Mahler would let no one interfere with artistic problems. Mahler decided the artistic profile of the house, while the *Intendant*, a sort of bureaucratic general manager, dealt with the administrative and financial complexities. Contrarily, some houses in Germany are now known as "producer's houses", being managed by a stage director – Rudolf Sellner in West Berlin, Walter Felsenstein in East Berlin, Günther Rennert in Munich. Bayreuth was always run by members of the Wagner family. Neo-Bayreuth was managed by Wieland and Wolfgang Wagner, both stage directors; since Wieland's untimely death in 1966, Wolfgang has been in charge. Some houses are run by composers: there was Georges Auric in Paris and Rolf Liebermann in Hamburg. But the world's four leading opera houses were run by men who are exclusively managers: Milan's La Scala by Antonio Ghiringhelli, a former shoe manufacturer (who served without getting paid); London's Royal Opera House, Covent

Garden, until 1970 by Sir David Webster, and now by John Tooley; the Vienna State Opera by Dr Heinz Reif-Gintl, Court Councillor and now by Rudolf Gamsjäger; and the Metropolitan, until his recent retirement, by Rudolf Bing who had had experience in the management of a wide variety of theatrical ventures when he took on this job in 1950.

Bing believed that current trends favour the managerial type for the direction of an opera house. He took it for granted that the manager was an opera enthusiast; no one else would have any business to be there. An artist managing a house, not unnaturally, tends to give preference to those works that he conducts or stages himself. Even with the best intentions, he cannot maintain a totally impartial attitude towards the entire repertory. Somehow, when Karajan was in charge of everything in Vienna, he always had better casts and more rehearsal time than other conductors, and consequently many first-rate conductors preferred not to conduct there. At least, that was the reason they gave (privately). For similar reasons, prominent stage directors were not too eager to work in Berlin or Munich. Besides, a prominent artist who must work hard at his own art will have far less time to cope with the endless administrative details of his job. Bing used to begin work at ten in the morning and rarely got home before midnight. In Vienna, in the early postwar years, the indefatigable Dr Egon Hilbert worked from the early morning until long after midnight coping with the problems of running an opera house in the occupied, impoverished, cold city.

The pressures of competition – among opera houses, and between opera and other forms of entertainment – have brought many changes in the past years. Earlier in the century, the leading opera houses in the German-speaking countries of Europe were ensemble theatres, performing many different works during long seasons, and achieving a high degree of artistic integration. In Vienna, Gustav Mahler, Felix Weingartner, Franz Schalk and Richard Strauss had formidable galaxies of stars at their disposal for almost the whole season, which lasted ten months. When Jeritza, Lotte Lehmann, Mayr or Slezak went to America for short periods, there was national mourning. (In Vienna, opera singers, once they become known, lose their first names, and are given only the article, *die* Lehmann, or *der* Piccaver.) At one time in the 1920s, Vienna had six great tenors under contract – Schmedes, Slezak, Schubert, Piccaver, Oestvig, Grosavescu. Today, a manager could plan a major part of a whole season based on each of them.

At that time, in Italy and other countries, the *stagione* system was the practice. *Stagione* is the Italian word meaning "season". A small number of works, rarely more than half a dozen, are performed during a short period, always with the same stars. The *stagione* is built around a few stars, promoting the individual star rather than the integrated art of the ensemble. After the *stagione*, the company disbands, possibly to meet elsewhere. This system suits the works of Rossini, Donizetti, Bellini, Verdi and Puccini better than those of Mozart, Wagner and Richard Strauss. It is still considered somewhat alien in the German-speaking countries, where it is said to be "less artistic" or "more commercial". (At this point, some German opera critics would go into the principles of *Kunst* and complexities of aesthetics.) The plain fact is that a fine *stagione* performance is artistically superior to a mediocre ensemble performance.

But the controversy between partisans of the ensemble and admirers of the *stagione* is not always distinguished for its logic. It often ignores the bitter truth: income taxes and jet travel have radically changed the situation and created, as some oldtimers say, a "debasement" of opera as an integrated art form. Today, the important singers want to make hay while the sun shines. For some, it doesn't shine long. They are afraid of staying too long in one place no matter how much they dislike travel. If you are not in demand internationally, you aren't "in". Your value (and the size of your fee) might go down on the international singers' exchange, where every voice has a price.

Years ago, Günther Rennert acquired a reputation for his good judgement in producing Italian operas with *stagione* stars, and ensemble operas with ensembles. But the trend towards the *stagione* is strong, and getting stronger. During his memorable eight years as *Operndirektor* in Vienna, Karajan developed a new kind of super-*stagione*. Knowing that even he couldn't tie the world's leading singers for six months or longer to the Vienna Opera, he devised a compromise: he would assemble the best possible stars and create a carefully rehearsed and well-integrated production of a single work. Such a production would be too costly for the financial resources of any one opera house. Karajan developed a co-operation between the Vienna State Opera and La Scala, where he'd also conducted for years. The expensive sets and costumes would be used by both houses, and the same singers would appear, a fine example of rational operatic planning. Later, other places were included. Karajan's *Il Trovatore* which he staged and conducted in Salzburg, was later performed in Vienna, Moscow, Berlin and Hamburg. A very beautiful production of *La Bohème*, staged by Zeffirelli and conducted by Karajan, travelled from Milan's La Scala to the Vienna Opera, to Munich, and back to Milan to be filmed for television. Karajan's detractors talked of the threatening spectre of an operatic Vienna-Milan "axis", and accused him of trying to create "a post-Habsburg empire".

After Karajan left Vienna, he continued to develop his ideas of a super-*stagione*, including all possible media – festivals, films, radio, television, announcing plans to "carry opera into millions of living rooms". His most ambitious project was his own production of the super-opera, Wagner's *Der Ring des Nibelungen*. Beginning with *Walküre*, he first produced the works for Deutsche Grammophon Gesellschaft; later, he staged the production at his private, and privately financed, Easter Festival in Salzburg; from there, he took part of the production to the Metropolitan Opera in New York; eventually he hopes to produce it for television or the movies. "A first-rate opera production is now so expensive that it can be financed only by a combination of several media", he says.

Conceivably, this procedure may create millions of new opera lovers, but it may also have a bad effect on individual opera houses. When the super-*stagione* offers a super-*Aida* as polished as today's super-recordings, it may eventually be sold at the supermarket of the future, along with canned fruit. Such a trend could lead to a complete internationalization of opera. The prominent houses might lose their individual profile. The Zeffirelli-Karajan *Bohème* was not identified with any opera house; it wasn't Vienna's or La Scala's *Bohème*, but the Zeffirelli-Karajan *Bohème*. Certainly it wasn't Puccini's *Bohème; he* got lost between the big names. It is no accident that, on the cover of R.C.A.Victor's luxurious *Carmen* album, the names of the stars and the conductor are printed in large letters, but the name of the composer does not appear at all. After all, Bizet only wrote the music.

Whether the "ensemble" opera is preferable to the *stagione* system is always good for an argument among opera *aficionados*. Conservative opera-goers claim that everything is beautifully and harmonically co-ordinated in the "ensemble" opera. However, the word "ensemble" evokes memories of an era that is, alas, gone forever. Fifty years ago, there was no argument. The court theatres in Austria and Germany employed the ensemble system. Elsewhere, the *stagione* was popular; certain *ad hoc* companies would perform during short seasons. The Metropolitan played only sixteen weeks a year. There were not as many opera houses as now, and there was a supply of good voices.

Even earlier, when the only works performed were Italian operas, only one system existed, though it wasn't known as a *stagione*. Almost all

singers, musicians and even stage hands and technical workers were
Italians; opera was an occupation for Italians. Companies were organized
and theatres built especially for baroque festivals, sometimes even for
special performances. Then the theatres were torn down and the artists
dismissed, and they would congregate elsewhere for another operatic
festival. Permanent theatres were built in Vienna, in some Italian cities,
and later in Paris, and there was the new necessity of setting up permanent
companies. At the time of Mozart, there were sometimes two ensembles
in Vienna, one for Italian opera and one for the German Singspiel. As
Mozart could depend on certain performers, he would write parts
especially for them. The part of Osmin, in *Die Entführung aus dem Serail*,
was tailored to the abilities of a great bass, Ludwig Fischer, whose voice
had a large range, yet (Mozart writes) "there is nothing coarse about the
lower notes or nasal about the top ones: the voice is smooth, unfalteringly
true, and in every way agreeable, and as an actor Fischer is equally at home
on the serious and comic stage". Mozart also admits that when he wrote
the first aria for Constanze, he was thinking of "the agile larynx" of
Madame Catarina (or Katharina) Cavalieri "who can cope with the most
difficult passages".

Today, some managers think that the trend towards the super-*stagione*
will have an unfortunate effect on singers, who develop best under a
variety of conductors and need the stimulation of change. Prominent
performers who are obliged to sing the same part over and over under the
same conductor are hardly able to develop their powers fully. Opera
lovers enjoy comparing the Met.'s *Aida* with Vienna's or La Scala's,
always hoping their own *Aida*, wherever they live, will turn out to be the
best. Record collectors have done this for a long time, comparing
Toscanini's *Falstaff* with Karajan's or Bernstein's. These delights would be
lost were there only one super-*Aida*.

The ensemble system still survives in the smaller opera houses of Europe
that cannot afford to hire the expensive international stars. The leading
houses compete for the services of the few top artists. At best, these houses
attempt to develop what Rudolf Bing in New York has called a "super-
ensemble", in which a number of prominent singers work together for
at least a large part of the season (no matter what sort of opera our
children are going to hear, it will be super – a super-*stagione* or a super-
ensemble). Bing claimed, with some justice, that the Metropolitan's
roster forms just such a super-ensemble, so far as singers are concerned;
to present *Turandot* with Nilsson, Price and Corelli gave him considerable

satisfaction. The situation is less super-ish, so far as conductors, producers and designers are concerned, but you cannot have everything.

There is a reason for the shortage of first-rate conductors at the Metropolitan, primarily a "singer's house". In America, a conductor's reputation is made on the concert stage, not in the orchestra pit, as in Vienna. New York audiences pay little attention to the conductor at the Met, unless he happens to be a star performer. In Vienna, they still ask, "Who conducts tonight?" which doesn't mean that they have an abundance of first-rate conductors. Young conductors prefer symphony conducting to the more stringent demands of opera. Famous conductors tend to be somewhat autocratic and some resented the autocratic manner of Rudolf Bing who dismissed several conductors when he took over in New York. Others left. One wanted to cast a work – a prerogative that the general manager claimed for himself, down to the secondary parts. Another wanted a première; Bing refused. A third wanted to conduct *and* produce a very popular work, which seemed to Bing too much of a risk. Yet a serious shortage of first-rate conductors is a grave handicap for an important opera house. Without superior conducting a performance may not rise above the level of routine. And routine is the arch-enemy of opera. Under Bing's successor, Göran Gentele, the style might have changed. However, following Gentele's death in a car accident in Sardinia in July 1972, Met. developments will be watched with interest.

Whether opera should be performed in the original language or in English was unequivocally answered by the Metropolitan's general manager: "Most of our subscribers know what happens in most operas. I have a feeling the majority of the audience does not want to be detracted from the music by the text which is often silly. A great many people feel happily lost in glorious melodies." Bing was vindicated by a long-time American opera fan who told him, "I don't care in what language you perform opera as long as I don't understand it". Performing opera in the language for which the music was written is artistically preferable; even the best translation cannot always follow the flow of the music. *Don Giovanni* sounds awful in German. *Carmen* was never adequately translated into any language from the original French. Opera lovers shouldn't regret missing the nonsense in the earlier Verdi operas or the often grotesque alliterations in Wagner's *Ring*. It is often argued that the charm and wit of some comic masterpieces – *Le Nozze di Figaro, Così fan Tutte, Il Barbiere di Siviglia* – are lost on audiences who don't understand the text. But even people who speak Italian do not always understand the subtleties of the libretto, since few singers have a clear enunciation; opera lovers can always buy the libretto in their own language and read the text, line by line. In the early years of Bing's regime, the Met. performed alternately the original Italian and an English version of *La Bohème*. The Italian original won hands down. Under no circumstances should an opera be performed in more than one language; even leading houses occasionally sin against this cardinal rule.

All prominent managers are accused of being "dictators". Most of them have admitted that opera management has to be a dictatorship. In Vienna, the famous co-management of Franz Schalk and Richard Strauss started auspiciously in 1919, and ended five years later after much bitterness and many recriminations. The deeper reasons will never be known. In Vienna, greatness was always suspect, and intriguers, sceptics and malcontents often made a common front against a great artist. The co-management of Karajan and Hilbert, that began in June, 1963, lasted only one year. In the summer of 1964, Karajan left the Vienna Opera. It has never recovered from his departure. Democracy is not ideal in an opera house, where a strong man is needed. "There often comes the moment of truth when one man must make the decision and take the responsibility", Bing said. He openly admitted that spectacular mistakes were made at the Met., and that they were *his* mistakes.

Asked by young people how one becomes an opera manager, Bing was apt to say, "Don't!" On second thought, he suggested they go to Europe and learn by experience. The manager should know about exact planning and careful co-ordination in his productions. The concept of grand improvisation is no longer valid. The manager must know all about budgeting, box-office reports, and the generally precarious economics of the theatre business. He should spend as much time as possible in the house; he should drop into the featured singers' dressing rooms prior to the performance, and go backstage again to say good night to them. Little courtesies do much to keep up the morale in an opera house, an institution of great sensitivity. The state of morale is evident in the level of the performances. An able manager spends at least part of each performance in his box, noting any symptoms of deterioration and sloppiness. He must also function in an emergency, when a star tenor is between crises or a *diva* between nervous breakdowns. He must convince them that they must sing "to save the performance". One famous manager describes the experience as upsetting:

The tenor (or the *diva*) is sitting next to a phonograph listening to an electronically beautified rendition of the glorious voice. For some reason, singers love to listen to the sound of their own voice when they claim to be unable to sing. The artist sings along inaudibly, with the mouth wide open, and watches in a mirror the action of the golden vocal cords. In the case of a *diva*, there may be intermittent crying spells. Having finished the recorded aria, the artist makes desperate, silent gestures intended to convey to the manager that he, or she, *has* to cancel tonight. There is just no voice left. A complicated argument then follows between the singer and the manager – an exchange of rational spoken persuasions and irrational silent protests. In the end, the great singer may be persuaded to make a supreme effort in order to save the performance. The expression "saving the performance", with its heroic undertone, seems to have a miraculous effect on the artist . . . Usually he, or she, sings very well that night.

Once in a while persuasion isn't enough. One night in December, 1959, when Birgit Nilsson was making her third appearance at the Met., in *Tristan und Isolde,* all three of the available tenors became indisposed. There are not many houses that have three Tristans available; some, actually, haven't even one. Bing resolved the crisis by persuading each tenor to sing one act – an effort, he hoped, for which each man's strained vocal resources might just suffice. In a short curtain speech explaining the unusual arrangement, Bing said, in a matter-of-fact tone, "Fortunately, the opera has only three acts".

All great opera houses now have a star problem. The Metropolitan in New York, as a result of geography, has a special problem providing understudies, or "covers", for the stars. In an emergency, a European house can usually get a replacement within a couple of hours. Not always though. Several years ago, a sold-out *Meistersinger* performance at the Vienna State Opera had to be cancelled twenty-five minutes *after* the scheduled beginning, with the people waiting in their seats. Through an administrative oversight, Wolfgang Windgassen, who was to sing the part of Stolzing, had not been notified, and was sitting in his country home in Bavaria while the Vienna management assumed he was in Vienna. By the time they found out, it was too late to get him, even by chartered plane. Refusing to be beaten, the management solicited other tenors but failed. Ernst August Schneider, a member of the management, had to announce the cancellation to the audience, and, of course, refund them. He admitted later that they should have arranged a different performance, say, *Così fan Tutte,* and refunded money to those who didn't want to hear it. Nothing hurts a great opera house more than a cancelled performance, both in terms of finances and public relations.

In 1963, a Saturday matinée of *Der Fliegende Holländer* at the Metropolitan had to be cancelled three hours before curtain time and was replaced by *Ariadne auf Naxos*. That was possible only because the sets for *Ariadne* (a technically rather simple, two-set opera) happened to be in the house, and because some of the *Holländer* artists could sing *Ariadne*. Even so, the first clarinettist had to be tracked down by the police at a track meeting in Jersey City, and brought to the Met. in a squad car.

The Met.'s backstage logistical problem has been solved by the fact that the new Metropolitan has sufficient storage space for all the sets that might be needed for half a season. But the problem of "covers" is becoming worse. "People don't seem to understand that singers often get sick", Bing has said. "New York's climate is not as bad as London's, but it isn't ideal for Italian singers." Until supersonic plane travel becomes a reality, the Metropolitan must be as self-sufficient as an aircraft carrier in the middle of the ocean. Occasionally it gets help from the City Opera in New York, Chicago, or San Francisco, but their basic policy is to have every part in every performance doubly cast. However, it demoralizes a singer to hang around backstage for weeks waiting for a call that may never come, and many good covers would rather sing twenty weeks in Hamburg or Munich than be paid for twenty weeks of not singing in Manhattan. Some singers can be paid off temporarily, but eventually they become dissatisfied and more power to them! (One of the Met.'s top artists cares so much about singing *all* of his guaranteed performances, that he signed his contract only after the management promised to pay him an indemnity, on top of his guaranteed fee, for each stipulated performance when he was ready to sing but was not scheduled. Bing respected such an attitude, though it complicated matters for the management.)

At the Metropolitan, the most efficiently run opera house in the world, advance planning has been developed to such a high degree that simply by glancing at a mimeographed chart General Manager Bing could tell which of his top artists would be available during each week of the following season. A green line meant yes; a red line, no. The fees and salaries of all performers are tabulated; there are cast lists of all performances in the future season, schedules of orchestral and choral rehearsals for each day of the season, the dates of the Met.'s future spring tours – certain auditoriums must be booked ten years ahead! – and statistics on how many times specific operas have been performed and how they did at the box office. (All that beautiful planning went out of the window in the autumn of 1969 when the very existence of the Metropolitan was threatened by the most serious labour dispute in its history; the season opened almost four months late.)

Nevertheless, Bing remained justifiably fond of his charts and figures. At the old Met. a full house would bring in $29,000; at the new one, the potential receipts are over $42,000.

Income also depends on popular taste. The Metropolitan management knows that certain operas are *always* sell-outs: *Aida, La Bohème, Madama Butterfly, La Traviata*. Others are too, when given with first-rate casts: *Der Rosenkavalier, Carmen*. Some depend on performers: *Salome* and *Turandot* will be sold out when Birgit Nilsson is available. But some of the greatest masterpieces are problematical at the box office. Verdi's *Falstaff* was a big hit at the Met. during the 1963–64 season, largely because of Zeffirelli's production and Bernstein's conducting. The following season, Bernstein was absent, and attendance declined. Alban Berg's *Wozzeck*, one of the very few operas since the days of Richard Strauss to be widely accepted as a "classic", did well at the Met. during the first season, when it was "a cocktail-party conversation piece", as Bing put it, but not the following season, although the production, the conductor (Karl Böhm) and nearly all of the cast were unchanged. Menotti's *The Last Savage* did well during its first season and very badly a year later.

In the summer of 1965, one year before the American première of *Die Frau ohne Schatten,* when Bing began to plan the 1967–68 season, he had to decide whether the Strauss-Hofmannsthal opera should be kept in the repertory a second year. Another possibility was to wait one year after the opera's first-year run, and take it back into repertory two years after the première. However, a complicated work such as *Die Frau ohne Schatten* might fall apart if not performed for a whole season, which would mean expensive rehearsals all over again. Reluctantly, Bing kept the work in the repertory for two successive seasons.

Almost half of Bing's working time was spent on "daily emergencies", the endless minute problems of a temperamental business. A singer is unable to learn a new part. A conductor has problems with the orchestra or the chorus. A top singer becomes ill. Once upon a time, famous singers went to the Metropolitan, and were paid more than any house in Europe could afford. The situation is now reversed: some European houses can afford to pay more for occasional appearances than the once "rich" Met. Years ago, Bing who was rarely shocked by anything, was somewhat

nonplussed to hear that Maria Callas was offered $10,000 for two per-
formances a night by the Hamburg State Opera. He realized that at a
top price of about a hundred dollars for the best seats, the Hamburg
Opera might break even. whereas the Metropolitan could ask such prices
only on opening night. Furthermore, the *Intendant* of the Hamburg
Opera could afford to offer this much money to Callas because she had no
competition among the singers of his house. But the general manager of
the Metropolitan would have been in serious trouble with half a dozen of
his top stars, who earned the Met.'s top salary, and had remained faithful
to his house for years. The frail structure of his top salary system would
have been in grave danger. When Bing invited Callas to appear twice in
Tosca at the Met. in 1965, he explained to her, regretfully, that he could
not pay her more than the Metropolitan's top salary. The prima donna
understood and agreed.

Money isn't the only concern; famous artists often care about the visual
attributes of fame. The manager has to spend much time, cunning and
skill on "the dressing room problem". ("Dressing room assignments and
appointments probably have caused as many prima donna fireworks as
any other single thing in the opera house", wrote Francis Robinson,
assistant manager of the Metropolitan.) At a gala evening in the old house,
when the programme offered one act of *La Traviata* with Sutherland, one
act of *La Bohème*, with Tebaldi, and one act of *Der Rosenkavalier* with
Della Casa and Schwarzkopf, the main managerial problem was the alloca-
tion of dressing room No. 10, traditionally the domain of the evening's
first soprano. After delicate negotiations, Tebaldi consented to move to
another dressing room, since she didn't have to do much dressing up for
the part of Mimi, the poor seamstress. Sutherland would have No. 10
during the earlier part of the evening, and Schwarzkopf during the later
part. Della Casa, though actually a soprano, was singing the mezzo part of
Octavian in *Rosenkavalier*, and so would take the first mezzo dressing room.

The sequence of solo curtain calls was another source of conflict at the
Met. until Bing established for each opera an escalating sequence, with
the last call being the most important. The order of battle was affixed in all
dressing rooms, and still creates violent disagreement. At the end of *Der
Rosenkavalier*, the Met.'s sequence of solo calls begins with Sophie, is
followed by the Marschallin, and ends with Octavian, after whom the
work is called, although dramatically and musically, the part of the
Marschallin is the most important. When Schwarzkopf was engaged to
sing the part of the Marschallin in two performances, Bing asked Della
Casa, the "regular" Marschallin, to sing the part of Octavian that she'd

sung years before at the Met. Della Casa consented after being assured that she would have the last solo call, though Schwarzkopf was clearly the star of the evening. Such decisions may seem ridiculous to an outsider, but they form the delicate fabric of which the structure of a great opera house is woven.

Every once in a while the managers of the leading opera houses speak wistfully of doing something about the top stars' monopoly, such as agreeing on the top price to be paid. But such an agreement would be no guarantee because it could easily be circumvented. Suppose a manager who had guaranteed the agreed top fee for ten performances then scheduled the singer for only six? That would increase the actual fee by forty per cent. Other singers might extol "tax-free" fees, with the management paying the tax, which now amounts to a considerable part of the fee in some countries. Famous Wagnerian *Heldentenöre* sometimes demand two guaranteed performances a week, which the Metropolitan cannot always do. The tenors point out that they lose money in New York. In Europe they may sing three times a week.

A celebrated singer's fee is established by demand and supply. The law works in the singers' favour. For years, a first-rate performance of *Walküre* or *Tristan und Isolde* depended on the availability of Birgit Nilsson; there was no one else in her class. (According to a story told around the Met., when an accountant helped Miss Nilsson with her income tax return and asked whether she had any dependents, she replied at once, "Yes, Mr Bing".) In the same way, a first-rate performance of *Lucia di Lammermoor* during several years called for Sutherland. Right now, lyrical tenors and *hochdramatische* sopranos are in short supply, and the best among them command top salaries. "The best" is not meant in an artistic sense, but rather in terms of vocal power and the ability to hold out exposed high tones. The Met., a large house, needs singers with a healthy volume and good vocal technique. Bing personally admired some "interesting" singers whom he didn't dare hire because, in spite of their great dramatic and musical ability, their voices might not be heard in the Metropolitan's huge auditorium. In moments of desperation, Bing was heard to say, "To appear at the Met. is a spectacular honour and should even be worth a financial sacrifice", but certain artists do not share this opinion.

Publicly, the managers of the leading opera houses constantly talk of the "need for co-operation", but privately each of them admits that he will stop at nothing to get the leading artists over the longest possible period. In this competition, Rudolf Bing did well, often acquiring great stars for as long as fifteen weeks. It is not just a matter of money. Bing's strongest weapon was the international prestige of the Metropolitan. Very good opera is occasionally performed in San Francisco and at the New York City Opera (whose devotees claim it superior to the "stuffy" Metropolitan) but Bing liked to point out that the Met. was the only American house "which counts on the international artists' exchange where a star's current value is reckoned". It is well known that successful Met. appearances attract recording, television and film offers.

The leading opera managers do not consider most of their stars lovable human beings. And strong dislike is widespread among many singers towards the managers. In time, when stars reach their ascendancy within a few years, many of them are overwhelmed by their fame. They often believe that the public expects a star to be "difficult". In the artistic medium of opera, violent emotions – love and hatred, pride and jealousy – are melodramatically magnified. Many artists carry their stage emotions into their private lives and seem unable, or unwilling, to separate the unreality of their stage life from the reality of their private life. Because they lead unusual lives, they conclude that they must be unusual people. And secretly, they are always terrified. Danger and artistic death are always one tone away. One cracked note may be the danger signal indicating the beginning of the end. It will be the talk of the musical community the next morning in Milan and Vienna, London and New York.

Some singers are afraid of being "exploited" if they behave in a natural, civilized manner. An experienced manager makes a careful distinction between normal nervousness, an occupational disease, and premeditated meanness. A sensitive artist suffers a great deal, won't speak a loud word on the day of a performance, terrorizes the household, comes to the opera house either very early or very late, and makes life miserable for everyone. But such an artist can be handled "with a mixture of understanding and toughness", according to a prominent manager.

But there is also the nasty artist – self-centred, unreasonable, impossible to deal with. Women are generally more difficult than men. One *diva* won't sing unless the furniture of her dressing room is completely changed, at each visit; nothing must remind her of other singers, her competitors. During a performance at the Metropolitan one *diva* suddenly demanded a solo curtain call after her next aria. It was explained that this was not done at the Met. (the policy was later changed). The *diva* threatened to leave the house. The general manager was summoned. Looking coolly at his wristwatch, Rudolf Bing said, "I shall give you exactly three minutes to go back on stage and continue. Otherwise, I'll have you thrown out of the Met. and sue you for tonight's entire house receipts. Incidentally, you now have only two and a half minutes left." The *diva* went on with her performance. There was no solo call.

Some years ago a temperamental tenor announced, two hours before an important rehearsal, that he was ill. Calling what he suspected was the artist's bluff, Bing sent an ambulance to his hotel; two sturdy men in white said they had come to take him to the hospital for treatment, "at the expense of the Metroplitan's general manager". The tenor experienced a miraculous recovery and sang at the rehearsal.

Another star sent Bing a doctor's certificate and a letter cancelling her contract the day before she was to join the Met.'s spring tour, not always as popular with famous singers as appearances at the opera house itself. Bing had no choice but to release the singer, which created confusion, confounding his carefully made plans. Five days later he was informed that the lady was singing in Europe. "We sued her", the general manager said. "She will not come back to the Met." In a more reflective mood, he once remarked, "I regret to say that attitudes improve as a singer's quality declines. As the voice deteriorates, the character becomes pleasanter. I find that artists are more often uneducated than genuinely temperamental."

All managers become more philosophical about criticism as they get older, but some are more so than others. One manager of a world-famous opera house often calls up music critics trying to convince them they may have been wrong. Others try to ignore all critics. After a rather sharp attack against a new production which Bing himself considered extremely good, he told a story about a clerk in a shoe store who had a standard answer for customers' complaints: "What do you mean, they don't fit?" the clerk would say. "They just don't fit *you!*"

He had a photograph in his office of his former enemy, Maria Callas. The picture showed her being kissed by Bing after her famous Metropolitan début, in 1956, as Norma; two years later, Callas was abruptly dismissed by Bing, after a terrible fight. Across the face in the picture two lines were written in black:

"Darling!"
"You're fired!"

THE CONDUCTOR

Originally, there was no conductor. A member of the orchestra players, usually the harpsichordist, would be in charge. Palestrina is said to have used a golden stick. Jean-Baptiste Lully used his violin bow to direct his fellow players. Later, Lully used a long ceremonial stick with which he would beat the floor. Carl Maria von Weber used a baton in Prague in 1814; Ludwig Spohr used it in Frankfurt and London, in 1820, but people didn't like the symbol of power. Mendelssohn introduced the baton in 1835 at the Leipzig Gewandhaus. Around 1850, the baton was used everywhere except by Johann Strauss, the waltz king, who played his violin in front of the orchestra and occasionally conducted with his bow. The *Kapellmeister* had been promoted from a *primus inter pares* to the *primus*. Berlioz and Richard Wagner made the conductor the musically and intellectually leading musician in charge of the orchestra.

At the opera house, the conductor's emergence as a superior force was a slow, gradual development. Gluck, Mozart, Beethoven and Weber personally supervised the production of their works. Mozart didn't have to put elaborate markings into his scores to clarify his purposes because he was present during all rehearsals of *Figaro* or *Don Giovanni*.

But when the composers died, and, too, the interpreters who had known the composers' original intentions, liberties were taken by singers and musicians. As early as 1813, Rossini deleted every ornament in the singers' parts in *Tancredi* because he was disgusted with their embellishing efforts. After a performance of *Don Giovanni* in London, in 1829 – only thirty-eight years after Mozart's death! – Mendelssohn wrote to Wilhelmine Schröder-Devrient, the great soprano,

> The other night I heard *Don Giovanni* given by the Italians. It was funny. Pellegrini sang Leporello, and acted like an ape. At the end of his first song he introduced a string of cadences out of any half a dozen Rossinian operas. The mandolin part in "Deh vieni" was played very delicately with the bow on a violin. The second verse was duly embellished and finished up somewhere in the skies.

Mendelssohn also wrote that Mme Malibran performed "a mad version of Zerlina, making her a wild, flirting Spanish country romp". The only singer he liked was the great Henriette Sontag as Donna Anna. The conductor was a very unimportant person, expected to provide the "accompaniment" while the singers provided feats of vocal *bravura*. This sad state of affairs lasted throughout most of the nineteenth century. On the playbill of Vienna's first *Die Walküre* no conductor was mentioned although Hans Richter was a famous musician, pupil and friend of Richard Wagner. When Nellie Melba sang in *La Traviata* at the Vienna Court Opera in 1900, Hans Richter thanked her for singing "Verdi, not Melba-Verdi".

In 1891, when Johannes Brahms visited Budapest, friends wanted him to hear a *Don Giovanni* performance at the local opera house. Brahms declined with thanks. "Nobody can interpret *Don Giovanni* for me. That is music which I can enjoy only if I sit down and read the score to myself" (this is reminiscent of Saint-Saëns who once said, "It is not a question of knowing what one prefers but what the composer intended to write"). As Brahms's friends insisted, he consented to go to the performance, and didn't regret it. He often shook his head in wonderment, exclaiming, "Excellent! Splendid! Remarkable!" Later he said, "At last – that's the way it ought to be done". During the intermission, Brahms went backstage, and threw his arms around the conductor, saying, "The best *Don Giovanni* I ever heard. Not even the Imperial Court Opera in Vienna can rival it". The conductor was a thirty-one-year-old musician named Gustav Mahler. Six years later, when Mahler was suggested as the new *Direktor* of the Vienna Opera, Brahms spoke up in his favour. After Mahler's first *Don Giovanni* at the Metropolitan in 1908, W.J.Henderson, the critic of *The Sun*, wrote, "Mr Mahler treated *Don Giovanni* not as a collection of set pieces for the singers, but as a drama in music, and the true nature of the noble old classic shone out as it has not in previous performances... The interest of the audience in the singers was heightened by the restoration of the continuity of dramatic thought."

As a sixteen-year-old student at the Vienna Conservatory in 1876, Mahler and his roommate, Hugo Wolf, talked about little else but the opening of Wagner's Festspielhaus in Bayreuth. They were unhappy because they couldn't afford to go. Mahler didn't go there until 1883, the year Wagner died. The performance of *Parsifal* remained "the loftiest and most agonizing of revelations". Two years later, Mahler was in Prague where he conducted *Don Giovanni, Meistersinger,* and the *Ring*.

Wagner had been in Prague in 1831 ("My stay in Prague was of great musical importance to me", he wrote in *My Life*) and met Dionys Weber who promised to perform Wagner's C major symphony. Weber had been present at the rehearsals of *Figaro* in Prague, under Mozart, and told Wagner about it. Wagner later became painfully aware of what many singers did to Mozart. He decided that this must never happen to his own scores, and he made sure by writing careful notation; there was no leeway for embellishments by the singers, but they were so complex that the conductor, until then a mere "accompanist", perforce became the opera authority; otherwise there would have been musical confusion. The era of the singers was ineluctably drawing to a close. In 1864, when

Wagner went to Munich at the summons of King Ludwig II, he prepared
a plan for the reform of the Bavarian theatre which included a new concept
of Mozart. He talked about it to Hans von Bülow who later conducted in
Meiningen and Hamburg, and to Hermann Levi who conducted Mozart
in Munich. Gradually, the idea emerged of preserving the scores of the
dead composers. Weber, Schumann, Mendelssohn, Liszt and finally
Wagner considered themselves the artistic heirs and deputies of the
old masters. Conducting became an important part of their activities,
not so much because they liked to conduct but because they felt obliged
to perform the works of Mozart and Beethoven as they ought to be
performed – according to the score. All conductors who grew up during
the time or in the shadow of Wagner were directly influenced by him:
Bülow, Levi, Richter, Artur Nikisch. Bülow's work was continued by
Mahler who in turn influenced Bruno Walter, Franz Schalk, Alexander
von Zemlinsky, Otto Klemperer. Richard Strauss, who began his career
in Meiningen as assistant to Bülow, had a strong influence on Erich
Kleiber, Clemens Krauss, Fritz Reiner, Karl Böhm, and on George Szell
who considered himself first and foremost "the servant of the composer".
Other outstanding conductors – Max von Schillings, Felix Mottl, Karl
Muck, Felix von Weingartner, Fritz Busch, Wilhelm Furtwängler –
were in various ways connected with the ideas of Wagner (as a young
conductor in Ulm, Herbert von Karajan would bicycle to Bayreuth to
hear Toscanini conduct).

As conductors, Gustav Mahler and Richard Strauss became the great
restorers of authentic Mozart performances. Strauss conducted Mozart
at Munich's Residenztheater, and later in Salzburg. Fritz Busch, head of
the Dresden Opera (Richard Strauss's favourite house) in 1934, took
his glorious Mozart style to Glyndebourne. Bruno Walter and Franz
Schalk, who had worked in Vienna with Mahler, continued the Mozart
tradition. It is still carried on in Vienna by Josef Krips and Karl Böhm.

In June, 1886, a young cellist named Arturo Toscanini conducted a
performance of *Aida* in Rio de Janeiro, because the regular conductor had
to cancel. Toscanini played the cello in the orchestra of La Scala on the
night of 5 February 1887, when Verdi's *Otello* was first performed. At
Verdi's express wish, Franco Faccio conducted; he was the first of the great
modern Italian conductors. Toscanini conducted *his* first *Otello* at the
Metropolitan in 1909, with Leo Slezak, who made his début that night.
And in January, 1954, Toscanini conducted his last opera performance in
New York, *Un Ballo in Maschera*. For sixty-eight years, Toscanini

exercised enormous influence. He made La Scala his theatre, and La Scala's orchestra became known as Toscanini's orchestra (not unlike the NBC Orchestra in New York that, later on, was especially created for him). Toscanini directed the artistic life of La Scala for only fifteen years, and never since 1929, yet his presence is still very strong. There were "melodramatic arrivals and stormy departures, angry ruptures and reconciliations", writes Claudio Sartori, but each come-back was better than before. In the early decades of this century, while Toscanini became closely associated with La Scala, and Mahler with the Vienna Opera, Sir Thomas Beecham became identified with Covent Garden; Fritz Busch (and later Karl Böhm) with Dresden; Furtwängler, Blech and Kleiber with Berlin; Clemens Krauss and Walter with Munich, and later with Vienna; Strauss and Schalk with Vienna.

But another type of star conductor had become prominent, the travelling conductor (an early one was Bülow who loved to travel). Nikisch, who conducted two of the best orchestras in Germany, the Berliner Philharmoniker and the Leipzig Gewandhaus, still found time to travel around and to fascinate his audiences. His successor, Wilhelm Furtwängler, never had fewer than two functions. At one time, he conducted the Leipzig Gewandhaus Orchestra, the Vienna Philharmonic, the Berlin Philharmonic and the New York Philharmonic, and he had time to conduct in Salzburg and elsewhere. Furtwängler, who also wrote philosophical and polemical essays, and tried to oppose the Nazi regime (until he resigned), became the symbol of German music. A conservative romanticist, he instinctively disliked the new perfectionism of the modern musical theatre and the kind of music-making exemplified by Toscanini. Furtwängler remained the great improviser, the last of his breed. Our era demands perfection: conductors who are able to perform with the sort of perfection that radio, television, and expensive recordings have conditioned us to expect. The present-day type of glamorous conductor is represented by Leonard Bernstein and Herbert von Karajan, both exceptional musicians and very similar in spite of their dissimilarities. Both exude a definite magic which is enhanced by their appearance. Both seem less interested in the classics than in their special field. Karajan loves Verdi and Wagner, Debussy (*Pelléas et Mélisande*) and Puccini. Bernstein is dedicated to Mahler and conducts only a few operas – *Médée, Falstaff, Rosenkavalier, Fidelio, Cavalleria Rusticana, Carmen*. And Georg Solti, for ten years music director of Covent Garden, made the Royal Opera House musically one of the world's greatest, ranging far from *Tristan* to *Falstaff* to Schönberg's *Moses and Aaron*.

Several years ago, George Szell, who was recognized some years before his death in 1970 as the foremost interpreter of classical music, said there was a growing shortage of first-rate conductors. The two world wars have killed off some potential talent, and in the past twenty years the traditional westward migration from Eastern and Central Europe has been cut off. During this time, opera has become big business, and the demand for able conductors is such that there simply are not a sufficient number for all the orchestras, opera houses, and summer festivals. Talented people who normally would serve an apprenticeship of several years under leading conductors, studying the musical repertory, learning their craft and taking time to develop artistically, are tempted to conduct too early, often with disastrous results (a young, brilliant, Japanese conductor was invited to conduct the first opera of his career, *Così fan Tutte* – in Salzburg, of all places). Karajan talks with asperity about "some young geniuses who never learned to hold a baton properly", remembering his seven-year apprenticeship as *Opernkapellmeister* in Ulm, Germany, where he had time to study the repertory. Formerly, in Salzburg and Bayreuth, the greatest conductors would appear at the zenith of their careers, "to conduct the masterpieces that had matured within them for a lifetime", Szell says. Nowadays, young conductors work there, conducting certain works for the first time in their lives. Some of them seem to owe their success to the rhapsodic elegance of their podium manners rather than to the quality of their interpretation. Some know nothing about the mysterious science of acoustics.

An opera house is judged by its acoustics, yet acoustics remain an enigma. The experts contend that by applying certain laws of physics and by using certain testing devices they can predict and determine in advance how a new auditorium will sound. The fact is, however, that several auditoriums built in Germany in the post-war years under the guidance of such expert consultants have turned out to have dreadful acoustics. Berlin's concert hall at the Hochschule für Musik, hailed in advance as Germany's finest auditorium, proved to be an acoustical atrocity when it was opened; in some seats disconnected noises seemed to be bouncing off the rear wall of the hall, in others multiple echoes closed in from all directions, while in others practically no sound at all could be heard. Although years of study had gone into the design, it was discovered, after the first concerts, that the ceiling and the side walls were all wrong in relation to one another and the size of the room. Later floor-to-ceiling hangings were put up on the walls to absorb some of the unwelcome noises. The Philharmonic Hall in New York's Lincoln Center also went through stages of sound correction and is still far from being perfect, though hundreds of thousands of dollars have been spent on acoustical studies and improvements. The sad truth is that scientists specializing in acoustics are on no surer footing when they make their forecasts than meteorologists are in making theirs. No one can say for sure what the acoustical qualities of an auditorium will be until it is finished, furnished, heated, and filled with musicians, singers, music and listeners. By that time it is very expensive to correct the acoustics, if they can be corrected at all.

The mystery deepens when one thinks of great old opera houses whose designers knew little or nothing about the science of acoustics but, by instinct or luck, produced auditoriums famous for their sound – La Scala, Venice's Teatro Fenice, Vienna's Court Opera, and the (old) Metropolitan on Broadway and Thirty-ninth Street. Happily, the new Met. also turned out to have excellent acoustics. Ideas about sound have changed, of course, like everything else. High frequency recordings have made our hearing more sensitive; when these recordings were first heard they were thought to sound too sharp (perhaps a semitone high in pitch), but came to be gradually accepted because they reproduced actual sounds more exactly than ever before.

Acoustics are determined by reverberation. In an auditorium, sound bounces off the walls, the ceiling, and the floor until the whole place is uniformly filled with it. If the source of sound stops, the sound remains audible for a while – sometimes as long as three seconds. The prolongation of sound *after* it has left its source is called reverberation. It strengthens sound, and is desirable, providing it does not interfere with succeeding sounds. The length of time that a sound can be heard after being originated is used as a measure of the auditorium's reverberation. If it is too short, the sounds one hears are muffled and "dead". If it is too long, the sounds jostle one another, syllables and phrases are hard to understand, and tones flow into one another and become confused.

The most favourable reverberation count, in an average-size opera auditorium, has been found to be from one and a half to one and eight-tenths seconds, or even longer. The bigger a house is, the longer the reverberation may be without blurring the enunciation. The Bayreuth Festspielhaus has a long reverberation, two and four-tenth seconds. Richard Wagner understood acoustics when he built this funnel-shaped house. Ordinary parallel walls often create dangerous reflections. Bayreuth has no boxes along the sides, which is all to the good, because boxes have a way of absorbing sound instead of reflecting it. The audience can hear every word in Bayreuth. Small voices seem to grow there, and the singers never have to strain.

Every listener absorbs sound – men, in their woollen suits, a little more than women in their silk dresses – and no opera house sounds the same when it is empty as when it contains two or three thousand living sound absorbers. In the perfect auditorium, which doesn't exist yet, the seats will be upholstered in such a way that each will absorb the same amount of sound when it is empty, as a person does when sitting in it. Designers like to install elegant materials, brocades and velours, all highly sound-absorbent. Acoustical experts don't care how the auditorium looks, as long as it sounds right. The auditorium of the Bayreuth Festspielhaus is ugly, and the seats are uncomfortable, but Richard Wagner knew what he was doing. To hear the low, sustained E flat in the beginning of *Rheingold* is a mystic experience. The tone is so low that one cannot distinguish when the silence ends and the sound begins; nor is one sure where the sound comes from; it might have come from the sides of the auditorium, the rear, or the ceiling. Slowly the orchestra begins to play the melodic passages, barely audible at first and gradually increasing in volume until the whole auditorium is filled with music – the music of the waters of the Rhine. In Bayreuth the brass doesn't sound brassy, and orchestral sound is round and blended, yet the instrumental groups can be clearly discerned, and a great conductor gets magically transparent effects from the orchestra. The strings, particularly the first violins, are somewhat subdued, such a minor flaw only reminding you that in acoustics, as in everything, there is no perfection.

Since Mahler and Toscanini introduced the primacy of the conductor into the opera house, the power of the famous singers has been broken. Today the leading singing stars are still tremendous box-office draws, but artistically it's the conductor who runs the show if he has the authority. When Bernstein, Böhm, Karajan, Kubelik, Abbado, Solti conduct, they can make or break the performance. This doesn't mean that the conductor should consider himself sacrosanct. No one understands this better than the great conductors. "The conductor must have complete respect for the composer's style. The composer's message, the substance of the music must never be changed," said George Szell. The elements of knowledge, style, imagination and taste are absolutely necessary; taste is very important. Haydn once told Mozart's father, "I tell you before

God and as an honest man that your son is the greatest composer I know, personally or by reputation; he has taste and, apart from that, the greatest possible knowledge of music".

Many prominent conductors now admit that this generation owes an everlasting debt to Toscanini who did much for the purification of taste. Toscanini, and Mahler before him, wiped out the arbitrariness of the post-romantic interpreters, and did away with the thick encrustation of interpretative nuances which had been piling up for decades and had mistakenly been accepted as "tradition". They did what skilful restorers of a painting do in bringing back the original masterpiece. The devotion to the composer, the fidelity to the work – all this is a matter of artistic discipline.

Would Toscanini's performances be called great today, if he were still alive? He was never doctrinaire, and sensitively reflected the style and taste of his time, but he was always faithful both to the composer's score and to the libretto. He established definite interpretations of Verdi which are as important today as when he made them; fortunately his recordings express the whole range of his artistry.

Singers, even the greatest, were always a little afraid to sing under him, because he was difficult and had a violent temper. But they admitted that he was difficult only because he wanted perfection. He insisted that they must sing only what the composer wrote: no *rubati, rallentandi,* or sustained notes were permitted. But his sense of perfection and feeling for accuracy were matched by taste and style. Italian writers said that he would give even the "La donna è mobile" an almost "ascetic" touch. They compare the intense dignity with which he approached the storm in the beginning of *Otello* to the fanatic power of the "Dies Irae" in Verdi's *Requiem.* Giuseppe Pugliese calls what is possibly his finest recording, *Falstaff,* "the highest example of moral and artistic achievement". Toscanini was human, and far from perfect, but he approached everything he did with an almost religious sense of morality. Not many leading conductors today can make that claim.

It is sometimes said that great performers at the moment of the performance "re-create" the music, which is more than merely performing it, "something that fuses together in one flaming unity all the elements of art, adding those of the spirit to those of the mind and senses," as Olin Downes wrote. Downes once used the word "re-creation" when he commented on a certain performance to Toscanini. Toscanini listened in silence. A few hours later, he sent Downes an envelope containing the copy of a letter which Verdi had written to Giulio Ricordi on the subject.

As to conductors' inspiration . . . to "creative activity in every performance" . . . that is a principle which forever inevitably leads to the baroque and untrue. It is precisely the path that led music to the baroque and untrue at the end of the last century and in the first years of this, when singers were told to "create" (as the French still say) their parts, and in consequence made a complete hash and contradiction of sense out of them. No: I want only one single creator and I shall be quite satisfied if they perform simply and exactly what he has written. I often read in the papers about effects that the composer never could have thought of: but for my part I never found such a thing . . . I deny that either singers or conductors "create" a work or work creatively – This, as I have always said, is a conception that leads to the abyss.

Unlike Wagner, Verdi was not concerned with theories and aesthetic ideas. Unlike Wagner, he was absolutely honest towards himself, and everybody else. His strong ideas on the subject were the result of what he'd heard musicians and singers in the opera house doing to the score, obviously leading "to the baroque and untrue". Even today celebrated star singers often take certain liberties with their parts under a weak conductor who doesn't know better or doesn't dare to protest. This is not "re-creation", but simply distortion. But at best, there is a certain re-creative force in the performance of a great, responsible artist so that the experienced listener who knows the work well suddenly has the impression he never heard it as clearly and convincingly and excitingly – yet it's all in the score. Even Verdi might not have objected to this kind of re-creation, because it arises from extreme artistic fidelity.

Unlike architecture and painting which are expressed primarily in terms of space and colour, music is dominated by the inexorable flow of time. Opera is a combination of audible and visual elements. Not all listeners, however, are as sensitive towards lighting and colours as towards tempo and pitch; they note a sour horn tone, but not a wrong light. An overture that starts with the wrong tempo is like a building erected on shaky foundations; the structure is bound to collapse. A false modification of the tempo, which occurs frequently during opera performances, breaks the flow of the music and ruins the unity of the work. There are conductors – some even quite well known – who are not thoroughly acquainted with the classics. They conduct beautiful phrases or fine-sounding sections of a movement, but fail to understand the overall structure of the score. A Mozart *andante* is different from a Verdi *andante*. Slow tempos have become slower, and fast tempos faster, than they were at the time when

Mozart's works were written; to a certain extent that also applies to Verdi and Wagner. Artists help to shape the music but they are also being shaped by it. Tempo is often a matter of the mind rather than of speed. Toscanini gave the impression that his tempi were slow when he conducted *Parsifal* in Bayreuth, but his slowness was never dragging (Theodor W. Adorno expressed doubts about Toscanini because he didn't feel the "poetic essence" of Toscanini's interpretations, and pointed out the contradiction between Toscanini's perfectionism and the "practical difficulties" that forced him to make compromises).

Tempo may be a problem but sound is more so – almost a mystery. Two different conductors of the same opera may get different sound from the same orchestra and the same cast. Some conductors haven't penetrated the mystery of sound and disregard it; others make a fetish of it, sometimes at the expense of taste and style. Think of the different nuances of warmth – the chaste warmth of the Countess in "Dove sono" in *Figaro*; the noble passion of Leonore's "Abscheulicher!" in *Fidelio*; and the lascivious eroticism in Salome's "Schlussgesang". A good conductor will wring different warmth from his performers. Above all, there must always be discipline, *controlled* passion. In his *Pelléas et Mélisande* Debussy didn't want a confused blur, but subtle clarity and poetic intensity. When Richard Strauss conducted his *Elektra* or Wagner's *Tristan* – two works in which the orchestra speaks with symphonic power and a dominant voice – one could always hear the score as well as the singers.

The opera conductor must be completely in control of the entire artistic apparatus. He must have a thorough knowledge of the score in order to react in a split second when a singer makes a false cue or jumps ten bars. An operatic performance may be studded with accidents so he must always be ready for impending disaster. The great conductors agree that conducting opera is more complex than conducting symphonies, and they had valuable training in the opera houses. Within the past eighty years, the position of *Opernchef* (opera chief conductor) at the German Theatre in Prague was held by Mahler, Klemperer, Kleiber, Zemlinsky, Steinberg, and Szell. For all of them, the theatre became a springboard to fame. Most conductors love to conduct opera because it gives them a wider berth for their artistic abilities, but it is becoming difficult to find the artistically satisfactory conditions that many great conductors demand – they want to be in charge, and need ample rehearsal time.

The great conductor who loves to conduct opera is faced with many problems: the stars don't like a rehearsal, and some may depart by jet for the other side of the globe after a few performances. Managers are sometimes more interested in box-office receipts than in artistic excellence. Producers try to run the whole show from the stage and resent strong conductors who try to run it from the pit. But the great conductors quite rightly insist that they must be in complete control of the orchestra, of the soloists, and the chorus on the stage. They, and only they, can weld all the components into an artistic unity.

THE PRODUCER

It is only in the past fifty years that the conviction has spread that opera isn't only to be heard but that it should be seen and understood. The time of the producer (*régisseur, metteur-en-scène*) had come.

Richard Wagner made the breakthrough when he developed his Gesamtkunstwerk, the "total theatre", in theory and practice. In the German-speaking countries, and later elsewhere, Wagner's ideas began to take effect. The concept of the *Musiktheater* is a German invention. Oskar Fritz Schuh, the noted German producer, considers it "the only real invention that the German theatre has made in the course of the last twenty years". Schuh writes in *Bühne als geistiger Raum* (stage as spiritual space),

> The realization of opera as a dramatic form is no easy task, for it has to serve two masters. Opera production is only good when both ear and eye are catered for. Opera leaves one dissatisfied, however beautiful the music and singing may be, if the acting and scenic arrangements are inadequate. And all scenic experiment is useless if the singing is not beautiful and the music is bad . . . Now that it is being generally recognized that opera must also be good theatre, it is often difficult to find a way of avoiding extremes . . .

The synthesis of all elements in the production of opera was a slow development. It is often said that Gustav Mahler in Vienna, around 1900, was one of the first artists who saw and tried to realize a new concept of opera. But as late as 1902, the ride of the Valkyries in the third act of *Die Walküre* was performed by officers of the Imperial Guard Regiment, dressed up as Valkyries, wearing wigs, helmets and armour. They would ride across the back stage on white Lippizaner horses that came from the Court stables. But Mahler who introduced precision, artistic integrity and uncompromising devotion into a medium known for high Cs, improvisation and sloppiness, demanded that the Lippizaner horses be brought to the opera house in the morning to be conditioned to stage thunder and lightning, and that they be taken around the house at night shortly before their performance so there would be no "incidents". The Lippizaners would go through the rehearsing routine stolidly, but at night they were nervous and unpredictable.

The permutations of the ride of the Valkyries during the past five decades are symptomatic of the change of popular taste in grand opera. After the Imperial Guard officers (who later became headwaiters, doormen and tennis coaches), Alfred Roller, Mahler's celebrated stage designer, constructed a sort of merry-go-round, with chorus boys dressed up as Valkyries sitting on flying wooden horses. Stage hands would turn the merry-go-round, and there were bolts of lightning and crashes of thunder. The action took place behind a dark veil. Through openings in the veil the "Valkyries" could be seen galloping away. Wagnerians called it "the greatest ride outside of Bayreuth", where real horses were still being used. After the first *Ring*, Tchaikovsky wrote,

You have probably heard Wagner's celebrated "Ride of the Valkyries". How we actually seem to see these fierce heroines flying on their magic steeds amid thunder and lightning! In the concert room this piece makes an extraordinary impression. On the stage, in view of the cardboard rocks, the canvas clouds, and the soldiers running about awkwardly in the background, the music loses all power of expression. Here the stage does not enhance the effect, but rather acts like a wet blanket...

Ten years after his merry-go-round, Roller designed a new *Walküre* production, with papier-mâché figures of early-Mobiloil-style flying horses, and with sexy pin-up Valkyries. The contours were silhouetted against a white backdrop, dramatically lighted by flashes.

Today we would laugh at such staging, but there was method in Mahler's integrity. In *Rheingold*, the three Rhine maidens were placed behind rocks, while lithe members of the corps de ballet were whirled through space in special flying machines hoisted on steel cables from the rigging loft. They were to be seen, and Mahler insisted they must move their lips as though *they* were singing. Their costumes were impregnated with lighting paint, a fine effect on the dark stage. In Mahler's production of Verdi's *Otello*, the wild sea was created by stagehands holding large sails on ropes, while other men blew air in through hoses below the sails. Mahler insisted that the movements of the sea be synchronized with

Verdi's music, but during the première the stagehands got mixed up and forgot all about the music. Fifty years later, Herbert von Karajan, in the production of *Otello* that marked the beginning of his short, happy life as Vienna's *Operndirektor*, showed Verdi's magnificent storm by having the flags of Venice blown by wind-machines – not much progress.

Mahler and Roller produced a new *Tristan und Isolde* in 1903, after "endless experiments and an immense amount of hard work", as Roller said. Colours were used to express specific symbols: the orange-red sail of the ship in the first act, the violet-blue background of the love scene in the second act, and the "cold pale grayness" of the third act when Tristan dies, under a lime tree whose foliage spreads all over the stage (this colour scheme has been imitated by many *Tristan* producers since). Max Graf, the Viennese critic, wrote: "The scenery actually reproduced something of the chromatic harmony of the music, subtle vibrations of light and colour producing an effect that was intrinsically musical".

There was no "producer" yet. Mahler acted as his own *Régisseur*. It was still the era of the conductor in the opera house. The Mahler-Roller concept survived them, which proves its validity. Some of their productions, such as their *Don Giovanni*, lived on for decades. After the First World War, when more people went to the opera than before, the productions of the past were no longer accepted. It was no longer possible for the tenor or the *diva* to make a haphazard entrance, sing an aria, and then walk off the stage. In Salzburg, Max Reinhardt began to experiment on a very large scale. In Vienna, the name of Lothar Wallenstein appeared on the bill under the heading "*Regie*" (*mise-en-scène*); he worked closely with Clemens Krauss, the conductor. In Berlin, in 1931, Carl Ebert staged a production of Verdi's *Macbeth*, with sets and costumes by Caspar Neher.

The producer reached full status after the Second World War. In 1951, Wieland Wagner and his brother Wolfgang launched the first post-war Bayreuth Festival with Wieland's production of *Parsifal*, one of his greatest, which has been shown for twenty years. Neo-Bayreuth's impact was immense. Wieland Wagner, who had been a painter before he became a producer, worked with lights and colours. He started by designing his own productions, including sets and costumes; many producers now like to do this. Wieland Wagner established the precedence of the drama over the music: "The music is of secondary importance in Richard Wagner's work because the music owes its importance to the dramatic idea", he wrote, following up the precept of Richard Wagner. Opera had come full circle since Mozart called poetry "altogether the obedient daughter of the music"

Wieland Wagner once said the luckiest thing that happened to him was that he had never known Richard Wagner. He never thought of him as "Grandfather", but as a major influence in musical history. His father, Siegfried Wagner, had to contend with the formidable memory of the *Meister* all his life, and then he had to contend with his mother, the formidable Cosima, the autocratic daughter of Franz Liszt. She ordered that everything must be done in 1930 as the Master had done it in 1876. By eliminating the *Deutschtümelei* of the *ancien régime*, Wieland Wagner saved Richard Wagner's work from becoming a museum piece, and gave it a universal meaning.

In 1936, when Wieland Wagner was nineteen, he became unhappily conscious of the papier-mâché castles, the pseudo-naturalistic forests, the fat ladies in helmets shouting lustily. He told people how he felt about it. All hell broke loose among the German traditionalists. Bayreuth was the most tradition-ridden town in all Germany; Hitler felt at home there. After the Second World War, when word got around that the Wagner brothers were planning to make a sharp break with the past, they were boycotted by the citizens of Bayreuth. The butcher and the baker refused to sell to them; no one wanted to work for them. They said, "Your grandfather would be horrified to see what you did". Wieland replied, "On the contrary, he would be all for it". Unlike most citizens, Wieland had carefully studied Wagner's writings. During the first Festival in 1876, he had told his artists, "Children, create something that's new, forever new. If you stick to the past, you'll be a sad bunch of artists". Wieland understood that Wagner would not have wanted to produce nineteenth-century theatre in the twentieth century.

Wieland Wagner had no use for conductors who think they can produce and producers who think they can conduct. Staging and conducting are actually diametrically opposed: the conductor interprets the work "from inside out", while the producer looks at it "from the outside in" (Richard Wagner, an able conductor, hired Hans Richter to conduct the *Ring* at the inaugural Festival, while he himself staged it). Wieland Wagner used colour and light to give form and atmosphere to the drama, and to the music. To him the colour of a costume was as important as the sound of an instrument; a false shade was as painful as a sour note. The singers were taught the meaning of the music *and* of the words; they had to express every nuance with as little gesture as possible, and with just the right volume of voice. Members of an ensemble, they had to give up all egocentric mannerism, and submit completely to the producer's instruction. (The first thing the Wagner brothers did was to re-educate the

singers, trying to make them momentarily forget that they were prima
donnas and *Kammersänger*. Total theatre knows no stars.) Wieland preferred to stylize and indicate, whereas others were explicit, but he tried his
best to avoid ambiguity. "Mystic ambiguity merely confuses the audience,"
he said. "It's one of the things that give us Germans a reputation for being
deep when we are merely vague."

When Wieland Wagner decided to use only a sparse décor and to
work mainly with lights, he developed what had been foreseen by the
genius of Richard Wagner who had said to his wife Cosima, in 1878,
"Ach, how I hate all costumes and make-up. Having created the invisible
orchestra, I wish I could have created the invisible theatre". Wieland reduced the stage props in his *Ring* to a symbolic round disc on which the
events took place. Reflections and the lights of the cyclorama did the rest.
Today the lighting directions for many contemporary productions form
complicated "scores". The detailed stage directions fill another volume,
with every step and gesture marked. This entails strict discipline by the
performers who must watch their steps as much as their tones. Substitute
singers must be trained to literally follow in their predecessors' steps.
Unfortunately, this is not always done in the big opera houses, where a
new production sometimes falls to pieces when the original cast disperses.
While it is possible to keep things together during a festival which lasts
only a few weeks, the artistic intensity is not sustained during the long
season at most houses.

There are exceptions. The productions of Walter Felsenstein, the
distinguished director of the Komische Oper in East Berlin, are outstanding for daring conception and painstaking execution. For Felsenstein, the
basic questions in opera are: why, when and how does the performer sing
and perform on the stage? He believes that in traditional opera (which
Bertolt Brecht contemptuously called "kulinarische Oper", culinary opera
cooked up to please the subscribers), "the singing is done only with the
empty voice, without concrete emotion. The notes are not fulfilled. Only
fulfilled sound is real, and thus dramatic". Felsenstein sums it up:

> When I am in charge, I produce music with my singers. It is imperative
> to recognize the dramatic function of music and song: that is musical
> theatre. To make the production of music and song on the stage into
> a credible, convincing, real and indispensable human utterance – that
> is its cardinal aim.

Felsenstein spends months of hard work with hundreds of rehearsals
on each of his productions. He doesn't work with international singing

stars who, because it might hurt their voices, would revolt against his treatment. Felsenstein's singers rehearse so thoroughly that they are virtually hoarse by the time the production is ready for performance. His admirers claim that he has produced some often-heard masterpieces intuitively and consistently, with a perfection never before seen on the stage. His detractors feel that there is too much emphasis on the stage, at the expense of the music. While Felsenstein won't admit it, the conductor is subaltern to the producer. He will cancel a performance when a member of the cast gets sick rather than permit a hasty replacement; while trying to show the composer's intentions, he will not compromise. A performance of *Don Giovanni* impressed Lord Harewood, writing in London's *Opera* magazine, "by the almost unique matching of dramatic action to music". When Felsenstein was rehearsing Verdi's *Otello*, he tried to create a convincingly realistic storm by taking his chorus members for several weeks of rehearsals to the wind tunnel of a nearby aircraft factory where they learned to stand up, and act, against a storm blowing with velocity 12. After a performance in East Berlin attended by Rudolf Bing, Felsenstein apologized because the storm hadn't quite come off. "Some of them behaved as though the storm were blowing only with a velocity 8," he said angrily. Such perfectionism is possible only in countries where *kultura* is subsidized to the point of prodigality, and opera has a very high budget priority. Felsenstein occasionally stages fine performances in the West, but he achieves his best results at East Berlin's Komische Oper.

The tacit admission of the producer's outstanding status in opera was made in 1956 when Herbert von Karajan, one of the most famous and most controversial conductors of our time, decided to conduct *and* stage his own productions when he took over the Vienna State Opera. "For years," he once explained to me, "I've suffered while conducting when I looked up on the stage and saw things there – the wrong lights, the wrong colours, the wrong movements – which I felt went against the very spirit of the music. I then decided that when I had the chance I would make the stage look the way *I* felt it." Karajan's second act of *Tristan* was a fine reflection of his impressionistic approach to the music.

Other great conductors have suffered similar frustrations, but didn't believe that conductors should or *could* be their own producers. Karajan's productions are almost always outstanding musically; however, the staging is often problematical. Amateur producers often have fine ideas but fail in the basic movements of people on the stage. Karajan once admitted to me that he sometimes had a hard time getting people on stage and off again in a convincing manner. Many of his productions are dim, even dark, and the audience, failing to guess what occurs on the stage, becomes bored. The late Ferdinand Jaschke, for fifty-five years stage director of the Vienna Opera, from Mahler to Karajan, called this "merciful darkness . . . when in doubt, be dim".

Ideally, the finest results are brought about by a great conductor and a great producer combining their efforts on the basis of mutual understanding and respect. A *Figaro* production in Vienna which was staged by Günther Rennert, the distinguished German producer, and conducted inimitably by Karajan, was a delight from beginning to end. Rennert staged *Figaro* out of the spirit of the music, and kept the stage activity at the relevant pace. "For me," Rennert once said, "it is important to make sure that there is no question of letting the piece be exposed to some typical fashionable principle of style, that is to say it should not be mis-handled merely to exemplify some so-called trend of the time."

("Felsenstein, Rennert and Wieland Wagner reformed the often mendacious, empty opera theatre and turned it into our credible and brilliantly thought-out musical theatre", wrote Walter Erich Schäfer, dean of Germany's opera managers, formerly Karajan's co-director at the Vienna Opera, and now in charge of the Stuttgart State Opera.)

A happy co-operation was the production of *La Bohème* in 1966: Franco Zeffirelli created beautiful costumes and sets – an impressionistic Latin Quarter, and the melancholy sadness of the third act, with snow flakes falling down slowly – and he pointed up the psychological subtleties of the music so beautifully conducted by Karajan. Everybody agreed that they had never seen and heard so many "new" things in this often shop-worn masterpiece. The production travelled successfully from Milan to Vienna and later to Moscow and Munich, without losing its wonderful charm. In New York, Zeffirelli staged a beautiful *Falstaff* production, conducted by Leonard Bernstein. In Vienna, Bernstein conducted another *Falstaff*, which was staged by Luchino Visconti. The Zeffirelli-Karajan team, however, followed up their wonderful *Bohème* with a *Traviata* production, which was such a flop that the Scala management had the sets removed a few months later.

In 1965, Carlo Maria Giulini found himself confronted with a conception of *Don Giovanni* at the Holland Festival which he couldn't accept – the production was by Virginio Puecher, the sets by Luciano Damiani – and offered to withdraw. Peter Diamand, the Festival director, said that "when a producer and designer became the dominant figures in an opera production, the conductor would have to take second place". "The gradual ascendancy of the producer to the place of power has occurred almost imperceptibly," Harold Rosenthal wrote in *Opera*. "It is true that we ourselves have probably encouraged the trend. Perhaps we have been so bemused by the stage spectacle, gorgeous costumes, and producer's gimmicks, that we have relegated music to the second place . . . If Giulini's action makes us all reconsider, his stand will not have been taken in vain. I would like to think that from now on, musical considerations will always come first." We should remember that "opera" derives from *opera per musica*.

Much modern opera producing is still under the cloud of German expressionism and the influence of psychoanalysis. Some producers ignore the musical approach, but in an opera there can be no other. Julius Rudel, the manager of New York's City Opera, once discussed the modern producer "who imposes unmusical ideas and keeps things moving every second in a kind of feverish counterpoint to the music. The visual *perpetuum mobile* is intolerable in opera where the music keeps things moving and intrinsically motivates". It is the music ultimately that decides success or failure (though a bad libretto may almost ruin some great music, as in *Fidelio*). Too many modern artists appeal only to the intellect, although opera is more often an emotional than an intellectual experience. Ingmar Bergman, the Swedish producer, believes that "the music is fundamental. It must be interpreted correctly; from this, one must build a production that is never allowed to wander off" (after Bergman's production of *The Rake's Progress*, Stravinsky said that he'd never seen a better production of his work). Bergman demands three months for rehearsal, with the conductor present all the time, no substitute artists after the opening, and absolute control of all performances, as Felsenstein. Not all musicians agree. In 1964 Rolf Liebermann, composer and *Intendant* of the Hamburg Opera, pronounced the work of producers and designers "the first prerequisite for the realization of our total work of art".

The danger of overproducing may lead to forced originality. Zeffirelli's "naturalism" occasionally appears intensely old-fashioned. When Fritz Wotruba, the great sculptor, was asked to design the sets for a new *Ring* in West Berlin, he created "Grecian air in Wagner's northern lands", and built a primordial arc-shaped landscape, with crystalline blocks standing out of the mist. Scene changes were assisted by projection of light and by vapours. The critics thought it was great, but the Berlin audience booed Wotruba.

The designer's function is often misunderstood. He should never forget that his work must be theatrical, in character with the opera itself. What goes well for *Pelléas et Mélisande* would be utterly wrong in *Der Freischütz*. The designer must clearly distinguish between operas where a setting contemporary to the period of its creation is required (*Le Nozze di Figaro*) and others where no such restriction applies. But what about *Aida*? Should he try to realize his own ideas of ancient Egypt, or Verdi's ideas of Egypt, or his idea of Verdi's ideas? In the case of *Falstaff*, Boito's and Verdi's ideas are quite different from Shakespeare's ideas. When libretto and music date from different periods – Hofmannsthal's *Rosenkavalier* goes back to the era of Maria Theresia, while Strauss's music is pre-World War I Vienna – should he follow the libretto or the music? The consensus is that the designer cannot ignore the music.

Some of the greatest operas are hard to stage because they contain many divergent elements. *Don Giovanni* has an enormous range of drama, from Leporello's *buffo* scenes to the Commendatore's terrifying appearance in the penultimate scene when Don Giovanni goes to his perdition. Prominent producers have tried many approaches, from naturalism to symbolism, and almost all have failed. The work is so complex that the sublime often becomes the ridiculous. In the Schuh-Karajan production in Salzburg, the giant shadow of the stony guest fell on the wall, reminiscent of the *laterna magica* scenes of our childhood, and there was laughter in the audience when there should have been horror. Wieland Wagner hesitated to stage *Don Giovanni* because he thought it should have been called "The Last Days of Don Giovanni". He saw Mozart's masterpiece as a drama of failure. The protagonist no longer gives the illusion of being a hero. The great seducer fails in everything he tries: Donna Anna resists; he has troubles with Donna Elvira; he cannot even get Zerlina, the little peasant girl; and when he serenades a servant girl, he reaches the borderline between the heroic and the ludicrous.

Carmen is another often mis-produced masterpiece. The drama is strong and clear, the characters are real, the mood is strong, the setting clearly established – yet there is rarely a wholly satisfying production. Staging reflects contemporary taste, and people's ideas are changing constantly. Was the composer's intention understood or distorted? Did the producer study the score and try to see it with no prejudice or whim? Did he place correctly the accents of the production so that they are synchronized with the music? Did he face the dramatic problem or did he evade it by diverting the audience's attention from the evolution of the drama to trivial detail? Didn't he overtax his resources? Did he consider the size of the theatre? It is as difficult to stage intimate works in a large house as it is to stage Wagner's *Ring* in a small one. In Bayreuth, Wieland Wagner solved the problem of the *Schusterstube*, the first scene of the third act in *Meistersinger*, by using a mediaeval wood-cut to show Hans Sachs's work room. The critics were delighted but they strongly opposed the symbolism of the second act. The mood of the *Fliedermonolog* pervaded the scene – two large, lilac-coloured balloons were hung up on top of the stage – but the towers and roofs of Ye Merry Olde Nuremburg remained invisible, which bothered many people.

Everybody agrees that we must have experimental productions but do they belong in a large opera house which is expensive to run, or on a smaller, experimental stage? Few people object to elephants appearing in the Arena of Verona during the triumphal march in *Aida*, yet the critics objected when Karajan brought hunting dogs on the stage of the Vienna State Opera, when the landgrave and his hunting companions appear in *Tannhäuser*. "The stage may well be regarded as holding a mirror up to nature but it is, of necessity, a distorting mirror," writes Sir Osbert Sitwell. "The situations that it reflects are the result of a selective process and must, therefore, be in some measure magnified or, on occasion, reduced." How can one show a sophisticated audience used to moon-flights and computers the miracle of the Holy Grail, in *Parsifal*, or the gold of the Rhine, without creating involuntary merriment? Producers are often accused of sinning against artistic integrity, of holding up the dramatic narrative, of ignoring the deeper meaning of the music. In one year both Marc Chagall and Oskar Kokoschka created designs, sets and costumes for *Die Zauberflöte*. It is a cheerful symptom that the "irrational" medium of opera once again attracts great artists, as it did in various earlier epochs, provided that the artists make a serious effort to understand *opera per musica*.

Once upon a time the producer was but a stage manager. Today an able producer is the guiding spirit of the performance. He doesn't have to be a trained musician but he should interpret visually what the composer tried to express in sound. He shouldn't consider himself the supreme arbiter of a "new style", but rather (as a good conductor does) the faithful servant of the composer without whom there would be no opera. There are producers who treat the musical and vocal elements of opera as though they were secondary. Something is wrong when people talk more about the brilliant staging of an opera than about the music, and the work itself.

ORCHESTRA, CHORUS, COACHES

Opera is often primarily identified with singers, "the stars of opera". Historically, however, they have remained almost without influence in the development of opera as an art form. Mozart's admiration for the great bass Francesco Benucci enhanced his decision to set Beaumarchais' *Figaro* to music, but he would have written *Figaro* anyway; Bellini would have written *Il Pirata* without the tenor Rubini; and Verdi didn't write *Otello* and *Falstaff* because of Victor Maurel, although Maurel himself may have believed so. Some operas are known as "singer's operas", "tenor's operas", "coloratura operas", because they owe their success to great singers or vocal ensembles. During the eighteenth and nineteenth centuries, the singers were the most important people in the opera house, often better known than the composers whose works they often wilfully distorted. No wonder many composers considered them a necessary evil.

The evolution of opera, from Monteverdi to this day, illustrates that the essential component at the opera house, from the composer's point of view, is the orchestra. Opera became exciting when Monteverdi created his timeless music drama – his orchestra created "the boldly arched, purely expressive, sculptured melody that was to haunt composers for a century" (Paul Henry Lang). Two hundred and twenty-eight years after Monteverdi's *Poppea*, Richard Wagner used his orchestra thus in *Tristan*.

"The history of opera shows the singer in a long battle with the orchestra, with the outcome never in doubt", writes Henry Pleasants. The public likes Wolfram's "Lied an den Abendstern" in *Tannhäuser*, but the "Lied" hardly compares to the symphonic poem performed by the orchestra in the second act of *Tristan*, where the voices are treated as vocal instruments. People love "La donna è mobile" in *Rigoletto,* paying no attention to the orchestral accompaniment, but Verdi's masterpieces are *Otello* and *Falstaff* where he uses the orchestra like a human voice. Puccini, generally considered a "singer's composer", used his orchestra poetically in the score of *La Bohème* and magnificently in *Turandot. Elektra* and *Der Rosenkavalier*, perhaps the most durable operas of Richard Strauss (though for different reasons), use the orchestra as the leading voice. In *Figaro* and *Don Giovanni*, the drama and the humour, the mood and the emotion, the passion and the irony are not in the singing voices but in the orchestra.

Then why is the orchestra's contribution to opera often treated in cavalier fashion by the management, the critics, the public? They comment on the singing, the staging, the lighting, but rarely on the orchestral playing, which is taken for granted. Many managers still think as Monteverdi did, when he was running the Teatro San Cassiano in Venice. He spent most of his budget on famous singers, and what little remained, on scenery, staging, chorus and orchestra. Today's great opera houses are ranked according to the great voices which they present, and possibly to the opulence of their productions, but not to the quality of the orchestra, which is noticed only when it plays very badly, or exceptionally well, as the Vienna Philharmonic occasionally does at the Vienna State Opera, or the Berlin Philharmonic during Karajan's Easter Festival in Salzburg.

The word "orchestra" derives from the Greek ορχηστρα, "a dancing place" – the part of the Greek theatre between the semi-circular seats of the auditorium and the stage, a few inches below the front row, where the chorus, from twelve to fifteen members, sang or spoke its comment (exactly where the orchestra pit is today). In his orchestra for *Orfeo* (1607), Monteverdi used violins, viols of three different sizes, end-blown flutes, cornets, trumpets, trombones, harp, harpsichords and three small organs. Some of the wind instruments could play only three different notes, but Monteverdi used his resources admirably. He made the strings the foundation of the orchestra which they've remained to this day, using *pizzicato* (plucked notes) effects, and inventing the bow *tremolo*.

Schütz, Lully, Purcell and Scarlatti used wind instruments in solo parts. Gluck became one of the first masters of modern orchestration. Berlioz, in his *Traité de l'Instrumentation* (later revised by Richard Strauss), quotes seventeen examples from Gluck's "new" orchestration. Gluck introduced the piccolo flute, found new ways of using the harp and the trombone, used arpeggios and string reiteration, and developed the use of the *tremolo*. He was feared by his musicians in Paris "because no pianissimo was delicate enough for him, and no fortissimo strong enough". When he conducted, the members of his orchestra received double pay since "the hardships of the rehearsals were considered unique" (no modern conductor may claim such a distinction). Gluck thought nothing of holding twenty or thirty rehearsals of a certain work (in Vienna, Wagner unhappily abandoned his production of *Tristan* after eighteen months of rehearsing the orchestra and the singers). One hundred and fifty years before Mahler made a fetish of *Werktreue* (fidelity to the score), Gluck had insisted on absolute faithfulness to the original.

The eighteenth-century orchestra was no miracle of accuracy. There were no standard tuning devices, and it was almost impossible for the orchestra to play in tune. The crescendo of the woodwinds was not spectacular. Gradually, the woodwinds began to form a self-contained choir. Valved trumpets and slide trombones were invented. Haydn, Mozart and Beethoven improved orchestral technique. Richard Wagner made the orchestra the expressive voice of his Gesamtkunstwerk. Richard Strauss wrote, "Wagner was the first who dared introduce virtuoso technique into all instrumental parts of the orchestra, something that Beethoven had indicated earlier in his last string quartets, but not in his symphonies".

Wagner's magnificent orchestration expresses drama, humour, action, passions and the subtle psychological nuances of his characters. The orchestration of *Tristan und Isolde* expresses the hidden thoughts and secret emotions of the characters. The characters on the stage may lie – there are many lies in the *Ring*, a story of betrayal – but the orchestra tells the truth. When the critics asked Gluck why Orestes in his *Iphigénie* appears so calm on the stage while the music is restless, he answered, "Orestes lies. The violas don't lie. Orestes killed his mother".

Wagner modernized the orchestra and gave it the prominence it deserved. He began to divide the strings into parts; sometimes the members of the first violin section play differently. He increased the number of woodwinds and brass. In order to cope with his technical demands, the musicians had to study their instruments. In Wagner's orchestra, nearly all instrumentalists became melodists. He introduced new tone colours and sound mixtures, introduced the "Wagnerian" tuba that had been invented in 1835 by the German bandmaster Wieprecht, and added the four-valve contrabass tuba (which is not called the Wagnerian tuba but was his idea). In *Rheingold,* he uses one cymbal hanging freely, touched lightly by the felt-covered drumstick of the kettledrums, to give the glittering acoustical impression of the gold.

Debussy developed the technique of orchestration into almost an art by itself. His shimmering orchestration of *Pelléas et Mélisande* resembles the colour poetry of the French impressionist painters: poetry had been turned into music. The twentieth-century Viennese composers changed the emotional colours of the orchestra, and introduced unheard-of contrasts and effects. In *Wozzeck*, Alban Berg creates an atmosphere of chaos and hallucination through classical forms. After Wozzeck murders Marie, the entire orchestra plays a terrifying *unisono* crescendo that builds up into supreme emotional suspense.

Opera lovers, a prejudiced breed, often consider *their* house the best. But there is no doubt that, among the world's leading houses, the Vienna State Opera has the best orchestra, the Vienna Philharmonic. For over a century the Wiener Philharmoniker has exercised a strong influence on Vienna's musical life, and remained the stabilizing element at the Opera. Singers come and go, conductors and managers are hired and fired, but the orchestra remains. Its first-stand artists are also prominent teachers, and the tradition of instrumental playing is handed down from professor to pupil. It was the ambition of the "good families" to have a Philharmoniker in charge of the children's musical education. Later, the young people became music lovers and opera enthusiasts and bought subscriptions at the Opera and the Philharmonic concerts. Ever since, there has remained an intimate contact between the orchestra and the public.

Nowadays, the dual position of the musicians – as members of the Philharmonic and of the orchestra at the opera house – creates complications. Playing at the State Opera, often under conductors of little distinction, is not an ideal training. As members of the Opera orchestra the musicians are state employees, playing a certain number of performances month after month. Eventually, they retire with a state pension. Some become music bureaucrats, unable to avoid the impact of the state bureaucracy. No other major orchestra on earth has such a tight schedule: playing a symphony concert at noon, and possibly a five-hour Wagner opera at night, as well as recording sessions, tours and other activities. But at best, the Vienna Philharmonic furnishes a magnificent opera orchestra. They instinctively synchronize their playing with the singing voices, even under a bad conductor who doesn't keep contact between orchestra and stage. No wonder that celebrated singers are often enthusiastic about the orchestra, one that makes the Vienna Opera primarily a musical institution, with a deep sense of tradition.

Since the Second World War, managers have begun to realize the growing importance of the orchestra. Prominent conductors demand better orchestras and more rehearsal time. (Karl Böhm had twenty-five orchestra rehearsals at the Metropolitan when he studied *Wozzeck*, but the critics agreed that the effort, and the expense, paid off.) Since Mahler and Toscanini, the standards of orchestra playing at the opera house have improved. In Bayreuth, Wieland and Wolfgang Wagner gave the orchestra its prominent place in the festival scheme: for years, the best instrumentalists from East and West Germany formed a great orchestra that would have pleased even Richard Wagner, who had created for his super-orchestra the "sunken" pit underneath the stage, which he called "the mystic abyss". It is a vast rectangular cavern sloping downwards under the stage. Only the conductor can be seen by the singers, and even he cannot be seen by the audience. The podium is screened by a wooden barrier. This is said to be the reason why some famous conductors have refused to conduct in Bayreuth; some modern conductors love to be seen. At La Scala's revival, in 1969, of Rossini's *Le Siège de Corinthe*, Thomas Schippers "distinguished himself by being the first conductor at the Scala to have a thin white spotlight directed at his head during the whole opera ... Who goes to the opera to see the conductor? Wagner had the right idea when he introduced the sunken orchestra pit in Bayreuth ... " writes Harold Rosenthal in *Opera* magazine.

Conducting in Bayreuth isn't easy. The conductor can hardly hear the singers, and they can't see him very well. Some conductors work in shirt sleeves, and some wear shirts that reflect light. The musicians don't hear the singers at all, and in some sections of the pit they don't even hear themselves. Under the circumstances, the conductor has a hard time keeping singers and orchestra together.

The chorus is often even more ignored by audiences and critics than the orchestra, yet it is older than the orchestra; indeed, in the Greek theatre, it had the function of an orchestra. Later, the chorus became an independent and important element in opera. Composers have found ingenious ways of using the chorus: Wagner employs the power of the chorus to characterize an important personage, as in the last scene of *Meistersinger* which culminates in the chorus' "Wach auf!" tribute to Hans Sachs. In *Lohengrin* and *Der Fliegende Holländer*, the chorus dominates long stretches of the action. In *Götterdämmerung*, it increases the dramatic tension. In *Fidelio*, Beethoven builds the prisoners' chorus, "Oh welche Lust!" into one of the most moving moments of the whole literature.

In *Carmen*, Bizet uses the chorus almost as a second orchestra. The members of the chorus lose their usual facelessness and become individual types. Puccini, a master of stage technique, uses the chorus effectively. Butterfly's first entrance, and the entrance of Scarpia in *Tosca* are dramatized by the chorus. In the second act of *La Bohème*, the chorus carries on the action. Puccini learned much from Verdi, who often expressed the emotions of the characters through, or against, choral accompaniment – in *Trovatore*, *La Traviata*, *Otello*, *Falstaff*. In the great climax of *Aida*, Verdi uses his protagonists and the chorus. In his late masterpiece, *Turandot*, Puccini uses the chorus as a super-protagonist.

This was done earlier in *Boris Godunov*. Mussorgsky made the chorus (the people of Russia) the hero of his opera and it expresses the people's emotions – fear and hope, humour and sadness. At various moments, it is weak or strong, benevolent or vicious, almost becoming a study in mass hysteria. Later, Benjamin Britten used the chorus prominently in *Peter Grimes*.

There would be no opera without chorus, but the chorus is usually taken for granted. When it is bad, it is blamed, yet it is rarely praised when very good. People have always noticed the pretty girls of the corps de ballet, but rarely the members of the chorus. Yet today much is asked from them. They must not only be able to sing, but should sing *together* which is not easy. Solo singing and chorus singing are altogether different. To-day's producers expect the chorus to move around and perform realistically and accurately, while singing difficult passages together, possibly in a foreign language. Felsenstein demands the same precision of his chorus that Toscanini demanded of his orchestra. The chorus at the Metropolitan sings in Italian, German, French, Russian and English.

At the great opera houses that have a large repertoire, the members of the chorus are expected to sing well, in proper pitch, without creating conspicuous attention. They have to learn the music of forty or fifty different operas. They are not supposed to look at the conductor; sometimes they must sing with their backs to him. When they move across the stage, they often don't hear the orchestra. If a singer makes a mistake, the conductor will try to help him. If a chorus member makes a premature entrance, he will be noticed like the proverbial horn playing a sour note. While the applause begins and the soloists take curtain calls, the chorus members are expected to leave the stage. Only rarely, in special operas, are they given a couple of curtain calls, by a producer and conductor who appreciate their contribution.

Why do people become chorus members? Possibly for the same reason they become second violinists: because they couldn't play first. Once in many years, a chorus member is noticed and makes a career as a soloist. But life isn't all resignation for the members of a good chorus: there is a special satisfaction in being an important element in the production of an opera.

There are other cogs in the machine that are never noticed by the public: members of the musical staff, *répétiteurs* and coaches who spend their artistic lives in dedicated anonymity. Yet without them there would be no opera. There would be no star singers, no prima donnas. Though the audience doesn't always realize it, it is a fact that their favourite singers are not born knowing their parts, and that they need help. A few singers are accomplished musicians, but the large majority relies on coaches. Some of the most famous singers have to have every single note, every syllable, played and sung to them over and over again, although, later, they must give the impression of complete identification with their part.

A singer doesn't have to be a born musician, but a good coach must be. He must have a strong sense of rhythm and a sharp ear. His work begins long before he starts coaching a singer. He must study the score, compare the piano score for possible mistakes and misprints with the orchestral score and, when in doubt, check with the conductor. Various editions may contain different ornaments. An *appoggiatura* – a note inserted between two other notes to give support or emphasis to a melodic line or harmonic progression – is often a source of argument. Even a well-made piano score is rarely a faithful condensation of the orchestral score. Is a staccato chord, marked 'ff' in the piano score, played *pizzicato* by the strings, or by the whole orchestra?

The good *répétiteur* emphasizes the musical line of the orchestra, and doesn't confuse the singer with details of the accompaniment, which the singer probably won't hear anyway when he performs on the stage. In duets, it is the *répétiteur's* job to accompany the singer and to sing the other part, so the singer will learn the entrance cues, and he must know the orchestral parts if he is to teach the singer the vocal score. Gifted singers may not always be endowed with a sense of rhythm or feeling for accuracy. The *répétiteur* must be strict and tough in his demands. He doesn't have to be a singing teacher – the singer may have his own teacher whom he visits periodically – but he should know, theoretically, a great deal about the art of singing. Occasionally he may have to demonstrate with his own (bad) voice how a certain phrase should be sung – phrasing is extremely important. The *répétiteur* must never allow a mistake to go unchecked, for it could easily become a bad habit with the singer. The coach must also be an amateur psychologist (should he be firm or lenient with a singer?) – and have the patience of Job.

The next stop is ensemble work. In many popular operas – *Le Nozze di Figaro, Meistersinger, Otello* and others – there are ticklish ensembles involving soloists and choruses. While the conductor works with the orchestra, the musical staff under the chorus master tries to get soloists and chorus together. Things may be further complicated when there is off-stage music, or special orchestras on the stage (as in the ballroom scene of *Don Giovanni*); then the producer begins to interfere, wanting people to act while they sing. Eventually, everything should be correlated under the conductor's beat.

Some modern houses use closed-circuit television, which gives people a chance to see the conductor from spots where they normally cannot. The chorus master or coach, who conducts the chorus backstage, doesn't then have to balance on a high ladder, holding up the score, in danger of falling at a dramatic moment. Eventually, there is a piano dress rehearsal, rehearsals with the orchestra, a final rehearsal, all requiring careful planning, timed well in advance. Sometimes more than one opera is rehearsed at the same time which complicates matters. Certain singers may be cast in both works. There are conflicting demands: a singer must be excused from a rehearsal because he or she sings at night in a performance. Guest artists arrive. Their time is always limited, but they, too, should be coached. Inexperienced but promising singers need help. But out of the confusion comes a performance. Afterwards, when the excitement is over, the applause, the ovations, the reviews, no one outside the opera house gives any thought to those members of the anonymous musical staff who made all this possible.

THE AUDIENCE

Very little is known about the audience in the opera house; nevertheless, neither the creative artist nor the performer can ignore it. In the last analysis, the audience decides what it does and doesn't like. Monteverdi watched the audience carefully. Mozart and Verdi often refer to the public in their letters. Beethoven was the exception, but he was never successful as a composer of opera.

Opera began as the cultured hobby of noblemen and princes of the church, emperors and kings. They enjoyed it, often appeared in opera as dilettantes, and paid for it, handsomely. In Austria, the Habsburgs did for opera what the Medicis in Florence did for painting. For centuries, the Vienna Opera was the Emperor's private domain. In Italy and Germany, the opera houses were court theatres, subsidized by the nobility and the church. The exception was The Most Serene Republic of Venice where opera from its very beginning was popular entertainment, performed for the people. When Monteverdi ran the first public opera house there, the Teatro San Cassiano, in 1637, he was confronted with the whims of popular taste. Even in Venice, however, a distinction was made between the haves in the boxes and stalls, and the havenots in the galleries. Nowadays, the people in the galleries often know more about the opera than the people in the expensive boxes, whereas in Italy and France, during the eighteenth and early nineteenth centuries, the rich were among the most discriminating members of the audience. In Austria and Germany, the burghers began to attend opera in the 1820s. In Vienna, in many houses of Germany, and in Italy, the galleries have remained an important segment of the audience ever since. They are passionate about opera, enthusiastic and critical. At La Scala or at the Teatro Regio in Parma, the habitués of *il loggione*, the gallery, are much feared by the artists. During the 1920s, when I was a member of the claque in the fourth gallery of the Viennese State Opera, the *Vierte Galerie* was the seismograph of success or failure. Up there were the young artists who would one day work in the orchestra or on the stage. They would stand in line the whole night to get a ticket to an "important" performance and would carry the heavy scores to the gallery, "controlling" the artists.

Many people who don't care for opera – because it's "extravagant" or "unreal" or "a hybrid art form" – consider the opera house a sort of private club for a few *aficionados*. In the United States this is a popular argument among those who are against public subsidy of opera. There is nothing private about opera in Italy, where it is one of the most popular forms of entertainment. And in Germany, France, in London and in many cities on the Continent, opera is winning new friends every day. The esoteric element has disappeared from the opera house, the purists and "true connoisseurs" of music now preferring chamber music or church music.

In America and England, surveys made in the past ten years established a few facts about the operatic audience. More women than men go to hear opera. In the United States, women account for 63 per cent, and in Great Britain for 55 per cent, of the audience. Among men, the majority are in the professions. According to *Performing Arts – The Economic Dilemma*, by Professors William J. Baumol and William G. Bowen, the educational level of operatic audiences is "extraordinarily high", and audiences are "well off financially". Relatively few people below the age of twenty and above the age of sixty attend opera (this is quite different in Europe). In the Anglo-Saxon countries, the legitimate theatre is attended most frequently, followed by orchestral concerts, opera, and the ballet.

Such studies are necessarily incomplete. Opera lovers are a very special breed. They rarely conform to any pattern. They fall in love with opera and usually stay in love with it. Some people go to gala premières and special openings, and are not seen at the opera house during the rest of the year, but they don't count. During the season, it's always the same people that go to the opera. The management of the Metropolitan believes that Italian, German and Jewish immigrant groups account for a considerable percentage of their habitués – the people whose parents used to go to the opera "in the old country".

However, the worldwide cultural revolution has brought many changes. People now hear first-rate opera on recordings, on the radio, and sometimes see it on television, and they become addicts. In the Communist countries, opera ranks high among the pursuit of "culture" – a development that was officially promoted first in the Soviet Union, and later in other countries – and audiences there have ceased to be middle class, because there is no more middle class. At the National Theatre in Prague, the Warsaw Opera, the Staatsoper in East Berlin, working-class people (meaning practically everybody because everybody works for a living) have become enthusiastic opera-goers. In Milan, the richest city in Italy, La Scala gives forty evenings each season for workers, at low prices, with the same casts that have appeared earlier in gala performances. In many other cities on the Continent special performances for workers and employees are given. The time may come, even in America, when the opera house is no longer a club for the happy few.

The age of tourism has also affected the opera house. In Vienna, a visit to the Staatsoper, or to one of the various festivals, is a must for foreign visitors. Nowadays, the expensive stalls and boxes at the State Opera are often occupied by "the foreigners". Some Viennese are there on subscription nights, or they queue up for hours to get the less expensive seats in the galleries, because they cannot afford to sit in the *Parterre*. The tourist at the opera is a pleasant phenomenon for the box office, but not necessarily for the performers. There are American tourists who attend the Vienna Opera, because the guidebooks tell them to. They are visibly astonished by the strange goings-on on the stage, and by the weird enthusiasm of the standees. Many wish they were elsewhere, and are glad when it's over.

The audience has become the last distinguishing element in the leading opera houses of the world. Star systems and air travel have created a *Gleichschaltung* of repertory, casts and artistic apparatus. The world's opera stages become sets of the same *stagione* during certain months of the year. September in Berlin, winter in New York and Milan, spring in Vienna and London, summer in Bayreuth and Salzburg. Same producers, same conductors, same singers. Not very exciting.

Only the audiences retain some characteristics of their own. Italians love opera and become excited by it. The Viennese and many Germans were "brought up on opera", and go, often dutifully. People in London go because they like it, although it's still somewhat "eccentric". And New York, as always, is a mixture of everything.

The Metropolitan's audiences like faultless, forceful singing. They care less about style and musicality, but there is a growing tendency towards better integrated performances (and at the same time, there is a tendency among audiences in Europe to judge performers by the strength of their high Cs rather than by their artistic conception of a part). Twenty years ago, quite a few people would leave before the end of a *Tristan* or *Don Giovanni* performance. Nowadays, they come in time for the beginning and stay to the end of *Die Frau ohne Schatten,* a true test of endurance.

Opera audiences in London are well informed and, on the whole, well mannered. They are not as enthusiastic as the Italians, and fortunately don't analyse all the time, as do many people in Vienna and Munich. The audience at La Scala is often overrated. There are always *cognoscenti* in the gallery, but the people in the stalls are often indifferent to lapses in musical taste. Once in a while there is a little scandal, and everybody is happy. But people speak wistfully about the great evenings when a gentleman in tails would become so upset by the tenor that he would throw his patent-leather shoe at him, or, even better, a mature tomato. No one is bothered by the fellow next to you humming the melody, which would never happen in Vienna or Berlin. There the atmosphere is hushed, rather like school: no one dares whisper or move. Local audiences are critical and uncompromising, except towards certain *Lieblinge* who get away with murder and even cracked notes. Viennese audiences are often unpredictable. They may cheer an ageing singer on the sentimental theory "you should have heard how well he sang fifteen years ago". Score reading is so popular that the State Opera has provided certain seat rows in the gallery with reading lights. The orchestra is carefully watched; a sour note by a horn player can create a minor disturbance. Unpopular conductors are booed even before they raise their baton, which doesn't seem fair. But fairness has never been a characteristic of the opera house.

To boo or not to boo has become a passionate argument among opera-goers. Hissing and booing (and whistling, which, until The American Influence, had been a sign of disapproval in Europe) were never restricted to the more "violent" opera houses in Italy – Parma and Naples – where operatic manners were known to be dangerous. Elsewhere every manifestation of displeasure was known as a "scandal at the opera house", duly reported in the papers the next morning. Such "scandals" were often "arranged" by a "clique" supporting a "competitor". There were precedents in operatic history – the violent "wars" between the partisans of Gluck and Piccinni in Paris, of Mozart and Salieri in Vienna, of Paisiello and Rossini in Rome. Wagner, as usual, had the field to himself; he managed to divide the audience into two vociferous and belligerent groups. Some opera houses try to prohibit such protestations in advance. The Vienna Opera displayed signs, "*Alle störenden Bei- und Missfallens- kundgebungen*" (all disturbing manifestations, for or against, are forbidden). For years, the programme of the Metropolitan requested the audience "respectfully but urgently . . . not to interrupt the music with applause". Such appeals are absurd and ineffectual. Why shouldn't people manifest their spontaneous reactions?

Indiscriminate applause, however, is as pointless as booing out of spite, of from supporting a rival singer. There is some belief that the dignified way to show one's displeasure is to remain silent, "to sit on one's hands". Silence can be utterly degrading, after a badly sung aria. But it may also be misunderstood by the singer as a sign of subdued approval. When in doubt, fellow opera lovers, clap your hands or boo.

THE CLAQUE AND THE CRITICS

The compleat opera house must have a claque. It belongs there with the general manager, the prima donna, the orchestra. An expert claque is more valuable than an amateurish clique, made up of admirers of the *diva* or the leading tenor. A trained member of the claque will never force his applause upon the public.

The claque is older than opera itself. It was known long before the Florentines began to experiment with opera in the late sixteenth century. Nero, who handled his public relations with a strong hand, had "a body of hired applauders". So had all dictators after him. Owing to their pedigree, the claqueurs in eighteenth-century Paris were called *les Romains*. They referred to each other as *chevaliers de lustre*, conscious of their ability to give brilliance to a lustreless performance. Until the end of the eighteenth century the names of the singers were not printed on the playbill. Ticket dealers were occasionally beaten up by angry customers, who, hoping to hear a prima donna, had been served a lustreless replacement.

In 1837, it was proposed in Paris that an official claque be introduced to educate innocent audiences and teach ignorant but well-meaning amateurs the subtleties of applause. (Fortunately, the proposal was not accepted. A bureaucratically run claque would soon lose its effectiveness.) The true claqueur is an educator. In Paris, many composers, authors and artists realized that it was safer to depend on organized applause than on the doubtful support of friends and admirers. "Observation for more than two decades has convinced me that the public is much better off in the hands of a claque than in the hands of a clique", writes Irving Kolodin. Alexandre Dumas *père* often consulted the *chef* of the claque about proper applause.

Hector Berlioz even distinguished between various kinds of applauding, from "creating as much noise as possible by striking one hand against the other . . . the fingertips of the right hand striking in the hollow of the left produce a sharp and resonant sound favoured by the majority of artists", down to "striking the two hands flat against each other which gives a dull and commonplace sound", and he defines it as "apprentice claqueurs' and barber's assistants' applause". Our opera houses are crowded with barber's assistants these days, and with veritable anti-claqueurs who applaud at the wrong time for the wrong singer in the wrong place. Unlike Rudolf Bing who got so irritated by the claque at the Metropolitan that he tried to stop their commendable activities, Berlioz well knew that

> . . . the claque has become a necessity of our time. In whatever shape or disguise, with whatever excuse, it has won its way everywhere. It reigns and governs in the theatre, at concerts, in the National Assembly, in clubs, churches and corporations, in the press and even in the salons. Whenever twenty people are gathered together to pronounce judgement on the sayings or doings or ideas of anyone standing before them, you may rest assured that at least one fourth of this jury has been planted among the other three fourths for the purpose of sparking them if they can catch fire . . . The claque at our theatres have become experts. Their profession has risen to be an art. People have often admired, but never adequately in my opinion, the wonderful talent with which Augustus [the claque *chef* of the Paris Opéra at the time of Berlioz] directed the great works of the modern repertory, and the high quality of advice he could give to authors on many occasions . . .

Berlioz concludes that, so far as good applause is concerned, "the public is absolutely of no use in the theatre". The general public should pay for being let in but should refrain from making undignified noises for the wrong person. How right he was! Today, good singing is widely and mistakenly confused with loud singing. The singers with the strongest vocal cords win the loudest ovations. Managers shouldn't try to forbid the claque, but instead encourage its artistic development. We remember the great Augustus from Berlioz's tribute but we've long forgotten, if we ever knew, the names of the managers of the Paris Opéra at the time of Augustus. The claque gives the opera house a much-needed element of enthusiasm. Berlioz reports that the claqueurs who came "from the ranks of commercial travellers, grounded cab drivers, poor students . . ." were opera-struck.

In my own claque days, most members of the claque at the Vienna State Opera were young musicians and singers and students, but there were also people of doubtful ancestry, and some black sheep from good bourgeois families who had deserted their family dinners in favour of a night at the Opera. Doubtless, an opera house needs the public, both the wealthy people buying expensive seats and making large contributions, and those in the galleries who will always send in a couple of dollars when an opera house is in trouble financially. But it also needs a claque that provides stimulation on dull evenings, orderly enthusiasm during great performances, and just rewards at all times.

The claqueur knows the score, has an understanding of the art of singing, is endowed with a sixth sense regarding the mood of the audience, and has perfect timing; he knows exactly when carefully started and built-up applause will have the greatest effect. Unless the applause begins at a certain moment – at the end of an aria, not too early, which might ruin the singer's last tone, and not too late, when the opportunity is gone – there may be disaster at the opera house. Inept applause that fizzles out ingloriously helps neither the singer nor the opera.

In his witty memoir, *Evenings with the Orchestra*, Hector Berlioz defined the professional claqueur as one who is "educated, shrewd, cautious, inspired". Each of these adjectives is fully justified. "Courageous" would be another. Under Gustav Mahler and some of his successors in Vienna, the members of the claque needed cool heads and steady nerves. They were often persecuted by the police who treated them like common criminals and disturbers of the peace. "Masters of the claquerie do not harbour love for overheated outsiders," Berlioz writes. "They show a distrust amounting to dislike for such adventurers of enthusiasm, *condottieri*, suicide squads, who rush in among them like fools and applaud without rehearsing first". He understood the claque. In Vienna, our carefully prepared actions were often frustrated by "overheated" members of a clique who would cut off a singer's aria during the last pianissimo, or irritate the public by entrance applause which is permissible only in exceptional circumstances – a favourite artist returning after a long absence. Verdi obviously expected applause after "La donna è mobile", yet not after Aida's "Nile" aria in the third act, which is so difficult that it often misfires – and Verdi knew it. Sometimes it is necessary to applaud "into the music". Only bold men with stout hearts should do this. Such applause must start with sufficient force and momentum that it literally stops the show. In Vienna, we often did this after the tenor's "Nessun dorma" in the third act of *Turandot* that ends with a high C. Puccini, possibly doubtful of tenors, or already so ill that he no longer cared, provided no pause for an ovation there. Unless applause hits the auditorium like lightning, it creates a shocking "disturbance".

In the great days of the Vienna claque under the unforgettable Joseph Schostal, we were welded into a precision instrument of musical timing and psychological skill. We would provide friendly guidance for the lukewarm subscriber, inject a healthy sense of competition among the artists, save many evenings from dullness, and generally contribute to the standard of the performance. The volume of our applause ranged from a mild shower after Cherubino's "Non so più" in *Figaro*, appropriate to the style of Mozart's lovely music, to a dramatic tumult after Iago's "Credo" in *Otello*. Schostal used to say, "It is the claque that makes the opera grand". He made the tactical decisions, often at the spur of the moment – whether an artist deserved applause, though he hadn't paid for it in advance, or whether one who had paid would get none, because he didn't deserve it. (Only the claque *chef* got paid. The members of the august institution were given free standing room tickets, and nothing else.) Schostal was incorruptible. He would even give the supreme accolade, a booming "Bravo!" at the end of the aria, to an artist who had declined a financial contribution to the claque *chef*. No wonder the claque often made headlines when the artist didn't. "The claque was in its usual top form," Julius Korngold, the music critic of *Neue Freie Presse* (and successor of Eduard Hanslick) wrote in his report. There were malicious reports that Schostal gave audible support to Korngold's son, Erich Wolfgang, the composer of *Die tote Stadt*. The truth is that we did support Maria Jeritza and Richard Tauber, the protagonists, who were usually in top form in this work, but we didn't applaud the composer.

Schostal loved opera so much that he took a busman's holiday listening to a five-hour performance of *Parsifal* during which, according to tradition in Vienna, there is no applause, allegedly because Richard Wagner wouldn't permit it, though in fact he did no such thing. Wieland Wagner once told me he hoped some day people would applaud after *Parsifal*, when the performance was good. Another, more sympathetic Viennese tradition is to applaud the appearance of Hans Sachs on the festival meadow in the third act of *Meistersinger*, particularly if he happens to be such a great Sachs as Paul Schöffler. The Vienna claque knew better than to applaud after the high B that comes towards the end of Don José's "La fleur que tu m'avais jetée", because we knew that Don José must still sing "Carmen, je t'aime". But some "overheated" outsiders didn't know it, and would ruin the tenor's greatest moment. After Zerbinetta's bravura aria, "Grossmächtige Prinzessin", in *Ariadne auf Naxos*, ignorant listeners would applaud after the final bravura sequence, though the poor girl raises her hand; she still has to sing "Sind wir stumm". Maybe Richard Strauss did it on purpose. He didn't like coloratura sopranos.

Berlioz, an able composer, admitted that "the art of the claque has affected musical composition". He spoke of composers who had ended their pieces "with the redundant, trivial, absurd and invariable formula called *cabaletta,* the little *cabal*, which calls forth applause ... When the *cabaletta* no longer worked, they introduced the bass drum into the orchestra, a big *cabal* now destroying both music and singers", and he asked what would happen at the opera house if a *cabaletta* sung in faultless style were succeeded by frightful silence? Irving Kolodin writes,

> Left to themselves, the members of the audience might respond only to those things to which they had an instinctive, pleasurable reaction. In such circumstances, a whole evening might pass with nothing more than a polite patter of hands, with never a bravo. Not only would the performers feel let down by this lack of attention, the public itself would likely conclude that it had witnessed a rather tepid affair. In such ways does the experienced claque render a service beyond the call of duty.

There are subtle gradations of applause, from "gentle indications of approval" to "wild outbursts of uncontrollable enthusiasm". A good claque is inspiring and effective, and all efforts to abolish it – in Paris in 1830, at La Scala in 1890, in Vienna in 1906, and in New York in the 1960s – have failed. Like a phoenix, the claque rises out of anarchy and confusion. As Berlioz admits,

> The claques at our theatres have become experts. Their profession has risen to be an art. Besides, the doings of the claque are part of the

fun: it is a pleasure to see it manœuvre. This is so true that were the claqueurs excluded from certain performances there would not be a soul in the house ... No, the suppression of the claque in France is happily a madman's dream. Heaven and earth shall pass away, but the claque shall stand.

That the critics be suppressed would be considered an undemocratic attack on the freedom of the press, but privately many artists and managers wish it were possible. Rudolf Bing publicly expressed a lack of respect for some of the music critics who attacked performances at the Metropolitan. "Criticism should be made a licensed profession", he once said. "Why should an experienced artist be subject to public ridicule by a young man who has just started in his job? There should be a school for critics, as there are schools for musicians and singers". He quotes Verdi, who once told one of Bing's predecessors, the young Giulio Gatti-Casazza, "Read the newspapers as little as possible but read most attentively the reports of the box office. These, whether you like it or not, are the only documents which measure success or failure, and they admit no argument and represent not mere opinion but facts. If the public comes, the object is attained. If not – no. The theatre is intended to be full and not empty. That's something you must always remember".

Operatic criticism should not be a young man's game. In Europe, an electrician, plumber or piano-tuner must pass examinations before he is permitted to practise his profession, yet a young man may be given a typewriter and is told to be a critic. Brillat-Savarin wisely said that no man under the age of forty should be entitled to call himself a "gourmet". Since knowledge of opera is as comprehensive, perhaps no man under forty should be an opera critic. Young people are apt to sacrifice their better judgement to a clever turn of phrase, and to make witty and brilliant, but also rather immature, statements at the expense of performers. Having been a music critic myself for many years, I now realize that in my younger years I was often more impressed by my own expressions of wit and brilliancy than by objective and musically founded appreciation. An egocentric artist is a pain in the neck, but an egocentric critic is worse.

In Germany, in the eighteenth century, Johann Adam Hiller and Johann Friedrich Reichardt wrote about music and opera. They were cultured men who knew a great deal about music (Reichardt corresponded with Goethe and engaged in polemics with Kant). Reichardt was the first critic to write in a highly subjective, first-person style, that has remained the prerogative of criticism. Once he admitted that he'd been so moved by Georg Benda's overture to *Ariadne auf Naxos* that he scarcely noticed the beginning of the first act. In England, Sir John Hawkins and Charles Burney published their musical essays in 1776. Both are still much quoted nowadays. Music criticism in France was both penetrating, such as Charles de Brosses', and prejudiced; however, the music critics of Paris were very often wrong about their own composers and artists. Johann Friedrich Rochlitz had great influence during the era of Beethoven. In Berlin, Ludwig Rellstab, who died in 1860, introduced musical criticism in his Sunday articles for the *Vossische Zeitung* (a violent diatribe against Spontini, then the musical Czar of Berlin, landed Rellstab in jail. Today's critics live less dangerously).

In Germany, the phenomenon of the composer-critic began rather early. Carl Maria von Weber, E.T.A. Hoffmann, Schumann, Liszt, Wagner and Hugo Wolf all wrote musical criticism. Most of them were what Paul Henry Lang rightly calls "musical politicians", more interested in "causes" than in music or performances. Fortunately there were also non-composing musical writers who were more concerned with aesthetics, and approached everything they heard with a healthy, often detached criticism. Paradoxically, Eduard Hanslick is best known for his well-remembered antipathy to the later works of Richard Wagner. Hanslick remains immortal as "Beckmesser" in *Meistersinger* – the greatest honour any music critic attained.

Hanslick used his column in Vienna's *Neue Freie Presse* as a musical court against which there was no appeal; he was dogmatic but not the narrow-minded misanthrope that Wagner made him in *Meistersinger*. He liked Wagner's earlier works, but objected to the "swollen eroticism" of *Tristan* and the mythology of the *Ring*. He was pragmatic enough to admit, in his autobiography, that the duty of the critic was "not to discourage production, but to recognize the genuinely felt and the spontaneously spirited in the art of the present and not degrade it superciliously by opposing it to the products of a defunct era. Different times create different conditions which necessarily change artistic values and tastes".

At that time, musical criticism in England was dominated by Henry Fothergill Chorley and James William Davison. In America, a number of influential critics wrote with great understanding, among them Henry Edward Krehbiel, Henry T. Finck, Philip Hale, Richard Aldrich, and James Gibbons Huniker. And in England there was also George Bernard Shaw, of whom Ernest Newman wrote, "His essays on opera strike me as being by far the most brilliant things that musical journalism has ever produced in England, or is ever likely to produce".

Occasionally, Shaw wrote terrible nonsense as well, though always brilliantly formulated, to be sure. He called Hermann Goetz, the almost-forgotten composer of *The Taming of the Shrew*, "the greatest symphonist since Beethoven". He wrote that Goethe loved *Les Huguenots*, but Goethe had died four years before the première. He called "blind hero worship . . . stupid", yet he worshipped both Mozart and Wagner; in spite of his passion for Wagner, he wished that "Tristan might die a little sooner" – a wish many opera-goers have shared with G.B.S. during the third act. Shaw despised Brahms and Bizet, but admired Mr Cyrill Kistler who had written two travesties of Wagner's *Ring*, called *Baldur's Tod* and *Kunihild*. Kistler, wrote Shaw, would flourish "when all the Mascagnis etc. are forgotten".

Nevertheless, Shaw often had excellent judgement. He wrote that "The superior intensity of musical expression makes an opera far more real than any play," which is the perfect case for the allegedly "artificial" medium of opera. Although he had heard ninety performances of Gounod's *Faust* he admitted it was "a travesty of Goethe" done by "the angelic Gounod". He disliked "Donizetti and Co.", which included even Verdi. He made fun of the "pure farce plot of *Othello*", and that applied to both Shakespeare and Verdi. His worst mistake, where he acted like Beckmesser, was in reference to Bizet's *Carmen*, which he called "the very smallest of small beer". The moral is, perhaps, that you should try to be amused by your favourite musical critic, but shouldn't take him too seriously.

Ludwig Rellstab wrote wisely that everyone who judges something is a critic, though he may not know what he speaks about – but he told those who did not know to speak about their likes and dislikes, and not indulge in aesthetic evaluations. Nowadays a great many critics indulge in lofty formulations on aesthetics instead of limiting themselves to their likes and dislikes. A few musically trained critics write for a tiny minority of professional "connoisseurs", while most of them write for "the public". In opera, they report on the performance rather than on the composition. A second-rate singer gets far more space than the composer. "This was the inevitable consequence of the requirements of modern journalism", writes Paul Henry Lang. "Musical criticism as divorced from reporting should be concerned with one thing only, to lead us to the work of art . . . The aim is not so much judgement as knowledge, the bringing of the critic and the reader to the enjoyment of art. And the task of this criticism is to convey and detect what the artist wanted to do and not what he should have done."

As Christian Friedrich Hebbel wrote, "Criticism should not be scissors which get snagged on a wart only to cut an artery; it should rather be a plough that ploughs a furrow only to sow in it seeds that will grow fruits."

THE CRITIC
(A Fairy Tale)

Everybody knows, of course, that we critics lead a wonderful life. We get free tickets to all performances at the opera house and sell the surplus at black-market prices. Usually we get two tickets, but for Karajan and Bernstein performances we get a whole box. The newspaper or magazine for which we write supplies us with dignified transportation to and from the opera house. In London we use a good-vintage Bentley, in New York a chauffeur-driven Cadillac limousine, like presidents and chairmen of the board. In Vienna we usually arrive in a carriage drawn by two white horses which didn't quite make the Spanish Riding School (though it is not true that our colleagues in Rome use a chariot from Metro-Goldwyn-Mayer's *Ben Hur*).

When we enter the opera house, immaculately dressed and suitably lofty in appearance, there are awed whispers and admiring looks among the bystanders. Little girls ask us to sign the programme. The ushers bow deeply. A high-ranking member of the management welcomes us and personally takes us to our seats (in Vienna I am addressed as "Herr Professor" at all premières. This is one of the highest-ranking local greetings. "Herr Doktor" is the lowest).

After the performance, we are often invited by the general manager for an intimate caviar-and-champagne supper during which he consults us on what operas to perform and whom to engage. We are the men who pull all strings, and we are considered Grey Eminences by insiders. Famous *Generalmusikdirektoren* ask our advice on the overture of *Wozzeck* and how fast the prelude to *Elektra* should be played, if at all. In our company these great men unbend and become almost human. They love us. They remember reverently that Schumann, Hugo Wolf and Debussy wrote music criticism.

A promising and strikingly handsome *diva* calls up with a promising ring in her voice, and invites us to come up to her place, any time, the later the better. The tenors adore us. When compelled to report that they forced their high notes or strained their lower ones, they call up to thank us for tactfully bringing these shortcomings to their attention. Sopranos praise us for our moral integrity and critical perception. Temperamental prima donnas are the nicest of all; they really have humility. They don't mind when we indicate the time has come for them to give up certain parts and move over gracefully. One lady, miscast as Octavian in *Rosenkavalier* – supposedly a seventeen-year-old gent from a good family – promised to tighten her pants and invited me to her next performance to show me the sartorial improvement. Yes, sopranos are lovable people.

It is a full life. You make friends wherever you go. Composers dedicate their works to you rather than to prominent conductors or *dive* whom they hope will perform them. Your brilliant comments are widely quoted over the radio. You are invited by television networks to address millions of opera lovers who need your advice and follow your counsel. You can make or break the greatest stars; one of your clever sentences will be their undoing. No wonder your perceptive and, oh, so prophetic reviews will be bound in red leather by a publisher whose imprint means both money and prestige ...

I could go on and on but an inner voice (baritone? contralto?) tells me that the day has come when children and the readers of this book must be told the facts of life. Children and the readers no longer believe in Santa Claus or in your favourite critic. *If* they ever had a favourite critic, which I personally doubt.

Children, the truth is that we critics are often disliked, sometimes misunderstood, occasionally maligned, frequently quoted out of context, and almost always ignored. We don't mind when we are resented by people who would resent us anyway, whether or not we write reviews. But it's hard on our artist friends who refuse to understand that though they are our friends, they are not exempt from our criticism.

It has been said that a critic should be endowed with knowledge, experience, taste, and a sense of style; maybe he should have wisdom too. But perfection, children, is rare – on both sides of the orchestra pit. As some singers are often out of tune, so some critics are often out of tact. That doesn't give a singer the right to condemn a critic "who can't even sing a scale". He isn't supposed to perform but to criticize – to differentiate between true and false, good and bad. Ignorance is inexcusable, but the performers should know that ignorant critics don't last very long.

I am doubtful of artists, musicians and singers who proclaim somewhat self-consciously that they "never read reviews". The critic is the voice of the public, and it does no credit to the performer to ignore his public.

You can't expect an artist to defend the right of the critic to express his opinion even if the critic's opinion be wrong. On the other hand, I will fight for the right of the performer to say in public what he thinks of his audience, and of his critics.

"Last night's performance of *Don Giovanni* was badly handicapped by a coughing, restless, uneducated audience. They applauded at the wrong moments and gave no support to the singers. Mr X., the critic, left the house before the last scene which he later described in his review as 'truly Gothic'. How the hell could he know whether it was true Gothic or phoney Baroque . . . ?"

There has been corruption in various spheres of public life, but so far as I know no real scandal has touched opera critics in the past few years. It is no secret that Giacomo Meyerbeer used to visit the important critics in Vienna before one of his premières to pay them his respect (and maybe something else too). Well, we know what happened to Meyerbeer. No composer has ever paid me anything, but modern composers are poor devils, and some of them expect the critic to pay for the drinks. Years ago, when I was a novice in this business, I foolishly accepted a dinner invitation from a lady singer whom I had highly commended for her recent performance. It was a good dinner; the lady's sautéed sweetbreads were as good as her *sotto voce*. Unfortunately, she gave a bad performance a few weeks later, which I felt duly bound to record. Ever since, the lady's husband has pointedly looked the other way when I am around. Perhaps he'd expected the sweetbreads to create a deeper bond between us. My mistake was in writing for an opera magazine about the lady's singing, when I should have reported for *Cuisine et Vins de France* about her cooking. Some artists will never learn that we critics write about the artist's performance, not his character. I've expressed praise for artists whom I do not respect as people, and I've been forced to criticize other artists whom I'm proud to call my friends. These are the pitfalls of the profession, the critic's eternal dilemma.

The truth is, children, that we often buy our own tickets; take the underground to the opera house; are admired and asked for autographs only when we are mistaken for a tenor; are considered a damn nuisance by members of the management; are noticed by pompous *Generalmusik-direktoren* only after we compare them favourably to Toscanini or Mahler; frequently get dirty looks from *divas*, hear unprintable comments from their escorts, and receive anonymous threatening letters from their admirers; we are often suspected of having been "bought" by someone we praise, and of having a "complex" against someone we criticize: we are held in lower esteem by publishers than people who write left-over recipes or compose crossword puzzles; and we know that all critics – before, during and after Schumann, Hugo Wolf and Debussy – were often wrong. Ourselves included.

Then why do we write reviews, making few friends and influencing even fewer people? Because we love music and opera.

So long, friends. See you at the next première!

Great Opera Houses

Not all theatres where opera is performed deserve to be called opera houses. Some have short seasons, and in others opera is performed sporadically. During the summer, al fresco opera is performed in several countries. The most famous open-air opera is given at the Roman amphitheatre, the Arena, in Verona, and at the Terme di Caracalla in Rome. The best open-air performances in France take place in Aix-en-Provence. Al fresco opera is not always pure enjoyment. In Augsburg, singers occasionally have to compete with the sound of planes, and in Cincinnati, at the Zoo, with the noise of the animals.

Obviously, I have no space to write about all the places where opera is performed. I've chosen the "leading" houses for their historic contribution to the art, and for the regularity and quality of their performances. I didn't include the Bolshoi in Moscow or other theatres in the Soviet Union because few of them feature the standard repertoire. And I didn't specifically mention the Teatro Colón in Buenos Aires and the Liceo in Barcelona, two large houses with beautiful auditoriums, because the seasons are short and they contributed little to the development of opera, though some of the most famous artists have occasionally appeared there. I've also omitted some houses that are important for the development of national opera (Budapest, Belgrade, Warsaw, Dresden, Lyon) or for modern opera (Hamburg, Darmstadt, Cologne). There is only so much one can try to do.

LA SCALA AND PARMA'S TEATRO REGIO

Toscanini once said, "There is no 'second' opera house on earth. There are only 'first' houses". Every important house considers itself the "leading" one. But the *Maestro* himself left no doubt that he considered, *naturalmente*, *his* house, Milan's La Scala, the world's greatest. In New York, Toscanini once reprimanded Geraldine Farrar, then a prima donna, by comparing her unfavourably to a member of La Scala's chorus.

Opera, grand and sometimes not so grand, is now performed in over a hundred opera houses and theatres all over the world. Some have a short season of a few weeks; others play more than ten months. Germany has more opera houses than any other country; Italy is in second place. In Western Europe and in the countries behind the Iron Curtain, even medium-sized cities have permanent opera companies. And a growing number of festivals are performing opera.

In a world-wide poll of opera-goers, La Scala might possibly emerge as the best-loved house of all. It isn't the world's largest house (that's the Metropolitan), or the most beautiful (that might be the Teatro Fenice in Venice). La Scala doesn't have the best orchestra (that distinction goes to the Vienna State Opera), or the most excitable public (the habitués of the Teatro Regio in Parma). But what makes La Scala unique is the atmosphere. In the homeland of opera it is a national shrine. At first nights, *prime*, and galas, tickets cost $22, but prices drop for later performances. In summer, there are forty *serate per i lavoratori* (workers' evenings) with tickets at $1 and standing room in the galleries at 30 cents, less than a cinema ticket. Workers buy their tickets at factories or local labour unions. Dr Antonio Ghiringhelli, for many years La Scala's *Sovrintendente* (general manager), an independently rich man, once said that La Scala charges Milan's rich people plenty for first nights so it can later sell cheap tickets to the workers. As a result of this admirable policy, La Scala now truly belongs to all Milanese. Poor and rich people go there with the same anticipations because they know that the cut-rate performances have the same casts, same conductors, same artistic standards.

In Milan, people have grown up with opera, know their traditions and have strong opinions about music, singing, staging. La Scala has a definite artistic profile – or style – of its own. It performs exciting lyrical drama, often conservatively but nearly always in good taste, with dedication to the composer's intentions, avoiding extremes but permitting some modern touches. Toscanini demanded that singers stop behaving like stars and create real human beings on the stage. Nearly everything comes naturally. No avant-garde experiments are made to *épater les bourgeois*, as in some German opera houses, where certain producers and designers consider themselves more important than the composers.

Tradition is not an excuse for sloppiness at La Scala, but a living force.

In 1839, La Scala became the artistic home of Giuseppe Verdi, when his *Oberto* was given, and remained his home until he died in 1901 at the nearby Grand Hotel. During the last days of his life the theatre was closed. Toscanini began his career there in 1898 and remained deeply attached to the house (which he called his "beloved mistress") until the end of his life in 1957. For over a century, La Scala was sustained by two great men of music. No other opera house can make a similar claim.

Toscanini's posthumous influence is strong at La Scala. Rehearsals are businesslike and intent; there is strict artistic discipline and integrity. During performances, everybody tries to be just a little better. Everybody at La Scala acts and talks as though Toscanini were still around the house. The older people, once his disciples, now indoctrinate the younger generation in his spirit. Whenever Toscanini happened to be in Milan, no decision was taken without consulting him directly, or through his daughter, Countess Wally Castelbarco, who still presides over the Association "Friends of La Scala", and is locally known as "Queen of La Scala".

"No other house has such a long, uninterrupted tradition of greatness", says Ghiringhelli, who was a disciple of Toscanini and came to La Scala after the Second World War to co-ordinate work on the faithful reconstruction of the bombed house. (Both La Scala and the Vienna Opera were destroyed late in the war by US Air Force crews who apparently mistook the opera houses for strategic targets.) Ghiringhelli, a wealthy industrialist who still runs his enterprises as a sideline, paid all his expenses and never took a *lira* from La Scala, often came at noon and stayed until midnight, attending every performance from his small box near the stage. As a result, even a routine repertory performance may become an artistic and emotional experience at La Scala. An opera house must not be judged by its sensational first nights, but by the level of the average performance.

From the outside, La Scala is disappointing. Built by Giuseppe Piermarini in 1778 on the site of an ancient church, the severe, neo-classical façade of *il Teatro alla Scala* (the Theatre at the Stairs), called after a flight of stairs that no longer exists, is a brown masonry box that compares unfavourably with the magnificence of the Paris Opéra, the Vienna Staatsoper, the new Met. But inside it is glorious, with Carrara marble, mirrors and chandeliers, statues of Verdi, Puccini, Rossini, Bellini, Donizetti and Toscanini, and a beautiful gold-and-cream-and-red auditorium, silk tapestries and deep rugs, and five rows of boxes. La Scala has space for 3,000 people, more than Vienna's 2,200, less than the Met.'s 3,800. Despite its size it exudes warmth and intimacy, and has miraculous acoustics, perhaps owing to two wooden ceilings. It is a lived-in opera house, and a much-loved one.

The Scala's general manager believed in careful planning, left nothing to chance or improvisation. Rehearsals and performances are scheduled a year ahead. Ghiringhelli spoke of his theatre as though it were a human being with a "soul". When La Scala travels, it takes the "soul" along with its sets, costumes, conductors, *comprimari*. Ghiringhelli considered La Scala a state-within-the-state that carried on artistic relations with other countries, and sometimes goes abroad on operatic missions: "When the Queen of England congratulated me, she was, in fact, congratulating the citizens of Milan who support La Scala. What happens here is more important than at any other theatre in Italy".

Contrary to a popular myth, La Scala is not "a singer's house". The hegemony of the star tenor and the prima donna ended when Toscanini took over, and La Scala became "a conductor's house", though in the past years the producer's position has much improved. The conductor is the artistic boss. He selects the cast, asks for rehearsal time, studies the work and – this is essential – conducts *all* performances, with the same cast (replacements are permitted only in case of illness). Thus a Scala production never deteriorates into routine and mediocrity which is the curse of many "first" houses. The conductor works closely with the producer, the production stage chief, the chorus master, and the artistic directors in charge of orchestra, ballet, backstage music. At La Scala a conductor conducts a work that he knows and loves – and not because he happens to be around. Even after the ninth performance, he may schedule a rehearsal to preserve the superlative finish of the original production. That doesn't mean there are no routine performances at La Scala, but much is done to cut their number to the unavoidable minimum. La Scala has an artistic commission whose members represent all departments, and judge each performance for possible flaws. Immediate steps are taken to remedy shortcomings.

Though La Scala is not a very modern house so far as stage machinery and lighting apparatus are concerned, its technical staff is famed for its efficiency. There exists a "school" of La Scala staging, and its "secrets" are handed down from one generation to the next. The backstage atmosphere is unusual. Stagehands don't play cards or read papers as elsewhere, but watch the stage and hold their breath when a singer tries for the critical high C, and so do wardrobe mistresses and ushers. Nicola Benois, the production stage chief, believes that no other house has such a pool of gifted designers, painters, sculptors, artisans – perhaps not surprising in the country of Michelangelo, Leonardo da Vinci, Cellini. Picasso worked here in 1954.

La Scala also has its own ballet school, founded in 1813; a school of singing, a sort of postgraduate course for promising young singers; a special school teaching the singing cycles of earlier centuries; and its own museum, just off the second-floor foyer. During the interval people wander around remembering the past as they see original scores by Donizetti, Bellini, Verdi, Puccini, the testament of Paganini, miniature sets, Verdi's writing desk from the room where he died.

Paradoxically, the tradition-conscious Scala is one of the world's most progressive opera houses. The management is constantly searching for new works; their shortage creates some serious problems. Every year, La Scala performs four modern works – by comparison, the Metropolitan rarely tries out a new work, and the Vienna Opera produces one, at the most. Of the sixteen operas produced each season, six are popular hits chosen from thirty box-office successes. La Scala's all-time hits are *Aida*, *La Traviata*, *Rigoletto*. As a rule, at least one work each by Rossini, Bellini, Donizetti, Verdi and Puccini is given; one by Mozart, not yet completely successful with the Milanese, and one by Wagner. They also perform three eighteenth-century works, and three important operas that are not yet popular in Italy. And two ballets, always with good music (Ravel, de Falla, Stravinsky), in accordance with Toscanini's rule that "the dance must not kill the music".

Popular successes are not repeated, year after year, as in other houses where *Aida* and *La Bohème* will always sell out. At La Scala, after two or three seasons, a popular success is taken off the repertory – though an exception may be Puccini's *Turandot* when the formidable Birgit Nilsson is available. Then, after a few years' pause, the popular work is done in a new production. They've had four new *Traviata* productions and three different *Rigoletto*s in the past twenty years. Even Zeffirelli's magnificent *La Bohème* is taken off, and in a few years they may produce a new one, not necessarily as good.

"Life is change", said Ghiringhelli. "We renew the settings of a work but remain faithful to its spirit". If a production doesn't work well, it is taken off. The Zeffirelli-Karajan production of *La Traviata*, following their sensational success with *La Bohème*, was such a flop that Ghiringhelli, in a magnificent fit of Toscaninian wrath, ordered the sets to be destroyed at the end of the season.

The Milanese are convinced that La Scala is incomparable. Once Ghiringhelli asked a noted Milanese critic why he was sometimes lenient with other companies but always tough with La Scala. The critic was astonished. "But after all, this is La Scala!" he exclaimed. La Scala's opening, on 7 December, the Day of St Ambrose, Milan's patron saint, is Italy's greatest artistic and social event of the year. The season lasts almost all year, and La Scala's four hundred employees get thirteen monthly salaries, health and social security benefits, and a pension at sixty-five. There is a strong *esprit de maison* among the fine orchestra and the first-rate chorus, each numbering more than a hundred; the not-so-great ballet of sixty, the excellent technical staff of a hundred; and the members of the administrative staff. There is also strong civic pride; to be able to say "I work at La Scala" is a patent of nobility in Milan – and that applies to seamstresses and ushers as well as to tenors and conductors. Famous singers admit they always learn something new at La Scala where the art of *bel canto* is thoroughly understood, and there is an instinctive feeling for "the divine marriage of drama and music". Foreign singers often have trouble learning La Scala's special singing style, a blend of clear phrasing, technique and breath control – the true *bel canto*.

La Scala's audiences are feared even by the greatest singers. "When they like you they love you, but when they don't, they sit on their hands", a famous singer says. In Milan, there is no excuse for bad singing. No one can fool a Scala audience. Elderly *aficionados* remember Toscanini's *tempi*, Caruso's high C's, Gigli's *legato*; everybody is measured up against the glorious past. La Scala's *chronique scandaleuse* is as old as the house.

La Scala has had its political scandals. In 1859, when Milan was still under the hated Habsburg yoke, the chorus in *Norma* began to sing, "War, war!" – whereupon the entire audience jumped to its feet and applauded. Then the Austrian officers in the audience beat the floor "with the same swords which months later they had to throw down in defeat on the battlefields of Magenta and Solferino", writes Giuseppe Morazzoni.

More recently, the stage of La Scala became the major battlefield for Maria Callas and Renata Tebaldi (minor skirmishes being fought at the Metropolitan in New York). The war of the *divas* even split the claque, some supporting "the Tigress", others "the Dove". Tebaldi became so upset that she left La Scala in 1953, and has never sung there since, though she keeps an apartment nearby in Milan. Callas also left, considering it "incompatible with my dignity as woman and artist".

Even Toscanini was not spared the holy wrath of the Milanese. In the middle of the 1903 season when the audience furiously demanded an encore which the *Maestro* wouldn't allow, Toscanini suddenly left the rostrum, the pit, the house, Milan and Italy, and the next morning sailed for Buenos Aires. Later, he was often booed by the galleries and cheered by the boxes (or vice versa), and there were fist-fights. When he conducted *Rigoletto* in the 1920s, the great Spanish tenor Miguel Fleta, a virtuoso of the high G (!!), climaxed "Questa o quella" with a ringing high tone on which he "sat", displaying more bravura than taste. Toscanini shouted "Stop it!" Fleta kept singing. Toscanini beat his baton against his desk. The people in the boxes supported Toscanini, and the galleries cheered Fleta, and there was wonderful bedlam. In the last act, Fleta repeated his defiance of Toscanini when he held out a very long high C at the end of "La donna è mobile". There was complete chaos, and Toscanini swore that Fleta would "never again" sing at La Scala.

After Puccini's death, Toscanini prepared the world première of his *Turandot* in 1926. He decided that Fleta was the ideal choice for the part of Calaf, and asked him to come to Milan. Fleta was so moved that he later confessed, "I would have sung for Toscanini, even for nothing". It was one of the few La Scala affairs with a happy ending.

Shortly after La Scala was rebuilt, Ghiringhelli decided to have a new building added in Via dei Filodrammatici which flanks the theatre. It was to be used for rehearsals, and later it was found to be suitable for recording sessions. Then it became a concert hall, and finally a small theatre, La Piccola Scala. It is now, in Ghiringhelli's words, "La Scala's daughter", with seats for 600 people, an orchestra pit holding a chamber orchestra of forty-five musicians, and a very modern stage with an electronically regulated lighting system. It is a beautiful, small theatre, harmonious and elegant, with excellent acoustics. The Milanese like to think that La Piccola Scala would have pleased Giuseppe Piermarini who built La Scala.

La Piccola Scala was opened in 1955 with Cimarosa's *Il Matrimonio Segreto*. On the bicentenary of Mozart's birth they gave *Così fan Tutte*. This was followed by Stravinsky's *Apollo Musagète*, Ghedini's *Ipocrita Felice*, Falla's *Retablo de Maese Pedro*, Scarlatti's *Mitridate Eupatore* and Donizetti's *Rita*. Ever since, La Piccola Scala has included in its repertory revivals and rediscovered works of the Italian seventeenth and eighteenth centuries, as well as modern works. Monteverdi's *Orfeo* was followed by Stravinsky's *L'Histoire du Soldat*.

Today La Piccola Scala has created its own artistic style, a small house where rarely performed works can be given, often by young artists who later graduate to La Scala. It continues the great Italian tradition, and helps to train talented singers. Being managed by La Scala, it doesn't try to compete with, but to complement, the larger house. La Piccola Scala is a great success.

All Italians agree that the most interesting among the country's "small" houses is the Teatro Regio in Parma, whose forty-one thousand people all seem to be opera-crazy. The Regio has space for only 1,300 people but it makes up in enthusiasm what other houses offer in size. Parma's musical tradition goes back to the fifteenth century. In 1618 it had a theatre for 3,000 people. Magnificent performances were given of Monteverdi's operas. During the reign of the Bourbons, the Parma opera house had the finest composers and singers of the epoch. Verdi was born in nearby Roncole and remains closely identified with the Parma Opera. The first Italian performance of *Les Vêpres Siciliennes,* under the title *Giovanna di Guzman*, took place here in 1855. Parma was the first state that joined Piedmont in 1859, and Verdi was chosen to personally convey the result of the plebiscite to Victor Emanuele in Turin. At the age of forty-six, the composer of "Va, pensiero, sull'ali dorate" (*Nabucco*) was already a local and national hero. Verdi represented Parma in the first Parliament of newly united Italy.

Another local hero is Toscanini, who was born in Parma, and played the cello in the Teatro Regio when he was a student. After his death, a local newspaper wrote, "Arturo Toscanini was a true *figlio del loggione* (a son of the gallery). In his *furie* and *carezze* he expressed the spirit of the gallery of our Teatro Regio". The furies and caresses, particularly the furies, of the sons of the Regio gallery are respected by opera lovers and artists all over Italy. The mightiest have fallen in this house, and the greatest singers have been booed. There is a story, probably not apocryphal, about a great tenor who had to carry his bags himself at the station, because he'd cracked a high note the night before, and the porters refused to help.

Today, signs on the highways point towards the houses where Verdi and Toscanini were born. (A famous heroine is Renata Tebaldi, born in Pesaro, who studied in Parma and started her career there.) Cleofonte Campanini, the great conductor, was also born in Parma. In 1914 he organized the competition that discovered Beniamino Gigli: a member of the jury, the tenor Alessandro Bonci, wrote "We have found *the* tenor". Not many tenors have said this about another. Bonci too began his career in Parma.

The Teatro Regio was opened on 16 May, 1829, with Bellini's *Zaira,* especially written for the occasion. The *figli del loggione*, who didn't like the opera, made Bellini furious. He later transferred much of the music to the more successful *I Capuletti ed i Montecchi*, based on Shakespeare's *Romeo and Juliet*.

Bellini was born in Catania, Sicily, and the Teatro Massimo Bellini, which opened in 1890 with a gala performance of *Norma*, started the current renaissance of Bellini's operas (Maria Callas, the greatest Norma of our time, may have helped, and so did Joan Sutherland, the great Amina in *La Sonnambula*). Catania's *figli del loggione* are tough too – in fact, they are pleased to hear that they may be even tougher than the Parmaggiani.

THE VIENNA STATE OPERA AND OTHER OPERA HOUSES IN VIENNA

No other opera house on earth means as much to so many who never go there, as does Vienna's State Opera. There is a local myth that all Viennese attend regularly, yet seven out of ten, according to reliable statistics, have never attended a performance (though tens of thousands of citizens walk through the auditorium, which is decorated with tens of thousands of flowers, on the afternoon preceding the *Opernball*). All Austrians love their Opera. Peasants in far-off Alpine valleys, wine-growers in the Burgenland plains, merchants in Salzburg, and employees in far-away Vorarlberg provide millions in taxes to subsidize an artistic extravaganza in Vienna.

The Staatsoper, is a national symbol, a spiritual concept, the sum total of Austria's arts, ideas and traditions. It was always considered a necessity, never a luxury. The Viennese would rather live without hospitals or schools than without an opera house; it has been that way for three hundred years. As well as the State Opera, there is also the Volksoper, performing lighter works, Singspiel and operetta, but often the same works that are given at the State Opera; it has happened that on the same night both houses performed *Die Zauberflöte*, the most popular work in Vienna. During the summer, opera is also performed at the Redoutensaal of the Imperial Palace, and at the venerable Theater an der Wien. On some nights, four opera performances are scheduled in this city of 1,700,000 people.

The enthusiasm for and sentimental attachment to the *Oper*, as the State Opera is called, grew out of the city's cultural climate that generated both the classical and modern epochs in music; it is the heritage of centuries. After a performance of *Lohengrin* in 1861, Richard Wagner wrote, "What was most affecting was the unbelievable unanimity of the whole audience. A shout of joy went up like the sound of a thousand trombones".

Wagner had come to Vienna after the *Tannhäuser* scandal in Paris. It was his first visit to Austria since his exile in 1849, and he was enchanted, as were so many before and after him, by the initial warmth and charm of the Viennese. On the morning after the *Lohengrin* première, however, he read the reviews of Eduard Hanslick and other local critics. They too showed "unbelievable unanimity" in the viciousness of their comments. In 1963, Heinrich Kralik, then the doyen of Vienna's critics, wondered whether "the demonstrative hatred, the unexampled hostility of the Viennese critics were not a sort of love-hatred perversion . . . It was typical of the inconstancy of Viennese audiences that the same people who had chuckled over Hanslick's devastating criticism of a work by Wagner in the morning would go to the Opera at night to applaud it".

Life in Vienna, that had begun for Wagner with "a shout of joy", ended in bitterness. After eighteen months of rehearsals, he had to abandon his plan to hear his first *Tristan* performed there. Biographers refer to his Viennese years as a time of unhappiness, but he did begin to think about *Meistersinger,* in which he saw the hated Hanslick as Beckmesser. Wagner wrote a twenty-page essay about the Vienna Opera suggesting drastic reforms. He was always the teacher who loved to lecture. He suggested that the *Oper* devote itself exclusively to German opera, "leaving Italian and French opera to the Italians and the French". The number of performances should be reduced by half, many to be devoted to the ballet. Fortunately, no one paid attention to his suggestions.

In 1872, Wagner returned to Vienna to conduct several "propaganda" concerts for his Bayreuth Festival. At that time, *Rienzi* was a great success at the Vienna Court Opera. Direktor Johann Herbeck's lavish production was the talk of the town. Even Emperor Franz Joseph I, not an opera fan, loved it and insisted that *Rienzi* be given as a command performance for his imperial and royal visitors. After the first bars, Wagner ran out of his box cursing the trumpet player. At the buffet, he was given a double portion of ice cream "to make him cool down". During the intermission he shouted at Herbeck and his staff. Everything was bad, he said; even the sets, much admired by His Majesty, were "all wrong historically". Wagner was furious, because he had earned no royalties for his early works, in accordance with an old agreement that the authorities refused to amend. But later he was pleased when his friend, Hans Richter, became chief conductor in Vienna, and returned to supervise the rehearsals of the Paris version of *Tannhäuser*.

Even now world-famous artists sometimes admit that there is a mysterious, affectionate bond between them and the Vienna *Oper*. "*Every*body has stage fright in Vienna but when all goes well, the rewards are terrific", George London once said. "The Viennese ask a lot but they give a lot in return". No other opera house radiates such warmth. Opera and real life are often interwoven in Vienna where everybody knows someone who sings at the State Opera (or, in turn, knows someone else who can get house seats). In Vienna, coffeehouses are called "Norma", "Papageno" and "Parzifal" [*sic*], and there are restaurants named "Falstaff" and "Rosenkavalier". A chain of pastry shops calls itself "Aida".

Very soon after the end of World War II, the opera-crazy Viennese contributed to the rebuilding of their destroyed Opera, even before they rebuilt their own houses. Streetcar conductors collected schillings from their passengers, soccer players from their fans. 5 November 1955 was the happiest day in Austria's post-war history: few Austrians could afford to attend the opening *Fidelio* performance, at eighty pounds a seat, but that didn't matter (some people camped four days and nights under the arcades, outside the house, in the raw November air, to get a standing ticket). The performance wasn't perfect, but that didn't matter either. To be an *Opernnarr* is a distinction in Vienna. The *Oper*, as every other opera house, has many dull or bad evenings, but on a truly good night sounds and sights, sets and lights, instruments and voices merge into a perfect work of beauty.

The State Opera is, geographically, at the heart of Vienna, where the elegant Kärntnerstrasse crosses the Ring, the *via triumphalis* of the Habsburg empire. Surrounded by museums and great hotels, old churches and the Imperial Palace, the opera house is a synthesis of French and Florentine neo-Renaissance with Venetian and Spanish neo-Gothic. An improbable mixture, the architects, Eduard van der Nüll and August Siccard von Siccardsburg, were criticized for their "Königgrätz", the Austrian equivalent of "Waterloo". Van der Nüll committed suicide before the building was finished, in 1869; von Siccardsburg died three months later. That house was famous for its mellow, soft sound. The postwar house has modern sound, better for people who were brought up on high-frequency recordings. The singers never have to strain, the instrumental groups or solo instruments can be clearly heard. The stage is one of the world's largest and most modern.

The season lasts from 1 September to 30 June and the orchestra, chorus and many soloists spend part of July and August in Salzburg at the festival. In Vienna, performances take place every night, except Christmas Eve and Good Friday. Ticket prices go from forty cents for a standing place in the galleries to twenty dollars on special nights. The Vienna Opera has probably the highest deficit of all opera houses on earth, close to eight million dollars a year.

Italian works are usually performed in Italian, *Carmen* in French, other operas in German. Verdi is the most popular composer, followed by Mozart, Wagner, Strauss, Puccini. Modern works are rarely performed though Berg's *Wozzeck* and *Lulu* are usually sellouts. Tradition is an artistic reality in Vienna where the orchestra, the celebrated Wiener Philharmoniker, plays from scores that contain the personal annotations of Gustav Mahler, Richard Strauss, Franz Schalk, Herbert von Karajan. For a long time after the death of Mahler, the singers and musicians at the *Oper* approached musical and technical problems by asking themselves, "how would he (Mahler) have done it?"

Mahler's ten years as *Direktor,* from 1897 to 1907, of the *Hofoper* (Court Opera, as it was then called), are still wistfully called "the golden age" of the Vienna Opera, comparable only to Toscanini's years at La Scala. (Neither Mahler nor Toscanini was able later to introduce the same strict standards at the Metropolitan.) Quite a few people who had helped to "eliminate" Mahler were later to regret it (which also applies to those who fifty-seven years later "eliminated" Herbert von Karajan). Both became suspect because they made no artistic compromises and boldly ignored the entrenched Austrian bureaucracy.

Yet Mahler had been appointed in 1879, after a distinguished career in Prague and Budapest, by Prince Montenuovo, the Imperial Court dignitary in charge of the Court Opera. He showed vision when he fought for Mahler, whose artistic principles would inevitably create many problems. Montenuovo thought it would be worth the struggle, and it was. After his predecessors, Wilhelm Jahn and Hans Richter, bearded Teutonic types, the clean-shaven, sensitive Jewish middle-class intellectual from a small Moravian town must have been a startling sight to the members of the Vienna Establishment at the turn of the century.

Mahler had conducted a performance of *Lohengrin,* after only one full orchestra rehearsal, which electrified the artists and fascinated the audience. Everybody was talking about "the small, slight, dynamic figure, with his finely chiselled and sensitive features". Once appointed, Mahler put his artistic ideas into practice with no regard for conventions.

During his ten years in Vienna, he established standards that have never been attained in Vienna since, and rarely elsewhere. "Mahler", wrote Bruno Walter, "was able to penetrate into the heart of the music, and to recreate the composer's dramatic vision from his music". Mahler's most often quoted statement, "Tradition ist Schlamperei" (tradition is an excuse for slackness), was also his most misunderstood. Mahler never implied that *all* tradition is slovenly, but distinguished between good tradition that must be preserved and bad tradition that is often used as an excuse for taking a shortcut or the easy way out.

Mahler radically changed the opera-goers' habits in Vienna. He ruled that the auditorium would remain in darkness during the performance. Latecomers would not be permitted to enter during the acts (Rudolf Bing was able to introduce this rule only after the new Metropolitan was opened). "The remarkable fact is not that Mahler was after ten years driven out", writes Kralik, "but that the easy-going Viennese for ten years accepted the dictatorship of this austere musician. The young people were fascinated, and yesterday's authorities were overawed. Mahler's ideas, his will, his aspirations were so unconditional, and he was so sure of himself, that he was as impervious to criticism, mockery and malice as he was to misunderstanding or to lack of understanding at all . . . Mahler's achievement was a phenomenon without parallel."

The Mahler era remains associated with a style of production close to Richard Wagner's *Gesamtkunstwerk*. Fifty years later, Wagner's grandsons used the same elements in neo-Bayreuth. With his great stage designer, Alfred Roller, and his chief conductors, Bruno Walter and Franz Schalk, Mahler carried out his revolutionary reforms. Mahler never pronounced lofty theories. He had ideas and carried them out. His *Don Giovanni* became the perfect synthesis of drama and music. His *Tristan* "gave full expression to the style, the taste and the progressive intellectual aspirations of the day", writes Kralik.

In fact, Mahler brought style and taste to everything he did. Under his direction, even the often-ridiculed grand opera, Meyerbeer's *Les Huguenots*, became truly grand theatre. Bruno Walter wrote that Mahler was "always bursting with ideas and energy". Mahler, according to Paul Stefan, the critic, said "I am beating my head against the wall but at any rate I'm making a hole in the wall". Singers, musicians, technicians were kept in a state of perpetual high tension. It was wonderful while it lasted – but of course, it couldn't last forever. In the end, Mahler made too many holes in the wall, and too many enemies. It is now said that he was chased out by "the revolt of mediocrity", the unholy combination of bureaucrats, gossipmongers, intriguers that has often driven out outstanding men from Vienna. Herbert von Karajan, who left the Staatsoper in 1964, after eight turbulent, always exciting years, will not be the last.

Vienna's most glorious house, though, is not *Die Oper am Ring,* but the nearby, older Theater an der Wien which was opened on 13 June 1801. Emanuel Schikaneder, who wrote the libretto of Mozart's *Die Zauberflöte,* was its first manager. Beethoven actually slept there (in a small room which Schikaneder had given him), and conducted his *Fidelio* in 1805, which was a failure. The following year, the Theater an der Wien was bought by the Gesellschaft der Kavaliere, an illustrious group of aristocrats – Prince Joseph von Schwarzenberg; Prince Franz Joseph Lobkowitz, one of Beethoven's patrons; Prince Nikolaus Esterházy, Haydn's employer; and others. Actually, the "theatre secretaries" were in charge, among them Joseph Sonnleithner, who first wrote the *Fidelio* libretto, and Georg Friedrich Treitschke, who wrote the final, successful version. The aristocrats tried to get control of the opera house which was still the Emperor's personal hobby. But their aims were not always strictly artistic, and His Majesty felt compelled to intervene.

"We have noticed with displeasure", it says in an *Allerhöchstes Handbillet* (a sort of court circular), "a grave decline, amounting to a public scandal, in the moral conduct of the actresses, dancers etc. engaged at the Court Theatres and at the Theater an der Wien; and further, that those chiefly responsible for this deplorable laxity are said to be certain gentlemen of rank employed in the administration." The Emperor ordered the gentlemen "to mend their ways", to avoid "more drastic measures". Thereupon most of the gentlemen lost their interest in the arts, and the Society was terminated in 1813.

The Theater an der Wien remained a haven of the arts in musical Vienna. The world of Nestroy and Raimund, Offenbach and Suppé, of the masterworks of the Viennese operetta is associated with the house. Johann Strauss's *Die Fledermaus,* the masterpiece of this genre, had its première there in 1874. Smetana's *The Bartered Bride,* which had had no success in Prague, began its international career in this theatre when the German translation was first performed in 1893. Four years later, *La Bohème,* the first Puccini opera in Vienna, was produced there.

After the end of the Second World War, the Theater an der Wien became the home of the exiled Staatsoper company, while the State Opera was being rebuilt. The era created the now almost legendary, often imitated Viennese Mozart style, under the artistic leadership of

Josef Krips. Egon Hilbert was the manager. When the State Opera was re-opened, there was ugly talk of turning the Theater an der Wien into a garage or a cinema. Fortunately reason prevailed; the City of Vienna purchased and renovated the house which was re-opened in 1962 with *Die Zauberflöte*. It is a lovely house. On some evenings, it is said, one may see Herr Beethoven standing there, leaning his back against the orchestra barrier as was his habit, shaking his head, not liking the conductor's tempi.

In 1962, Karajan resigned and briefly left Vienna, after issuing an ultimatum to the Austrian government. His conditions – that the State Opera be autonomous, independent of the heavy-handed bureaucratic machinery that often interfered with artistic matters – was accepted and Karajan returned. He received an ovation from the staff of the *Oper*, and promised to make it "the best in the world". During the 1962 festival, Karajan conducted memorable performances of the *Ring, Tristan, Parsifal*. Nevertheless, two years later, he was forced out, as Mahler had been, and once more the Vienna Opera failed to be "the best in the world".

OPERA IN NEW YORK

Not so long ago opera enthusiasts in Europe would talk condescendingly about the Metropolitan in New York, where most of them had never been. Similarly, some operatic "America-Firsters" now like to run down the leading European houses. Among the ignorant chauvinists on both sides of the Atlantic are music critics who ought to know better. Today the leading houses have a similar repertory, the same conductors and stage directors, the same leading singers.

The Met. is a house of many extremes, like everything in America. Performances vary bewilderingly from dull to brilliant, from improvisation to integration. The sets may be wonderful or terrible. When Rudolf Bing joined the Metropolitan in 1949, he took the productions of *Carmen* and *Aida* out of the repertory because he "couldn't bear to look at them". The visual element is now an important component of new productions. Bing brought to the Met. prominent designers – Eugene Berman, Rolf Gérard, Oliver Messel, Cecil Beaton, Oliver Smith, Teo Otto, Caspar Neher, and others – and he hired prominent directors from the legitimate theatre – Margaret Webster, Alfred Lunt, Peter Brook, Jean-Louis Barrault, Tyrone Guthrie. Bing gave his designers and stage directors rank and authority equal to those of his conductors. He made it clear that he was the one who would resolve all conflicts. Partly as a result, there is a shortage of first-rate conductors.

In the running battle that Bing waged with his critics from the beginning of his years in New York, he was accused of turning the Met. into an "Italian house", of neglecting Wagner, and of avoiding contemporary works. Doubtless, Italian operas are more popular with the Metropolitan audiences. And Bing always made it clear that he was not an ardent Wagnerian (he is not quite sure whether he has ever heard an entire performance of *Siegfried*). As evidence of Bing's "conservatism", some critics laid special stress on the fact that only once did he open the Met.'s season with a world première, Samuel Barber's *Antony and Cleopatra*. Its only other world première during his regime was Barber's *Vanessa*. Neither work was a spectacular success. At the Met. there is rarely an American première of operas that have already been performed abroad. Works that do not draw well at the box office are rarely revived, the repertory consisting mainly of surefire favourites.

"The Met. has been called a conservative house," Bing said. "It has to be. If I had unlimited funds available and could do exactly as I please, I would try to get the best artists on earth – the conductors, producers, designers and singers I happen to consider the best – and I would try to offer the best possible productions of operatic masterpieces. The function of the Metropolitan Opera House is not to become a home for contemporary opera but to preserve the great works of the literature in excellent modern frames." Bing's operatic philosophy, which sometimes led him to compare the Met. to a museum, was strongly attacked by several New York music critics, who pointed out that much more varied repertories were being offered in some European houses. Bing's answer was that he had been supported "by the extraordinarily loyalty of the American public". The Met. is almost always sold out except when a modern work is given.

Bing speaks wistfully about the tranquillity that characterized the Met. under the regime of Giulio Gatti-Casazza, who managed the house from 1908 to 1935. Gatti-Casazza never bothered to learn English. He never went along on the Met.'s spring tour. As soon as the short season was over, he returned to Italy. He didn't have to worry about money. At the end of the season, he would tell his board of directors how large the deficit was, whereupon Mr Otto H. Kahn and a few others would write out their cheques.

Mahler and Toscanini conducted at the Met. Artur Bodanzky, who would be a star conductor today, was available most of the time as house conductor. Year after year, Caruso came for the opening night, stayed through the entire season, and sang two or three times a week. During one season, he made fifty-three appearances. The singers then were not distracted by offers from other media. It has been "a singer's house" since it opened in 1883; the great singers were the stars; the opera itself was incidental to those who paid to support it. The American millionaires, making up the Metropolitan's deficit, knew no more about opera than Andrew Mellon or Henry Clay Frick knew about old masters. They operated on the same principle: all they had to do was to get the very best. A reporter wrote, "Tiaras flourished among the boxes and conversation interrupted the music except when some favourite singer sang a popular aria". It wasn't very different from what went on in the eighteenth-century opera houses in Venice at the time of Monteverdi. Singers would send their secretaries to rehearsals, when they were not in the mood to attend. The productions were lavish, and the singing was often very good.

Bing remains convinced that "the standing of an opera house depends on the quality of the singing stars it attracts". When he had to choose between two equally competent artists, an American and a foreigner, the American got priority. Otherwise, the better artist was hired. "The Met.'s public wants to hear the best voice, not the best American voice. I admit that sometimes the voice it hears is only the second best, because there is no one else who is better." It is known among artists all over the world as a no-nonsense house, where people get on with their business with a minimum of hysterics. There are problems, to be sure; when an opera house has half a dozen "leading" bass-baritones, each of them feels that he is *the* leading one, and his opinion will be buttressed by his wife, his friends, his relatives, and his admirers. It is impossible to convince a singer of the superiority of a colleague. When a member of the board of directors suggested to the general manager that it might be desirable to explain his views on artistic matters to important singers "in a way that would not upset them", Bing replied, "There is no use trying because singers are bound to be upset most of the time anyway".

No opera house can be better than its public. When Bing went to New York he discovered that many people would arrive late, spend half an act at the bar, make noisy entrances in the middle of a pianissimo, and leave early. The Metropolitan lacks an essential element which makes a great house – the part than can only be contributed by the audience. Opera-goers in New York do not "live" opera the way the citizens do in Milan or Vienna. Yet things could be much worse. Eugene Bonner wrote in *The Club in the Opera House*,

> With the establishment of what was, in effect, a sort of Republican Court at the opera house, the parterre boxes gradually took on the semblance of individual drawing rooms where the hostesses – during the intermissions, when they were not distracted by the music – could receive visitors. The majority of these consisted of unattached and eligible males who either had seats in less exalted parts of the house or simply bought General Admission and cruised the boxes until vacancies presented themselves.

Monday night was "society night" at the Metropolitan because Monday was dancing night at Delmonico's, where the Patriarchs Club, the Assembly, and the Family Circle Dancing Class held forth. Society people would appear in their boxes at the Metropolitan around 9 p.m., after dinner, regardless of curtain time, and move on later to other functions. Monday night is still black-tie night at the new Metropolitan, although Bing, following the example of Gustav Mahler, no longer permitted latecomers to be seated during the acts. A special hall with a close-circuit television screen is provided for them. Champagne is no longer served from the bar to the boxes, and it is not good manners to be seen at the bar during the acts. It is doubtful whether the Metropolitan Opera will ever be in the mainstream of cultural thinking in the United States, but at least the Met.'s audiences are developing.

New York's "other" opera house, the City Center, was founded in 1943 at the instigation of Mayor Fiorello La Guardia, Newbold Morris and Morton Baum, "to present opera with the highest artistic standards, while maintaining the civic and democratic ideas of moderate prices, practical business planning and modern methods". The City Opera has shown imagination and courage, taste and energy, proving that relatively little money can go a long way. The old theatre had 3,000 seats, the new house has 2,700 seats. In 1946, the City Opera gave the American première of Strauss's *Ariadne auf Naxos*. It also gave the first performances in America of Bartók's *Bluebeard's Castle*, Von Einem's *The Trial*, Frank Martin's *The Tempest*, Britten's *A Midsummer Night's Dream*, and Strauss's *The Silent Woman*. It had its share of world premières – Copeland's *The Tender Land* (1954), Robert Kurka's *The Good Soldier Schweik* (1958), Hugo Weisgall's *Six Characters in Search of an Author* (1959). The theatre was the first to remove the colour bar in opera, when Camilla Williams, in 1946, sang the title role in *Madame Butterfly*. In 1951, for the opening night of his second season as manager, Bing gave the Negro dancer Janet Collins an important part in the ballet of his first *Aida* production, which he still considers his biggest single achievement at the Met.

The City Opera's musical director, Julius Rudel, is also a competent manager (both Bing and Rudel were born in Vienna). Quite a few people in New York, especially among the younger opera enthusiasts, feel invigorated by the artistic atmosphere of the City Opera, which, they say, has nothing of the old-fashioned dignity of the Metropolitan Opera, just across Lincoln Center Plaza. The operas are well staged and designed, and completely conducted and sung. While the City Opera cannot hire the Met.'s expensive international stars owing to its more limited budget, it has discovered gifted young American singers. Some of them have later gone to the Met. The management is unafraid to perform such popular works as *Porgy and Bess* and *Die Dreigroschenoper* because both are folk operas. Competition is healthy though the august Metropolitan feels that occasionally there may be too much competition. A few years ago, when the Met. was preparing a new production of *Der Rosenkavalier*, for which it had acquired the performing rights for New York City from Boosey & Hawkes, the American publishers of Richard Strauss, Bing refused to let the City Opera share those rights. The rich, great Met. was severely criticized, and, although Bing was under strong pressure to give in, he didn't.

The Metropolitan was only once in its history threatened by serious competition: between 1906 and 1910, when Oscar Hammerstein I, the formidable impresario with an almost obsessive desire to produce opera, put up the Manhattan Opera House, at Eighth Avenue and Thirty-fourth Street. Against the powerful, entrenched Astor-Morgan-Vanderbilt directorate and Wall Street's financial forces that stood behind the Metropolitan, Hammerstein was underdog and challenger. The American public and the press were enthusiastically on his side. He had flair, showmanship, gambling instinct. The newspapers loved him. It was a relief to have an "opera war" in Manhattan on the front pages, instead of another revolution in South America. The music critics of the big papers became unaccredited war correspondents. They watched Hammerstein with fascination. He had no outside backing and financed the Manhattan Opera House with the profits from his own vaudeville house, the Victoria Theatre. It was a sporting contest rather than an operatic one. Hammerstein belaboured the Metropolitan with its own weapons, importing the greatest stars he could get: Melba, Calvé, Bonci, Renaud. He couldn't get Toscanini, who was at the Met. but got the next best conductor, Cleofante Campanini, who had earlier conducted there, but disliked the interference of the financiers and society ladies and left.

Hammerstein did incredible things. Everybody knew that *Aida* was the Metropolitan's top box-office hit; Caruso sang the part of Radames sixty-four times. Hammerstein produced his own *Aida*, and scheduled it on the same night that it was being given at the Met. The Cup Final spirit had infected everybody at the Manhattan Opera House. During the first interval, news reached the Manhattan, which was completely sold out, that the Metropolitan was half empty. There was pandemonium back-stage; singers, stagehands, musicians, the conductor and Hammerstein formed a circle and danced a triumphal war dance.

At the Metropolitan, there was a bleak mood of despair. On "Melba nights" the Manhattan began to look more and more like the Metro-politan, as the elegant members of the Diamond Horseshoe set made the hazardous journey to "that house" on Eighth Avenue. It was reported that some defectors even *liked* the performances at the Manhattan Opera. Hammerstein's *Rigoletto*, with Melba and Bonci, was called by the *Times* "the best production of *Rigoletto* seen in New York for many years". In 1907, the Met. tried unsuccessfully to stop Hammerstein from produc-ing *La Bohème*, with Melba, claiming that it had obtained exclusive rights to all Puccini operas from Puccini's publishers, G. Ricordi, in Milan. At the end of Hammerstein's first season, his public accountants announced that he'd made a profit of 11,000 dollars. The Metropolitan finished its season with a loss of 84,039 dollars. During the 1908–09 season, Hammerstein made a profit of 229,000 dollars, while the Met. had a loss of 205,201 dollars. The following season New York had *three* opera houses – the Metropolitan, the Manhattan, and the recently opened New Theater. Certain operas, such as *La Bohème* and *Cavalleria Rusticana,* were given by all three houses and always sold out. New York had temporarily gone opera-mad. The city's population had increased by 700,000 people during the first decade of the century and many of the new immigrants were Italian-born opera enthusiasts.

At the end of the 1909–10 season, the directors of the Metropolitan conceded defeat. Hammerstein received from them a cash settlement of over eight million pounds, in return for which he agreed not to produce opera in New York and America for the next ten years. Hammerstein had won his four-year opera war. He had over a million dollars in cash, still owned his Manhattan Opera House, and had gained a worldwide reputation as a genius among opera managers. He had made New York opera-conscious for the only time in history, and had advanced the cause of opera in Manhattan by at least fifty years.

In 1624, only a few years after opera was launched in Florence, King Ferdinand II had an Italian work – we don't know which one – performed for his aristocratic guests at the Castle in Prague. It is believed that Draghi's *La pazienza di Socrate con due Moglie* (which sounds like a fascinating subject) was given at the court in Prague in 1680, and we know that Giovanni Federico Sartorio's opera *La rete di Vulcano* was performed in 1704. In 1723, *Costanza e Fortezza*, composed by Johann Joseph Fux for the coronation of Charles VI, was presented in a specially built amphitheatre to accommodate 4,000 people.

The National Theatre in the Fruit Market, which opened in 1783, remains one of the oldest (and most beautiful) houses in existence, preceding both the Theater an der Wien in Vienna and the beautiful opera house in Venice, La Fenice. The Prague house, called first after Count Nostitz, then after the Estates that helped to build it, and now Tylovo Divadlo, after the Czech playwright Josef Kajetán Tyl, made musical history when Mozart wrote for it and conducted there *Don Giovanni* and *La Clemenza di Tito*. Operatically, Prague remains one of the world's great cities.

Prague's Národní Divadlo ("National Theatre") was opened in 1881, burned down a few weeks later, was rebuilt and reopened in 1883, and ever since has remained the spiritual focus of the Czechs' national and musical life in Bohemia. It was always a splendid opera house, where great composers, conductors and singers worked. Otakar Ostrčil, a first-rate conductor, brought Janáček's *Excursions of Mr Brouček* to Prague, and gave Berg's *Wozzeck* in November, 1926, one year after the world première in Berlin. There were such demonstrations of protest that eighteen days later the city authorities forbade further performances. Today the National Theatre is combined with the Smetana Theatre (the former German Theatre). Soloists, conductors, ballet and the production staff are shared from a common pool; each theatre has its own orchestra and chorus. What with Saturday and Sunday matinees, there are about fifteen opera performances every week; occasionally a Mozart work is performed at the historic Tyl Theatre. The repertory is dominated by Czech opera, but includes the standard works of the classic and romantic composers. The beautiful house remains a shrine in the country's cultural life.

COVENT GARDEN

To some people, "Covent Garden" means London's fruit and vegetable market; to opera-goers and ballet fans, it is synonymous with the Royal Opera House. Opera has been irregularly performed there since 1734 though it only became a full-time operatic institution after the Second World War.

The present building is the third on the site. The first was erected by John Rich, who had made a fortune with his production of *The Beggar's Opera,* in 1728, at his theatre in Lincoln's Inn Fields. Rich opened the house in 1732 with Congreve's *The Way of the World.* The second work given was *The Beggar's Opera.* During the 1730s and 1740s, Handel was associated with the theatre. His operas *Atalanta, Alcina* and *Berenice* were performed there. But mostly it was drama that was given.

On 30 September 1808, Rich's theatre burned down. He built his second theatre on a piece of land "contiguous to Bow Street, Hart Street and Covent Garden" belonging to the Duke of Bedford, whose forebears had received it from Henry VIII when the monasteries were dissolved (Covent Garden had originally been "Convent Garden" and there the monks of Westminster buried their dead). On 18 September 1809 the second theatre opened with *Macbeth,* with Mrs Siddons and Charles Kemble, and with "the musical entertainment", *The Quaker.* There followed the famous O.P.Riots (Old Price Riots), when the public protested energetically against the expensive tickets sold by the management (in our age of inflation and steadily rising prices, some O.P.Riots by an enraged public might not be a bad idea).

During that period "various unrecognizable versions of Mozart's operas were given, generally with 'additional numbers' by the theatre's musical director, Henry Bishop", writes Harold Rosenthal, the Covent Garden historian. In 1824, Charles Kemble, then the manager of Covent Garden, asked Weber to write an opera especially for his theatre. At that time three London theatres – Covent Garden, Drury Lane and the Lyceum – were playing Weber's *Freischütz* "to full houses", and Kemble not unreasonably wanted to cash in on the composer's popularity. Weber first considered Faust, but then decided that Oberon would be his subject, and approached the English writer James Robinson Planché to write the libretto (Planché later wrote the English versions of *Die Zauberflöte* and

Le Nozze di Figaro). Weber came to London in March, 1826, conducted his *Oberon* at Covent Garden on 12 April, and died two months later in the Great Portland Street home of Sir George Smart, an English musician.

In 1847, Covent Garden, after some structural alterations, became the Royal Italian Opera. An Italian company gave successful performances of Rossini's *Semiramide*, with Giuletta Grisi. In 1851, Frederick Gye, the son of a wealthy tea and wine merchant, took over the management. He produced the first English performances of Verdi's *Rigoletto* and *Il Trovatore*, and Meyerbeer's *Le Prophète*.

In 1858, the house burned down again, was quickly rebuilt and re-opened the same year with Meyerbeer's *Les Huguenots*. The performance had to be stopped after the fourth act. It was midnight and one dared not profane the Sabbath by performing the fifth act.

From 1858 until 1939, opera was merely a feature of the London "Season", when opera was strictly an entertainment for society and "Evening dress was indispensable in stalls and boxes". The opera house had its greatest period under Augustus Harris, from 1888 to 1896, when Nellie Melba, Nordica, the de Reszkes were the great stars. French, Italian and German operas were given in the original language. Covent Garden became known as "the Royal Opera House", no longer "the Royal Italian Opera". After the death of Augustus Harris a Syndicate carried on in his tradition. Caruso, Scotti, Destinn and Tetrazzini often sang in London. Wagner was performed under Hans Richter who suggested that operas be given in the language of the audience. In 1908, Wagner's entire *Ring* was given, with the blessing of Frau Cosima. It was an enormous success; so was *Meistersinger*. Ever since, the British have been a strong Wagnerian contingent in Bayreuth and elsewhere.

The Syndicate, under and after Harry Higgins, decided that what the public really wanted was "star" opera, and the plan of setting up a permanent English company was dropped. It was a lavish age, and its most extravagant spectacles were the state performances. Not even the imaginative French surpass the English in the splendour of their colourful pageantry. Artistically, these evenings were mixed blessings. The state performance in 1897, commemorating Queen Victoria's Diamond Jubilee, featured the third act of *Roméo et Juliette*, the second act of *Tannhäuser*, and the fourth act of *Les Huguenots*. It wasn't great fun for music lovers, but not many of them were present. Yet Augustus Harris gave London some of its finest opera seasons. He was knighted in 1891, not for his services to music and opera, but because he happened to be

Sheriff of the City of London during the visit of Kaiser Wilhelm II. Such are the rewards of an artistic life.

In 1910, Sir Thomas Beecham introduced Strauss's *Salome* and *Elektra*, and founded the Beecham Opera Company, which became the British National Opera Company when Sir Thomas, after a financially disastrous season, felt compelled to retire. The new company arranged performances at Covent Garden until the almighty Syndicate decided, in 1924, that it didn't want British opera, but international opera seasons. Until 1939, there were ten-week seasons, in summer, mostly German opera, under Bruno Walter and Sir Thomas Beecham, with Lotte Lehmann, Olczewska, Melchior, Schorr, Mayr; and Italian opera, with Gigli, Stabile, Pertile, Pinza, Ponselle, Pampanini, Caniglia. "Many of these performances provided evenings of wonderful singing, but the productions as such were often nonexistent, and the ensemble in such operas as *Falstaff* and *Don Giovanni* was not of a very high standard", writes Rosenthal. In fact, it was Glyndebourne and the visit of the Dresden State Opera in 1936 that illustrated the beauty of the ensemble, "not a collection of star singers gathered together for a few weeks each year, often not meeting one another until a few hours before the performance".

During the First World War, Covent Garden was a furniture depository; during World War II, it was a dance hall, managed by Mecca Cafés. After the last war, it reopened under the management of Boosey & Hawkes, the music publishers. In 1946, David Webster, a department store executive with a flair for opera, became General Administrator. During his administration, Covent Garden became one of the world's great opera houses, the only one able to keep up with the Milan-Vienna-New York triumvirate. Covent Garden is still handicapped by the lack of rehearsal and storage space, high costs and insufficient state subsidies. However, the original, small Treasury grant of twenty-five thousand pounds has increased to nearly a million, and Covent Garden now performs opera and ballet between ten and eleven months each year.

Today, Covent Garden has become an accepted part of the musical life in London. Opera is no longer considered "an irrational entertainment", and certainly not one limited to "society". Since the war, a generation of genuine opera connoisseurs has emerged. Like the Metropolitan, Covent Garden performs most works in the original language. Sir David Webster created the atmosphere, which is all-important to a great opera house. A skilled administrator, until his retirement in 1970, he ran his house efficiently. Covent Garden is said to make fewer changes in announced repertory and casts than any other major house. This is no small claim, especially when one considers the hazards of London's climate. In 1971, John Tooley became general administrator, with Colin Davis as musical director in place of Georg Solti. The staging is often first-rate. The people in London understand the stage, and some of the greatest operatic producers, among them Zeffirelli and Visconti, have had both triumphs and trials in Covent Garden. (The London music critics are now among the world's best, though there is no longer a Shaw or a Newman among them.) Sir David always understood the need for first-rate conductors, and even induced Otto Klemperer to appear in Covent Garden. Under the leadership of both Georg Solti and Colin Davis the orchestra often plays with exquisite beauty. The woodwinds and brass were always very good, and the strings have acquired more colour and warmth. The singing is often first-rate; a generation of fine British singers is now admired in London and in opera houses everywhere. And London audiences are no longer lukewarm; there have been terrific ovations, and also refreshing scandals, when the reticent British were heard booing and hissing. It is still customary in opera circles in Milan and Vienna to shrug off London. Yet Covent Garden years ago managed to put on Arnold Schönberg's *Moses und Aron* – something neither Milan, New York, nor Vienna dared do. It was a great performance, and it was a popular success. There is no doubt that Covent Garden belongs in the Big League.

THE PARIS OPÉRA

The Paris Opéra, officially known as Théâtre National de l'Opéra, has a great history, a dull presence and a doubtful future. Founded in 1669, it was once the focus of operatic sensations and dramatic scandals. In the days of Rameau, Gluck, Cherubini, Wagner, the Paris Opéra generated excitement, controversy and occasionally produced beautiful opera.

Today the average Frenchman thinks of the Opéra as a musical museum, rather stuffy and bureaucratic. It is the most ornamental of the world's great opera houses, and the least meaningful. Jean Louis Charles Garnier, the great architect of the Deuxième Empire, put everything good and expensive into his Palais – marble, sculptures, staircases – nevertheless, it is a cold house, and its performances are rarely stimulating.

Paris has several fine orchestras, but they are not playing at the Opéra. Conductors, musicians, singers, stage directors, stage hands perform a routine that would not be tolerated in the kitchen of La Tour d'Argent or in the work rooms of Balmain. The scenic and choreographic possibilities of the house are enormous, and the ballet can be very good. The company has some good singers, but no effort is made to forge them into an ensemble. Characteristically, the Opéra was very good in the early 1940s, during the German occupation. The Germans "suggested" what to play (for instance, Pfitzner's *Palestrina*, which no one in Paris understood or cared for), and how to rehearse, and they brought in German conductors and stage directors. Four-fifths of the better seats were reserved for members of the Wehrmacht and Party people. The French were graciously permitted to sit up in the galleries but, as people now say, "who wanted to go there anyway?"

Forty years ago, people went to the Opéra on certain nights, because it was a social "must". On Mondays and Fridays, according to Baedeker, "evening dress was *de rigueur* in the orchestra seats and *premières loges*". Subscribers would appear wearing canes, capes and opera hats. They were permitted to spend the interval in the Foyer de la Danse, a gold-and-mirror-filled vestibule behind the big stage, where gallant sugar-daddies could express their admiration to the ladies of the Ballet. "The Foyer de la Danse", it says in the Memoirs of Bachaumont, "is the most sought-after place at the Opéra".

Things have changed now, and people no longer shout "bis!" ("repeat!") after Isolde's *Liebestod*, but the repertoire is rarely exciting ("To be performed at the Opéra one must be either dead or almost dead", a modern French composer says). It is a bureaucratically run enterprise; it has a steady deficit although it plays almost twelve months a year, longer than any other house. More than four hundred people draw regular salaries throughout the year, with civil-service contracts, and paid vacations. There are regular performances on Monday, Wednesday (ballet), Friday, Saturday night and Sunday afternoon. Sometimes there is an extra soirée on Sunday night. On Thursdays, prominent artists may rent the Opéra; only *very* prominent ones, like Paderewski, Kreisler, Heifetz have done it. The Opéra does much for its ballet; it is the only institution of its kind, which educates its own corps de ballet.

The present house is the twelfth home of the Paris Opéra. Of the other eleven, three burned down. The present Palais Garnier owes its existence to an attempted assassination. On 14 January 1858, one Felice Orsini hurled a bomb at Napoleon III and Empress Eugénie, as their carriage was passing through the Rue le Peletier. The royal couple was not hurt but a number of other people were killed. Napoleon decided to build a new opera house, "more splendid than all the previous ones". Garnier was not narrow-minded about his Palais: whole streets and blocks of houses were torn down, and the magnificent Avenue de l'Opéra was created, the only large street in Paris without trees so as to permit an unobscured view of the building. The Opéra stands at the intersection of seven important streets.

Years ago Georges Auric, the composer, was appointed administrator of the Réunion des Théâtres Nationaux Lyrique (as the French bureaucrats call the merged Opéra and Opéra-Comique) by André Malraux, the Gaullist Minister of Culture, who predicted the Paris Opéra would again be a place for "world events". But behind the administrator there are 13 faceless figures – members of parliament, civil servants and varied "personalities" – who have much to say about budget, repertory, contracts. M. Malraux wanted to see Debussy's *Pelléas et Mélisande* at the Opéra, although Debussy never wanted it performed there, knowing it would be destroyed in the huge, cold house. It was a disaster.

It is a muddled house. The choruses refuse to sing in any language but French, while the principals sing in German (in Wagner operas), or in Italian, when performing Verdi. It has taken the more popular works, such as *Carmen*, from the intimate and more artistic Opéra-Comique. Gounod's *Faust* is the most popular work. Wagner is very popular as well, mostly performed by guests from Germany. The Opéra has derived a certain amount of fame from its gala balls, elegant charity affairs, and Lon Chaney's film *The Phantom of the Opera*. Everyone wants to go to Paris, but does anyone wish to go because of the Opéra?

However, all this may change now that Rolf Liebermann has been appointed the new director, and Georg Solti as chief conductor.

GERMANY

Operatically, Germany was never split. West German artists appear in East Germany and vice versa. For several years, the orchestra of the Bayreuth Festspielhaus was made up of the best instrumentalists in both Germanys. The repertoire is similar on both sides of the Iron Curtain, though there is somewhat greater emphasis on Russian operas in East Germany. Even the infamous Berlin Wall has not completely divided the city's operatic life. Although East Berliners cannot go to West Berlin to hear opera, nor West Berliners to East Berlin (though West Germans may go there), the most famous opera artist in East Germany, Walter Felsenstein, *Intendant* and absolute ruler of East Berlin's Komische Oper, lives in his comfortable house in West Berlin, and commutes through the Wall.

Most of the fifty-odd opera houses in both Germanys were totally or partially destroyed during the Second World War, but all have been rebuilt. West Berlin, Hamburg, Münster and Cologne created modern opera houses of daring design. In Aachen, Frankfurt, Düsseldorf, Hannover, Wuppertal tradition was blended with modern elements. Munich rebuilt the Bavarian State Opera along traditional lines. The East Berlin Staatsoper, Unter den Linden, originally built by Knobelsdorf under the reign of Frederick the Great, and opened in 1742, was faithfully reconstructed in "Berlin Forum" style, with its austerely classical façade, and baroque and rococo touches, down to the smallest detail.

The East Berlin State Opera is the showplace of East Germany, and probably the most important house behind the Iron Curtain. (Other houses, such as Moscow's Bolshoi Theatre or Prague's Národní Divadlo, are famous but not for well-integrated performances such as the East Berlin house offers with its great orchestra, the famous Staatskapelle, and a large ensemble.) It is a house with a violent history. During the Seven Years' War it was closed. Under Napoleon's occupation the theatre became a storage depot for bread. In 1843, the opera burned down and was quickly rebuilt. Under the Hohenzollerns it became the official *Hofoper* (Court Opera), one of the world's great opera houses. Muck, Strauss, Kleiber, Blech and Furtwängler were among the State Opera's conductors. It was then Berlin's first opera house, while the Städtische Oper had the more popular function of Vienna's Volksoper. After the First World War, when Berlin became the theatre capital of the world, the Städtische Oper gave the State Opera tough competition, and lucky Berliners had the choice of hearing opera conducted by either Wilhelm Furtwängler or Bruno Walter on the same evening.

During the Nazi regime, Goering was the State Opera's protector, while Goebbels considered the Städtische Oper his *Protektionskind*. When the State Opera was bombed out in 1941 by the Royal Air Force, Goering gave orders that it must be rebuilt and reopened a year later, and it was. In 1945 it was bombed again, by the Soviets (historians may one day explain the aversion of bombardiers in World War II to opera houses).

After the war, while Unter den Linden was still a ghost street, the Staatsoper was faithfully reconstructed, though with a little too much emphasis on marble (not unlike the Moscow subway). After seeing the rubble outside, and the ruins of the Crown Prince's Palace and the old Royal Library, it was a strange sensation to step into the rebuilt opera house with its profusion of crystal mirrors, chandeliers, carpets, marble walls. In those days the basement buffet was the only place in East Germany where anyone could buy food without a ration card.

The fame of the house is based on the Staatskapelle, always one of Germany's great orchestras. (East Germany has two other outstanding orchestras: the Dresden Staatskapelle, and the Leipzig Gewandhaus Orchestra.) The Berlin Staatskapelle has a typically "Prussian" sound: excellent woodwinds and brass, but as the strings are not sweet, the orchestra's sound is sometimes sharp rather than luscious. The staging, sometimes dull and provincial, can be stunning and revolutionary; most leading East bloc houses offer such contrast. The performances are well rehearsed and there is a sense of discipline in the house. The artists are among the best-paid citizens in East Germany; this is, of course, a reflection of Soviet *kultura* policy. Tickets are low-priced and very hard to get (though a certain contingent is kept for Western visitors paying in hard currency). Most tickets are distributed among workers' groups and Party bureaucrats. There are no budget problems. *Kultura* has priority and the government makes up the deficit. No opera house in the Communist world ever publishes its balance sheets.

I'm often asked whether there is a basic difference between opera houses in the East and the West. There isn't, on the stage or in the orchestra pit. The days of revolutionary staging are over. Productions of *Aida* or *Carmen* are not questions of *Weltanschauung*. The difference becomes obvious only after the curtain falls and the lights go on in the auditorium. Audiences in the East are not as well dressed as in the West; but this is a superficial factor. Eastern audiences are restrained and often self-conscious and there is no warmth in the house. People keep away from each other. An East German publication explained that in the days of Frederick the Great the opera house was "the salon of the feudal regime, with no inner meaning for the people". I sometimes left the Lindenoper (as the Berliners call it) with the impression that the opera had once more become "the salon of the regime".

The most interesting opera house in Berlin, East *and* West, is Felsenstein's Komische Oper. Completely rebuilt in the late 1960s to his specifications, it is completely the creation and reflection of the great producer. The orchestra is second-rate, the conductors are usually of little importance, and there are no international stars. The only star is Felsenstein, who has created the perfect ensemble – so perfect that he would rather cancel a performance, if a leading performer were ill, than replace him with someone who might disrupt the clockwork precision of the production. No other house could afford Felsenstein's rehearsal methods for any length of time. He spends months on a new production, making no compromise with his ideas. Occasionally he produces in the West, but to appreciate his style and painstaking work, one has to see the productions at his own house. They run from the superb to the whimsical, but they are never dull. He loves to produce works that are not in the repertory of many houses – Janáček's *Cunning Little Vixen*, Strauss's *Die Schweigsame Frau* – but he has done stunning, original things with the greatest master-pieces, such as *Don Giovanni* and *Otello*.

West Berlin's opera house, once called Städtische Oper, now Deutsche Oper Berlin, in Bismarckstrasse, was re-opened in 1961, a modern, sober, rather cool auditorium, matter-of-fact and democratic (it certainly looks more modest than the Staatsoper, across the Wall, in the "People's Democracy"). The best thing about the building are the foyers, filled with light, glass, stone, with ash-trays on the walls, and a great deal of space to see and be seen. Opera-going in Berlin is neither a religious service as in Vienna nor a spiritual one as in Milan, one simply goes to hear an opera. Gustav Rudolf Sellner, a noted producer, was the general manager; his successor is Egon Seefehlner, a Viennese, who once worked under Karajan. (Director-for-life of the great local orchestra, the Berlin Philharmonic, Karajan does not conduct at the Deutsche Oper.)

The orchestra and the chorus are said to be among the best in West Germany's opera houses. Lorin Maazel, the American conductor, was *Generalmusikdirektor,* and there are quite a few American singers in the ensemble. The chorus, under Walter Hagen-Groll, and the ballet, under Kenneth MacMillan, have made much progress in the past years. West Berlin is a "modern house", open to contemporary works. Schönberg's *Moses und Aron* has been in the repertory for years, and some works of Hans Werner Henze and Boris Blacher were first performed in West Berlin.

Modernists argue that opera, as a living part of the contemporary theatre, should be housed in a contemporary décor. "These strange twentieth-century people use scientific devices such as dictaphones, teleprinters and airplanes as a matter of course in their professional life but as soon as they go to the opera they step mentally into a coach-and-four and shut their minds to all evidence of the modern world", wrote K. H. Ruppel, the German critic. Most people ignore modern opera and only want to hear the classical works in antiquated settings, among boxes, pillars, stucco, velvet and plush. Technical perfection, of course, is expected to be as good as that of recordings.

There is not a single opera house in all of West Germany that has the national and international prestige of the Vienna Opera, Milan's La Scala, or the Metropolitan. Instead, several good houses compete for prominence and leading artists. The Bavarian State Opera in Munich, the city of Richard Strauss, is a first-rate ensemble opera, specializing in the works of Mozart, Wagner, Strauss, Pfitzner. Hamburg had the oldest opera company in Germany, established in 1678, produced the first German-language *Otello* (1888), the first *Eugene Onegin* (1892), in Tchaikovsky's presence, the first *Peter Grimes* (1947). Mahler, Klemperer, Böhm, and Leopold Ludwig were among its musical directors. Rolf Liebermann, the *Intendant*, made Hamburg the most progressive opera company of all. Over fifty contemporary works have been staged in Hamburg since 1946.

The Stuttgart Opera has, possibly, the most closely integrated ensemble of all, owing to the policies of its admired *Intendant*, Walter Erich Schäfer (who served for a while as administrative director of the Vienna State Opera under Karajan, but wisely left after becoming ill and unable to stand the strain). The Stuttgart house, called Württembergische Staatsoper, has a very large repertoire, a fine roster of artists, a very good orchestra, and probably the finest ballet ensemble in Germany, one of Europe's best. Wieland Wagner often rehearsed his productions in Stuttgart, before taking them to Bayreuth; a large number of his singers came from Stuttgart.

In South Germany, the climate is more emotional, closer to that of Italy, than in the cool, intellectual latitudes of Northern Germany. People prefer the old masterpieces and are somewhat reluctant to accept modern works. Even in Hamburg, Berlin and Cologne, where many new works are performed, it is admitted that they rarely sell out the house. In Germany, as elsewhere, opera appeals primarily to the emotions. Even the restless, ambitious, German technological supermen forget their computers and become romantics-at-heart when they listen to the love duet in the second act of *Tristan* or the trio from *Rosenkavalier*.

The finest opera performances, however, are heard during one month only in Bayreuth's Festspielhaus. In the early 1960s, during the great days of Wieland Wagner, Bayreuth offered the richest experience in the contemporary musical theatre. The Festspielhaus is a styleless, red-brick building – with what are probably the best acoustics in the world. The climate is often hot and humid. Wieland and Wolfgang Wagner had the problems of managers everywhere – rising costs, uncertain subsidies, strong competition, and a growing scarcity of robust Wagnerian voices able to execute Richard Wagner's inhuman vocal demands. Everything is exaggerated in Bayreuth, an unfriendly town with unfriendly people: performances start at four in the afternoon and seem endless; intermissions last over an hour, and the seats are as uncomfortable as everything else.

But at best, the artistic climate was invigorating under Wieland's personality, the enthusiasm was contagious, and the tension strong and happy. Some of Wieland Wagner's productions are already classics: his *Parsifal, Der Fliegende Holländer, Götterdämmerung*. Some people say that Bayreuth couldn't exist if the annual festival were to last longer than a month; as it follows a month of rehearsal, the tension just couldn't last. But while it lasts it's wonderful. Where else could you find an uncomplaining orchestra at the final rehearsals of *Tristan und Isolde* or *Die Meistersinger* playing on successive nights from 7 p.m. until 3 in the morning?

The four *Ring* evenings, still the most important productions of the festival, which also features regular *Parsifal* performances and two other Wagner works, are often stunning. What Wieland Wagner did with an empty stage, a cyclorama, and many lights in *Parsifal* was magical and an impressive lesson to designers and producers elsewhere who clutter their stages with props and people, but fail to evoke the spirit of the work. From the opening scene in *Rheingold*, when stage and auditorium seemed flooded by the blue-green waters of the Rhine, to the closing, apocalyptic scene in *Götterdämmerung*, there were moments of unforgettable beauty. Wieland and Wolfgang Wagner achieved Richard Wagner's drama of the *Gesamtkunstwerk*.

TOO MANY FESTIVALS

A festival should be approached with dedication, presented with devotion, remembered with happiness. Above all, a festival must have an idea, a theme, a *raison d'être*. The mere fact that a great composer once slept there, or that a music-loving prince had built a castle with a small theatre in the vicinity is not sufficient excuse for a festival.

Bayreuth celebrates the genius of Richard Wagner. Originally, Wagner decreed that *Parsifal*, a "stage dedication festival play", was to be given there, and nowhere else. Half a century later, Hugo von Hofmannsthal, Richard Strauss and Max Reinhardt devoted themselves to the idea of performing opera and drama in the perfect artistic climate of Salzburg. The memory of Mozart strengthened the idea.

Since the end of the Second World War, festivals have mushroomed all over Europe. Their origin is often similar. A dead and defenceless composer, whose image appears on souvenir ashtrays and candy boxes, is drafted as the (unpaid) star attraction. A few (well-paid) big-name artists are hired. Beautiful posters are printed and sent to the travel agencies. There may be some lofty talk about "culture", but the hard thought is of money. Thus a beautiful idea deteriorates into mere business.

There are now a dozen "big" festivals and perhaps three times as many "smaller" ones scattered all over Europe (I use the terms "big" and "small" the way travel agents use them). An enthusiastic festival visitor might be kept on the run from early May (Florence) to early October (Berlin) rushing from Glyndebourne to Wiesbaden and on to Aldeburgh, Prague, Amsterdam, The Hague, Vienna, Spoleto, Aix-en-Provence, Bayreuth, Salzburg, Bregenz, Lucerne, Verona, Schwetzingen, Edinburgh, Munich, Bath, Recklinghausen, and Zurich. "*Das sind nur die Namen; nun lernt sie singen!*" David complains in *Meistersinger*.

Festivals are just another symptom of this age of civilized anxiety. In a hurry to soak up culture, people tolerate small rooms, big prices, large crowds, suffering second-rate performances, which would be unacceptable at home. It is no longer like making a pilgrimage.

Fortunately, the festival inflation is limited by the available supply of artists. There are just not enough Almavivas, Alberichs and Aidas for all scheduled events, therefore, some singers commute between the festivals, over the *Autobahnen* of Europe, as do conductors and stage directors. Managing a major festival has become an exercise in brinkmanship and demands virtuosity in logistics (fortunately, Bayreuth, Munich and Salzburg, whose important festivals occur at the same time, are separated only by a few hours of *Autobahn* travel). At a pinch, last night's Amfortas becomes tonight's Don Giovanni.

Quite a few festivals are managed by businessmen, who care more about financial profit than artistic integrity. The performances are often badly rehearsed, because rehearsals are expensive. The whole production may be haphazardly thrown together. Prominent artists spend their time between performances at a nearby spa, taking a cure. "Why not?" one of them said to me, not long ago. "My reputation is established in the great opera houses. These tourists here don't know the difference anyway."

Once, the idea of the festival was to give the best possible performance under the best possible conditions. Enormous difficulties had to be overcome in Salzburg in the "good" years between the two world wars, when Toscanini, Furtwängler and Walter gave their memorable performances there. People still talk about the early days of Glyndebourne, a praiseworthy exercise in devotion, teamwork, and taste, when Fritz Busch and Carl Ebert were in charge. Glyndebourne still conveys a festive feeling to artists and listeners. "Here there is still a certain intimacy and simplicity", wrote Günther Rennert later. "As a logical development of our cultural mission it now remains to tap the sources of Mozartian and Rossinian opera . . ."

There are glorious moments during the long festival summer in Europe, but finding them takes knowledge, patience, experience, and, above all, luck. I had such moments in Bayreuth, but I always attended the dress rehearsals, never the gala performances, dominated by snobs and fashions. To me, Wieland Wagner's *Parsifal* remains the greatest festival experience of our era.

A few hours, and light years, away is the Baroque wonderworld of Salzburg. Above Salzburg, there hovers the heavenly music of Mozart, with its ever-present undercurrent of sadness. The visitor is captivated by the landscape and atmosphere, the fairy-tale visions of lighted towers against the black sky and the sounds of music in the air. Even the *Schnürlregen* – the dreary, monotonous rain – comes down in a steady rhythm.

But Salzburg has never quite recovered from its post-war trauma, when it was headquarters of the American forces in Austria, a wide-open place where anything went, while the military police weren't looking. Dear Mozart would have quite a shock if he were to see the Salzburg merry-go-round today, the espresso cafés, cinemas, drugstores, cakes and squares named after him. The ten-million-dollar Festspielhaus was to be the crowning achievement of the thriving Mozart industry. Unfortunately, it is not very suitable for the performance of most of Mozart works, and is often used for Verdi and Richard Strauss and Mussorgsky. Yet Salzburg's Mozart is probably still the best, because the Mozart style is still alive there. The Vienna Philharmoniker are hard to surpass when they play Mozart on a good evening.

A different festival, and one of the best, is Vienna's contribution known as *Wiener Festwochen*. Throughout late May and June the city is literally filled with music: in the three opera houses, half a dozen concert halls, parks and squares, churches and courtyards. The music ranges from highbrow Mahler and Schönberg to popular open-air concerts by the Fire Brigade Band. The attitude is casual: no fuss, no special exploitation. Foreigners are welcome, but it's really a festival for the Viennese. There is a constant interplay between past and present, stage and life. Old people remember Bruckner and Mahler; even I remember Strauss and Pfitzner. Now a coffeehouse, the Palais Auersperg, which was the headquarters of the provost-marshals during the Four-Power Occupation, was once the home of the legendary Marschallin, who inspired Hofmannsthal when he wrote *Der Rosenkavalier*. I myself remember the elderly gentleman, known to be the prototype of the Baron Ochs von Lerchenau. In Vienna, one is never sure whether something happened on the stage or in real life.

The main problem is abundance. On a typical evening one has the choice between opera performances and concerts, a recital or a Bruckner work performed at St Stephen's Cathedral, a Schubertiade in the house where Schubert was born, or a serenade in Heiligenstadt where Beethoven wrote his Pastoral Symphony. No matter where you go, if you are lucky, you will have the true festival spirit in your heart.

Opera as a Business

AN ACCOUNTANT'S NIGHTMARE

Opera is an accountant's nightmare. No opera house on earth has ever managed to break even, let alone make money. Grand opera is the costliest extravaganza among the performing arts. Invariably a great deal of money is lost. In 1967, a ten-week season in Chicago, playing to 97·4 per cent capacity, broke all box-office records, yet ended with a record deficit of $526·300.

The complexity of its operation makes opera equivalent in cost to the combined economic burdens that beset symphony orchestras, the legitimate theatre, and the ballet. Opera has expensive scenery, elaborate costumes, the most complicated lighting and technical machinery, and a large technical staff. An opera house also needs a permanent orchestra of eighty to a hundred members, a chorus of about one hundred men and women, a ballet company of fifty people. A performance of *Aida* requires several leading stars, supporting singers, a large orchestra, the full chorus, the ballet, and a large number of extras; from three to four hundred people are involved in it, including the technical staff. Furthermore, different operas with different casts are given from one night to the next. This increases the cost of rehearsals. The star performers in opera are the most highly paid artists in the performing arts. No opera house likes to divulge what it actually pays, but it is no secret that some are now earning four to five thousand dollars a performance. They appear on the labels of the expensive recordings, and people want to hear them in the opera house.

The managers of the leading houses have tried in vain to fight the stars' monopolistic demands. The stars want big money, except when they sing at the most prestigious festivals, such as Bayreuth or Salzburg, where they are sure of a worldwide radio audience. The situation isn't much different from the problems Monteverdi had in 1639 when he became director of the Teatro San Cassiano in Venice. He had to import the great stars on *their* conditions. During the 1964–65 season, when the Metropolitan's total expenses were 9.9 million dollars, the singers alone received over 1.5 million. During the 1968–69 season, when the total expenses were 17.4 million dollars, the singers had been paid $3.6 million – 21 per cent of the total. Monteverdi wouldn't have been surprised.

In the past ten years, the annual deficit of the Metropolitan has increased from $800,000 in 1960 to $4,300,000 in 1969. In 1970, it was almost $7,000,000, after the costly settlement of the long labour dispute which nearly defeated the august Metropolitan. Being one of the few privately subsidized houses, it publishes its figures. The Vienna State Opera, a publicly subsidized house, doesn't publish exact balance sheets, but it is no secret in Vienna that of the annual $10,000,000 subsidy for the state theatres, the Staatsoper receives around 80 per cent.

The Metropolitan Opera, known as "the giant of the live performing arts", is not big by American business standards; it is dwarfed by the smallest of the five hundred largest corporations in the United States. The Metropolitan's board of directors has reacted to the mounting deficit with astonishment, resignation and, occasionally, desperation, but the members find it easier to meet a deficit when they know about it well in advance. Rudolf Bing always correctly predicted the deficit a year in advance, in a carefully prepared budget resembling that of a small European nation, and usually the management was able to adhere to the budget to within one per cent ("The board is not happy with the deficit but at least they know they can trust the management's figures", Bing has said).

It takes the Met.'s expert management several weeks to assemble the annual budget in its final form. The next season's performances are scheduled, contracts with the artists are drawn up, the exact number of orchestra and chorus rehearsals are determined, and the physical costs of new productions are estimated down to the special nail polish for the *diva* singing the part of Turandot. Of every dollar, 43c are spent on artists, 38c on other payroll expenses, and 19c on non-payroll expenses such as scenery, costumes, building operations, administrative expenses. Obviously it's the people that cost most in opera. The Metropolitan's expenditures per performance have increased in the past twenty years at an average annual rate of 4.4 per cent. Several years ago, the costumes for a new

La Traviata production cost over $75,000, including a few dollars for the imitation tiaras worn by Flora's party. Material and workmanship must be first-rate. "Make-believe" is a thing of the past. The great scene in the first act of *La Traviata* must have the sparkle of a diamond twice as large as the Ritz; otherwise, the production may be considered a flop. Europeans used to deride the American habit of applauding a particularly beautiful set after the curtain rises, but now the sets in Europe are becoming more lavish, and audiences are beginning to applaud.

The Met.'s budget experts know that fewer stage rehearsals are needed for *Traviata*, with its intimate scenes performed by two or three people, than for *Turandot* with its large mass scenes. Conductors, chorus masters and stage directors invariably ask for more rehearsal time than the management feels it can afford.

The management depends on guesswork and a prayer, however, when it comes to estimating future box-office receipts. During the 1968–69 season, the Met. received 64 per cent of its expenses from ticket sales, 15 per cent was other income, and 21 per cent were contributions. (By comparison, the Paris Opéra covers only 25 per cent of its expenses from ticket sales, and the Vienna State Opera about 30 per cent.) In 1966, when the Metropolitan moved into its new house in Lincoln Center, it was suggested that all of its 3,788 seats be sold on a subscription basis. This would ensure sold-out houses throughout the season, and enable the management to predict future income precisely. But this would mean that no one would ever be able to step up to the box office and buy a ticket for any one opera he wanted to attend.

At the Metropolitan, subscription tickets are no cheaper than ordinary ones, unlike at other leading opera houses. Almost half of the twenty-one thousand Met. subscribers add a twenty-per-cent voluntary contribution to their cheques, which is unique in the operatic world. The regular season has gradually been expanded from eighteen weeks in 1949 to thirty-one weeks. Instead of six long subscription series, there are now twenty shorter ones. The development is towards fewer non-subscription performances and a greater number of seats sold to subscribers on sub-scription nights, and there will probably be new subscription series be-cause this means guaranteed income. Subscribers send in their cheques for the next season by 1 May. Thus, during the summer months, the Met. is able to invest considerable sums of money which generates additional income.

The subscriber buys only the right to his seat on a certain evening. Basically, the management presents him with the old favourites in the best possible dress. Even the New York City Opera is now forced to follow the subscription policy of the Metropolitan.

When Bing took over, he was told "you cannot play opera in New York on Tuesdays". Instead, there were to be exhausting trips to nearby Philadelphia. Bing surprised a lot of people when he decided to play opera in New York on Tuesdays, and give up the trips to Philadelphia. Opening night, once the private preserve of the Monday-night subscribers, was taken out of the subscription system and offered on a first-come-first-served basis to anyone willing to pay $50 a seat (a great many people who feel they must attend opening nights, not necessarily because they love opera, would gladly pay a thousand dollars for the privilege).

The Met. has had to scramble for money ever since it was founded, in 1883, when Henry E. Abbey, the first general manager, lost over $600,000 during its initial season. Though for many years the Met. was known as a "rich" house, the management was constantly struggling to extract enough money from rich patrons and not-so-rich radio listeners just to keep its head above water. Nowadays over a hundred leading companies are contributing on an annual basis as patrons of the Metropolitan. Bing's initial production of *Don Carlos*, in 1950, was the gift of Mr and Mrs Gilbert Kahn "in memory of their parents' close and affectionate connexion with the Metropolitan Opera". For some thirty seasons, Texaco has been the exclusive sponsor of the Metropolitan's Saturday afternoon performances, with the Texaco Metropolitan Opera Radio Network covering all fifty states, Puerto Rico and Canada. Eastern Airlines pledged $500,000 for a completely new production of Karajan's *Ring*. Glen Alden Corporation pledged $150,000 towards new productions of *Cavalleria Rusticana* and *Pagliacci*. The gifts from Mrs John D. Rockefeller, Jr., included new productions of *Carmen, Die Meistersinger von Nürnberg, Der Rosenkavalier, Il Trovatore* and others. An anonymous donor gave the Met. the production of *Die Frau ohne Schatten*, "in recognition of the interest of the late Mrs Izaak Walton Killam". Who could deny that New York is a wonderful place?

Until a few years ago, it was un-American to favour public subsidies for the Metropolitan (and the other permanent opera companies in the United States). The argument was advanced that opera is performed "for a tiny privileged minority", and that in an egalitarian society, the majority shouldn't be made to pay for the minority. A Stanford Research Institute study in 1962 reported that in America "there are more piano players than fishermen, or at least people who pay for fishing licences", and that there were "more theatre-goers than boaters, skiers, golfers, and skindivers combined". Similar comparisons could doubtless be made for opera goers, and one might arrive at interesting figures concerning the number of people who love to listen to opera on the radio and on recordings. Perhaps "the privileged minority" isn't so tiny.

And there is another side to the problem. Harold C. Schonberg, music critic for *The New York Times*, wrote in a magazine article in 1963,

> We do have some of the best opera singers in the world – but they are not in America. Most of them are solidly entrenched in the European opera houses. Naturally. Where else can they go? The sad fact is that America has only one major opera house, the Metropolitan.

A Rockefeller Panel Report on "the cultural boom" reports that "of the 754 opera-producing groups in the United States, only 35 to 40 are fully professional, and not more than 10 of these provide performances more than fifteen days in the year". An analysis by Professors William J. Baumol and William G. Bowen (*Performing Arts – The Economic Dilemma*), published in 1966 by The Twentieth Century Fund, reaches some sober implications for the future of the performing arts in America. Costs mount and revenues don't keep pace. (In 1960, the Metropolitan's operating income was $6,000,000 and its total expenses $6,800,000. In 1969, the income was $13,900,000 but the expenses were $17,400,000.) August Heckscher, Director of The Twentieth Century Fund, and formerly a Special Consultant to President Kennedy, stated in the Foreword,

> Others have faced the fact that the live performing arts cannot expect to pay for themselves without subsidies, direct or indirect ... but the present report goes beyond this recognition. It is not only that the live performing arts do not pay for themselves, but that, within the developing economic system, they will show deficits of increasing size ... A study of higher education twenty years ago would have shown something like the outline of the crisis which now confronts the live performing arts. The educational crisis has now largely passed because new resources have been mobilized ... Something of the same kind will, we hope, take place in the case of the arts.

Heckscher's hope has not been fulfilled since he wrote this. In the early 1970s, the live performing arts were in worse economic trouble than ever. Even some of the celebrated American orchestras with large endowment funds have financial problems, yet orchestras are more liberally supported in the United States than opera companies. Today not only the state and federal governments but also private sources – foundations and individuals

– place priority not on the arts, but on the problems of the ghettos and the cities. And, according to Internal Revenue Service statistics, a great many people who make deductible donations prefer to give to religious activities, community chests, the American Red Cross, hospitals and educational institutions, with the arts way down on the scale of donations. "Roughly half of the nation's large corporations give something to the arts, but most of them give very little; about half of those contributing allocate less than one per cent of their total donations to this purpose", writes the Rockefeller Panel Report.

In the United States, opera was never subsidized by the federal government. The State Department occasionally subsidizes concerts by American artists abroad. Both the Eisenhower and Kennedy administrations advocated support of the arts. President Kennedy in 1963 created an Advisory Council on the Arts, but it never became operative. The following year, Congress established the National Council on the Arts on a permanent basis, with an annual expenditure of $150,000. It was a modest beginning. Eventually, the financial commitment is to be $10,000,000 annually for all the arts – as much as tiny Austria puts up for its state theatres. In France, the government provides almost $10,000,000 for the five national theatres, among them the Opéra and the Opéra-Comique.

In spite of the long tradition of opera in America that goes back to 1735 opera never caught on as in Europe. Only four major companies exist: the Metropolitan, the New York City Opera, the Chicago Lyric Opera, the San Francisco Opera. There are also some smaller, specialized younger groups, the Santa Fé and Central City summer opera, and some professional opera-producing groups. In the past twenty years, the popularity of opera has steadily grown in the United States, both in the number of performances and the size of the audiences. The Metropolitan now performs for over three-quarters of a million people a year; and there is an extensive series of summer opera in Lewisohn Stadium. The Met. is very often sold out – but when an unpopular modern work is performed, capacity may fall off to 80 per cent (which the management considers a "disaster"), from $42,000 for a full house to about $34,000. Since it now costs $60,000 to put on a performance, even a drop of $5,000 is disastrous. Six performances of a not-too-popular work may cost the Met. $30,000. Two such productions a year can increase the deficit by over $60,000. Yet ticket prices have gone up at a rate of over 6 per cent a year. A good seat now costs $17.50. Attendance, once close to 97 per cent, has slipped to 85 per cent of capacity.

At the New York City Opera, the capacity decreases from 65 to 39 per cent when a modern work is given; the expected revenue loss is almost $4,000. The City Opera is extremely popular with partisans of contemporary opera, and justly so. The management considers a fifty per cent capacity a considerable success; quite a few partisans, it would seem, talk a lot about modern opera, but rarely bother to attend. Contemporary works require more rehearsals (and thus higher production costs) than repertory opera. Since the modern work is only performed a few times, the production costs cannot be spread over a large number of performances. People who often criticize the opera managers' "conservatism" ought to study the financial reports. They should also read the annals of the labour disputes at opera houses.

All opera managements must deal with various unions; the management of the Metropolitan deals with thirteen different unions. The five-and-a-half-month labour dispute late in 1969 came to an end when agreements were signed with the various unions representing the orchestra, stagehands and front-of-house personnel, and with AGMA, representing the principal artists, chorus and ballet. The new contract provided orchestra members with an average annual income of $16,500 which reached over $21,000 by 1971-72. The Met. now has the highest-paid orchestra in the world. The top technicians make as much as the musicians and lesser principals. Senior chorus members get $15,000 and senior ballet members over $11,000. No other opera house pays such salaries; and none makes it so complicated for foreign artists to appear there. An Italian, who years ago came to sing briefly at the Met., appeared off-Broadway and made a few television appearances; he had to join the American Guild of Musical Artists for his work in opera, the American Federation of Television and Radio Artists for his television appearances, and Equity for his stage appearances; had he appeared in a movie, he would have had to become a member of the Screen Actors Guild.

THE CASE FOR SUBSIDIES

Of the hundred-odd opera houses on earth, only those in the United States are not supported by some form of official subsidy. In 1940, after an urgent radio appeal, 166,000 opera-lovers from coast to coast contributed more than a million dollars to help buy the deed of the Metropolitan's old building, on Broadway and Thirty-ninth Street. During the 1968-69 season, the Met. received almost $4,000,000 from individual donors.

It was never that way in Europe. Ever since Emperor Leopold 1 of Habsburg made up the deficit of a hundred thousand guilders, after the operatic festival of 1666 celebrating his marriage to Infanta Margaret Theresa of Spain, emperors and kings, aristocrats and princes of the Church, and, after them, governments and taxpayers continued to pay for opera.

A very special case is that of La Scala in Milan. Its organization and financial background are unique. In 1921, Toscanini, "under the spiritual protection of Verdi" (writes Giuseppe Morazzoni) created the "autonomous corporation of La Scala". He decreed that La Scala must "always" keep its artistic and economic autonomy. (In 1962, Karajan accomplished something similar in Vienna. But unlike the case of Toscanini, the bureaucrats engineered Karajan's departure in 1964, from which the house has not yet recovered. Like Mahler before him, Karajan was driven out by an unholy alliance of the musical bureaucrats, the press and "public opinion". Opera history always repeats itself in Vienna.)

Toscanini wanted neither a privately supported house like the Met. nor a straight state-opera house as in Vienna, Hamburg or Paris. Most important of all, he had the autonomy codified into law. There would never be any undignified hustling for money, as in New York. La Scala receives no special contributions from private patrons. Such gifts would not be tax deductible in Italy. Half of its budget is covered by ticket sales: La Scala takes in more money than the other twelve Italian opera houses together. Until recently, the 50 per cent deficit was made up by the City of Milan, through a small tax on movie tickets, and by the Provincial Government, through a tax on the national soccer pool. Such taxes are possible only in the operatic atmosphere of Milan. Would New Yorkers be willing to support the Met. through a small tax? I wonder.

By 1967, all Italian opera houses – most were broke – were getting some state subsidy from Rome. Ghiringhelli, La Scala's general manager, helped with the reorganization of Italy's opera houses, but made sure that La Scala's autonomy was not touched. The management now deals with a large "administrative council" where all groups supporting La Scala are represented: city, province, state, guilds and unions, institutions and even composers. The administrative council doesn't interfere with the management's artistic decisions. The walls of the council's conference room are hung with pictures of Verdi and Toscanini and photographs showing the ruins of the destroyed house in 1943 – a subtle reminder of what has been achieved since by the present management.

Vienna's State Opera is handsomely subsidized by Austria's taxpayers.

The Austrian government spends more money on its state theatres than on its foreign service: an admirable policy that should be followed elsewhere. In Vienna, opera has always been the quintessence of Austria's cultural past. Many hospitals and schools are in a deplorable state, Vienna University is hopelessly crowded, scientists cannot be appointed to teaching jobs for lack of funds – yet the State Opera was rebuilt at a cost of $10,000,000; and in Salzburg, a sumptuous Festspielhaus that is used less than thirty days a year was built for $9,000,000. But the State Opera has its troubles too. It was never efficiently managed; Karajan was said to have spent too much money, but his successor, Egon Hilbert, spent even more, and got less for it; ever since, angry voices have been raised at the Austrian Parliament demanding more efficiency. It is never revealed to what extent the State Opera's expenditures are covered by ticket sales; probably not more than one-third. It has been said that the government contributes 600 Austrian schillings ($24) to every seat in the house, every night.

London's Royal Opera House, Covent Garden, has had as many financial crises as the Metropolitan, and has often been on the brink of disaster. Although opera isn't considered as important as in Milan or Vienna, it seems agreed that "there'll always be a Covent Garden", and that it must be subsidized. For a short time in its proud history, in the truly golden days of Caruso and Melba, Covent Garden broke even, under the management of Harry Higgins and Neil Forsyth, but those days are gone forever. In the post-World War II era, Covent Garden was kept alive by a £25,000 grant from the Arts Council. Now, the government subsidy is £1,250,000 – enough to support a season of eleven months; the opera shares its season with the Royal Ballet. Seat prices are slightly below those of New York, Milan and Vienna, the most expensive on a most expensive night being £7·80.

In the Communist countries, grand opera has high priority on the list of *kultura* musts. All opera houses are generously supported by the state. Budgets are secret, as everything else, but must be very high, because ticket prices are low, and productions often very expensive. At his Komische Oper in East Berlin, Walter Felsenstein could afford to spend two years and 233 rehearsals preparing his production of Offenbach's *Tales of Hoffmann*. West Berlin opened its new opera house in September, 1961 (about half the budget is subsidized by the Senate of Berlin). East Berlin had re-opened the State Opera eight years earlier. The East German government provides what is needed to make the State Opera the country's cultural showplace. The situation is similar in the Soviet Union and in the Eastern Bloc countries. In these houses there is a dramatic contrast between the marble staircases and people's shabby shoes, their clothes and the gold leaf on the walls.

In 1961, Carl Ebert, one of the great old men of opera, who returned to the Met. after re-opening the West Berlin Opera, said, "America will just have to understand that you can't have opera without subsidy". The American argument against subsidies is out-dated and meaningless. It is claimed that political pressure might be exerted on managers were an opera house to be publicly subsidized. But the time is past, when kings and aristocrats were able to install their lady friends as prima donnas (unless their lady friends be genuine prima donnas). The very thought that men of the calibre of Karajan, Ghiringhelli or Schäfer might be "influenced" or accept subsidies "with strings attached" is too ludicrous to be taken seriously. At La Scala, Ghiringhelli once told me, "No one ever worked here who was recommended by a Minister or Senator". Bing proved his independence in more ways than the members of his board of directors liked. In Vienna, Karajan never attended foolish cocktail parties, and on occasion treated members of the government with proper condescension.

The annals of the Metropolitan show that more influence was exercised in the old days by wealthy millionaire donors, particularly by their wives, than in European houses, where aristocrats or government officials held the purse strings. The Vanderbilts, the Morgans, the Kahns were sometimes far less subtle in their approaches than any finance minister in a European country would ever have dared to be. It is also absurd to claim that pressure could be exerted on the programme of a subsidized opera house. The repertory is more often dictated by the available voices than by the wishes and whims of the managers. During the First World War, the Met. did not play Wagner for some time, and during the Second, it might not have performed *Madame Butterfly*, if some people had had their way. Fortunately, cooler heads prevailed. There will always be some attempts at pressure regardless of subsidies. A manager with a sense of artistic responsibility and civic attachment will simply ignore them. If he doesn't, he shouldn't have been made manager in the first place.

Thirty years ago, even the members of the boards of great symphony orchestras were strongly opposed to federal aid. The arguments ranged from the pathetic to the idiotic. It has been said that government grants "might discourage private giving", as in Europe. But most of the existing tax laws make no allowance to private donors; besides, the state subsidies come from taxpayers' money. A favourite argument is that "the small percentage of people who enjoy opera does not qualify it for public support", or "if opera cannot pay for itself, the fault is with opera . . ." This sounds like the hoary, Philistine argument, "Why should so many be forced to pay for a few?" Austria's Burgenland winegrowers, Alpine peasants and simple people who never go to their State Opera, yet pay for it, are more sophisticated than the vast majority of the American public that pays for the oil-depletion allowances of a few millionaires. Oil-drilling is a high-risk business, but so is opera. In Europe, the education of opera-goers begins at an early age. It adds to the prestige of the community and the country, attracts visitors, and increases tourism. The example of Austria is interesting: tourism is the small country's second-largest industry, and a visit to the highly subsidized Vienna State Opera is a "must" with most foreign visitors. Perhaps the "absurd" subsidies pay off in unexpected ways.

An overriding argument has been the alleged dangers of public control. (Rudolf Bing once said he wouldn't cherish the idea of sitting in a Washington Congressional Committee room, facing half a dozen senators.) But again, Europe should be an example. There the performing arts, mostly under government support, have remained free from political pressure and interference.

Admittedly, both private and public support have their dangers. In America, the artists must always fight to get to the top and stay there, which is as it should be. In Europe, artists with state contracts and pensions need not worry about next month or next year; at the Vienna State Opera, a contract artist, who has been with the house for ten years, cannot be dismissed and is assured of a state pension (for many years this was believed to be law; not long ago, it was discovered that the practice was based on a letter of a former *Intendant*). Such economic security doubtless enables some to concentrate on their artistic work; others, however, develop an art-bureaucratic mentality and slide into mediocrity. At the Vienna Opera, the members of the orchestra who are, so-to-speak, government employees don't speak of performing, as artists should, but of "*Dienst machen*" which means "rendering a service". This is the real danger of government support: that it may stifle the arts (though it doesn't limit the artist's freedom). This danger exists when one considers the range of extremes in opera houses on the Continent, where an evening of extraordinary achievement may be followed by a dreadful routine performance. In the provincial towns of Germany there is a widespread notion that attending an opera performance is the citizen's "cultural duty" ("If my father could stand it, I can stand it too"). This may make an opera performance an indifferent experience, on both sides of the pit. Then opera is in trouble.

Some sort of public support seems inevitable for the performing arts in the United States, particularly for opera which is becoming just too expensive for the enthusiasts who so valiantly support it.

Success in Opera

Fidelio was an utter flop in 1805, yet succeeded only nine years later, after two complete revisions. Rossini's *Barbiere* displeased the audience in Rome at the première, but was a hit the second night: same cast, same opera. Why? Verdi's *La Traviata*, now universally beloved, created a terrible scandal in 1853 at the Teatro Fenice in Venice. The sets, costumes and characters were criticized as "modern" and "unconvincing". The title role was sung by a rather well-fed lady, whom the audience was amused to see die of consumption in the last act. In 1863, there was the historic *Tannhäuser* scandal at the Paris Opéra, which caused Wagner to withdraw the work. The failure of *Carmen*, in 1875, didn't "break Bizet's heart", as is now claimed, but probably hastened his death. In 1904, a hostile audience at La Scala sat "unmoved, in glacial silence" through the première of Puccini's *Madame Butterfly*. The next morning, Puccini heard newspaper vendors under his hotel window shout, "Puccini's flop". "I was in the depths of despair", he wrote to his friend Fraccaroli. "I thought I should never again touch a note". The next morning, he began to revise the work, combining the second and third acts; fourteen weeks later, it was a huge success at the Teatro Grande in Brescia. It has been a smash hit ever since.

Contrarily, some instant successes have since vanished from the stage: Meyerbeer's *L'Africaine*, Ambroise Thomas' *Hamlet*, d'Albert's *Tiefland*, Leoncavallo's *Zazà*. As in other art forms, longevity almost always implies artistic quality. A composer's best-known works may not be his masterpieces, but they appeal to the public. It may not appreciate the sublime masterpieces: *Falstaff* is less popular than *La Traviata*, and *Ariadne auf Naxos* never had the success of *Rosenkavalier*. Success in opera depends on many elements – timing, taste, fashion, and the nationality of the listener, though the truly great works have become international. *The Bartered Bride* (Prague) and *Boris Godunov* (St Petersburg) now belong to the whole world.

The Italians originally considered opera a *dramma per musica*: conflict of characters on the stage, drama that was made more deeply human through music, probing into the depths of thought and emotion. Prose is the first step, poetry the second, and song the third in expressing subtle shades of feelings. The drama may begin on a gay note, as in *La Traviata* or *La Bohème;* and a comic masterpiece, such as *Figaro*, may have serious undertones at the end. Some great masterpieces – *Don Giovanni, Die Meistersinger, Boris Godunov* – combine tragic and comic elements. Melody seems an important element of popular success – though Richard Wagner would disagree; *he* was able to break all the rules, creating the exalted melodies of his orchestral symphony. No one has ever explained what creates an "immortal" melody. Richard Strauss (whose *Rosenkavalier* waltz is reminiscent of the *Dynamiden* waltz by Joseph Strauss) once called Cherubino's "Non so più" the ideal melody, because "it goes on and on". Some Italians would prefer "La donna è mobile", "Di quella pira" (*Trovatore*) or "Che gelida manina" (*La Bohème*). Next to great arias, vocal ensembles form an ingredient of popular success. Mozart and Verdi, Wagner and Strauss were masters of the ensemble: it may be amusing (the finale in the second act of *Figaro*), moving (the quintet from *Meistersinger*, the trio from the last act of *Rosenkavalier*), or heroic and exciting, as in most Verdi operas.

Perhaps the single most important ingredient is a dramatic libretto, which gives the composer a chance to write exciting music (*Il Trovatore, Tosca, Lucia di Lammermoor*). A dull libretto defeats even good music, as Tchaikovsky and Weber learned. The libretto should have a moving, possibly feminine, character: Violetta in *La Traviata*, Mimi in *La Bohème*, the *Marschallin* in *Rosenkavalier*, Marguérite in Gounod's *Faust*.

Wagner, as so often, breaks this rule, too. The only sympathetic character in his *Ring* tetralogy is Brünnhilde, and even she doesn't always manage to break the tedium caused by a galaxy of first-rate scoundrels. Neither Eva (*Meistersinger*) nor Isolde are particularly sympathetic persons, and who but Lohengrin could possibly like Elsa? Yet all of Wagner's operas have immense dramatic conflict. Good taste is not always an element of success: what is in good taste in *Tosca* or *Salome*? Style is not a prime necessity. *Fidelio*, a work with a complete style break, partly *Singspiel* and partly moving drama, has become successful – and there are no singable melodies either. But Beethoven's enormous humanity moves audiences.

Comic operas have their own laws of failure and success. The exhilarating frivolity of *Figaro* is pure enchantment, but the more sophisticated humour of *Così fan Tutte* is not always appreciated. The audience is often confused by the capricious happenings and not always sympathetic towards the characters on the stage. *Falstaff* is a perfect story; everybody likes a lovable crook. The success of Wagner's *Meistersinger*, his best libretto, is due to his feeling for dramatic contrast: the wise Sachs, the romantic Stolzing, the bizarre Beckmesser, the sexy heroine. There is tension: everything seems lost at the end of the first act, and pretty confused at the end of the second. Yet *Meistersinger* lasts five hours and seems much shorter than a great many operas which last only two. This is what makes success in opera.

Opera on Television

Opera on television is an enormous challenge and one that could bring enormous rewards. "Opera at home" enlarges the vision of millions of people watching the perdition of Don Giovanni, Octavian presenting the silver rose to Sophie, the coronation of Boris Godunov, and the death of Carmen. A country might become a nation of opera lovers ...

Unfortunately, the challenge hasn't been met as yet. One of the most successful opera presentations of the past decade was recently televised: Puccini's *La Bohème*, the memorable La Scala and Vienna production by Zeffirelli, conducted by Karajan, that enchanted opera lovers everywhere. But the television version was disappointing. Opera lovers found they saw *too* much (meaning things they didn't want to see), while those unfamiliar with opera didn't understand what was going on. After a while, even the beautiful arias became monotonous. The programme which began in beauty ended in boredom, though the show lasted less than two hours.

Some day television will master the problems of opera. When the first gramophone records were made in the early years of our century, musicians had only contempt for the new medium. Today some musicians have contempt for the perfection of modern recordings: some acoustically "improved" recordings of live performances remind them of too much make-up on a woman's face. The era of radio also began amidst prejudice and dark forebodings, yet radio performances are now often admired.

Opera and television are diametrically opposed forms of artistic expression. Opera began as an aristocratic entertainment and later spread among the people. Contrarily, television began as a medium for the masses, and sometimes reaches great moments when it appeals to people with taste. As television is very expensive, it is only under pressure, as a sort of glorified cultural duty, that a network will put on an "artistic" programme, such as an opera. While opera wins new addicts every day, it cannot compete with soap opera or Westerns: it doesn't have such universal appeal.

There are also vast technical problems. Opera is basically static. (In another Karajan television experiment, *Carmen*, filmed at the Salzburg Festival, succeeds only when one sees the singers at close range, but not while they are singing; Don José's tortured face while Carmen is teasing him; perhaps this is a solution for presenting opera on TV.) Television producers either show singers at close range singing an aria, or they let the camera wander aimlessly. Both methods have their drawbacks. Looking at the celebrated tenor through the pitiless eye of the television lens, we notice his double chin, the strange contortions of his mouth, and there may be a ludicrous effect during the most dramatic moments. But is it permissible for the camera to perform a descriptive lecture of Sevilla while the poor fellow tries for a high C? In the end one has neither an opera nor a movie.

Another problem arises when celebrated singers neither look nor act like the characters they portray. Opera plots, which are often preposterous, may provide a televised performance with touches of unwanted humour. Opera lovers feel like closing their eyes in such moments, content and relieved only to hear the music. And many people find it impossible to accept the basic fact that characters in opera sing when they ought to be speaking to each other.

Furthermore, the television viewer doesn't see the action from a safe distance, across the orchestra pit, but is plunged into the middle of the drama, thus destroying the all-important barrier between his own reality and the seeming reality of the stage, where baritones, after being stabbed to death, revive to bow to applause. On the television screen an actor-singer's gesture, which would be acceptable on the stage, often looks ridiculous. Singing is, at best, a very difficult, demanding activity, and it is uncomfortable, to say the least, to watch the intimate vocal efforts of one's beloved prima donna or star tenor as she or he attempts a high C. Again, one feels like closing one's eyes. And television doesn't always deliver as much as one would like to hear. Details get lost. Rarely is the unity between stage and orchestra achieved, that we take for granted in the opera house. Instead, the orchestra sounds like "background music".

The film has mastered the medium of the drama. *Henry V* and *Romeo and Juliet* gave Shakespeare almost a new dimension, when they were translated to the modern cinema screen. Opera on television shows only what the camera sees; the choice is not made by the viewer, but by the producer and the cameraman. At the opera house, the public may switch from one part of the stage to another, whereas on television, the camera forces the audience to follow the camera. But opera-goers are usually individualists who don't like to be told what to see.

Production techniques create more problems. In Italy it is customary to pre-record the opera beforehand. This ensures the best sound quality. Later, the original cast must mime its own recordings while the music is played back. This, naturally, leads to contrived gestures. Sometimes other singers, who look better than the original singers, mime the pre-recording. This approach may offer better acting, better acoustics, more space. But there is always a strain when artists have to sing in trying conditions of heat and glare, and something of the spontaneity of a fine performance is lost. Perhaps the direct method will be found to be the best, in the end. "The limitations of the medium must be borne in mind", writes Lionel Salter, a British television producer. "So long as many viewers have only small-screen sets, spectacular large-crowd works, or operas with casts large enough to be confusing seem doomed to failure'.

The television producer of opera must please both the opera lover, who should enjoy the production almost as if it were live opera, and the majority of viewers who, not caring about opera, might be made to look and listen for a couple of hours. Most producers agree that "a fast-moving story, which the viewers can understand and follow, is essential, even if they cannot catch the singers' words; not too many principal characters; each of them clearly defined and characterized in make-up and costume, so that they cannot be mistaken ... one should be able to follow the story without being told it beforehand" (Rudolph Cartier).

This means that the word is more important than the sound, that the voice has precedence over the orchestra. The performance shouldn't last longer than a hundred minutes. Some producers, mindful of the fact that every opera loses through presentation on a small screen, try to show things in close-up that sometimes get lost on the large stage; or certain characters are shown alone during a climax, while on the opera stage they may be surrounded by other people. Yet there is the danger that the opera-goer, used to the larger frame, will perversely miss the other people, though they are not needed dramatically.

The camera magnifies every change of expression in the face of the singer. Cartier writes,

... it is the producer's job to help the cast with their characterization and interpretation, particularly as they have hardly any chance to do so *during* singing. Singing is a major job in itself, and therefore I put all the facial expressions and movements if possible into the bars between sung phrases. I know that singers don't like that, but they soon realize how important it is, and co-operate.

Another British producer, George R. Foa, admits that "the thrill of an exciting performance under ideal conditions in a great opera house would seem almost impossible to substitute", yet "the loss of size is counter-balanced by greater mobility of action and richness of detail". The great problem is that the screen presents only small fragments of what is seen on the whole stage. "The medium has its dangers", says Foa. "It could be very irritating to see Tristan in close-up against an out-of-focus background meeting a close-up of Isolde running towards him in similar nondescript conditions."

Opera was created for the lyrical stage. Perhaps in order to succeed operas will have to be especially written for the new medium of television. The emotional impact of a great opera is such that it is almost impossible to "adapt" it for the new medium. Opera remains a very demanding art form.

Is There a Crisis in Opera?

Years ago, Pierre Boulez declared in a controversial interview that "no opera worth mentioning" had been composed since Alban Berg's *Wozzeck* and *Lulu*. Berg died in 1935. Boulez specifically singled out Hans Werner Henze's *Der Prinz von Homburg* as "an unfortunate dilution of Verdi's *Don Carlos*", and turned down Günther Schuller's *The Visitation*, a blend of jazz with twelve-tone music which failed, according to Boulez, "because the jazz forfeited its characteristic of improvisation . . .' Boulez thought Schönberg had been right when he said, "The middle road is the only one that does not lead to Rome". Boulez turned down Boris Blacher's *Zwischenfälle bei einer Notlandung* (Incidents on an Emergency Landing) which "was written in our time but is in no way modern . . . Is that modern music just because Blacher uses electronic methods? Reminds me of the plays at the beginning of the century when people thought they were being modern because they had a telephone on the stage."

Boulez believes there is no such thing as a modern opera because there is no congenial collaboration between librettist and composer. He wonders what might have happened in a collaboration between Brecht and Stravinsky in the 1920s. "The text must really be conceived directly for the musical theatre; it must not be an adaptation of literary material. Literature set to music is sterile." It may be that Jean Genet "could fuse modern music and modern theatre together". He is impressed by Genet's *The Screens,* the scene in which the Algerians are abusing the French, but no longer in words. They draw the insults on the stage. At the end of the scene the set is ready.

Boulez also objects to the new German opera that looked very modern "from the outside; inside, they remained extremely old-fashioned. Only with the greatest difficulty can one present modern operas in a theatre in which, predominantly, repertory pieces are played. It is really unthinkable". Then he made the extravagant statement that gave an otherwise sensible, sound interview worldwide publicity: "The most expensive solution would be to blow up the opera houses". He also objected to modern producers, "who are still hobbling along far behind the times . . . Did you see the so-called realistic production of *Rigoletto* by Zeffirelli? Idiotic! A theatre or film audience would laugh itself to death over that kind of performance. The opera audience is something else entirely."

Boulez divides the public into three groups. The first considers itself "cultured" and goes to "the music museum". The second lives in the present and listens to the Beatles. Boulez considers a Beatles record "cleverer and shorter than a Henze opera". And there is a small third group independent of, and sometimes above, the taste of the bourgeois society. Boulez concludes that opera lives in the ghetto. It can be compared to a church in which, at best, eighteenth-century cantatas are sung.

The theories of Boulez have been challenged by the modern composer Rolf Liebermann, former *Intendant* of the Hamburg State Opera, where modern opera is much cultivated. Liebermann believes that everything can be done in traditional houses, "on the sole condition that one accepts the conventional stage, audience seating and the orchestra pit . . . Beyond that any wish can be fulfilled: electronic installations, stereophonic loudspeakers, stage mechanism." Perhaps what we really need is not a new opera house or even a new stage, but a new genius able to write the truly modern, post-Berg opera.

Much of Boulez's criticism is preposterous. It was a good exercise in *épater les bourgeois*. (Boulez conducted beautiful *Parsifal* performances in Bayreuth, the super-museum, and revealing *Pelléas* performances at Covent Garden, not generally considered a platform for modern art.) But he did touch the nerve of much that causes worry to the lovers of contemporary opera. There is the serious danger that the opera house could become the twenty-first century's music museum where the great standard works will be admired as are Leonardo da Vinci's *Mona Lisa* or Michelangelo's *Moses*. Once again, the villain is Richard Wagner. When he wrote *Tristan und Isolde* over a century ago, opera was no longer entertainment for the masses, as in Venice and Parma, but "edification" for the few. The suffering is terrible during the dull, empty stretches of recitatives in the *Ring*, though some people maintain that it is great music. There are no tunes in *Tristan* that can be sung or hummed. There are almost no tunes in Verdi's later masterpieces, *Otello* and *Falstaff*.

Eduard Hanslick, never the fool whom Wagner ridiculed in *Meistersinger*, wrote, after the première of *Otello* in Milan, in 1887,

> ... We demand of the opera composer beauty and novelty of musical ideas, particularly melodic ideas. And from this point of view *Otello* strikes me as less adequate than *Aida, La Traviata,* or *Un Ballo in Maschera.*

Absolutely right. A modern critic, Henry Pleasants, agrees:

> Contemporary composers would have done better had they not dismissed the fact that *Aida* is still more popular than either *Otello* or *Falstaff*, and always will be. Their error was in listening to the critics rather than to the box office. About this even Verdi, for whom the box office was never an institution to be taken lightly, may have been deceived. By the time *Otello* was produced he had achieved a position in the hearts of his countrymen and others where failure would have been next to impossible.

> There are no tunes in *Elektra*, a greater masterpiece, though much less popular, than *Rosenkavalier*, with its famous waltz theme. And Puccini's masterpiece, *Turandot*, closer to *Otello* than to *Aida*, will never be as popular as *La Bohème*. *Turandot* has the better "technique" and contemporary composers often consider technique more important than melody and music.

Alban Berg's *Wozzeck*, written in 1921, is the only modern opera that has become an international box-office hit. Neither *Turandot* (1926) nor the later works of Richard Strauss are "contemporary" operas in the sense of a new musical idiom. Every art form must change and evolve, in order to stay alive. Opera, however, has almost stood still since the death of Puccini, Berg, Strauss. Managers admit that most modern works are performed as an artistic obligation. "The total lack of creative talent in the operatic world today poses the critical question whether opera is a viable art at all, and whether it can claim sufficient *raison d'être* to justify the immense financial outlay that it entails", wrote Heinrich Kralik, the Viennese critic.

The revolution in the operatic world is not visible at first glance. The repertoire of the big houses is made up of the classical, romantic and post-romantic works that are everywhere accepted by the public. Mozart, Verdi, Wagner, Puccini and Richard Strauss remain generally the most popular composers. The legitimate stage is always interested in new things; not so the opera house.

It no longer tolerates the prima donna or the star tenor who cannot act, or singers who express emotions in clichés. The new concepts of neo-Bayreuth, and of the few creative producers, have increased the visual and dramatic attraction of the operas; star conductors have given new life to their readings of the score. Managers have been trying to enliven the repertoire by performing "re-discovered" baroque or pseudo-romantic works. Great performances of Monteverdi and Bellini operas, that were half-forgotten, are always exceptional, because not many singers today can execute the *bel canto* demands of these composers. The masterpieces of the Italian and German opera remain the backbone of the repertoire. Certainly no opera house could built its repertoire on the basis of contemporary works.

Janáček, who died in 1928, wrote wonderful operas which are now slowly being discovered. They may not be "modern", but they are timeless. Stravinsky's *Oedipus Rex* and *The Rake's Progress* are occasionally performed, so are Benjamin Britten's *Peter Grimes*, *Billy Budd* and *A Midsummer Night's Dream*.

Most modern operas are unsuccessful because most modern composers write cerebral music, confusing "technique" with "music". Music is an emotional art, no matter what some fashionable musicians may say. Without feeling, there can be no music. Even the brilliantly intellectual music of Anton von Webern contains emotion, though it is distilled and disciplined. Modern composers, who claim they can do it without feeling, wind up as musical mathematicians or construction workers, though they may consider themselves architects. The greatest musical architect, Johann Sebastian Bach, was a man of powerful emotions who built cathedrals out of feeling. Compared to him, today's "architects" can't even build a weekend bungalow.

Using brains instead of feelings, many contemporary composers have turned opera into logarithmic exercises that please a tiny minority of esoteric snobs and avant-garde critics, who claim that emotions are out and asceticism is in. The composers' idiom is not melody and song, but parlando and declamation. They use the orchestra not as a singing voice, but as a mechanism expressing theory or shock. They wilfully ignore the evolution of opera since 1600 that shows a steady development of the orchestra and harmony. Almost all are unable to integrate drama and music, as Mozart, Wagner and Verdi did. Strauss who understood this, but was unable to coerce himself in tuning down the voice of the orchestra, often told his disciples that the singer's words must be clearly enunciated and understood even above the fortissimo din of the orchestra in *Elektra*. (Strauss's foremost disciple, Karl Böhm, keeps the orchestra of a hundred down to a chamber-musical level.)

The greatest contemporary composer, the late Igor Stravinsky, wrote operatic works that don't, however, have the genius of his early orchestral masterpieces, *Petrouchka* and *Rite of Spring*. Paul Hindemith, a master of the contrapuntal style, never won a large public with his operas, *Cardillac* and *Neues vom Tage*; *Mathis der Maler* was more successful in the concert hall than on the stage. Carl Orff has a personal style, using popular tunes and recitatives with artfully blended dissonances but his *Carmina Burana* remains an interesting experiment. Ernst Křenek has wavered between popular opera (*Jonny spielt auf*) and serious (*Karl V*). Kurt Weill, gifted and brilliant, will long be remembered for his (and Bertolt Brecht's) version of *The Beggar's Opera* (*Die Dreigroschenoper*), but the European critics refuse to consider Weill a "serious" composer, which is both unfair and idiotic. Some day George Gershwin may be recognized as the eminently "serious" composer of *Porgy and Bess,* but today the unwritten rule is that a composer must not have a "commercial" success if he wants to remain "serious".

The contemporary composer's lot is not an easy one. How is he to compete with the popularity of *Aida, La Bohème, Carmen?* Modern composers complain about the "libretto problem". Greek and Roman subjects are unpopular with their public: Stravinsky's *Oedipus Rex,* Orff's *Antigonae,* Britten's *Lucretia,* Honegger's *Antigone,* Liebermann's *Penelope.* Historical subjects were also disappointing: Milhaud's *Christophe Colomb,* Honegger's *Jeanne d'Arc,* Einem's *Dantons Tod,* Hindemith's *Mathis der Maler.* Legends (Werner Egk's *Irische Legende* or Henze's *König Hirsch*) were no more successful than adaptations of books and plays – Britten's *Billy Budd* (Melville), Liebermann's *Schule der Frauen* (after Molière's *Ecole des Femmes*), Malipiero's and, later, Barber's *Antony and Cleopatra.*

Modern themes have been disappointing: Dallapiccola's *Volo di notte,* Boris Blacher's *Zwischenfälle bei einer Notlandung.* But Blacher's pupil, Gottfried von Einem, has shown originality and taste in *Dantons Tod* and *Der Prozess* (with a libretto written by Blacher after Kafka's *The Trial*). He turned Dürrenmatt's play, *Der Besuch der alten Dame,* into a successful opera. Britten has been accused of eclecticism, but he has written two good modern operas, *Peter Grimes* and *Albert Herring*; and

Michael Tippett and Richard Rodney Bennett have written English operas. Will they survive? It is too early to tell. That also applies to Malcolm Williamson (*The Violins of St Jacques*), who was accused of writing "diluted Schönberg", while Gian Carlo Menotti (*The Consul, Amelia Goes to the Ball, The Saint of Bleecker Street*) was accused of "diluting Puccini". In Germany, Hans Werner Henze has been successful with *Elegy for Young Lovers* and *Die Bassariden*, and Bernd Alois Zimmermann with *Die Soldaten*. Diluters and compromisers haven't fared well with modern critics, who wait for Boulez, Stockhausen or Ligeti to write *the* modern opera.

Perhaps the real crisis in contemporary opera is the growing emphasis on intellectual achievement. Since Schönberg, much of modern music has moved from emotion to intellect. Schönberg himself was a great master of post-Wagnerian emotion (something he didn't like to hear), as witness *Transfigured Night*. His monodrama *Erwartung*, a single-voice recitative that is a *tour de force*, is a study in terrifying emotion and tension. His often emotional masterpiece, *Moses und Aron*, is becoming progressively more popular. Bartók never wrote operas; his *Bluebeard's Castle* remains an exciting promise.

Today, only Henze and Britten are full-time opera composers. Messiaën, Lutoslawski, Boulez, Stockhausen have shown a noble disregard for the medium. Some of them claim that modern opera needs a modern, experimental stage, but that is irrelevant. Modern opera has reached an impasse because few creative people are interested in it.

Pierre Boulez in France and Karlheinz Stockhausen in Germany have experimented with electronic music. They use sounds emitted by electric frequency generators, filtering the harmonics, altering the timbres and creating new tonal shades. There are no more scales with fixed intervals, leaving Schönberg's twelve-tone music far behind. Intonation becomes flexible; rhythmic combinations are possible that the human mind couldn't create: computerized music. The question remains whether the pilots of these new experiments are hypnotized by purely technical problems, and whether these experiments run against physical and psychological permanency in human nature.

Some critics claim that modern music must not provide pleasure, entertainment, distraction; rather, it should be strictly an intellectual discipline. Others consider the various musical systems as a means of displaying advanced technical mastery which should stimulate intellectual response in the public. The public is bewildered or bored, but rarely amused or pleased or moved. In 1948, Pierre Schaeffer wrote that "concrete expression in music consists in constructing objects in sound, not as until now with numbers and metronomic measurements, but with fragments of time snatched from the cosmos, these fragments being the grooves on the recording disc." The system uses objects in sound (noises?) as its raw material.

All these experiments run counter to the expression of feeling, and are against the operatic stage. Possibly, they create shock effects. No one can tell whether they will have more than a passing impact.

The four-hundred-year-old history of opera reveals a phenomenon that may leave some hope. For some unfathomable reasons, the great achievements in opera were always made in the second half of the century – Lully, Gluck, Mozart, Wagner, Bizet, Verdi, Puccini and Mussorgsky. Maybe the great twentieth-century genius in opera is still to come. Of course, there have been prominent exceptions: Monteverdi, Pergolesi, Bellini, Rossini, Beethoven, Strauss. In the preposterous medium of opera every rule has at least two exceptions. Opera may be on the critical list right now, but it will never die.

Epilogue

TONIGHT: FIGARO

The last act of *Le Nozze di Figaro* is coming to an end. Susanna has sung her most beautiful aria, "Deh vieni, non tardar". It sounds like a "simple" piece but Mozart – who could write the most complicated music with an apparent lack of effort, as only true genius can – worked hard on this aria. He rewrote it several times before he was satisfied.

Susanna's aria is followed by a sequence of errors and wild complications which explain the opera's subtitle, *La Folle Journée*, "The Mad Day". The complications are interrupted by a wonderful love duet of Figaro and Susanna, and come to an end with the Count's getting down on his knees, begging his wife to forgive him.

Mozart might have been shocked to learn that the Countess, on whom he lavished so much love and affection, in the end went the way of all flesh. In the third play of Beaumarchais's *Figaro* trilogy, *La Mère Coupable* (*The Guilty Mother*), the Countess has become mother of a child by Cherubino. Poor Cherubino, known as Léon d'Astorga, received the news while fighting a war, and replied on the back of the Countess's letter, using the last drops of his life blood. The Almaviva home now includes little Léon, named after his father, and the Count's illegitimate daughter, Florestine. Fortunately, Mozart never knew about these complications; the play was written one year after his death.

Mozart's *Figaro* ends with a choral-like andante, followed by a merry finale. All's well that ends well, and the maddest day in opera is also the happiest. In the Beaumarchais play, the characters step towards the footlights at the end, and speak a rhymed refrain: Susanna says, "Deep truth is hidden in our merry, mad play. Forgive its serious moments, for the sake of the fun, even if you should have disliked them . . ."

In the da Ponte-Mozart *Figaro*, which has some very serious moments, we are not asked to forgive and forget them. They belong there because Mozart's theme is not social inequality, as in the work of Beaumarchais, but love. Love with its many facets. Cherubino's boyish adoration of the older Countess. Love's unhappiness (the Countess). Love as erotic passion (Count Almaviva). Love turning into jealousy (Figaro). Love that may become hatred (Marcellina) and which turns into vengeance (Bartolo). Love as pure bliss (Susanna) and love as fulfilment (Susanna and Figaro). And, finally, love that forgives everything: that is pure Mozart. "His heart remained that of a child", writes Romain Rolland, "and beneath all his music we seem to hear a simple demand: 'I love you. Please love me.' "

The greatest musical comedy in opera is a comedy of love.

Index